NEW PLAYS USA 1

Edited by
James Leverett

Introduction by
Michael Feingold
*American Playwriting: the State of the Art,
the State of the Union*

THE PLAYS

A Prelude to Death in Venice
Lee Breuer

Dead Souls
Tom Cole

FOB
David Henry Hwang

Still Life
Emily Mann

The Resurrection of Lady Lester
OyamO

Winterplay
Adele Edling Shank

Theatre Communications Group/TCG

New Plays USA 1
ISSN 0731-4523
Cloth ISBN 0-930452-23-2 $17.95
Paper ISBN 0-930452-24-0 $ 9.95

Printed in the U.S.A.

CONTENTS

Preface
James Leverett   vii

Introduction
American Playwriting: The State of the Art,
the State of the Union
Michael Feingold   xi

A Prelude to Death in Venice
Lee Breuer   1

Dead Souls
Tom Cole   31
Translated and adapted from the novel by Nikolai Gogol
and the Moscow Art Theatre stage version
by Mikhail Bulgakov and Constantin Stanislavski

FOB
David Henry Hwang   109

Still Life
Emily Mann   153

The Resurrection of Lady Lester
OyamO   225

Winterplay
Adele Edling Shank   289

About Theatre Communications Group/TCG   371

New Plays USA 1

Preface

"Two years in the making!" That's what press ballyhooers used to shout about the latest Cecil B. DeMille parting of the Red Sea. You don't hear that phrase much anymore, perhaps because spending time no longer packs the publicity wallop that spending money does. "Megamillions in the making!" is the new headline. But I want to resurrect the old one for a moment, because it has real meaning for the book you are holding. *New Plays USA 1* was two years in the making, and more. Those years saw the birth and first growth of a new process of getting plays to those who want and need to read them—a way specially fitted to the demands of this vast country and with no precedent here or elsewhere.

That process is aptly named *Plays in Process.* In the Introduction to this book, Michael Feingold describes the situation which brought the project into being: the present decline of play publication which cuts off script availability at a time when many new plays are being written and many theatres, new and old, are interested in staging them. How to repair this severed connection between playwrights, theatres and the public and thus to facilitate the continued life of new works on stages everywhere?

An idea evolved to use the facilities and connections of Theatre Communications Group, the national service organization for nonprofit professional theatre. TCG has a constituency of some 200 of these institutions—also variously known as regional, repertory and resident theatres. They are the source for the great majority of new American plays being done today on stages—commercial, noncommercial and educational —in every section of this country. Why not mobilize these wonderful resources by asking the TCG theatres to submit the new works they are presenting in a given season—dramatic translations and adaptations included—to a selection process on a national level? Then circulate the scripts chosen in this process to other theatres and organizations such as colleges and universities where people are likely to read, study and produce them. The Ford and Rockefeller Foundations and the National Endowment for the Arts liked the idea enough to give it the necessary financial send-off and *Plays in Process* began.

With a project so untried in a country so large, there were naturally some fears. First, of course, would we get enough good plays, given those perennial dire assessments of the state of American playwriting? Would the plays come from just a few large theatres in a couple of urban centers? Would we get just one kind of play—say, the much maligned realistic family drama?

We still have some fears two years later, but they are none of the above. *Plays in Process* has circulated 28 play manuscripts to a subscribership of noncommercial theatres, educational institutions and other nonprofit organizations. (In order to encourage production of new works in the nonprofit sector, only these kinds of organizations are eligible to take part in the *PIP* script circulation project; individuals and commercial organizations may not subscribe.) The 28 *PIP* scripts were selected from some 150 nominations made by more than 50 nonprofit professional theatres of every size, location and artistic complexion. The roster sounds like another chorus of "America": They came from the Magic Theatre in San Francisco and Mabou Mines in New York, from the Milwaukee Repertory Theater Company and Florida's Asolo State Theater. Add to those plays produced in Los Angeles, Seattle, Dallas, Chicago, New Haven and many more places.

As for the quality and range of the plays, the six in this volume tell the tale. In his Introduction, Feingold correctly denies that the selection committee used the "Noah's Ark" principle for its choices. We simply chose from the 28 scripts, all of which pleased us, the six anthology entries which pleased us most. It was accidental that we picked a play by an Asian-American, one by a black, two by women, a major new translation, a daringly experimental performance piece, a documentary about the aftermath of Viet Nam and a hyperreal family drama.

Or was it accidental? As Feingold suggests, chosen as they were from among the best plays being produced throughout this country, naturally they reflect this country in all its diversity. They help to form the necessary literary foundation of a national theatre located, not in some stoney edifice where a few come to exorcise their cultural obligations, but in a mosaic (Feingold's word) of theatres, existing in various places in various ways, filling the special needs of the many nations of the United States.

The parts of the mosaic, however, are flung across this vast country; and we are often terribly myopic when we try to judge the whole. The next time some pundit opines how dreadful the last Broadway season was, the usual nodding chorus will sigh, "Yes, it is always thus in the American theatre." But what is—or, more to the point, *where* is—the American theatre which they are so glumly assessing? The most important achievement of *Plays in Process,* and now *New Plays USA 1,* is to help bring into focus a larger picture of the state of the art. I can do no better than to introduce you to some vital, vibrant parts of our theatre gathered from many points on the geographical and artistic compass. They will speak to you directly and eloquently about the whole:

Experimental theatre poet Lee Breuer has toured his *A Prelude to Death in Venice* in this country as well as Belgium, Brazil, France and

Italy—appropriate, because it takes place somewhere between Thomas Mann's Italian Venice of art, eros and death, and Breuer's Venice, California of film and fast talk. At the play's center is John, a dummy—that *is,* a puppet suspended in his James Dean jacket between two pay phones.

The savagely comic premise of *Dead Souls,* Nikolai Gogol's panoramic novel of the 19th century, is that, under a twist of Russian law, a businessman could buy up dead peasants ("souls" as they were called) and then make a fortune using them as collateral for huge mortgage loans from the government. Tom Cole is the first to adapt this rich, timelessly pertinent, hilarious epic for the American stage from Stanislavski's renowned Moscow Art Theatre production.

In David Henry Hwang's *FOB,* a Chinese restaurant becomes the scene of a battle, part American comedy, part Chinese opera. Two Asian-American college students meet a new immigrant "Fresh Off the Boat." Their confrontation is social, sexual and mythical; their weapons are dress, language, cars, hot sauce and swords.

Still Life by Emily Mann documents with testimony taken from actual case histories the legacy of violence carried over from Viet Nam into the present-day lives of a veteran, his wife and his mistress. The wife: "War: He said it was the best sex he ever had." The mistress: "Men: They were programmed to fuck, now they have to make love. We don't like them in the old way anymore. And I don't think they like us, much. Now that's a war, huh?"

OyamO's *The Resurrection of Lady Lester* summons up the jazz genius of Lester Young in a play suffused with his special music and poetry. Like interwoven melodies, we experience his childhood, his one-nighters, his women (including the one he named "Lady Day"), his rise to the top of his art and his death.

Using the hyperreal style which she pioneered, Adele Edling Shank creates in *Winterplay* an affluent suburban Christmas in California down to the last detail: a turkey, a car, the right wine, the son and his male lover, the daughter allergic to everything but plastic and obliged to communicate only through closed circuit television. Materialistic America catches up with itself.

This is *New Plays USA 1,* the *first* of an intended series of yearly anthology "manifestos" (Feingold's word again) of American dramatic literature. They will be chosen, like this one, in a process that includes writers and theatres throughout this country.

Thanks to the focus that *Plays in Process* and *New Plays USA* have provided, the Literary Services department at TCG, which is responsible for these projects, has also become the dissemination point for all sorts of information for those who write for the stage and those who provide stages for that writing.

For a project as ambitious as *Plays in Process* to be set into motion, the advice and support of a great many people is necessary. The members of the *PIP* and *New Plays USA* selection committee are as varied and accomplished as the plays which they chose: actor Robert Christian; playwrights Gus Edwards and Corinne Jacker; scenic designer Karl Eigsti; translator and critic Michael Feingold; former director of the National Endowment for the Arts Theatre Program Ruth Mayleas; author and critic Julius Novick; scholar and academic leader Howard Stein. My gratitude to all of these pioneers.

And my special thanks to Arthur Ballet, whose vision and support gave birth to *Plays in Process;* Richard Sheldon and Gayle Counts who, while they were at the Ford Foundation, joined with the National Endowment for the Arts and the Rockefeller Foundation in funding a risky new venture; my associates in TCG's Literary Services department, David Izakowitz and Gillian Richards; Katy Brooks, director of publications at TCG, who helped bring the book into being; Gordon Davidson, Richard Nelson, Lloyd Richards and Lanford Wilson for their concern, commitment and encouragement.

James Leverett
January 1982

American Playwriting:
The State of the Art, the State of the Union

Michael Feingold

The nice people who produced this volume sometimes introduce me at public forums as "America's oldest living dramaturg." It isn't true—I flatly deny the canard that I translated Ibsen for Mrs. Fiske—but it does entitle me to begin this Introduction with the phrase "when I was a boy." So: When I was a boy, American playwrights—the few such creatures that existed—were on Broadway. At least, that was all I knew about it, growing up in Chicago in the 1950s. Oh, occasionally one heard of a playwright popping up on what was called *Off* Broadway, but this was rare, and it was assumed that the playwright in question would be moving north to Broadway as soon as his commercial credentials had solidified.

As for theatre outside New York, very little was left of the indigenous movement that had vanished in the 1890s as railroads brought stars in touring companies all over the country, and had boomed again in the 1920s, when all the stars went to southern California to become two-dimensional objects on a large screen. The upheaval wrought by World War Two, followed by the advent of television, had brought this movement down to a murmur. Around the country, a few theatres were doing what was called "stock"—generally remaindered Broadway plays of 10 years earlier—and a few remnants were left of what had been condescendingly baptized "little theatre." There were also a few hardy pioneers of what is now a thriving network of resident theatres around the country: Eccentric, gutsy, tenacious men and women (mainly women), determined that their city should have a serious theatre in it—Zelda and Tom Fichandler in Washington, Margo Jones in Dallas, Herbert Blau and Jules Irving in San Francisco, Nina Vance in Houston; the list is not really very long. In my own home town, a band of young loonies calling themselves The Second City set up a theatre next door to the cabaret where they improvised satirical sketches and tried to keep Chicago in touch with Off Broadway and Europe. But there was no national sense of a connection among these very different phenomena, and none of them had much to do with playwriting as such, as yet.

I really thought, when I was young, that there was one serious playwright in America, a man with the imposing name of Williams Miller Inge. As time went on, this triple-barrelled organism separated into its various components in my mind, and the Chicago Public Library yielded up to me the secret of its many and various predecessors in the field. The library also showed me, one aisle over in the stacks, that Europe had had a much longer and more varied history of playwriting. The European plays I read seemed to me more mature, more wide-ranging, with a soberer and deeper view of life; the Americans, on the other hand, offered a racy vividness of language, a speed and directness of action, an eagerness to please that appealed to me strongly, and still does, complicit though it may be with superficiality.

Reading plays, however, led me inevitably to read criticism, and since critics are on the whole people whose first interest is seriousness, by the time Williams Miller Inge became three separate artists for me, I had lost interest in American plays and was loudly and prematurely proclaiming my contempt for the shallow culture in which I was growing up. The generation just ahead of mine was being represented Off Broadway by a new three-headed hydra named Albee Gelber Richardson, but this extravagant creature barely entered my consciousness, busy as I was going to Fellini and Bergman movies, reading Brecht, and memorizing long screeds from Shaw. I kept a secret soft spot in my heart, though, for our native trash, and if I can still reel off a good two paragraphs of Shaw at his most earnest, I can also, with prodding, recall most of the major wisecracks from *The Man Who Came to Dinner.* Somehow I knew even then that, trashy as it was, it was our own; and that fact was in some way important.

Like me, the people who founded America's resident theatres in the 1950s and 1960s were Europe-oriented and past-oriented. They wanted an alternative to the trashiness of Broadway, with its one or two serious prize exhibits balanced precariously, like poisoned and bruised maraschino cherries, on top of a load of escapist whipped cream. Their first impulse was to take from abroad what they could not find at home: English actors (or actors trained in England); English directors; English or French plays, varied with whatever classics had been lately revived in London or Paris. Later Germany, Scandinavia, Eastern Europe, Russia (this last depending on the State Department's mood at any given moment) were added to this mix. More slowly and tentatively, the American past crept in, usually in the form of a "romp" or "end-of-season treat" for the audience: Many of you reading this will be too young to remember the eyebrows raised when the APA, a national touring company whose lofty repertoire included Pirandello, Sheridan, Chekhov and *War and Peace* (the Erwin Piscator adaptation, if you please), added to its list George M. Cohan's *The Tavern.* To the eyebrow-raisers' surprise, the production was not only successful with audiences, but demonstrated that Cohan in his trivial way had certain things in common with Pirandello. To compound the felony, the same clever director (Ellis Rabb) went to the staid Phoenix Theatre—Pirandello, Chekhov, Brecht and *Coriolanus,* yet—and demonstrated that Dion Boucicault's Civil War melodrama *The Octoroon* had something in common with *The Cherry Orchard;* by this time the highbrows' eyebrows were shooting through the ceiling, but the early American repertoire was established as playable. Where, however, was the contemporary American repertoire?

The answer, confusing as it may seem linguistically, was Off-Off Broadway: While directors and actors were spreading out across the country, or starting theatres wherever they happened to be, the playwrights were heading for New York. As there was virtually no room for them in the calcifying commerical system, they started what was in effect a wildcat theatre, with the aid of some young directors with unconventional ideas, and some benevolently wacked-out parent figures, like Ellen Stewart and the late, beloved Joe Cino. Where the resident theatres were solid, hieratic, middle-class, Off-Off Broadway was rowdy, flimsy, Bohemian. Where the regions honored Ibsen, O'Neill, Shakespeare, the Elizabethan thrust stage and the box set, Off-Off invented plays in all shapes and sizes, productions that were environmental or imagistic or audience-participatory, where you might be asked by the actors to go down a slide or put on a party hat and yell "Surprise!" The resident theatres' models were the Schiller Theater, the Comédie-Française and the Old Vic; Off-Off's models were old movies, medieval strolling players, Gertrude Stein and the original production of *Ubu Roi,* with Gémier waving a toilet brush as a scepter and Yeats moaning, "After us, the savage god."

I exaggerate this dichotomy for purposes of simplification. Actually, the theatre being the nomadic profession it is, there was cross-fertilization between the two sectors almost as soon as they were born. Nor do I mean that one took more risks than the other: After the cultural lulling of the Eisenhower years, to be serious *or* funny on the American stage was an incredible risk, if you were for real about it, and the resident theatres got themselves into every bit as much trouble as the Off-Off theatres, and sometimes over the same things. The New York City Police closed down John Vaccaro's Play-House of the Ridiculous under pressure from the Indian consulate (which took offense at Ronald Tavel's *Indira Gandhi's Daring Device*—solve the population problem by freeze-drying untouchables), and the Hartford Stage Company was menaced with obscenity charges when Jacques Cartier directed Genet's *The Balcony*. Minneapolis audiences streamed for the aisles in horror at the sight of Rochelle Owens' *Futz!*, a keystone play of the decade, and in Philadelphia the police sat all through Andre Gregory's production of Anouilh's *Poor Bitos*, to make sure the public wasn't unduly inflamed by the sight of an actress's bare breast. In New Haven, the Yale Rep's season ad was censored by newspaper editors who couldn't bring themselves to print the filthy title, *'Tis Pity She's a Whore*, and Long Wharf's sedate subscription audiences showed their displeasure with David Rabe's *Streamers* and David Rudkin's *Afore Night Come* by hurling their programs at the actors during the curtain calls. Whether from European tradition or native innovation, the American theatre was getting a terrific shakeup on all fronts.

A shakeup, however, is merely a sign of creativity: The theatre was also getting established in the public eye, as a part of the community, as an institution that deserved government support, as a set of phenomenal growth cases—the Harris Poll investigations in the mid-1970s revealed to a startled public that the American theatre was actually a boom industry, at a time when very little else in the United States was. These far-flung, diverse theatres were beginning to sense their connection to one another, to take their places in a mosaic picture called "Our National Theatre"—a little kitschy and awkward, a little overly Europe-influenced, like many native works of art, but with a zest that was all its own.

One sign of this awareness was that the nonprofit theatre's two sectors began to develop their own opposing trends, their own dialectic: Cities blessed with a particularly staid resident theatre suddenly found themselves growing counter-culture theatre groups in opposition to it. Off-Off theatres found themselves being put on a stable administrative basis, discovered classical theatres springing up next door and sometimes even had to trim their sails to suit their subscribers. Most surprising of all, the commercial theatre, which had virtually been declared ready to lie down and die, was discovering the profit potential of both the resident theatres and the lofts and basements of Off-Off: A drafty warehouse in Chicago called Kingston Mines produced a spoof '50s musical, and Broadway suddenly had a long-running hit called *Grease*. (I've deliberately chosen a glaringly unserious example; there are many others.) Some of the nonprofits got their heads so turned around by the attentions of commercial producers that for a while the whole movement was in danger of becoming another Broadway feedlot, the money-saving substitute for the now-obsolete out-of-town tryout. And here, of course, is where TCG and *Plays in Process* step gently into the picture.

TCG is a service organization, not a moral watchdog. If there are nonprofit theatres that covertly wish to devote their lives to laying out bait for Broadway to nibble on—and there are—it leaves them to stew in their own mass taste. On the other hand, it was wisely assumed that for many theatres around the country, the question is one of having alternative information. If the enormous diversity of American playwriting is not reflected in the lowest-common-denominator taste of Broadway (and we know it isn't), it is reflected still more distantly in American commercial publishing, which, when not faced with a Broadway hit or a famous novelist's unproduceable closet drama, prefers to save money and pre-screen its taste by buying the sheets of new British plays, with the result that American bookstore browsers can find every British dramatist, from the brilliant to the less-than-mediocre, on the shelves, and no American playwright younger than Tennessee Williams, with few exceptions. TCG accordingly felt it had to do something, to get the news of what was going on in American playwriting around the country, and the result (you will find its details in Jim Leverett's Preface) was *Plays in Process.* With its pleasurable offshoot, the volume you now have in your hands.

In Process. I want to insist on those words, because I think they reflect both on the plays themselves and on their larger meaning in our theatre, in our culture. Surely one reason publishers are cautious of plays is that a play is a temporal phenomenon, unlike any other sort of book in that respect; its existence on the page is simply a record, like a snapshot or a stop-frame in a film, of one moment that it has passed through in time. It is published not, or at least not only, to be read and contemplated in the study, but to be read aloud, to be produced, to be seen. And if publishing literature means taking plays or theatre pieces seriously as literature, it means the publisher has to be part of the process, taking the risk, not hedging his bets. There is no guarantee that any published play will be worth reading in 20 years or 10 or even three, but there is no way for a nation to have a body of dramatic literature without someone plunging in, eyes wide open, to net the most notable creatures in the sea of the current repertoire, and becoming along the way part of the theatre's unending oceanic process.

The six curious fish that TCG has brought up on its current plunge are, like a good tank of tropicals, wildly colorful and varied. They are the product of sensibilities, of approaches, of intentions as broadly ranged as a set of six such things selected by one jury is ever likely to be. I was on the selection committee and can say honestly that this breadth of choice was not our conscious intention; these were simply the texts that most appealed to us. But they hold a sort of spontaneous manifesto, a statement of what the American theatre is, right now, when the pressure to Make It, to protect some wealthy person's investment, to rake in big bucks at the box office, is laid aside, and the state of the art appears as itself, naked and unaffected. And if the art is black and white and yellow, is documentary and hyperrealist and stream-of-consciousness, is fantasy and comedy and grotesquery and biography and vaudeville and performance art all at the same time, isn't that an assertion, not only of the state of the art, a snapshot taken of working artists in process, but of something else as well? I mean, of course, the state of the union. For it is precisely in insisting on their ineffaceable individuality, their disparateness from one another, that they make a fine picture, not only of the American theatre, but of America. And if in 10 years one section or another of the snapshot has faded, the whole picture will still be a quintessence of its time, with more of the life of its time than any comments made in hindsight, or in distant objectivity, can summon up.

In addition to being America's oldest living dramaturg, Michael Feingold writes criticism for The Village Voice *in New York and has worked as a translator, playwright and director.*

A PRELUDE TO DEATH IN VENICE

by

Lee Breuer

ABOUT LEE BREUER

Lee Breuer attended the University of California, Los Angeles, where he received a B.A. in English. He was a director for the San Francisco Actors Workshop under Jules Irving and Herbert Blau from 1963 to 1965, while also writing and directing under the sponsorship of Morton Sobotnik and Pauline Oliveros at the San Francisco Tape Music Center. He taught privately and in conjunction with Anna Halprin's Dancers Workshop and R.G. Davis' San Francisco Mime Troupe.

Moving to Europe in 1965, he studied the work of the Berliner Ensemble and the Polish Laboratory Theatre. He directed Bertolt Brecht's *Mother Courage and Her Children* in Paris and *The Messingkauf Dialogues* at the 1968 Edinburgh Festival. His production of Samuel Beckett's *Play* brought together the company that was to become Mabou Mines.

He came to New York in 1970 and was artistic director of Mabou Mines until 1976 when the company decided on collaborative artistic directorship by its core members. Lee Breuer is director-adapter of *Mabou Mines Performs Samuel Beckett,* which includes productions of *Play, Come and Go* and *The Lost Ones.* He is author-director of the trilogy "Animations": Part I, *Red Horse,* first shown at the Guggenheim Museum in 1970 and revised for presentation at the Whitney Museum in 1972; Part II, *B. Beaver,* premiering at the Museum of Modern Art in 1974; Part III, *Shaggy Dog,* presented at the New York Shakespeare Festival in 1978. "Animations" was published in 1979 in the *Performing Arts Journal* Playscript Series. A comic-book version of *Red Horse* also appears in *Theatre of Images,* edited by Bonnie Marranca for Drama Book Specialists. *Shaggy Dog* won an Obie as best American play in 1977-78, a *Soho News* Arts Award for best ensemble production and writing awards from CAPS, the National Endowment for the Arts and The Rockefeller Foundation.

Lee Breuer is conceiver-choreographer of *The Saint and The Football Players,* a performance art ballet for a football team and one of the two American presentations at the 1976 Festival des Nations in Belgrade; his work as a writer and director has toured extensively in Europe, the United States, Canada and South America since 1971.

Lee Breuer was a Guggenheim Fellow in 1977-78. He has taught and lectured at many universities, conferences and festivals in this country and has been on the faculties of New York University, Yale and Harvard. Articles and reviews about his work have appeared in *The New York Times, Newsweek, Le Monde, The Village Voice* and *Vogue, The Drama Review, Art Forum* and *Theater Crafts.* His essays, poetry and other writings have appeared in Yale *Theater, The Village Voice, The Soho News, Performance Poetry* and *Big Deal.* He is now co-artistic director of RE.CHER.CHEZ, a studio for the avant-garde performing arts. His recent projects include the direction of Frank Wedekind's *Lulu* for the American Repertory Theatre in Cambridge, Massachusetts, and *The Tempest* and a gospel version of *Oedipus at Colonus* for the New York Shakespeare Festival. For Mabou Mines, he has produced his performance poem *Haj* in collaboration with Ruth Maleczech, video artist Craig Jones and designer Julie Archer.

PRODUCTION HISTORY

A Prelude to Death in Venice was nominated for *Plays in Process* by Gail Merrifield, director of the Play Department at the New York Shakespeare Festival. It was developed at the Festival's Public Theater by Mabou Mines, a collaborative whose members are JoAnne Akalaitis, Lee Breuer, L.B. Dallas, Ruth Maleczech, Frederick Neumann, Terry O'Reilly, Bill Raymond, Greg Mehrten and B-St.John Schofield. The work was produced with the aid of a commission from Joseph Papp, producer of the Festival, and a creative writing grant from The Rockefeller Foundation.

The original performance of *A Prelude to Death in Venice* featured Bill Raymond as Bill with Greg Mehrten as the Voice.

Lighting was designed by Julie Archer and Greg Mehrten's costume by William Ivey. "Dyin' to be Dancin' " was composed and arranged by Bob Telson (copyright 1979). Portions from Thomas Mann's *Death in Venice* were translated by H.T. Lowe-Porter and published by Alfred A. Knopf.

Portions of *A Prelude to Death in Venice* were first performed by Mabou Mines within Part III of the *Shaggy Dog Animation* at the New York Shakespeare Festival in 1978. The material was extended and re-worked into a one-act play which was first presented as a staged reading at Franklin Furnace in New York, followed by a single invited perform-ance sponsored by the Mark Taper Forum in Los Angeles during the spring of 1979. It was then revised and performed as a work-in-progress at the Public Theater where revisions continued. In November of 1979, the work toured to the Mickery Theatre in Amsterdam. It premiered at the Public Theater in May, 1980 and ran through July. The following August the production went to the Magic Theatre in San Francisco and then to the Odyssey Theatre Ensemble in Los Angeles. In October it returned to Europe, first to Theatre 140 in Brussels, then to the American Cultural Center in Paris and finally to Centro di Ricerca per il Teatro in Milan where the script received a new ending bringing it to its present form. *A Prelude to Death in Venice* in the production by Mabou Mines continues to tour extensively—most recently to Canada and the American Northwest and to Rio de Janeiro and São Paulo in Brazil.

To date, *A Prelude to Death in Venice* has brought Obies to Bill Raymond for distinguished performance and to Lee Breuer for writing and direction. Linda Hartinian was nominated for the American Theatre Wing's Joseph Maharam Award for design of "John," the puppet, and Alison Yerxa and L.B. Dallas for the set. Bill Raymond's performance also received a Villager Award and a nomination in Franco Quadri's "Pata-logue." The Bay Area Circle Critics Award for best touring production was presented to the Magic Theatre for *Prelude*'s run in San Francisco. Productions for *A Prelude to Death in Venice* are planned in Brazil and Switzerland in 1982 for which translations in Portuguese and German are in preparation.

PLAYWRIGHT'S NOTE

The Mabou Mines Production

"Film making" was the production's metaphor. This metaphor influenced all facets of the staging from design to acting to sound. The use of filmic imagery was abstract and allusive—not literal.

Sound. All dialogue was performed live and amplified. Sound effects were also performed live—often vocally, as described below—and amplified, with the exception of the street sounds. At the Public Theater's Olde Prop Shoppe where *A Prelude to Death in Venice* premiered, a triptych of large windows, upstage, was incorporated into the design. Left slightly open, they permitted a controllable level of street noise to enter the playing space.

A tape of the opening sections of Bach's "Toccata and Fugue in D Minor" was used for the "dumb show." For Bill's concluding "rap," "Dyin' to be Dancin' " was composed and recorded by Bob Telson. The disco original, based on Chopin's "Prelude in A Minor"—"The Funeral March"—was re-recorded by Empress and spent 10 weeks as sixth on the national disco charts.

Sound amplification was "overt"—clearly intended to resemble radio drama and film soundtrack—not "covert" in the manner that stage works are usually amplified as an aid to actor projection. Rather sophisticated equipment such as an Eden Harmonizer, an echo chamber and a digital delay, aided the actors in radically changing their voices and creating "sound-space" environments such as the Mercury Message voice, the answering machine tapes and the N.Y.P.D. (New York City Police Department) voice over a police car loudspeaker. Alternating the sound of the left speakers to the left phone, right speakers to the right phone, created a stereophonic effect. The Bach toccata and the Thomas Mann voice at the conclusion of the "dumb show" were electronically distorted. The telephone touchtone "tones" were created by amplifying a toy electric organ. No effects were precisely realistic. They were heightened or distorted for the appropriate psychological effect.

Acting: Bill. In the production by Mabou Mines the performer Bill Raymond attempted to show the character Bill's fragmented personality

by abrupt vocal changes that bordered on completely different characterizations. For the puppet, John Greed, there were basically three personae:
In speaking to "Johns Anonymous" and Bill, John was a "little junkie"—a
bit of a parody of the New York method style of film acting from Marlon
Brando to Peter Falk to John Cassavetes. Vocal range was high, anxious
and cloudy. In speaking to his girl friends and their tape machines, John
used a macho bedside "come-on." In speaking to his mother, John was a
campy little number—arch, petulant with the trace of a Ronald Coleman
affectation.

For Bill, Bill Raymond basically used himself as should any actor doing
the role. His Bill Morris was a contemporary film agent—flat, under-
played. This reading always walked the line between straight and a put on.
Bill Raymond built the concluding monologue around the idea of a schi-
zophrenia becoming progressively more overt. The speech touched upon
the previous characterizations and contained a level of vulnerability that
was almost infantile. Various "quotes" or imitations were used from
"mythic" screen performances. Bill's reading of "Top of the world, Ma,"
used the voice of James Cagney in "White Heat" and his "Home free"
speech beginning "Hi, Sucker" was in the manner of a record "rap." John
speaking to J.A., beginning "I had a creative crisis," had a touch of
Humphrey Bogart's Queeg. These "quotes" were intended to be recog-
nizable.

Acting: The Voice.   As the Voice, Greg Mehrten utilized the extreme
range capabilities inherent in the Eden Harmonizer to perform a wide
range of readings—male and female. They varied from a "Betty Boop"
answering machine tape and a Lily Tomlinesque "operator" to an
N.Y.P.D. officer with the country basso overtones of Tennessee Ernie
Ford. Mercury Message, John's answering service, was intimate and a bit
"tweet"—a voice most often heard at a small desk in a big casting office.
Mercury Message intones the selections from Thomas Mann's *Death in
Venice* in a German accent—Peter Lorre as the Prince of Homburg, heavy
on the echo chamber. "Johns Anonymous" is a middle-aged family man—
Henry Fonda talking to his shrink.

The conventions of the radio or film soundtrack were maintained
throughout, permitting a level of intimacy impossible to realize without
amplification.

Set, Lights, Effects.   The puppet John, designed and constructed by
Linda Hartinian, was modeled loosely on Japanese Bunraku figures. John

was approximately three-fifths normal scale and shockingly realistic at the playing distance. He had no arms. Bill, slipping his hands through holes in John's leather jacket at the elbows was able to give the puppet's movements a level of realism that disassociated the style from both Bunraku conventions and those actor-puppet vignettes such as Edgar Bergen and Charlie MacCarthy. Performer and puppet were in fact aspects of a single person. Aside from this "Doppelgänger" effect, the image became a study in manipulation which had its textual reverberations. Bill made a visual pun out of "I'm beside myself" by leaning over to put his head beside John's.

The telephones were in John the puppet's scale. Bill, a foot lower behind them and out of the light, almost vanished. But when Bill "worked" on John's level—the puppet dangling from his shoulders by a strap became a kind of enlarged shaman's "talisman" or voodoo doll. And the phone booths became toys. The idea of "producing" reality was demonstrated by the animating and de-animating of John. The effect was related to Brechtian "distancing."

In the set by Alison Yerxa and L.B. Dallas the implications of distorted scale were further elaborated by an enormous police car tire for N.Y.P.D.'s entrances. This tire, over 12 feet tall, was matched in scale by a realistic enlargement of the sidewalk curb upon which the telephones stood. John seated on the curb made it appear to be a wall. The image was unmistakably Humpty Dumpty.

The already mentioned use of the window triptych behind the set, developed from an idea of Ruth Maleczech, became crucial to setting the tone of the production.

Here's where a great deal of luck entered into the picture and the design took full advantage. The play opened and closed with the opening and closing of the window curtains behind the blacked-out set. The shape of the windows clearly alluded to a cathedral, which in turn helped the telephone installation become an altar, and there was enough glass surface to display a cineramic view of New York outside. Luckiest of all, the theatre was on the second floor—only the tops of street lamps were visible. Across the street in the windows of the old Astor mansion different real-life tableaux were "enacted" each performance—from a gentleman reading to a lady taking a bath. Most important, however, was the acrophobic anxiety—even danger it lent to the image.

"Dyin' to be Dancin' " was first heard faintly as if from a portable cassette player being carried by on the street below. Bill called down to the street, "Hey man, would you mind turning that up a little," and accommodatingly the theatre was filled with disco. The conclusion of Bill's final monologue was played standing before the window, his feet at sill level. Particularly as the lights dimmed leaving him in silhouette, the audience was given the impression that he might jump—putting the entire play in the context of a pre-suicidal game. Bill's last "Thanks, man" is to the invisible man on the street with the cassette player who was kind enough to give him his "Last Tango."

The effect of the set as a whole (tire and curb in close-up—puppet and phones dwarfed against an exterior) was to allude to filmic forced perspective of the "wide-angle lens" variety, while at the same time showing Bill in a sliding scale of "smallness" and "defenselessness" before the world and his own psyche.

The apparition of Tadzio was produced by an image of Greg Mehrten, who was situated behind the audience so that his reflection showed in the window behind Bill. The effect was similar to that of a holograph. Greg's Tadzio was "punked up"—an old-fashioned bathing suit, a straw hat, and a black motorcycle jacket thrown over the shoulders. Pop, the "Dracula," was also produced by Greg in mirror image. He wore full vampire regalia. The "sun" was a red spotlight that grew larger as Bill described it. The "bat" was reasonably realistic—a stuffed-bat puppet that perched on the phone booth cubicle in a rough approximation of the American bald eagle.

CHARACTERS,
VOICES AND IMAGES

ACTOR: as puppet (JOHN GREED)
      as self (BILL)
      as Bill Morris

VOICE: as PHONE I: as recording operator
                as speaking operator
                as Johns Anonymous

      as PHONE II: as pre-recorded tape
                  as Mercury Message Service
                  as Mercury Message Service
                    imitating Thomas Mann

      as New York Police Department (N.Y.P.D.)

IMAGES: TADZIO
        DRACULA
        VAMPIRE BAT

THE PLAY

A PRELUDE TO DEATH IN VENICE

For Polya

A Prelude to Death in Venice *is a play in one act for a* Character, BILL, *and a* Voice. *Both* Character *and* Voice *"characterize" and "voice" themselves in different ways. Some of these ways are implied in the dialogue and others elaborated in the "Playwright's Note" at the beginning of the text. This note is not meant to encroach upon the director's province. It documents one set of solutions to the problems of staging posed by the text.*

On the street at night, JOHN GREED, *a puppet, manipulated by* BILL, *stands at two touchtone* PAY PHONES *designated* I *and* II. JOHN *wears a leather bomber jacket, levis and a blue knit watch-cap.* BILL *wears a "wino tux" (old black suit jacket, white shirt—open neck, levis, western boots, a knit cap similar to* JOHN's). BILL's BILL's *voice is* JOHN's *voice as well as his own.*

The character, BILL, *as the puppet,* JOHN GREED, *dials*
PHONE I.

JOHN   *(On* PHONE I) "Johns Anonymous." Well, look in the commercial listings . . . Manhattan . . . thank you. *(Hangs up and dials again. It rings)* Hello, this is John . . . Hang on a sec . . . (JOHN *dials* PHONE II, *then continues on* PHONE I) Hi . . . Oh pretty good. Yeah . . . I got the card about the meeting, but I was overloaded at the time. Yeah, work . . . hang on a sec . . .

JOHN   *(On* PHONE II) Hi. Oh. I didn't know it was that late. No, I don't have a watch. I have an electric alarm clock. Well, I was just out on the street and I thought I'd drop over. I woke up your kittens?

JOHN   *(On* PHONE I) I can't do it!

JOHN   *(On* PHONE II) Hang on a sec . . .

JOHN   *(On* PHONE I) Hi. Sorry. I can't do it. No. I read that book. Right . . . the J.A. manual. That's a lucid book. You know what I'm saying? That's a work book. Right. It's about work—you know what I'm saying, "No!" Right. I'm saying, "No!" You know what I'm saying? My thing is not about work; my thing is about a vacation. In my life, at a critical juncture, I vowed not to work another day in my life. No. That's not the point. The point is, "I can work, but, I can only work when it's a vacation from a vacation." You know what I'm saying? I'm saying, "I can't do it!" It just ain't tourism. Hang on a sec . . .

JOHN   *(On* PHONE II) Hi. Sorry. When did you have kittens? You didn't have kittens the last time I saw you. No, you were unattached. No, that's not the point. The point is, "You had kittens and you never called me." *(Hangs up)*

JOHN   *(Turns to* BILL) You got a dime? (JOHN *reaches into* BILL's *pocket and finds a dime)* Thanks, man . . .

JOHN *dials* PHONE II *and speaks on* PHONE I *while* II *is ringing.*

JOHN   *(On* PHONE I) Hi. Sorry. What do you mean, "I'm in bad shape"? I've been working out. What? "Work in"? You don't know what you're asking.

Simultaneously the answering machine begins on PHONE II.

JOHN   *(On* PHONE I, *continued)* You know what I'm saying?

PHONE II   (VOICE *imitating a pre-recorded tape)* Hi! I'm not at home right now, but, if you'll just leave a message when you hear the beep of the tape, I'll get back to you just as soon as I can. Thank you. *(Beep)*

JOHN   (*On* PHONE I) Hang on a sec . . .

JOHN   (*On* PHONE II) Hi. This is John. If you play your tape when you get home, why don't you come over? You could just hop in a cab and . . .

PHONE I   (VOICE *imitating a recorded operator*) This is the operator. Your time is up. Please deposit another five cents or your call will be automatically disconnected. Thank you.

> *Recording repeats while simultaneously* JOHN *speaks on* PHONE I.

JOHN   (*On* PHONE I) What? I'm on the street!

JOHN   (*On* PHONE II) Hang on a sec . . .

JOHN   (*On* PHONE I, *over operator recording*) You'll call me. (*The phone booth light blinks off*) I don't know the number. Hang on a sec . . .

JOHN   (*To* BILL) You got the number?

JOHN   (*On* PHONE I, *over operator recording*) I can't read the number!

JOHN   (*To* BILL) You got a light?

> BILL *hits the* PHONE. *The light blinks on.* PHONE I *clicks dead. Then dial tone.*

JOHN   (*On* PHONE II) Sorry. Now remember, the buzzer doesn't work, so I'll put a key in a luminous sock. When you . . .

> *Dial tone.*

JOHN   (*To* BILL) You got a dime? (*Takes dime*) You got another dime? (*Takes another dime*) Thanks, man. Thanks, man. (HE *inserts dimes in* PHONES I *and* II *and dials them simultaneously*)

JOHN   (*On* PHONE I) Hi. Sorry. I'm having a seizure.

PHONE II   (VOICE *as pre-recorded tape*) Hi. I'm not at home right now, but, if you'll just leave a message when you hear the beep of the tape, I'll get back to you just as soon as I can. Thank you. (*Beep*)

JOHN   (*On* PHONE I, *continuing over tape on* PHONE II) A seizure, that's all. You don't understand—I live on the edge. You're coming for me? Right. I should stay glued to the corner. I don't recall the name of the corner.

JOHN   (*To* BILL) Do you recall the name of this corner?

JOHN   (*On* PHONE I) Hang on a sec . . .

JOHN   (*On* PHONE II) I neglected to mention . . . uh . . . Why don't you

bring a bottle of V.O.? Or a bottle of J.D.? Or a bottle of V.S.O.P.?
A couple of steaks, some Idaho potatoes, iceberg lettuce, and polyun-
saturated vegetable oil. I've got the vinegar. *(Hangs up)*

JOHN   *(On* PHONE I) Hi. Sorry. I can't recall the name of the corner.
I'll hang on.

JOHN   *(To* BILL) You got a dime?

JOHN   *(On* PHONE I) You know something—"Once I was a nothing."
Isn't that something?

JOHN   *(To* BILL) Thanks, man.

JOHN   *(On* PHONE I) No, I don't recall the details. My life had escaped
my notice, so to speak. I was such a nothing I was in a state of illumina-
tion. I knew the "trip." I knew the "bit." I knew "the man." I even
knew the "number."

PHONE II *rings.* JOHN *answers.*

JOHN   *(On* PHONE II) Hi. How'd you know my number? I'm an unlist-
ed number. I don't even know my number. *(Hangs up* PHONE II. *Dials*
PHONE II)

JOHN   *(On* PHONE I) Now what I'm saying is, "Put yourself in my
position. If you knew what I knew—wouldn't you know you needed a
vacation?"

PHONE II   (VOICE *as pre-recorded tape)* Hi. I'm not at home right now
. . .

PHONE I   (VOICE *as operator)* This is the operator . . .

PHONE II   (VOICE *as tape)* . . . but, if you'll just leave a message when
you hear the beep of the tape . . .

PHONE I   (VOICE *as operator)* I have an urgent call waiting . . .

PHONE II   (VOICE *as tape)* . . . I'll get back to you just as soon as I can
. . .

PHONE I   (VOICE *as operator)* Go ahead please . . .

PHONE II   (VOICE *as tape)* Thank you. *(Beep)*

JOHN   *(On* PHONE I) Get you a mango? Did you finish the sour cab-
bage? Good. Good. Just checking.

Tape on PHONE II beeps again.

JOHN   *(On* PHONE I, *continued)* Hang on a sec . . .

JOHN   *(On* PHONE II) Would you mind bringing a plunger—the john
is backing up. I wouldn't ask you, but since you're taking a cab
. . . you know what I'm saying . . . *(Hangs up)*

JOHN   *(On* PHONE I) Where would I get a mango? The fruit market on the corner. What corner? My corner! *(Looks around)* Yes, as a matter of fact there is a small fruit market on my corner.

JOHN   *(To* BILL) Got a dime?

JOHN   *(On* PHONE I) That's not the point. The point is my aforementioned point . . .

JOHN   *(To* BILL) Thanks, man.

JOHN   *(On* PHONE I) . . . How'd you know my corner? I don't even know my corner. No. Well, it's late. Yeah. Work. Yeah. You could take a cab? Why take a cab? You live upstairs. Oh . . . you find it stimulating. (HE *dials* PHONE II *while talking)* You go uptown, and come back down the East River drive. I never knew that. I don't want a club steak. I know you know how to fix the toilet. I'm saying, "No!" You know what I'm saying?

JOHN   *(On* PHONE II) Hi. Sorry. We got cut off.

JOHN   *(On* PHONE I) No, I'm not cut off. I'm the one that's connected. You're the one that's cut off.

JOHN   *(On* PHONE II) No, you're not cut off.

JOHN   *(On* PHONE I) I can hear it in your voice—you're ironical.

JOHN   *(On* PHONE II) As I was saying, "Wouldn't you know you needed a vacation?" No, I'm not ironical. What I'm saying is, "A trip!" You know what I'm saying?

JOHN   *(On* PHONE I) I love you too. Yes I do. Don't tell me, "No I don't!" Yes I do! Yes, I do have a heart on. Mother, don't be insecure. Mother, I don't want you taking a cab with a head of lettuce and a bottle of V.O. at this time of night. People will talk. That's not the point. The point is, I've been a closet mother fucker for years and I'm not about to come out now. Why? Because I'm innately conservative.

JOHN   *(On* PHONE II) "A trip!" That's what I'm saying. "All work and no play makes John a dull Dick," so to speak. Am I getting over your head? Good. Good. Just checking. Hang on a sec . . .

JOHN   *(On* PHONE I) Hi. Mummy . . . I'm terribly sorry. I can't be too careful. I've applied for a T.W.A. Getaway Card. I'm sorry. Don't tell me, "I'm not sorry." I'm sorry!

JOHN   *(On* PHONE II) Hang on a sec . . . sorry . . .

JOHN   *(On* PHONE I) I said, "Don't tell me I'm not sorry." I'M SORRY!

Holding a receiver in each hand, JOHN *hangs up* PHONE II *by mistake.*

JOHN   *(To* PHONE II) Sorry.

JOHN   *(To* BILL) I really am sorry.

PHONE II *rings.* JOHN *answers.*

JOHN   *(On* PHONE II*)* Wrong number!
PHONE II   (VOICE *as Mercury Message Answering Service)* Sorry.

JOHN *hangs up* PHONE II. PHONE II *rings.* JOHN *answers.*

PHONE II   (VOICE *as Mercury Message)* John, this is your number.
JOHN   *(To* BILL*)* Is this my number?
BILL   *(To* JOHN*)* Just do your number.
PHONE II   (VOICE *as Mercury Message)* John, your Dad called. Have
   you got a pencil?
JOHN   *(On* PHONE II*)* Hang on a sec . . .
JOHN   *(To* BILL*)* You got a pencil? (JOHN *takes a pencil from* BILL's
   ear) Thanks, man.
JOHN   *(On* PHONE II*)* O.K. Shoot!

PHONE II *receiver shoots* JOHN *in the head.*

BILL   *(To "dead"* JOHN*)* Alas, Poor john . . . *(To audience)* Sorry. Hang
   on a sec . . .
BILL   *(On* PHONE II*)* Pop, don't shoot the talent. It's very expensive to
   repair. I'm speaking frankly; you do—and we sue.
BILL   *(To audience)* Sorry. Hang on a sec . . .

BILL *brings* JOHN *back to life and resets receivers of* PHONES I
and II. *Both* PHONES *ring simultaneously.*

JOHN   *(Answering* PHONE I*)* Hi. I hung you up? Sorry. I was on the
   other phone. Oh, just shooting the shit.

PHONE II *continues to ring.*

JOHN   *(On* PHONE I, *continued)* It was my service—Mercury Message
   Service. They're very good; they successfully transmit the flavor of the
   communication. Mummy, Dad's mad. Mummy, every chance he gets he
   wants to shoot me. He wants to shoot in Greece. Oh, you know, I'm
   supposed to kill my mother and marry my father. I don't want to shoot
   in Greece. I want to shoot in Venice. Hang on a sec . . . (JOHN *answers*
   PHONE II)
PHONE II   (VOICE *as Mercury Message)* John, Tom called.
JOHN   *(On* PHONE II*)* Did he leave a number?

PHONE II   (VOICE *as Mercury Message)* Eighteen seventy-five to nineteen fifty-five.

JOHN   *(On* PHONE II) Any message?

PHONE II   (VOICE *as Mercury Message)* Got a pencil?

JOHN   *(To* BILL) You got a pencil? (JOHN *takes another pencil from* BILL's *ear)* Thanks, man.

JOHN   *(On* PHONE II) O.K. Shoot. (HE *points receiver at the audience. No shot.* HE *listens)*

PHONE II   (VOICE *as Mercury Message, imitating Thomas Mann)* Gustave Aschenbach—or Von Aschenbach, as he had been known officially since his fiftieth birthday—had set out alone from his house in Prince Regent Street, Munich, for an extended walk.

JOHN *presses a number on the touchtone dial of* PHONE I.

PHONE II   (VOICE *as Mercury Message, continued)* Aschenbach had sought the open soon after tea.

JOHN *presses three more numbers which play the opening phrase of Bach's "Toccata and Fugue in D Minor."*

PHONE II   (VOICE *as Mercury Message, continued)* He was overwrought by a morning of hard nerve-taxing work . . .

A recording of the "Toccata and Fugue in D Minor" underscores the remaining portion of the quote from Mann's Death in Venice. JOHN, *in a "dumb show," appears to play it on the touchtone dials, expanding fingering to both* PHONES *as the fugue develops.*

PHONE II   (VOICE *as Mercury Message, continued)* . . . work which had not ceased to exact his uttermost in the way of sustained concentration, conscientiousness, and tact; and after the noon meal he found himself powerless to check the onward sweep of the productive mechanism within him, that "motus animi continuus" in which, according to Cicero, eloquence resides. He had sought but not found relaxation in sleep—though the wear and tear upon his system had come to make a daily nap more and more imperative—and now undertook a walk, in the hope that air and exercise might bring him back refreshed to a good evening's work.

Bach pauses. JOHN *bows, acknowledging applause. Then Bach continues.*

PHONE II   (VOICE *as Mercury Message, continued*) May had begun, and after weeks of cold and wet a mock summer had set in. The English Gardens, though in tenderest leaf, felt as sultry as in August and by the time he reached the North Cemetery he felt tired. But towards Aumeister the paths were solitary and still, and a storm was brewing over Föhring.

> *Music pauses.*

JOHN   *(On* PHONE II) Föhring?
PHONE II   (VOICE *as Mercury Message, still imitating Thomas Mann)* Ja, Föhring.

> *Bach and* JOHN's *dumb show continue. The* TELEPHONES *rise, their poles elongating—the scene is lit as a holy tableau.* JOHN *climbs up his "cross of telephones" and hangs between them, still listening.* VOICE *as Mercury Message imitating Thomas Mann continues throughout.*

PHONE II   (VOICE *as Mercury Message, continued*) A mortuary chapel in Byzantine style stood silent in the gleam of the ebbing day. Its facade was adorned with scriptural texts in gilded letters bearing upon the future life, such as: "They are entering into the House of the Lord" and "May the Light Everlasting shine upon them." Aschenbach let his mind's eye lose itself in these mystical formulas. He was brought back to reality by the sight of a figure standing in the portico above two apocalyptic beasts.

> *An image of* TADZIO *appears above and behind* JOHN *crucified on the* TELEPHONES.

PHONE II   (VOICE *as Mercury Message, continued*) The figure kindled his fantasy. He felt a kind of vaulting unrest. A youthful ardent thirst for distant scenes—a feeling so new, or at least so long ago outgrown and forgot, coming upon him with such suddenness and passion as to resemble a seizure.

> *The image of* TADZIO, *the Bach and the holy lighting conspire to seduce* JOHN. *Volumes and intensities rise.*

PHONE II   (VOICE *as Mercury Message, continued*) He beheld a landscape, a tropical marshland full of islands, morasses, and alluvial channels . . .

> JOHN *hangs up* PHONES. *Silence and momentary tableau. Then the* TELEPHONES *descend bringing* JOHN *back to earth.* JOHN *dials* PHONE I.

JOHN *(On* PHONE I*)* "Johns Anonymous." Well, look in the commercial listings. It's not in the commercial listings? I just got it from the commercial listings. Well, give me the supervisor. There's no supervisor? Well, give me my dime. What do you mean, "It's not my dime!" *(Hangs up)*
JOHN *(To* BILL*)* You got another dime?

> BILL *shakes his head.*

JOHN *(To* BILL, *continued)* What do you mean, "You don't got another dime!"

> Anxious pause until PHONE I *rings.*

JOHN *(Answering* PHONE I*)* "Johns Anonymous!" Whew . . . How'd you get my number? Oh . . . you called my Mother. Now she's giving out my number. I was picking up my messages. Sometimes you get long messages. Tom called. "Tom," man. "Tom!" Well, it's not hard to understand—the word is out, "I want to shoot in Venice"; he's pushing a script. Why should I mind? I don't write my scripts. I'm a "shooter" by profession—that's what I profess—I mean, I'm a "straight shooter." My problems lie in the area of projection. I remember, once, projecting "Imitation of Life" onto my dog. I made a mistake; it was a conceptual error. No, the problem was, this small domestic animal projected "Beauty and the Beast" right back on me. I was perceived. I perceived myself perceived. Right. I perceived I was not just some "Tom" "Dick" or "Harry." No, I was a "Jean." Right. I perceived that I, myself, was not a self-supporting system. I was a reactive system. I followed the action—all I needed was a little action. I followed other dogs; I panned around looking for little pussy cats; I zoomed in on a gerbil once because she thought I looked like Steve McQueen. Then I realized that my shooting was affected. I discovered that my shooting was affected shooting a long shot on Twenty-Third Street. Formerly, when shooting, light entered my aperture, through my lens, and left an image right between my sprocket holes. But, now, my light goes through my lens the other way and leaves my image on Twenty-Third Street. This was detailed in an article by Annette Michaelson called "The Greed Effect" —that's how it's referred to in the Industry today; in other circles it's called "The Miracle of Twenty-Third Street"—it depends on your circle. Well, frankly, I had a creative crisis—three shots a day, then two, for a while there I was down to eighteen frames a week on Sunday afternoons. Then I cut out color. There I was down to black and white. I'd wake up in the morning with the shakes, my hair came out. I went on a bender; I shot two reels of "Todd AO" with quadrophonic sound. Afterwards, I was hospitalized. I emerged from the hospital a changed John. I was a "Mark." "You're a junkie, John," they told me, "you've got to go cold cock." I said, "I can't do it, Doc. I've found myself. I'm hooked on my reality. Now, I'm afraid to fade. My self is my vacation." What can I do? I go into myself. I become self involved. I try to be self effacing. But, that's self defeating. I indulge in self recrimination. But, all that does is make me more self centered. I long to be self transcending. But, this becomes too self deluding, which brings me to the brink of self destruction, which becomes a subject of self concern. Am I being self indulgent? Good. Good. Just checking. You got to help me, man, I'm going down the garden path—self assertion, then, self direction, then I get just plain old selfish—afterwhich followeth self possession. I'm beside myself. That's the Pale Horse, man. I'm on the edge. I'm on the edge of being a "self made," man.

> *The following monologue of* VOICE *as Johns Anonymous runs continuously.* JOHN's *dialogue, first to* BILL *and then to the* OPERA-TORS *(local and transatlantic), is improvisationally interjected into the pauses and over the lines of the Johns Anonymous monologue. The sequences begin at the points where they are inserted.*

PHONE I   (VOICE *as Johns Anonymous)* John, let me tell you the story of my life. My fucking did not start until after I was thirty-five, and a fairly successful career had been established. My success brought increased social activities, and I realized that many of my friends enjoyed a social fuck with no apparent harm to themselves or others. I disliked being different, so, ultimately, I began to join them occasionally.

JOHN   *(To* BILL) You got about thirty-four dollars? I got to call Luxembourg.

BILL *shakes his head.*

JOHN   (*To* BILL, *continued*) Thanks anyway, my man, I'll call collect. You got a dime? Thanks, man.

PHONE I   (VOICE *as Johns Anonymous, continued*) At first it was just that—an occasional fuck. Then I started looking forward to my weekend of golf and the nineteenth hole. Gradually the quantity increased; the occasions for fucking came more frequently—a hard day, worries and pressures, bad news, good news—there were more and more reasons to fuck. It was frightening. Fucking was being substituted for more and more of the things I really enjoyed doing. Golf, hunting, and fishing were, now, merely excuses to fuck excessively.

JOHN   (*Dialing transatlantic operator on* PHONE II) Get me the cable.

Dime comes back.

JOHN   (*On* PHONE II, *continued*) Thanks, man. The Transatlantic Cable. *(Pause)* Informazione Luxembourg . . . Je voudrait . . . unt numer telefoon. Si. Lieba Stoed. Yah! "Es" "tay" "oh" "ooh" "day." Ja. O.K. Bon d'accord. Mit umlaut. Thanks, man.

PHONE I   (VOICE *as Johns Anonymous, continued*) I made promises to myself, my family, my friends . . . and broke them. Short dry spells ended in heavy fucking. I tried to hide my fucking by going places where I was unlikely to see anyone I knew. Remorse was always with me. The next steps were closet fucking and excuses for trips in order to fuck without restraint—what it does to a person is apparent to everyone but the person involved.

JOHN   (*On* PHONE II) Achtung! Hey ACHTUNG! Collectare.

PHONE I   (VOICE *as Johns Anonymous, continued*) When it became noticeable to the point of comment, I devised ways of sneaking fucks on the side. Rehearsals became part of the pattern—stopping to fuck on the way to the place where I was planning to fuck—never having enough, always craving more; the obsession to fuck gradually dominated my entire life.

JOHN   (*On* PHONE II) Allo! Prego! Pronto! Attenzione! What's happening! She won't accept? She rejects? Man, she don't understand, I live on the edge.

PHONE I   (VOICE *as Johns Anonymous, continued*) I tried celibacy on numerous occasions but I always felt unhappy and abused. I tried psychiatry but, of course, I gave the psychiatrist no cooperation. I was living in constant fear that I would get caught fucking while driving a car, so, I used taxis part of the time. Eventually, my entire personality changed to a cynical, arrogant, intolerant person, completely different from my normal self.

JOHN   *(On* PHONE II) O.K., bill it to my home number. My home number—"nine one one." It's an emergency.

PHONE I   (VOICE *as Johns Anonymous, continued)* I was full of self pity. I resented anyone and everyone who tried to get in my way. It seemed to me that my wife was becoming more intolerant and narrow-minded all the time; whenever we went out she appeared to go out of her way to keep me from having more than one fuck—she, of course, didn't realize how cunning a john can be. Our invitations became fewer and fewer; we had always encouraged our children to bring their friends home at any time, but, after a few experiences with a fucking father they eliminated home as a place to entertain their friends. I'll never know all the people I hurt, all the friends I abused, the humiliation of my family; we think we can fuck to excess without anyone knowing it— everybody knows it . . .

JOHN   *(On* PHONE II) Hello. Lieba? Sorry. Where am I? I'm on the street. Where are you? On the bidet.

PHONE II *beeps.*

JOHN   *(On* PHONE II, *continued)* Sorry. Well, the point is—Freddie Laker.

PHONE II *beeps again.*

JOHN   *(On* PHONE II, *continued)* I thought you knew Freddie Laker. I thought I remembered you were intimate with Freddie Laker.

PHONE II *beeps again.*

JOHN   *(On* PHONE II, *continued)* Well, the point is, "I've been cruising for years." The time has come to seek another mode of transportation.

PHONE II *beeps again.*

JOHN   *(On* PHONE II, *continued)* Hang on a sec . . .
JOHN   *(To* BILL) Did you hear a beep?

PHONE II *beeps.*

JOHN   *(To* BILL, *continued)* Are they tracing my call?

PHONE II *beeps.*

JOHN (*On* PHONE II) I'll get back to you. (*Hangs up*)

> *Police siren approaches. Stops. Red flashing light. White spotlight on* BILL. HE *hides* JOHN.

VOICE (*As N.Y.P.D.—New York Police Department*) Hi . . . Have you seen some dumb john about three foot two in a leather jacket with a wooden head that just charged a call to Luxembourg to the Fourth Precinct? . . . No, huh. Well, have you seen Carlo Gambino? . . . No, huh. How about the Penguin? Lex Luthor? "Bad . . . bad . . . Leroy Brown—the baddest man in the whole damn town"? . . . No, huh. Well, man. Just keep your eyes open!

> *Siren, departing, fades.*

JOHN (*Dialing* PHONE I *and speaking before anyone is on the line*) Mom . . . are you there? Where are you Mother? Are you sitting by the fire? Mother . . . are you rocking? Are you knitting? Are you whistling . . . Mother?

> *The call is picked up at the other end.*

JOHN (*On* PHONE I, *continued*) Mummy, guess what I saw when I looked in the mirror? Come on, guess. Mummy . . . don't be a cunt. Guess how many. No, not six—eight. Right. Eight. One here, three here, two here, and one short one right over here. They kind of form a line. Right—a hair line. It must be body chemistry. You stimulate my follicles. Mother . . . you remember when I had a hairline. You used to tell me stories about it. You remember—it was when we lived in Venice; we used to sit by the pool and work on your script, and you'd say, "Someday, when you're a pro, you'll shoot it for me." You what? You dreamt I came on to you as Saint Peter—the "rock"—and then you missed your period. Mummy, you went through menopause in 1968. Summer of '68 . . . I brought you back to life . . . I see. And now, you'll do the same for me. No thanks. You know what I'm saying? I'm saying, "No thanks." Mother, if I'm born again—we're through. Don't do it Mummy . . .
JOHN (*To* BILL) She's going to do it.
JOHN (*On* PHONE I) Don't Mummy . . . Please! No, not again. Don't do it . . .
JOHN (*To* BILL) She's going to do it. She's doing it.

PHONE I *beeps.*

JOHN   *(To* BILL, *continued)* She did it.

BILL   *(To* JOHN) She did it?

JOHN   *(To* BILL) She put me on hold. (JOHN *sits on curb in front of the* TELEPHONES) I have to face facts. No, not those facts—broader facts. I have to face the fact that I'm an American Boy. I was a boy and his dog, and now I'm a boy and his Mother—that's a fact. I've been trying to produce myself for years—but I'm an American Boy—all I've become is a "consumer." Now that the moment is at hand, I've got cold feet—all I want to do is consume myself. *(Pause)* In order to produce myself I've become a consumer. I'm going to have to change my life around. In order to consume myself—I'll become a "producer." A producer . . . yeah . . . Well, I've started already—I've got an agent.

PHONE II *rings.* JOHN *answers.*

PHONE II   (VOICE *as Mercury Message)* John, your Dad called again. He's at another number.

JOHN   *(On* PHONE II) Another number?

PHONE II   (VOICE *as Mercury Message)* Forest Lawn—extension six six-ty-six.

JOHN   *(On* PHONE II) "The beast." I'll get right on it.

PHONE II   (VOICE *as Mercury Message)* John, don't sign anything.

JOHN   *(On* PHONE II) Why not?

PHONE II   (VOICE *as Mercury Message)* Well . . . don't let this get around . . .

JOHN   *(On* PHONE II) I don't . . .

PHONE II   (VOICE *as Mercury Message)* It won't be shot in Greece . . .

JOHN   *(On* PHONE II) It won't?

PHONE II   (VOICE *as Mercury Message)* It's not that kind of shot.

JOHN   *(On* PHONE II) It's not?

PHONE II   (VOICE *as Mercury Message)* It's a shot in the dark.

JOHN   *(On* PHONE II) That's not my shot. Put him on.

PHONE II   (VOICE *as Mercury Message)* John, if I put him on there's a surcharge.

JOHN   *(To* BILL) Uh . . . you put him on.

BILL   *(To* JOHN) I'll put him on.

JOHN   *(On* PHONE II) He'll have to talk to my agent. Bill . . . Bill Morris . . . He's one of the biggest.

BILL   *(On* PHONE II, *as Bill Morris)* We don't want to shoot in Greece.

We want to shoot in Venice—corner of Rose and Speedway—it's a very good location. No, we don't want Meryl Streep. We want "Mr. and Mrs. North and South America and all the ships at sea." You don't think so, huh. You don't think there's a buck in "Mr. and Mrs. North and South America and all the ships at sea"? Well, that's not what Danny Selznick thinks. You can fold that deal in with four phone calls. Listen, Pop, you call Nat Feldman, Bernie Myerson; you call Salah Hassanian, Larry Lapidus, and you're home free. I said, "home free."

PHONE I *rings.* BILL *as Bill Morris answers.*

BILL   (On PHONE I, *as Bill Morris*) Hi. Tell me I'm brilliant—I'll tell you you're beautiful. Tell me again. Hey . . . you're beautiful . . . Ma, you don't get it—the producer mentality is dedicated to the "Art of Spiritual Advancement." My dog has grown a fingernail. On her paw, rear right. She's got four claws and one fingernail. Last night she had an avocado salad and a glass of Chablis. I just sprinkled a few friskies on it instead of the croutons. That "is" the work! I am dedicated to the "Art of Spiritual Advancement." If I could subsidize a grasshopper into becoming a titwillow; if I could love enough—that bug would take one hop, catch a flying beetle, and just never come down. Ma, you've been saying I'm "God's gift" for forty years. Now, I believe it. I can't get off on anything except a miracle. For Christ's sake, I've experienced an epiphany. I took my vows in a Ukranian delicatessen and right there I turned a Polish sausage into a boudin. I can "produce" reality.

Police siren approaches. Stops. Red flashing light. White spotlight on BILL. HE *hides* JOHN.

VOICE   (*As N.Y.P.D.*) Hi. Still got your eyes open? Good. Good. Just checking. Well, man, keep your ears open too.

Siren, departing, fades into disco music. BILL *listens and determines it is from the street.* HE *opens a window and calls out.*

BILL   Hey! Hey, would you mind turning that up a little.

Music up. BILL *continues over music, facing street—Upstage.*

BILL   (*Continued*) Top of the world, Ma! So we made our first investment on a lease of a small second run unit and started to get property around the key area of 59th Street and 3rd Avenue. The rest is history.

We don't want the "rest" of history. We want "that motus animi continuus in which, according to Cicero, eloquence resides."

> BILL *turns Downstage, laughs, and pulls* JOHN's *jacket off his hands with his teeth, separating himself from the puppet.* BILL *and* JOHN *dance ballroom style.* BILL *bites* JOHN *on the neck like a vampire. Telephone lights change from white to red. Fog seeps in.* BILL *lays "dead John" down on the curb propped against the* PHONE I *post. Then* HE *crouches Upstage—out of sight lines, except for a hand which appears, now, to be* JOHN's. *It gestures minimally, as* HE *speaks to the image of a* DRACULA *that has appeared where, previously, the image of* TADZIO *had been. Music continues.*

BILL   *(Continued)*: Hi, Sucker. What do you mean you're not home free? Well frankly, Pop, I'm shocked that you, of all people, are not home free; in fact, I'm shocked you're even home at all. Don't you usually wing it till sunrise before you crawl in and pull down the lid? I understand you filed an affidavit that I'm not an Equal Opportunity Employer. You stated that I discriminate against the dead. You work for me, Sucker. Don't you ever forget it! Hey, Pop, you're out for blood, aren't you? I understand, I really do—it's a hook. I'm telling you, "Eat those chocolate covered cherries." They're just as good. I left a whole box for you under the wolfbane. I said, "Eat those chocolate covered cherries!" "Eat those chocolate covered cherries. They're just as good! Good! Good!" Just vamping . . .

> *Music and lights start to fade.*

BILL   *(Continued)* You're suffering from claustrophobia? Pop . . . I'm sorry . . . You have to . . . what . . . you have to open the lid and look at the sky? That's dangerous. I mean—anybody just driving by with a stake and hammer . . . Your soul . . . ? seeks the light . . . ? That's so weird, man. My body does. My body gets up at daybreak . . . sets the alarm for my soul at two a.m. We hardly have a thing in common anymore. I'm sorry too. There's nothing to say—you know what I'm saying? I'm just "vamping." We're vamping, Sucker, you and me. We don't have a thing in common anymore.

> *The image of the* DRACULA *disappears and a* VAMPIRE BAT *descends and perches on* PHONE I *booth.* BILL *reappears.*

BILL   *(Continued)* We do? (BILL's *hand disassociates from* JOHN, *entirely de-animating the puppet, which* HE *disposes of out of sightlines)* Uh huh . . . uh huh . . . uh huh . . . hey, do you mind if I bum one of those chocolate covered cherries? (BILL *materializes the cherry magically, unwraps it and eats)* Thanks, man. (BILL *assumes* JOHN's *position against* PHONE I) Uh huh . . . well, why don't we have lunch sometime —a late lunch. Who would you like to eat? Well, it's business too—I want to incorporate. I want to incorporate in two states—"yours" and "mine." I want to work up a joint proposal. I need a little subsidy. Yeah, that's my point—supernatural subsidy. Well, you know the people, man . . . I mean . . . shit, man, you know Croesus. Right now I'm just a piece of chalk on the blackboard of myth. You got another chocolate covered cherry? *(Again* BILL *materializes the cherry magically, unwraps it and eats)* Thanks, man. Well, I was going to wait to get into this over lunch, but, if you've got a minute, I could pitch it to you. All I want is a "development deal." Uh huh . . . and pursuant to our previous discussion, Pop, I want to shoot in Venice. PLEASE. Thanks, man. I want to shoot you sitting in the fog, on a bench, on a beach in Venice. We'll use fast film 'cause there's not much light. There's not much color. I'm on your lap. I'm down inside your overcoat like a kangaroo in a pocket. Well, that's my shot. Yeah, that's my point—it's a "lap" dissolve. You got another cherry? *(Again* BILL *materializes the cherry magically, unwraps it and eats)* Thanks, man. I want your shoes off, and your feet in the sand, and your eyes on the water, and your hair in the fog. You know, it's Venice before the mist burns off—it's "vamping" weather. (BILL *sits between* PHONES *facing the street—Upstage)* And I say to you, Pop, "How do you do." How does a "doer" do . . . or die . . . And you say, "You vait for de sun, son, like any uder sucker." Now . . . dissolve to the sun.

The sun appears in the night sky over the street.

BILL *(Continued)* The sun comes right down Pico Boulevard beating every yellow light. The "son" is looking for you. *(Music, lights and effects fade)* I want to die in my father's arms looking at the sea. Repeat after me . . .

BILL sings to the tune of "Row, row, row your boat." The VOICE, *as a child, joins the round faintly.*

BILL *(Continued)* I want to die in my father's arms looking at the sea. I want to die in my father's arms. Repeat after me . . .

Round repeats. Music barely audible, lights and effects out. BILL *silhouetted at the window.*

BILL   *(Continued)* Yeah . . . well, just bring along one of your standard contracts. Yeah . . . yeah, I'll sign in blood.

VAMPIRE BAT *flies off.*

BILL   *(Continued)* Jesus Christ . . . what a primitive . . . (BILL *calls through the window into the street)* Thanks, man . . .

INTERVIEW
WITH LEE BREUER

I say there is no fantasy. It's all alive.
. . . What is born of yourself is not under your control. It is under the control of the influences of your life, the stories in your life. I believe firmly in the archetypal imagery, in the idea of control by the ancestors, in the idea that you are given a voice, that a character is simply an aspect of the *persona* of yourself, that you are never one thing, that you are constantly giving off energy the way an atom would radiate. All of this energy is characters: they come back to find you. You give up aspects of yourself: some of them are identical, many others appear to be you, but they are not.
    John the puppet was born because I walked around New York with a leather jacket and a blue hat. I asked myself: now, what is my purpose in walking around New York with a leather jacket, I shouldn't be walking around with a jacket, I'm 40 years old. I loved to wear a leather jacket. Why? Because John is born of a necessity, of the need that found me when I was 16. John is born of the problem of my 16th year. John is an attempt to supplant loss, to deny the future, it is a character born of the necessity of my life . . .
    . . . The creation of John was a purging of my John. Once I had him as a puppet I could kill him in myself. For me, the act of creating is an act

of killing . . . when I want to kill John I write the John. It is an act of killing. An act of purging, in a sense. It is an attempt to purify and it's like gouging out, and you throw up characters. This is essentially the drama of creating. It is a way of saving the self, because this something, this character, is making you sick.

. . . Being an artist is a real thing. Loving, being afraid of dying is a real thing. But I think there are very few real things that I really understand. What I understand very well are the clothes that they hide in, the coats and hats, the illusion and the covers: this is the theatre of the world, this is the illusion of the world, and my part as a craftsman is to understand illusion, to be able to create illusion. In a way, I feel that in world terms my job is to be a magician, in an attempt to perceive the truth.

The way I've chosen, I think, is the *via negativa.* Through my "Animation" plays (the trilogy consisting of *Red Horse,* 1970; *B.Beaver,* 1974; and *Shaggy Dog,* 1978) I have eliminated as not true the Horse, the Beaver, the Dog, and in *Prelude,* John, so far. This has taken 12 years. What I now find is that at least the truth is that it is not that.

. . . Why a script? What kind of speech act is a theatre text? Asking for love. That's the precise answer. That is the speech act. In theatre terms we call it an action. It is the action of a literary text. It is an offering and a hope that there will be a response.

Adapted from an interview
with Nicoletta Cherubini
Paris, 1980

DEAD SOULS

Translated and Adapted

by

Tom Cole

from the stage version
of Nikolai Gogol's novel
created by Mikhail Bulgakov for
Constantin Stanislavski and the
Moscow Art Theatre

ABOUT TOM COLE

Tom Cole was brought up in Paterson, New Jersey, took his undergraduate degree at Harvard and a graduate degree there in Slavic Languages and Literatures. He taught Russian and literature at the Massachusetts Institute of Technology in the post-Sputnik years and worked as an interpreter at the American Exhibition in Moscow, 1959, when Nixon quarreled with Khrushchev in the model kitchen—a scene with distinctly Gogolian overtones.

In the 1960s and early 1970s Tom Cole's fiction appeared in *The Atlantic, Esquire,* and other magazines. His first published story (which was set in Russia) won the Atlantic "First" award, while others were included in an anthology of best fiction from *Esquire* and three times in the yearly O. Henry Prize collections. His novel, *An End to Chivalry,* won the Rosenthal Award of the National Institute of Arts and Letters in 1966.

He has worked in the writing, direction and production of numerous films, both dramatic and documentary, during the past 10 years, chiefly in collaboration with Joyce Chopra. Their subjects range from community health in Nigeria to female adolescence in Waltham, Massachusetts; four of those films have won Blue Ribbons at the American Film Festival, and twice the Cine Golden Eagle. As part of his film apprenticeship, he also served as "script doctor" for feature movies, but was given early parole for good behavior. At present he is working with director Irvin Kershner on new feature film projects.

His first play, *Medal of Honor Rag,* was produced by the Theatre Company of Boston in 1976, and then at the Folger Theater in Washington, the Theatre de Lys in New York (where it was a nominee for the Drama Desk and Obie awards), the Annenberg Center in Philadelphia, the Pittsburgh Public Theater, Actors Theatre of Louisville, Milwaukee Repertory Theater and other regional theatres throughout the country, in addition to productions in England and Australia. *Medal of Honor Rag* is in production for "Playhouse," a Public Broadcasting Service national telecast in early 1982, directed by Lloyd Richards. The Milwaukee Repertory Theater commissioned Tom Cole's next play, *Fighting Bob,* producing it on the main stage in 1979 and touring it in 1980. That tour led to the Off-Broadway opening of *Fighting Bob,* at the Astor Place Theatre, in November, 1981. Having enjoyed his rapport as writer-in-residence with the Milwaukee Rep and director John Dillon, he agreed to try a new translation for the theatre of a Russian play, provided that it be a major work to challenge that growing company to its limit. This adaptation-translation of Gogol's *Dead Souls* was the result.

Tom Cole also translated *Letter to a Teacher* from the Italian and will undertake a contemporary Russian play for Joseph Papp and the Public Theater as soon as the Cold War thaws enough for rights to be secured.

PRODUCTION HISTORY

Dead Souls was nominated for the *Plays in Process* series by John Dillon, artistic director of the Milwaukee Repertory Theater Company, Milwaukee, Wisconsin. It was presented there from January 25 through March 2, 1980.

John Dillon and Sharon Ott directed. The set was designed by Stuart Wurtzel, costumes by Carol Oditz, lighting by Arden Fingerhut, properties by Sandy Struth, and music by Mark van Hecke. The cast was as follows:

CHICHIKOV .... Larry Shue
LANDOWNER, CLIENT OF CHICHIKOV .... Robert Martin
PETRUSHKA, SERVANT TO CHICHIKOV .... Jon Banck
SECRETARY OF THE STATE MORTGAGE BANK.. Henry Strozier
GOVERNOR OF AN OUTLYING PROVINCE .... Earle Edgerton
GOVERNOR'S SERVANT .... Carl Thomas
GOVERNOR'S WIFE... Diane Johnson

GOVERNOR'S DAUGHTER ....Dana Barton
POSTMASTER, IVAN ANDREYEVICH .... Henry Strozier
PRESIDENT OF THE COURTS,
IVAN GRIGOREVICH .... Ritch Brinkley
ANNA GRIGORYEVNA, HIS WIFE .... Marge Kotlisky
SASHA, HIS SERVANT .... Rick Weber
POLICE CHIEF, ALEKSEI IVANOVICH .... John P. Connolly
POLICEMAN .... Robert Martin
PUBLIC PROSECUTOR,
ANTIPATOR ZAKHARYEVICH ....Herbert Mark Parker
SOFYA IVANOVNA,
FRIEND OF ANNA GRIGORYEVNA..........................Peggy Cowles
FATHER KYRIL .... Victor Raider-Wexler
KOPEIKIN ....Herbert Mark Parker
MANILOV .... James Pickering
LIZANKA MANILOVA, HIS WIFE ....Judy Dorrell
SOBAKEVICH .... Daniel Mooney
PLYUSHKIN .... Victor Raider-Wexler
MAVRA, HIS HOUSEKEEPER.. Jane Brown
PROSHKA, HIS BOY SERVANT.................................. Kurt Knuth
NOZDRYOV .... William Leach
MIZHUYEV, HIS BROTHER-IN-LAW .... Jack McLaughlin-Gray
KOROBOCHKA ....Rose Pickering
FETINYA, HER SERVANT ....Dana Barton

The first stage production of *Dead Souls* was presented in 1932 by the Moscow Art Theatre under the direction of Constantin Stanislavski. The production was part of the Moscow Art's season at the City Center in New York. It opened there on February 4, 1965.

PLAYWRIGHT'S NOTE

Gogol's hilarious and tormented novel resisted dramatization for almost a century after its appearance in 1842, although more than a hundred attempts were made, in Russian, to adapt the story and characters into a form suitable for the stage. The problems, in brief, were a narrative line too rich, sprawling, picaresque, and a gift for verbal flight too extravagant to be compressed into playable drama.

Still, *Dead Souls* beckoned, because of its characters—perhaps Russia's most celebrated gallery of grotesques—and the savage comic potential of its premise: that under a twist of Russian law a businessman could make a fortune traveling about and buying up dead peasants (or "souls" as they were called) and then using them as collateral for vast mortgage loans from the government. Here was a promise of laughter and a powerfully absurd imagery for stage, if only a play could be made to work without destroying the elusive, madly logical "feel" of the world Gogol had created.

Finally, in 1932, the Moscow Art Theatre managed it by pooling the formidable talents of Mikhail Bulgakov, Constantin Stanislavski, and its own extraordinary acting company. Bulgakov, both a novelist and man of theatre (as Gogol himself had been), served in a capacity that combines our notions of writer-in-residence and dramaturg. Working closely with the company and Stanislavski (not without some fireworks) he fashioned a clear, playable structure, a vehicle by which the actors could present characters whom the Russian audience long had craved to see and hear. Much had to be sacrificed of the novel's lavishly entertaining detours, but under Stanislavski's direction in the twilight of his career, this efficient version of *Dead Souls,* entered the repertoire of the Art Theatre and has remained as a solid classic, through various revisions, both in Moscow and in the overseas tours of the company. One of the leading actors, V. O. Toporkov, wrote that it took him 10 years, but he finally did figure out how to play the impossible role of Chichikov. (See "Two Footnotes on Characters," following.)

When it came time for an American translation of the play, we found Bulgakov's framework useful only up to a point, for we could not rely, as he could, on an audience already familiar with every nuance of the characters to be portrayed. It seemed necessary to reach for more of Gogol himself, for the implications of his wild premise: after all, we did have an audience familiar with the nuances of business corruption on an epic scale.

The present version is, therefore, an adaptation of an adaptation, fleshed out by revisiting parts of the novel which Bulgakov had excluded, allow-ing a few more wild Gogolianisms to enter in, even if they complicate the picture at times. The translation is in part of Bulgakov's Russian version and in part of newly dramatized passages from the novel. There are even tidbits snatched from elsewhere in Gogol's inimitable work—certain of his refrains that show a human situation at once funny and heartbreaking to the extreme. Or, as it has been described elsewhere, a situation "too hopeless to be serious."

Two Footnotes on Characters

Chichikov.   The difficulty of playing Chichikov, the central character and schemer, would seem to be that he is a chameleon who must react according to the incredible humors of those whom he confronts, while retaining a center of his own (however empty it may seem). There is also the danger of an episodic quality in his going from one to another with his scheme, unless each scene be done as if it were an entire, short play. Toporkov has written interestingly on both these points. (See *Acting, A Handbook of the Stanislavski Method,* edited by Toby Cole and Lee Strasberg, Crown Publishers, New York.)

I regard Chichikov as an ideal candidate to hold the 19th Century Banality-of-Evil title. It has been said of him that his "psychological leit-motiv is complacency, and his geometric expression roundness." He is business-as-usual. He is purest essence of *poshlost'*, a key word in the Gogolian lexicon, often translated by dictionaries as "vulgarity" or "trite-ness," but pinpointed in Chichikov's incarnation of it as "self-satisfied inferiority," or, even better, "placidly ambitious inferiority."

Nozdryov.   If Chichikov provides the spine of the play, then Nozdryov provides the stimulus, the shock, which repeatedly jolts the nervous sys-tem into wild twitchings. He is the inveterate liar who has the integrity of believing everything he says. He "lives exclusively on the inspiration of the moment. Everything, every notion, every chance thought, every momentary feeling is turned outward, let out in a torrent of words that flows on uncontrollably. . . ." In Russian, his speech is utterly unpredicta-ble, full of private emotion, more expressive and pungent than anyone else's. In the translation, he has been given certain colorations—*"Oi, oi,"* and *"nu"*—which could be taken here as Jewish, because of their use by American comedians, but are in fact among the many Russian expressions borrowed by Yiddish. He is not Jewish; he is a good-for-nothing Russian landowner. But he is "Jewish" if that means warmer, livelier, a madcap, and something of an outsider amid the smug provincial establishment.

Music and Design.
The text of this play cannot possible convey the vastness of Russia nor, in particular, the feel of the Russian road that so dominates the novel, evoked by the brilliance of Gogol's language.

In the original production by the Milwaukee Repertory Theater, music and design had to perform these acts of creation. The composer and musical coach was Mark van Hecke, who wrote original songs to give resonance to the action. He taught the entire cast to sing them, in Russian. (For a copy of his music-and-effects tape, or for his services, he can be reached at Milwaukee Repertory Theater, 929 North Water Street, Milwaukee, Wisconsin 53202.)

Directors John Dillon and Sharon Ott, in collaboration with the designers, found a way to project Gogol's peculiar Russian landscape onto a smallish stage in Wisconsin. (For one thing, they had peasants roll each new setting in on wheels and then curl up asleep, or "dead," until the next scene change.) For directors' notes, they can be reached at the theatre's address, listed above.

CHARACTERS

CHICHIKOV
LANDOWNER, client of Chichikov
PETRUSHKA, servant to Chichikov
SECRETARY OF THE STATE MORTGAGE BANK

Provincial Officials
GOVERNOR OF AN OUTLYING PROVINCE
GOVERNOR'S SERVANT
GOVERNOR'S WIFE
GOVERNOR'S DAUGHTER
POSTMASTER, Ivan Andreyevich
PRESIDENT OF THE COURTS, Ivan Grigorevich
ANNA GRIGORYEVNA, his wife
SASHA, his servant
POLICE CHIEF, Aleksei Ivanovich
POLICEMAN
PUBLIC PROSECUTOR, Antipator Zakharyevich

Other Townspeople
SOFYA IVANOVNA, friend of Anna Grigoryevna
FATHER KYRIL
KOPEIKIN

Landowners
MANILOV
LIZANKA MANILOVA, his wife
SOBAKEVICH

PLYUSHKIN
MAVRA, his housekeeper
PROSHKA, his boy servant
NOZDRYOV
MIZHUYEV, his brother-in-law
KOROBOCHKA
FETINYA, her servant

NOTE: In the Milwaukee Repertory Theater production, there were 17 men and seven women performing 28 roles, plus three stagehands dressed as peasants. There were five doublings: Secretary of State Mortgage Bank/Postmaster; Landowner (Chichikov's Client)/Policeman; Governor's Daughter/Fetinya; Plyushkin/Father Kyril; Prosecutor/Kopeikin. Other doublings are possible, involving the Police Chief, the President of the Courts, Lizanka Manilova, and servants.

SETTING

Russia in the 1830s. Costumes and sets should probably have an exotic air about them. There are multiple sets which can be stylized.

THE PLAY

DEAD SOULS

ACT I

Prologue 1

Alone on the stage, dwarfed by an enormous portrait of Czar Nicholas I, a self-important bureaucrat has his lonely supper. HE *is* SECRETARY OF THE STATE MORTGAGE COUNCIL—*akin to a lower Cabinet post.*

Enter CHICHIKOV—*a man "neither too fat nor too thin; not old, but not so young either . . ." HE is a member of the gentry, but not the higher gentry; holder of rank in the Civil Service, but neither at the top nor the bottom. In brief, a "middling" kind of man.*

CHICHIKOV *has a bottle of champagne in hand, and behind him trails a pathetic wreck of a* CLIENT, *a landowner who has come on very bad times.*

CHICHIKOV   Ah, Mr. Secretary, sir!

SECRETARY   Mr. Chichikov? Surely, it can't be you again! Tell me I'm mistaken. All morning, in my office, you're there, like the plague. In the evening, at my supper table, you track me down.

CHICHIKOV *pops the champagne bottle, placatingly.*

SECRETARY   *(Continued)* My dear, dear fellow. I know you're doing your job. But I've told you—I cannot do anything for you, in this case.

CHICHIKOV   Mr. Secretary, sir. With all due respect. I won't budge from this spot until I get some decision from the State Mortgage Bank in this matter. My client is leaving!

SECRETARY   Your client is a total financial wreck.

CHICHIKOV   *(Pours some champagne for the* SECRETARY*)* Ah, Mr. Secretary. Human frailties, you know, are infinite in number, like the sands of the sea.

SECRETARY   You can say that again. Lost half his fortune at cards, drank away the other half, just squandered the whole pile, in the grand manner. You expect the Imperial Government to extend a mortgage loan to save this, this . . . *(Pointing at the* CLIENT*)* You expect *me* as representative of . . . *(Suddenly threatening)* Do you know before whom you are standing?!

CHICHIKOV   Yes, of course, and I honor you, sir, I—

SECRETARY   No! That! *(Meaning the picture: the Czar) That* is before whom you are standing! Who is that?

CHICHIKOV   That's Nicholas . . . our beloved Emperor . . .

SECRETARY   Beloved, my foot! That is truth and vengeance, rolled into one! That is pure justice, uncorrupted by mercy! And what do I say when he takes me aside, insignificant worm that I am, and says, "Why did you do it?" Do I say, "Your Omnipotence, (Thrice-Noble Sire,) I squandered the State treasury, violated my sacred trust, all because of this solicitor, Chichikov . . ." "Chichikov?" says he. "Bring him here!" "Oh, do not harm Chichikov," I beg. "Why he has butter in his veins instead of blood, milk pours from his eyes . . ." "He is pernicious, evil, and corrupt." "But, Your Majesty"—you see? I keep pleading for you—"Chichikov? Such a mild, middling kind of man. How could I know his aim was to undermine the State?" *(Adopts the Czar's voice)* "The whip! Ice! I will have you both plunged naked into Lake Baikal! I will flog all the skin from your bodies, and let you discuss this transaction while your wretched nerves and flaccid muscles freeze to your splintering bones! And in spring, when you thaw, the wolves will eat you..." *(His own voice again)* That's what will happen, Mr. Chichikov. That's what Nicholas will think of your proposition.

HE *goes on eating. Both* CHICHIKOV *and the* CLIENT *quail under the Czar's terrible threats. But* CHICHIKOV *persists, as always.*

CHICHIKOV   But it's not because I'm a kind fellow, Mr. Secretary. That is not the reason.

SECRETARY   What then?

CHICHIKOV   My client is a man of property. He owns peasants.

SECRETARY   You want to put up his serfs as collateral?

CHICHIKOV   I do. Sir.

SECRETARY   How much? Per head?

CHICHIKOV   Two hundred rubles, for each soul.

SECRETARY   *(Guffaws)* . . . Two hundred rubles per soul! . . .

CHICHIKOV   Sir, the State Mortgage Bank—

SECRETARY   The State Mortgage Bank was not founded to prop up gamblers and drunkards!

CHICHIKOV   Your Honor, why so harsh? What ruined his estate, when you get right down to it? Bad harvests, hoof-and-mouth disease, a crooked steward . . . This could happen to anybody.

SECRETARY   The answer, Mr. Chichikov, is "no." It is absolute, and final. Now, do you have anything else to say to me?

CHICHIKOV   Yes. *(Takes out a large packet of bribe money)* If you'll be so kind, sir, as to allow me . . . *(Thrusts the money toward the* SECRETARY*)*

SECRETARY   Oh, well, there is always another side to a complicated question like this . . . *(Takes the money)* Are we, the protectors of the people, to be rigid, like Pharisees? We of the State Mortgage Council are here, Mr. Chichikov, to help forward-looking agriculturalists like your worthy client. *(Counting the money)* Ah, I'm not alone on the Council, you know. There are others, . . .

CHICHIKOV   The others, too, will not be left out in the cold. Heaven forbid! I have served in Government. I understand.

SECRETARY   Well, then, let's have a look at those papers.

CHICHIKOV   *(Holding the papers back)* There is—may I broach it?— one little circumstance. I have prepared this mortgage list for you, but half the peasants on it have, well, died. Just so there won't be any catches, later on . . .

SECRETARY   You represent quite an estate! A total shambles, and half the people dead, in the bargain.

CHICHIKOV   Please, Mr. Secretary . . .

SECRETARY   Well, let's look at it this way. On the Government's last Census Report, all these dead souls you worry about, are they listed in fact as dead, or alive?

CHICHIKOV   They're *listed* as still alive, of course. They were alive, then. But when the next Census is taken, they—

SECRETARY   Not another word! You know these peasants: One dies, another crops up, it all works out in the end. As long as they are still officially listed as alive on the Census Report, and the taxes are paid on them, to me they are alive. Your client pays tax on this whole list? *Every single name?*

The CLIENT *sways.* CHICHIKOV *holds him up.*

CHICHIKOV   Oh. Oh, yes.

SECRETARY   Well, there. They live. Mr. Chichikov, I go by the letter of the law. That's all I need to know. *(Begins to take mortgage lists from* CHICHIKOV)

CHICHIKOV   *(Sudden change of expression; strikes forehead)* Aaah!! (CHICHIKOV, *who was supporting the* CLIENT, *lets him drop)*

SECRETARY   What's that?

CHICHIKOV   Oh, nothing. Nothing at all. *(Picks up* CLIENT *again)*

SECRETARY   Ah. Well, let's get the paperwork started on this little mortgage of yours . . .

SECRETARY *exits. As soon as* HE *does,* CHICHIKOV *bolts from the spot, dropping the astounded* CLIENT *still again, in his excitement.*

CHICHIKOV   Petrushka! Petrushka! Petrushka! (CHICHIKOV *runs in circles, trying to find* PETRUSHKA) I know he's here. I can smell him. Petrushka!

Ultimately, from a pile of discarded rags or old coats—which HE *resembles—*PETRUSHKA *emerges, scratching, yawning, and drunk.* HE *is* CHICHIKOV's *valet and driver.*

PETRUSHKA   Master? . . .

CHICHIKOV   You foul, drunken sot! You . . . garbage heap!

PETRUSHKA   Yes, sir. That's right, sir. *(Waves his whip)*

CHICHIKOV How did you get in here?

PETRUSHKA How did I get in here?

CHICHIKOV That's what I asked you. I've been looking for you!

PETRUSHKA Don't know how you found me, Master. Didn't know I was here, myself.

CHICHIKOV I smelled you. *Yekh.* Can't you do anything about that?

PETRUSHKA God's will, Master. *(Opens his foul, old coat and sniffs inside)* The Lord works in strange ways.

CHICHIKOV He does! He does! Petrushka, harness up! My fortune lies ahead! I've seen the way! Finally! *(Pointing to the* SECRETARY's *table)* The Secretary has shown me the way! I can make my fortune out of dead souls.

PETRUSHKA *(Regains his vitality, swings his whip, calls)* Fly, you lads, fly! Tprrr . . .

Music, Change of light.

ACT I

Prologue 2

On the road. PETRUSHKA *drives.* CHICHIKOV *sits in their carriage on a lonely road across the Russian countryside.*

CHICHIKOV To the Governor's. Yes! That's where we'll start.

PETRUSHKA Hup, Hup! Fly, lads, fly!

CHICHIKOV Will it be said of me someday that I left nothing to my children? That I was an improvident father? That I bequeathed rags and starvation? God forbid! *(Crosses himself)* Of course, I have no children. That is true. But someday the Lord will bless me with progeny, and for them I will make my millions. For them only, I will go through any trial, it is all for them, Petrushka! . . . The little rascals . . . The way is clear now, it lies before my eyes clear as the mileposts of this road . . . The taxes. All I have to pay are the taxes, and they'll bless me for it. *(Taken aback)* Oh! Land! You can't buy peasants without land. Blockhead! What do I do? Petrushka! Ah! Transfer! I can have them transferred to . . . Kherson District, yes, land is being given away over there. Of course, it's a desert, but then again, all my peasants will be dead, God rest their souls . . . *(Crosses himself)* God, what province is this? The roads are abominable! Are we near the Governor's yet? Petrushka? Petrushka! Are you asleep?

PETRUSHKA   *(Mumbles)*

CHICHIKOV   You fungus! You reeking, rotted turnip!

PETRUSHKA   Yes, Master, To the Governor's. Steady, lads, fly now

    . . .

ACT I

Scene 1

The GOVERNOR, *surrounded by his fancy needlework, sits at a tambour, working on a new embroidery.* HE *wears a dressing gown, with the Order of St. Anne around his neck. As* HE *works,* HE *sings to himself a coy popular tune, about flirtation.*

SERVANT   *(enters)* A certain Pavel Ivanovich Chichikov, by rank Collegiate Councillor, desires to be in your august presence.

GOVERNOR   Chi-chi-kov? Give me my frock coat!

The SERVANT *helps the* GOVERNOR *into his frock coat, through another verse of the song—preferably, on the subject of old age being foolish enough to fall in love with youth.*

GOVERNOR *(Continued)* Show him in.

Exit SERVANT. *Enter* CHICHIKOV.

CHICHIKOV Your Excellency! *(Deep, flattering bow)* No sooner had I penetrated the gates of your fair city than I felt it incumbent upon me to pay my respects to its lords and foremost citizens! And above all, to present my humble person, mute with reverence, to Your Excellency himself.

GOVERNOR Oh. Well. Most happy to meet you. Won't you sit down?

CHICHIKOV *sits.*

GOVERNOR *(Continued)* Rank of Collegiate Councillor, you say? Where did you serve?

CHICHIKOV Sir, the path along which I have served our sacred Russia commenced in the Treasury Department. Ultimately, it went on to . . . other places. Just for one example, the Erection Commission.

GOVERNOR The erection of what?

CHICHIKOV The erection, Your Excellency, of the Cathedral of Christ Savior, in Moscow! Yes! I went on to serve in the Privy Council, Your Excellency. And thence, to the Customs.

GOVERNOR The Customs? You're not here, I trust, in official capacity?

CHICHIKOV I have left all that far behind, sir. I am nought but an insignificant worm making my way through this vale of sorrows. Patience is my only virtue. Patience and humility, and what have I received in turn from my enemies along this arduous path of service to my country? *(Leans close)* Dare I mention intrigues? Plots against my very life? Neither pen nor paint could possibly picture it all. My life, Your Excellency, could well be likened to a frail bark, tossed amid the waves—

GOVERNOR A "frail?" . . .

CHICHIKOV Bark! Your Excellency.

GOVERNOR And where, Mr. Chichikov, do your travels take you now?

CHICHIKOV I journey, sir, to find some corner of Russia where I might peacefully pass the twilight, and yet, just to have the privilege of witnessing the kaleidoscopic turnings of this earth and its people—

GOVERNOR Kaleidoscopic?

CHICHIKOV Kaleidoscopic, Your Excellency . . . that, in itself, so to speak, is the most vivid of studies, a deeper science, a book that lives and breathes.

GOVERNOR Oh, quite true. Quite, quite true.

CHICHIKOV For one example, to enter this province, which is fortunate enough to be under Your Excellency's care, is to enter Paradise.

GOVERNOR   Oh no, Mr. Chichikov. My goodness! . . . Why?

CHICHIKOV   Your roads: pure velvet.

GOVERNOR   *(Smirks shamefacedly)* Oh . . . Mmm . . .

CHICHIKOV   Governments which raise men of wisdom to lead them, deserve the highest praise.

GOVERNOR   Oh, my dear, dear . . . what's your name again?

CHICHIKOV   Chichikov. Pavel Ivanovich Chichikov, Your Excellency.

GOVERNOR   My dear Pavel Ivanovich, we're having the wee-est of parties this very evening. May I beg you to be present?

CHICHIKOV   I should consider it a most particular honor, Your Excellency. *(Rises and bows)* And now I beg to take my leave. Ah! *(Stops in feigned admiration, before the embroidery)* . . . but who sewed this sumptuous border?

GOVERNOR   *(Modestly)* Oh, that's just for a little purse. I'm working on it myself.

CHICHIKOV   No! Remarkable! *(Bows again)* But now I must . . . if you'll allow me . . . *(Withdraws, bows, exits)*

GOVERNOR   *(Races off to find his wife)* At last, there is a man in town worth talking to! A philosopher! Sterling qualities! . . .

ACT I

Scene 2

The Party. Salon of the GOVERNOR's *house. Card tables. Sound of harpsichord in the distance.*

At cards: POLICE CHIEF—*hearts,* PRESIDENT—*clubs,* PROSECUTOR—*spades. Ad libs.*

PRESIDENT OF THE COURTS   *(Banging down a card, violently)* Get lost, you Tambov peasant!

POLICE CHIEF   *(Bangs down card)* Off with you, you slut of a priest's wife!

PUBLIC PROSECUTOR   *(Picking up)* The queen! I've got her, Aleksei Ivanovich. Got her by the mustache!

SERVANT   *(Approaching)* Your Excellency, Pavel Ivanovich Chichikov.

GOVERNOR   Ah, Chichikov! So glad you could come.

CHICHIKOV   May I ask after Your Excellency's health?

GOVERNOR   A bit of pain in the lower back.

CHICHIKOV   It will pass, Your Excellency. With God's help. Just refuse to pay any attention to it.

GOVERNOR   *(Leads CHICHIKOV to his WIFE)* Here, my sweet, let me introduce you: Collegiate Councillor Pavel Ivanovich Chichikov. The man I told you about. *(Continues introductions)* Our Public Prosecutor, Antipator Zakharevich . . . The President of our District Courts, Ivan Grigorevich. Aleksei Ivanovich, Chief of Police. *(To CHICHIKOV)* How do you find our provincial society?

CHICHIKOV   Provincial? Your Excellency, this is not a province, this is Paris itself! But tell me, are there also any considerable landowners in the district? Oh, agriculturalists, owners of many peasants?

GOVERNOR   Oh, yes, of course!

CHICHIKOV   I wouldn't mind meeting some of them, too. If it's not too much trouble.

GOVERNOR   Why, my dear Pavel Ivanovich, just say the word! Say the word . . . Here . . . *(Turns to MANILOV, passing by)* Allow me, an introduction: Squire Manilov, Mr. Pavel Ivanovich Chichikov.

POLICE CHIEF   Excellency!

PUBLIC PROSECUTOR   *(Approaching)* Your deal!

> GOVERNOR *withdraws to card table.* CHICHIKOV *and* MANI-LOV, *having exchanged greetings, are at ease with each other.*

MANILOV   And how does our little town strike you, Mr. . . . Mr. Chichikov?

CHICHIKOV   Delightful; and a society most civilized.

MANILOV   How do you find our Governor? Is he not the last word in respectability?

CHICHIKOV   Absolutely. The very ultimate. Respectability can go no further.

MANILOV   It's amazing—his gift for making any man feel welcome, regardless of rank. The delicacy and tact, of his bearing . . .

CHICHIKOV   An urbane and most estimable man, and quite the artist:

He was showing me a purse, of his own workmanship. Only a rare lady's hand could embroider so deftly.

MANILOV   But, might I be so bold, what is your opinion of our Police Chief? Is he not a very pleasant man, himself?

CHICHIKOV   An extraordinarily pleasant man, and so intelligent. A most distinguished gentleman.

MANILOV   Ah, Mr. Chichikov! And the Governor's wife?

CHICHIKOV   Well, that's simply a case of the most utterly distinguished woman I have ever had the pleasure of knowing . . .

MANILOV   And the President of the Courts, too, don't you think?

CHICHIKOV   Oh yes! Yes! Yes!

MANILOV   And the Public Prosecutor?

CHICHIKOV   Do you spend all your time in the country?

MANILOV   Most of the time. Once in a while we do come to town, in order to bask in the company of cultured people. Otherwise you go to seed, you know, all the time out in the wilds . . . It would be different if there were a trace of decent society out there. If there were, for example, just one man *(Significant look at* CHICHIKOV*)* with whom one could chat, from time to time, on subjects such as . . . respectability, proper courtesies, the little niceties that make life worthwhile . . .

CHICHIKOV   I could think of nothing better, for my part, than to live in solitude, drinking in the joys of nature.

MANILOV   Mr. Chichikov, would you consider doing me the honor of a visit to our humble retreat?

CHICHIKOV   I'd consider that not only a pleasure, but a sacred obligation as well . . .

MANILOV'S WIFE   *(Approaching)* My darling, open your darling mouth, I'm just dying to pop this devilish little pickled mushroom inside . . .

MANILOV   Mr. Chichikov, permit me to present my wife, Lizanka. Lizanka, this is Pavel Ivanovich Chichikov . . . Don't forget us, now. Just fifteen miles from the city gates. Manilovka Estate—ask anybody. *(The* MANILOVS *withdraw, toward the buffet)*

CHICHIKOV   *(Takes out his notebook and precisely records the data on* MANILOV*)* The estate is called "Manilovka" . . .

SOBAKEVICH   *(Suddenly looms up behind; gruffly)* Come and see me, too.

CHICHIKOV *is startled, turns around.*

SOBAKEVICH   *(Continued)* Name's Sobakevich. (SOBAKEVICH *steps forward, treading heavily on* CHICHIKOV's *foot)*

CHICHIKOV *(Tries to conceal the pain, bowing and holding out his hand)* Chichikov. Yes, yes, the President of the Courts was speaking of you just today, sir. *(Sits down)* A splendid man.

SOBAKEVICH Who's that?

CHICHIKOV The President of the Courts.

SOBAKEVICH Maybe on first glance. Except for being a Freemason, he's probably the biggest fool the world has yet managed to produce.

CHICHIKOV *(Stunned)* Oh, yes, well, there isn't a man born without some failings. But, but, the Governor, take the Governor: There is an outstanding person!

SOBAKEVICH A barbarian. A Visigoth.

CHICHIKOV Visigoth? What are you saying?

SOBAKEVICH I'm saying he's the number one thug of the district.

CHICHIKOV Come now! The Governor? I must say, I'd never thought that. Quite the contrary, he seems, if anything, almost too gentle.

SOBAKEVICH Gentle-schmentle, the man's a thug! For a kopeck he'd cut your throat. I know them all for what they are, a cult of swindlers. That's this whole town: one swindler rides another swindler's back and lashes a team of swindlers forward. Judases, every one; sellers of Christ. Maybe there's one man . . . the Public Prosecutor . . .

The PUBLIC PROSECUTOR *appears behind* SOBAKEVICH's *back.*

SOBAKEVICH *(Continued)* Who is a decent human being . . .

The PUBLIC PROSECUTOR *smiles.*

SOBAKEVICH *(Continued)* but if truth be told, he's also a swine.

The PUBLIC PROSECUTOR disappears.

SOBAKEVICH *(Continued)* But come see me. That's an invitation. *(Bows)* Cult of swindlers . . . *(Withdraws, muttering)*

GOVERNOR *(Takes* CHICHIKOV *by the arm again)* Most esteemed Pavel Ivanovich, you'll have the wisdom to resolve our dispute: Is a woman's love lasting, or not?

CHICHIKOV Well, on that score, the Greek philosopher Diogenes—

SERVANT Your Excellency, Mr. Nozdryov.

GOVERNOR *(Heavily)* Oi!

Enter NOZDRYOV, *not sober, with one of his mutton chops par-*

tially missing. Following is NOZDRYOV's *brother-in-law,* MIZ-HUYEV, *also drunk.*

NOZDRYOV   Hullo, everybody! Your Excellency! Wha . . . wha . . . wha . . . why, there's ye olde Judge . . . Hullo, hullo to the Police Chief, too. *(To* GOVERNOR*)* My broth'-in-law, Mizhuyev. W'd you believe, Y'r Excellency, I've raced straight over here from the Market Fair?

GOVERNOR   I think I detect signs of that, yes.

NOZDRYOV   Your Excellency! I introduce! My broth'-in-law, Mizhuyev!

GOVERNOR   Overjoyed to meet you. *(Bows stiffly, withdraws)*

NOZDRYOV   Gen'l'men, gen'l'men, congratulate me, I've done it—blown every last kopeck. Shot my entire wad like never, never before! Tried the roulette, won two jars of pomade, then lost my four best trotters, and, believe me, every other blessed thing! Look, no watch. In fact, no watch-chain! Gen'l'men! My broth'-in-law, Mizhuyev.

POLICE CHIEF   Watch-chain? You've lost half your whiskers, man!

NOZDRYOV   Half?

GOVERNOR   Here, meet Pavel Ivanovich Chichikov.

NOZDRYOV   Wha . . . wha . . . what brings you to our precincts? Eh? Come, let me embrace you for it, darling man, come, let's have a kiss. Who is this?

GOVERNOR   Pavel Ivanovich Chichikov.

NOZDRYOV   Good, good! Where have you been traveling? Myself, brother, I've just come from the Market Fair, feels like a whole squadron just spent the night in my mouth. Well, give me a kiss, you dear man, you! What, you're not acquainted? My broth'-in-law, Mizhuyev; we were just talking about you this morning.

CHICHIKOV   About me?

NOZDRYOV   Just wait, I said to him, just see if we don't run into Chichikov tonight!

PRESIDENT OF THE COURTS *laughs, waves his hand in disgust, withdraws.*

NOZDRYOV   *(Continued)* What a damned pity, that you couldn't be with us!

CHICHIKOV   Me?

NOZDRYOV   Thee. Ekh, Chichikov, what would it have cost you to come along? Eh? The Fair was splendorous! Oh, *mon frere,* did we live it up!

The Champagne we had—Clicquot twice over! Would you believe it, at lunch I drank—all on my own—seventeen bottles of champagne.

MIZHUYEV   No, no that you didn't do, no seventeen bottles.

NOZDRYOV   As a man of honor, I'm telling you, I did.

MIZHUYEV   Say what you like, as anything you want, but I'm telling you you didn't even drink ten.

NOZDRYOV   Want to bet on it, that I'll drink seventeen bottles right now? Put up your rifle, the one you bought in town.

MIZHUYEV   I don't want to bet.

NOZDRYOV   Yah, yah, you'd lose your rifle just like you lost your cap. *(To* CHICHIKOV) Ekh, Chichikov, my dear friend! Now, why couldn't you have come along? Really, you're just a disease-ridden pig for that, you're worse than a cattle breeder! Come on now, give us a kiss! I love you, you're beautiful! *(To* MIZHUYEV) Mizhuyev, see how the fates have thrown us two together? After all, what is Chichikov to me, or I to him? He arrives *here,* from God know where, and I live here myself! Think on it! *(To* CHICHIKOV) What's your plan for tomorrow?

CHICHIKOV   I'm going to visit Squire Manilov, in the country. And then, some other man.

NOZDRYOV   What, "some other man"? The hell with him, get rid of him! Come see me, instead!

CHICHIKOV   That I can't do, I have business to attend to.

NOZDRYOV   I'll bet you're lying! Who wants to bet? *Nu,* just tell us, who is this "some other man"? Does he have a name?

CHICHIKOV   Well, . . . it's Squire Sobakevich.

NOZDRYOV   *Who?*

CHICHIKOV   Sobakevich.

NOZDRYOV *explodes into laughter.*

CHICHIKOV   *(Continued)* What's so funny?

NOZDRYOV   *(Howling)* Oi, oi, have mercy, hold me, I'll crack wide open!

CHICHIKOV   There's nothing to laugh at here. I gave him my word, and I'm glad to say I shall honor it.

NOZDRYOV   Well, you won't be so glad when you get there. You're a lunatic, if you think you'll find a . . . a decent hand of cards there, or a lively bottle of something with a bit of the devil grinning inside it. I say, the hell with Sobakevich! Come along with me, right now! It's only five miles, altogether! (NOZDRYOV *pulls and clutches at* CHICHIKOV)

CHICHIKOV   Let go, please! I shall call on you the day after tomorrow, if you insist.

NOZDRYOV   Well, darling man, I'm glad to hear it! I think I might kiss you for that! Yes! *Vivat! (Kisses* CHICHIKOV) Three cheers for Chichikov! Ready?

ACT I

Scene 3

At MANILOV's.

MANILOV   My dear Mr. Chichikov, I'm afraid our dinners here are not such as would be brought to you across the parquet floors of the world capitals.

CHICHIKOV   Ah, but agreeable conversation and fine manners are better than food.

MANILOV   Might I ask you to pass on ahead to my study?

CHICHIKOV   Please, do me the favor of not fussing so much over me. I'll follow you.

MANILOV   Oh! No, Pavel Ivanovich, no, no. You are a guest.

CHICHIKOV   Don't trouble yourself, please: Go ahead.

MANILOV   No, you'll forgive me, but I cannot permit a guest of your level of education to pass behind.

CHICHIKOV   What does education have to do with it? Permit me, please: Go ahead!

MANILOV   No, good sir, if you'll permit me: Go ahead.

CHICHIKOV   But, why not permit me? I insist . . .

MANILOV   Well, just because, I—

THEY *look at each other, and both try to go through apologetically, sideways. Of course,* THEY *get stuck and have to unravel themselves. Finally,* THEY *pass into the study.*

MANILOV *(Continued)* Well, this is my little den.

CHICHIKOV What a delightful room! . . . Most valued friend, it is unfortunate, but there comes a time when the poetry of life must yield to business.

MANILOV Permit me, first, to beg you to make yourself comfortable in this particular armchair.

CHICHIKOV If you'll permit me, I'll just sit right here.

MANILOV Permit me not to permit you that. This armchair, you see, is especially assigned for guests of honor. Whether they like it or not, there they must sit . . .

THEY *sit.* CHICHIKOV *leans forward to start his business, but* MANILOV *halts him again.*

MANILOV *(Continued)* Permit me to offer you tobacco and a pipe. A mild blend, you'll find.

CHICHIKOV If you'll permit me, I don't smoke. The medical profession tells us it dries the membranes of the throat.

MANILOV Ah! Our conversation already grows rare, brilliant. Although if you'll permit me to take a position, philosophically, I should say that smoking a pipe is healthier than the taking of snuff directly into one's nose . . . And so, here you are gracing our home with your visit. Such joy you have given us already, like a . . . day in May, a . . . holiday of the heart!

CHICHIKOV I'm afraid I don't have a great name to offer, nor even high rank.

MANILOV You have everything, and more than everything!

CHICHIKOV Squire Manilov, you're too kind! I'm just an average fellow, and nothing more!

MANILOV Oh, Pavel Ivanovich! How good it would be if we two, somehow, could live together, under one roof, or better still, in the shadow of some kind of . . . elm, or whatever, to be able to contemplate . . . things, to explore the depths, or follow the trail of some science, you know, into the unknown, and stir our souls to the very roots so that they could just soar . . . up . . . and up . . .

CHICHIKOV Ah, yes, I can picture that: Up . . . and up . . . *(Glances about)* But while we still touch earth, if you'll permit me, that little matter of business. Just a trifle, really. Would you happen to recall how recently you filled out the Census and Tax Report on the serfs in your possession?

MANILOV I should say, well, quite a while ago. Or I really should say, more exactly . . . I don't remember.

CHICHIKOV   In any case, have many of your peasants died since that time?

MANILOV   Oh, they've died, they've died . . . But might I ask in return, for what purpose you would need to know such things?

CHICHIKOV   You ask me, for what purpose? *(Deep breath)* I will tell you the purpose: I am in the market to buy peasants.

MANILOV   Ah. You want to buy some of my peasants. I'll have some brought in.

CHICHIKOV   No, wait, it's not that . . . not quite, or exactly . . . so to speak, peasants . . . uh, I like to buy them dead.

MANILOV   What?

CHICHIKOV   I am proposing to buy up dead souls, if you have any around.

MANILOV *drops his pipe. A pause.*

CHICHIKOV   *(Continued)* . . . I thought, since you might have some cluttering up your inventory, you could transmit them to me—cause me to have them—souls, I mean, not quite living any more in one sense, but very much alive according to the letter of the law. Taxable property. You do see? *(A pause)* You find this conversation awkward?

MANILOV   I? . . . awkward? . . . no . . . nothing you say could ever seem awkward, to me. But . . . forgive me, my education was not so brilliant as yours. Your every word contains meanings which are hidden, to my dull mind. And so—ah! That's it! You have been speaking symbolically. Your significance lies hidden within rhetorical flourishes which you affect, for beauty of style. I quite understand.

CHICHIKOV   No. I mean just what I said. Dead souls. *(A pause)* And so, old fellow, if there is nothing standing in the way, why, God bless us, we can go right ahead and draw up the contract.

MANILOV   What, what? Draw up a contract? On dead people?

CHICHIKOV   Oh, no, no, no! Good heavens! Not dead people. Legal entities, my dear sir. Legal entities. Our deed of sale must record them exactly as on the last Government Census. This is a legal question. I am one accustomed never to deviate from the letter of our laws. The State Treasury of our sacred Russia will even profit from it! Yes! Who do you think receives all the legal fees, for processing our deeds of sale?

MANILOV   So your supposition is—

CHICHIKOV   —that this will do good.

MANILOV   Ah, if it will do good, that's a different matter.

CHICHIKOV   Now, what's left? Ah, yes, just the little question of a price.

MANILOV   A price? What price? If you'll permit me, I grant them to you without profit on my part. And as for those legal fees for the deed, I take that cost upon myself.

CHICHIKOV   *(Carried away, kisses* MANILOV's *hands)* My dear, dear friend! Oh! . . .

MANILOV   Pavel Ivanovich, I have all along, you see, been searching a way somehow to prove the sincere attraction, the magnetism of our two spirits . . . And peasants who have died are, in a certain sense, nothing but trash.

CHICHIKOV   Not trash at all! Absolutely not trash! If only you knew what a blessing you bestow by this supposed trash on a man without fortune or high birth. *(Sudden change of tone)* You know, it wouldn't be a bad idea to put through that deed of sale right away. Just make out a detailed list, each peasant by name, please. And if you could drop into town with it yourself . . . to close the deal, you know?

MANILOV   Oh, rest assured. I'll be apart from you no longer than a day or two.

CHICHIKOV   *(Takes his hat)* Well, then, it's the briefest of good-byes.

MANILOV   What's this? You want to go already? Lizanka, Pavel Ivanovich is abandoning us!

MANILOV'S WIFE   *(Entering with two bonbons)* Oh, and I was just about to pop a few bonbons into both your mouths. *(Coquettish)* But then, I suppose we must be boring to Mr. Chichikov. *(Pops a bonbon into* MANILOV's *mouth)*

CHICHIKOV   Boring? *(Touches his breast)* Madame, here, here, yes, here is the place, in my heart, where the pleasures spent with you will be memorialized for all time. Ah, if only it could come to pass, indeed how good 'twould be for all of us to live together, if not under the same roof, then at least close by in the neighborhood. Farewell, dear lady. *(Kisses her hand)* And farewell, my newest and most valued friend. *(Embraces* MANILOV*)* See you in town.

CHICHIKOV *and* MANILOV *embrace, wordlessly.* CHICHIKOV *exits, and can be heard whistling or singing as* HE *leaves, in smug triumph.*

MANILOV   *(Alone)* How fine it would be to live with him on the green bank of some river . . . Or build a home with a high, lofty belvedere, so that we could see all the way to Moscow . . . and that's where we would take our tea, on that high belvedere, under the open sky . . . From the house itself we could lay out a passageway underground, to that river, and then across the river put up a bridge, and construct little shops along the bridge itself . . . and we'd have merchants, shopkeepers, sitting there to sell the little odds and ends the peasants need for survival . . . And then, use it as a carriageway to go out with Chichikov to enjoy cultivated society . . . Chi-chi-kov! What a harmonious name! . . . And the Czar, our monarch and emperor, would find out about this celebrated friendship and would wish to bestow upon us the appropriate rank. Chichikov and I, as generals! . . . General Manilov. General Chichikov . . . *(His face changes)* But, they are dead?! Aren't they?

ACT I

Scene 4

At SOBAKEVICH's. *A portrait gallery. A thrush in a cage. Massive furniture.* SOBAKEVICH *and* CHICHIKOV *emerging from dinner, with a certain amount of belching and staggering.*

NOTE: *As* SOBAKEVICH *is an overwhelming, bear-like man,* CHICHIKOV *must try either to create an equally impressive front, or somehow contrive to dance around the edges of that solidity; quite different maneuvers from those that worked with* MANILOV.

SOBAKEVICH   You won't find a dinner like that in town.
CHICHIKOV   Well, the Governor doesn't keep a bad table.
SOBAKEVICH   Nonsense! Here, we serve you a saddle of mutton stuffed with buckwheat—you can see what you're eating! But that French scoundrel of a Governor's cook, he'll take a cat and skin it for fricassee, he'll coat a frog all over with sugar and expect you to pop it into your mouth! I wouldn't touch it, and I wouldn't touch oysters, either; I know what oysters are like; and those sickly diets peddled by French or German doctors who have no idea how to cope with a real Russian stomach! In my house, if I have pork, then put the whole pig on the

table! If it's mutton, I say fetch the whole sheep! My gallery! *(Pointing to enormous statues)* Mavrocordato, Greek commander . . . Kolokotroni, Greek general, wars of independence . . . Bagration, one of ours, look how skinny . . . That's my pet thrush. What did you want to ask me about?

CHICHIKOV Ask you? Oh, nothing serious, just . . . the way to Squire Plyushkin's house, after I leave you. Is it to the left or the right from your gates?

SOBAKEVICH Plyushkin?! I would not even advise you what road to take! Plyushkin! That dog! That miser! He starves his peasants, they die off like flies!

CHICHIKOV Really? Like flies?

SOBAKEVICH *(Breaking in)* I'm waiting.

CHICHIKOV For what?

SOBAKEVICH The point.

CHICHIKOV The point?

SOBAKEVICH The point of your visit.

CHICHIKOV The point . . . Here is the point. *(Pacing; judicious, solid)* Travelers from all foreign nations are astounded at this Russian Empire, which has, in its majesty, many interesting and unusual features.

SOBAKEVICH Name one.

CHICHIKOV Easily, sir. Our Russian law, going back to its ancient foundations in the *mir,* or village commune—

SOBAKEVICH You're not interested in the law.

CHICHIKOV I'm not?

SOBAKEVICH You're a businessman. That's why I'm talking to you.

CHICHIKOV There is one law that interests me very much. It says that all Russians who have completed their mortal journey are still equal to the living, in the juridical sense, until the next government census. This can create quite a burden for the major landowner—like yourself, sir— obligated to keep paying taxes on all his serfs, or souls, no longer living except in the impartial justice of the tax rolls.

CHICHIKOV *watches him, carefully.* SOBAKEVICH *watches back, just as carefully.*

SOBAKEVICH You want dead souls!

CHICHIKOV Yes . . . no . . . well, non-existing.

SOBAKEVICH You mean, dead.

CHICHIKOV Yes.

SOBAKEVICH *(Breaking in)* Fine. I'm ready to sell.

CHICHIKOV Sell? Ah . . .

SOBAKEVICH   Not to make it too steep for you, what do you say to one hundred rubles a head.

CHICHIKOV   *One hundred?!*

SOBAKEVICH   What, surely that's not too expensive for a man like you.

CHICHIKOV   We really don't understand each other at all. Eighty kopecks per soul; that's a perfectly fine price.

SOBAKEVICH   Ai, ai, ai, you should be ashamed to let such a sound come out of your mouth! Eighty kopecks? Not even one ruble for a soul. Come now, let's do business. Name a real price.

CHICHIKOV   I can't, my dear sir. Believe me in all conscience, I can't . . . Well, I'll add half a ruble per head.

SOBAKEVICH   Why so stingy? These are not bark sandals I'm selling you. Some other swindler would cheat you, he'd sell you rubbish instead of good souls. But mine are all like heart of oak, all choice, top selections; if not master craftsmen, then strong healthy peasants at the least. Just you take a real look at someone like Mikheyev, the carriage maker, for instance: he'll do everything, down to the upholstery and veneer himself.

CHICHIKOV   Please, I—

SOBAKEVICH   And Milushkin—the bricklayer! He'll build you a perfect stove, fit it into any house you like.

CHICHIKOV   If you permit me.

SOBAKEVICH   Or, Maksim Telyatnikov, the shoemaker: His needle just pierces the leather and out comes a pair of boots, and what boots, you'll never see boots like that again! And not a drop of liquor passes his lips! I stake my head on it! That's the sort of people they are!

CHICHIKOV   Why number all their virtues for me now? What good are they? These are dead men! All of them!

SOBAKEVICH   *(As if remembering)* Well, yes, they are dead. On the other hand, if you take the men who are now living, what good are most of them? They're flies, not men!

CHICHIKOV   But still, they exist; while these others are just a dream.

SOBAKEVICH   No, no, not just a dream! Let me tell you what kind of a man Mikheyev was: *(Makes huge gesture to show his shoulders)* He wouldn't even fit into this room. Try to find another like him, you'll see what a dream is!

CHICHIKOV   My dear Sobakevich, this whole thing's a bit odd, don't you think? I mean, this entire subject is simply . . . damn it! What good are these men? Who needs them?

SOBAKEVICH   But you're the one who's trying to buy them, so they must be needed? Yes?

CHICHIKOV   Two rubles. That's it.

SOBAKEVICH   Then I'll give you my final word, too: fifty rubles.

CHICHIKOV   You know I can go somewhere else and get them for nothing.

SOBAKEVICH   Well, you know, you'd better be careful where you go. Just between us, this kind of transaction is not strictly . . .

CHICHIKOV   Sir, I am impeccably within the law. If you don't want to sell, then it's goodbye. Yes! Goodbye, Mr. Sobakevich!

SOBAKEVICH   *(Rises)* Now just a moment, just a moment! *(Takes* CHICHIKOV's *arm, and in the process, treads heavily on his foot again)* Oh, have I hurt you, sir!

THEY *sit,* CHICHIKOV *to nurse his foot.*

CHICHIKOV   No, no, it's clear, I'm just wasting my time. I'd really better hurry off. As soon as I can walk.

SOBAKEVICH   Please. I have something pleasant to say to you. *(Sits close to him)* Remember my first price? What would you say to—a quarter?

CHICHIKOV   Twenty-five rubles? No. Nor even a quarter of a quarter. I will not add one kopeck.

SOBAKEVICH   You know, to you a human soul is worth no more than a boiled turnip. The least you could do is offer me three rubles.

CHICHIKOV   I can't do that. Two and a half.

SOBAKEVICH   I give up, there's nothing to be done with you. I'll take a loss, but that's the way I am—just like a dog, I can't help wanting to make my fellow creatures happy . . . Now I suppose we'll have to make out a deed of sale? Just so everything is in order?

CHICHIKOV   Of course.

SOBAKEVICH   Well, so there it is, I will have to go to town for the signing. I'll take my advance now.

CHICHIKOV   Advance? What for? When you get to town, you'll get all the money at once.

SOBAKEVICH   That's the way it's done, and you know it. That's why it's called an advance.

CHICHIKOV   But I don't know how I can give it to you. I really didn't bring any money with me . . . Well, here . . . I've got ten rubles.

SOBAKEVICH   Fifty, or the deal is off!

CHICHIKOV   I don't have it.

SOBAKEVICH   You have it.

CHICHIKOV   Well, . . . here's another fifteen for you . . . Twenty-five rubles in all. Receipt, please.

SOBAKEVICH   A receipt? What for?

CHICHIKOV   You can't tell; anything can happen. If you don't mind.
SOBAKEVICH   Well . . . give me the money first!
CHICHIKOV   I have the money right here, in my hand. Look! As soon as you write out the receipt, you can take your money.
SOBAKEVICH   Now, how can I write a receipt? First, I have to receive the money!

> THEY *both hold on to the bills.* SOBAKEVICH *writes the receipt.* CHICHIKOV *hands over the money.*

SOBAKEVICH   *(Continued)* This bill is a bit old, you know? . . . You wouldn't want any souls of the female gender?
CHICHIKOV   No, thanks very much.
SOBAKEVICH   Well, then . . .
CHICHIKOV   I have one request to make of you: that we keep this business strictly between ourselves.
SOBAKEVICH   But that goes without saying. We're men of the world. Goodbye. Thank you for dropping in.
CHICHIKOV   Oh, ah . . . the way to Plyushkin's? To left or right, you never told—
SOBAKEVICH   *Plyushkin?! Plyushkin?!* That dog!
CHICHIKOV   Never mind, never mind, I enjoyed our conversation. Goodbye. (CHICHIKOV *exits*)
SOBAKEVICH   *(Watching from the window)* What a scoundrel!

ACT I

Scene 5

At PLYUSHKIN's. *Neglected, fantastically overgrown garden. Rotting columns. Terrace, piled with rubbish. Sunset.*

A FIGURE *in nondescript gown and serf-woman's cap, going over and over the pile of junk as if it were dearest treasure. Keys dangle from the belt of the gown.*

CHICHIKOV *(Coming to terrace)* Good woman! Say, good woman, is your master—
PLYUSHKIN Not home! . . . What do you want?
CHICHIKOV Business.
PLYUSHKIN That's different.

Silence.

CHICHIKOV Well?
PLYUSHKIN Well, what?
CHICHIKOV Where's your master?
PLYUSHKIN Here.
CHICHIKOV *(Looking about)* But where?
PLYUSHKIN What's your problem, sir, what are you—blind? Can't you see. Good heavens, I'm the master!
CHICHIKOV Oh? Oh, yes, I have heard about you, sir . . . Squire Sobakevich spoke to me of your . . . thrift and rare abilities in managing your estate, sir, and so I felt it behooved me to make your acquaintance and personally pay my respects. Sir.
PLYUSHKIN I beg you, sir, take a seat. It's a while since I had visitors, you see. We Russians have taken up a filthy habit; we keep visiting each other! . . . And so our estates fall into rot. I had my dinner already, sir, a very long time ago, and my kitchen, you see, is so narrow, and the chimney has fallen to pieces, you can't start up the stove because the whole place will catch fire.
CHICHIKOV Oh. I see how it is.
PLYUSHKIN And this is the miserable part of the story: I don't have a single wisp of hay for you, not on the entire estate! And how could I have extra, anyway, with only a little wee piece of land—and any day now you'll turn around and I will be going out begging, on the streets, in my old age . . .
CHICHIKOV And yet, people seem to have told me that you own over a thousand serfs.
PLYUSHKIN Who? Who told you that, sir? A thousand souls! Well, you go right out there, go ahead, take a count, and see where you get.
CHICHIKOV One . . . two . . .
PLYUSHKIN These last three years, the damned fever, has killed off a whole barnful of my peasants.
CHICHIKOV A whole barnful?

PLYUSHKIN   I'm too old, sir, to start telling lies.

CHICHIKOV   You have my sympathies, dear Squire Plyushkin. My condolences, and my sympathies. And not to waste any more of your valuable time, I come to the point: I am ready to pay the taxes for you on all your peasants who have so grievously died of late.

PLYUSHKIN   What? What? Ah, you . . . you've been serving in the Army.

CHICHIKOV   The Army?

PLYUSHKIN   Oh, you Army people are the worst—horse races and carousing, using up all the money your father left you on . . . Do you know what you squander your money on, sir?

CHICHIKOV   No. No, I don't.

PLYUSHKIN   On *actresses!* You spend your money on *actresses,* and you drink champagne until you're red in the face, and then you come around here kissing my hand and calling me "Uncle," hoping to borrow, sir, to borrow! I'm no more your Uncle than you're my grandfather! Don't tell me about the Army! I simply won't listen! No, no, no!

CHICHIKOV   But I was in Civil Service. And I have not come to borrow, but, as I said, to give.

PLYUSHKIN   But, but . . . Civil Service, eh? You're sure you are not in the Army? I don't understand you, sir. If you mean what you say . . . *(Struggling with an impossible thought)* Why, *you'll lose money!*

CHICHIKOV   I am happy to lose some money, out of respect for you, sir. For I see before me a fine old man, and I see what he has had to suffer through because of his good nature—

PLYUSHKIN   Oh my good Lord, yes! Oh, my God, it's true! All because of my good nature! Oh, my good sir, oh my, my . . . benefactor! Oh, my Lord in heaven! Oh, my holy Saints! *(Pause. Complete change of expression: Back to the suspicious, the joyless)* But how, may I inquire, do you intend to do it? Will you pay the taxes every year?

CHICHIKOV   Well, here is what we'll do. Let's write up a deed of purchase, just as if they were all still alive, and you were simply selling them to me.

PLYUSHKIN   Yes, yes—a deed of purchase . . . A deed of purchase, sir, it . . . costs something.

CHICHIKOV   Out of the same respect for you, I am ready to take even that expense upon myself.

PLYUSHKIN   You . . . lovely man! You! Benefactor! Every blessing be upon you, and upon your children! Yes, your darling little children! Proshka! Proshka!

Enter PROSHKA, *a house serf, a boy of 13 in boots much too large.*

PLYUSHKIN *(Continued)* Just take a look, good sir, at that mug of his. Stupid, as a block of wood, but just try putting anything down and he'll make it disappear in two seconds! *(To* PROSHKA) *Nu,* what are you here for, you young idiot? What are you standing here for? Get out the samovar, do you hear? And here, here, take this key, go find Mavra. Give it to her, tell her to go into the storeroom, there's a slice of that Easter cake Aleksandra Stepanovna brought us three years ago. Tell her, we're going to have it for tea! Wait! Where are you going? Now you listen, carefully: That slice of cake, I think, probably has a layer of mold on it, just on top. So tell her to scrape it off with a knife—but don't throw the crumbs away! Feed them to the chickens, you hear? *(Suspicious of* CHICHIKOV *again)* You know, sir, it wouldn't be a bad idea to put through that deed of purchase right away. You know how it is: A man may be alive today, but tomorrow God knows what will happen.

CHICHIKOV Right away! This minute! Of course, you'll have to go to town to sign the final papers.

PLYUSHKIN To town? How? Leave the house all alone? My peasants are all thieves or swindlers, sir. In one day they'll strip this house so there won't be a peg left to hang my coat on!

CHICHIKOV Don't you have anyone in town that you know? A friend, well, an acquaintance whom you could entrust with the deed?

PLYUSHKIN Acquaintance? What acquaintance? They're all either dead, or we got . . . Ach, wait! Good Lord, how can I have none? I have one! Of course I have one! The President of the Courts, himself, that's who! He used to come and visit me, in the old days. Do I know him? Of course I know him! When we were little boys, we climbed fences together, we played, like . . . friends . . . Do you think I should write to him? *(Pause. A brief ray of warmth passes over* PLYUSHKIN's *face)*

CHICHIKOV Why of course, write to him.

PLYUSHKIN *(Suspicious again)* There was a clean sheet of paper lying right here. I don't know where it could have disappeared to . . . My people are just unfit . . . scoundrels! Mavra! Mavra!

Enter MAVRA, *in ragged clothing, with the wedge of Easter cake on a plate.*

PLYUSHKIN *(Continued)* You thief! Where did you put that piece of paper?

MAVRA   Honest to God, sir, I ain't seen it! Except you mean the bit you cover the brandy glass with.

PLYUSHKIN   I can tell by your eyes, you filched it!

MAVRA   But what do I want to snitch it for, Master? It's not much good to me, is it, as I don't know how to write, Master.

PLYUSHKIN   You're lying! You took it to the sexton! He can scrawl a few words, so you took it to him!

MAVRA   The sexton? He can get his own paper. He's never seen your scrap of paper!

PLYUSHKIN   You wait and see, on the terrible Day of Judgement, the devils will roast you alive for this, on their red-hot horns of fire!

MAVRA   But what are they going to roast me for, if I never even held your notepaper in my hands? But there it is! Look, it's lying right there! You're always putting blame on me, for nothing at all!

PLYUSHKIN   Ooh, what a foul temper she has! Ooh, how she carries on! *(Starts to write. To* MAVRA*)* Now go fetch me my sealing wax and a little fire. No, wait! You'll bring me a good tallow candle, and tallow— the trouble is, it melts, it burns away, it disappears, and there's nothing left, it's pure loss . . . Just bring me a splinter of wood! *(To* CHICHIKOV*)* By the way, do you happen to have any friends who might be interested in buying runaway peasants?

CHICHIKOV   And what kind of numbers are we talking about?

PLYUSHKIN   It must be sixty or so, by now. Every year, a few more run away.

CHICHIKOV   No, I don't have any friend interested in that kind of deal. But if you really feel so strapped for money, then I myself am ready to give . . . twenty-five kopecks for each fugitive soul.

PLYUSHKIN   Yes sir, yes . . . Dear sir, it's your business, but cou!dn't you tack on just two or three little kopecks more?

CHICHIKOV   Why, of course, I can tack on five kopecks, if it would please you. Now, you say sixty runaways, more or less . . . ?

PLYUSHKIN   Seventy-eight.

CHICHIKOV   Seventy-eight, at thirty kopecks a head, makes . . . *(Pause, for one second)* Twenty-three rubles . . .

PLYUSHKIN   Forty kopecks.

CHICHIKOV   Forty kopecks. Please write a receipt.

CHICHIKOV *makes a slight movement.* PLYUSHKIN *pounces on it, as a sign that* HE *might be ready to go.*

PLYUSHKIN   What's this, getting ready to go so soon?

CHICHIKOV   What? Oh, yes . . . Yes, time to go.

PLYUSHKIN   And what about our tea?

CHICHIKOV   Thank you kindly. But, no.

PLYUSHKIN   Proshka! Put the samovar away! And this cake! . . . No, I'll put the cake away, myself. *(The receipt is written . . .* PLYUSHKIN *receives the money and hides it in his housecoat)* I have an excellent little liqueur. Here . . . Someplace . . . My people are such thieves, sir! But wait, . . . *(Rummaging in a cabinet, finds decanter covered with woolly dust)* Isn't this it? It was my late wife who made it, but then one of our housekeepers did criminal negligence, just throwing it back here and didn't even cork it up, the slut! Gnats and flies and all kinds of things got crammed in there, but I dug all that out myself, and now, you see—it's really quite clean, I'll pour you a glass.

CHICHIKOV   No. I've drunk, I've eaten. Time to go.

PLYUSHKIN   What? You've eaten and drunk already? But, of course, you can recognize a man of breeding anywhere. He doesn't eat, and yet he's already full! Farewell, then, my dear boy. And God bless you! (HE *sees* CHICHIKOV *out, and then returns. Alone)* I shall give him my pocket watch as a present. Yes, it's a good silver watch, not one of those fake bronze ones. Of course, it isn't working right now, but he can get it repaired for himself. He's still a young man, he'll need a good pocket watch so that he can be even more appealing to his future bride! *(Thinks a moment)* Or no—maybe it's better to leave it to him when I die, in my will: Then, he'll remember me . . .

ACT I

Scene 6

At NOZDRYOV's *house. Bright day. Dinner is ending. On the wall: Sabres, two rifles, a portrait of General Suvorov.* NOZDRYOV *in striped, short, Asiatic coat.*

NOZDRYOV   No, now you try it, it's a mixture of Burgundy and champagne. Goes down like sweet cream. (HE *pours*)

MIZHUYEV   *(Dead drunk)* Well, I'm going.

NOZDRYOV   Uh-uh-uh-uh! I won't let you!

MIZHUYEV   Come on, don't start insulting me, old friend, I've got to go.

NOZDRYOV   "Got to go!!" That's nonsense, that's trivia, we've got a hand of cards to play.

MIZHUYEV   No, old boy, you play one yourself, but I'm out. My wife will be lodging a law suit against me, honestly, I've got to go home and tell her about the Fair.

NOZDRYOV   Oh, your wife . . . can go to . . . It's not as if there's anything important you're going to do, with her!

MIZHUYEV   No, old boy, please, she's really such a good wife. She's faithful, and she respects me, and does so many little things for me, she made me this wonderful little cap, but I lost it at the Fair . . . believe me, it just brings tears to my eyes . . .

CHICHIKOV   *(Quietly to NOZDRYOV)* Let him go, what good is he now?

NOZDRYOV   *(Quietly in response)* You're right. Lord, I hate these sentimental types! *(Aloud)* All right, the hell with you! Go home, nuzzle your wife, you—fig's testicle!

MIZHUYEV   No, brother, don't call me a fig's testicle! I owe my whole life to her, she's so good and tender and sweet . . . She'll ask me . . . what did I see at the Fair . . .

NOZDRYOV   Well, go. Make up any kind of crap and tell her.

MIZHUYEV   No, I can't listen to you take that attitude to her . . .

NOZDRYOV   Then clear out and go running to her! Here's your cap.

MIZHUYEV   Yes, all right, I'm going. Forgive me, dear brother-in-law, that I can't stay.

NOZDRYOV   Go! Get out!

MIZHUYEV   I'd be sincerely glad to stay, but I can't.

NOZDRYOV   Then go to hell!

MIZHUYEV *leaves, still apologizing.*

NOZDRYOV   *(Continued, watching through window)* What a piece of trash he is! There he goes, dragging himself home! A lot of rich detail his wife will hear from him, about the Fair! . . . That trace-horse of his isn't so bad. I've wanted to get my hands on it for a long time . . . Can't get him on a price, he's a real fig's testicle . . . Well, I'll show you my property. You can see the boundary: Everything on this side of it is mine. And on the other side, too—all the woods that look blue over there, that's mine, and also whatever is on the other side of the woods, that's also mine . . . *(Gets out a pack of cards, splits open the wrapping and shuffles with amazing dexterity)* Well, to help pass the time, I'll set up the bank with three hundred rubles.

CHICHIKOV   Oh, just so I won't forget. I do have a little request to make of you.

NOZDRYOV   What?

CHICHIKOV   You have to promise first that you'll carry it out.

NOZDRYOV   If you want.

CHICHIKOV   Word of honor?

NOZDRYOV   Word of honor.

CHICHIKOV   All right, here is my request: You probably have quite a few . . . ah, deceased peasants, who have not yet been crossed off the government's census?

NOZDRYOV   Some, that's right. So?

CHICHIKOV   Transfer them to me, in my name.

NOZDRYOV   To you? What for?

CHICHIKOV   Well, I just want them. I need them.

NOZDRYOV   Ah, there's some kind of dark plot here. Come on, 'fess up, what it is?

CHICHIKOV   What dark plot? From such a trifle you can't have any kind of plot.

NOZDRYOV   Then, what do you want them for?

CHICHIKOV   A kind of . . . whim came over me.

NOZDRYOV   Fine. Until you tell me, I won't do it.

CHICHIKOV   But look here, my friend, that's not fair. You gave your word and now you're going back on it.

NOZDRYOV   Well, that may be, but I'm still not going to do it until you tell me.

CHICHIKOV   I need dead souls in order to gain some status in society, for my—

NOZDRYOV   Oh, you're lying, you're lying!

CHICHIKOV   All right, all right, I'll tell you more simply. I'd like to get married, but—this I tell you in confidence—my future in-laws are amazingly ambitious people, they—

NOZDRYOV   Oh, you're lying! You're lying again!

A storm cloud comes over them.

CHICHIKOV   This is growing offensive. Why, exactly, must I be lying?

NOZDRYOV   Well, I know you, I know all about you, you see. You're a criminal mentality, through and through, from your head to your *pupik.* I tell you this as a friend. If I were a judge, I'd hang you from the nearest branch. Damned if I wouldn't! I tell you this frankly and sincerely, as one friend to another.

A pause.

CHICHIKOV   If you don't want to give them to me, then sell them.

NOZDRYOV   Sell them? But I know you, Chichikov. I'll bet you're not going to give me much for them. Are you?

CHICHIKOV   Well, aren't you the fine fellow, yourself! What are they to you—diamonds, or what?

NOZDRYOV   Well, listen, just to show you that I'm not some money-grubbing type, I won't take a penny for them. Just buy my stallion from me, and I'll throw the peasants into the deal, for nothing.

CHICHIKOV   But what in the world do I want with your stallion?

NOZDRYOV   What do you mean by that? Look, I paid ten thousand for him; I'll let you have him for four.

CHICHIKOV   But I don't want your stallion, God bless him!

NOZDRYOV   All right, all right! Good. Then buy the chestnut mare.

CHICHIKOV   I don't need the mare either.

NOZDRYOV   Try this: For the mare and for that gray horse you see, I'll take from you—altogether—two thousand.

CHICHIKOV   But I don't want any horses at all.

NOZDRYOV   Then you can sell them, you'll get three times as much for them at the first fair.

CHICHIKOV   I think it would be better for you to sell them yourself, since you're so sure you can triple the price.

NOZDRYOV   But I want you to get the profits!

CHICHIKOV   I'm grateful for the good thought, but I don't want any horses.

NOZDRYOV   All right, then buy some dogs. I'll sell you a certain bitch, she'll just raise a chill all over your body. Pedigreed, borzoi, huge whiskers like a mustache, a coat that stands out like bristles, rib-cage like a barrel, and velvet fluff for a paw—She'll never make the tiniest mark on the earth!

CHICHIKOV   And why do I need a dog with mustaches? I'm not a hunter.

NOZDRYOV   You don't want dogs. Then, buy my barrel-organ. A real hurdy-gurdy.

CHICHIKOV   A hurdy-gurdy? Why? Am I some kind of German, to go up and down the streets begging money?

NOZDRYOV   But this isn't that kind of hurdy-gurdy that Germans drag around. This is an organ! Pure mahogany! . . . (HE *pulls* CHICHIKOV *over to the hurdy-gurdy and grinds out "Marlborough Went to the Wars . . ." In the distance, sounds of thunder beginning)* Here's what we'll do: I'm going to give you the hurdy-gurdy and all the dead souls, and you give me your carriage and throw in three hundred rubles, and that's it.

CHICHIKOV   And how will I travel, without my carriage?

NOZDRYOV   I'm going to give you another. Come on to the coachhouse, you'll see: Just needs a paint job and she'll be a beautiful little *britzka!*

CHICHIKOV   No.

NOZDRYOV   But why don't you want them?

CHICHIKOV   Because I don't want them, and that's it!

NOZDRYOV   You're such a . . . I don't know what to call you! I welcome you here, thinking we'll be like friends, comrades together. But now it's clear what you are. You're slimy, two-faced! You're duplicitous, that's what you are!

CHICHIKOV   But not a fool! You tell me—why should I acquire things that are absolutely of no use to me?

NOZDRYOV   Please, you're wasting your breath. Now I know you through and through. You're even worse than I thought you were. All right, listen, we'll play some cards. I'll stake all the dead souls on one card. And the hurdy-gurdy, too.

CHICHIKOV   But that means, we're leaving it all up to chance.

NOZDRYOV   What, chance? Who's talking about chance? This is luck, and if it's on your side, you can win a hell of a pile today. (HE *deals)* You don't want to play?

CHICHIKOV   No.

NOZDRYOV   What scum you are! A real fig's testicle! You know, I was on the verge of giving those dead souls to you free? But now you're not getting a damned thing! Offer me three kingdoms, you still won't get 'em. *(Shouts)* Porfiry! Go down to the stable, tell them no oats for this bastard's horses! Let 'em eat hay . . . I wish I had never set eyes on you!

CHICHIKOV   *(Enraged)* Petrushka! Carriage! *(Gets his hat)*

NOZDRYOV   No! Wait! Listen, listen, we'll play a game of checkers! You win, and the peasants are all yours! This isn't cards, we're not talking about leaving it to chance. What's cards anyway?—it's all cheating and marked decks and outright dishonesty. This is skill, all skill . . . And I should warn you, I hardly know how to play the game.

CHICHIKOV   *(To himself)* Mm . . . truth is, I didn't play too badly in the old days, and I don't see what kind of tricks he can pull on a checkerboard. *(Aloud)* Well, all right, if it has to be, I'll play a game of checkers.

NOZDRYOV   The dead souls against a hundred rubles?

CHICHIKOV   Fifty will be enough.

NOZDRYOV   What sort of a bet is fifty rubles? Let me throw in one of my medium puppies, or a gold seal to go on your watch chain.

CHICHIKOV   If you want.

NOZDRYOV   How many pieces will you give me to start?

CHICHIKOV   What for? Why should I give you a handicap?

NOZDRYOV   At least, let me have the first two moves.

CHICHIKOV   No, I won't. I'm a poor player, myself.

THEY *begin to play.*

NOZDRYOV   We know you, we know what kind of poor player you are . . . *(Makes a move)*

CHICHIKOV   It's been years since I've held a checker piece in my hand . . . *(Makes a move)*

NOZDRYOV   We know you, we know what kind of poor player you are . . . *(Makes a move)*

CHICHIKOV   Haven't touched a checker piece for—Whoa! . . . Whoa! What is this? Put it back.

NOZDRYOV   What?

CHICHIKOV   That checker piece, that's what! And that other one, too— wait! *(Gets up)* No, no, my dear fellow, it's just impossible to play with you! I just don't play that way . . . with three pieces at the same time!

NOZDRYOV   Why do you say three? That was by mistake, one got moved by accident. I'll put it back, I'm sorry.

CHICHIKOV   And where did this other fellow come from?

NOZDRYOV   Which other fellow?

CHICHIKOV   That one, right there. Out of nowhere, he's going to be a king!

NOZDRYOV   Now, that's too much! As if you don't remember . . .

CHICHIKOV   I remember very well. You just nudged it over there! *This* is its square, right here!

NOZDRYOV   How—that square? I can see, old chum, you like imagining things!

CHICHIKOV   No, dear fellow, I'm afraid it's you who imagines things. But it's not going to work with me!

NOZDRYOV   What, pray tell, do you take me for? A cheater? That's what you're saying?

CHICHIKOV   I don't take you for anything, but I'm never ever going to play with you again, as of right now! *(Sweeps all the pieces together)*

NOZDRYOV   No, you can't back out now! The game is begun! *Les jeux sont faits!* You've got to finish the match! It doesn't matter that you've wrecked the board, I remember every move! *(Starts to put pieces back)*

CHICHIKOV   No, sir, I am not going to play with you.

NOZDRYOV   So, so, you're saying you won't play? *(Advances closer to CHICHIKOV)* Give me a straight answer!

CHICHIKOV   I would play an honest game, with an honorable man, but I can't do that here.

NOZDRYOV   Oh, you can't, can you? Oh, you can't, can you? You villain! You filthy sow! You see you're losing, so you quit! I'll make you play. We'll beat it into you! *(Whistles) Fire! Chinko! Cherkai! Wolf!*

Ferocious barking comes closer.

NOZDRYOV   *(Continued)* Beat him! Thrash him! Porfiry! Pavlushka! . . . Beat him!

Flings himself at CHICHIKOV. SERVANTS *come with clubs.* PE-TRUSHKA *runs in to help his master.* CHICHIKOV *tries to hide.*

NOZDRYOV   *(Continued)* Porfiry! Forward, lads! Storm the barricades! *Courage!*

Whistles. Shouts. Barking. Sound of thunder. With PETRUSH-KA's *help,* CHICHIKOV *makes a desperate escape.*

ACT I

Interlude

On the road. Night. Lurid glimmerings. Thunder. Storm. Rain.
PETRUSHKA *and* CHICHIKOV, *driving headlong through darkness.*

CHICHIKOV   Where are you going? Where is the road? *(The carriage
lurches)*
PETRUSHKA   I give up. Where is it?
CHICHIKOV   You're drunk!
PETRUSHKA   God's will, Master . . .

Thunder. Dangerous joltings.

CHICHIKOV   What are you doing? You'll turn us over!
PETRUSHKA   No, sir, no, no. It's not good to turn people over. I know
that. I'll never turn you over, Master!

*The carriage turns over. Shouts. Muddy squishings. More thun-
der.*

ACT I

Scene 7

At KOROBOCHKA's. *Stormy night. Lamp burning. Samovar.
Icon.*

KOROBOCHKA   A bit of tea, sir?
CHICHIKOV   Not a bad idea, little lady. If you'll forgive us for this hasty
arrival.

KOROBOCHKA   Not at all! Not at all! Such a dreadful storm! In what terrible weather the good Lord has brought you to us. What thunder! I've had a candle before the icon all night . . . You'd better have something with your tea, sir. I've got some fruit brandy, in that flask.

CHICHIKOV   Not a bad idea, either, little lady. Fruit brandy it will be . . . And would you be willing to tell me your family name again? I'm still a bit distracted . . .

KOROBOCHKA   Korobochka. Widow of a Collegiate Secretary, sir.

CHICHIKOV   A widow?

KOROBOCHKA   You should lie down and rest! What you must have been through on the road. Oh, my Lord, sir, your back is all covered with mud, just like a hog's! We should rub that with something warm! Lie down and rest. Take your shoes off. Would you like to have your heels tickled? My late husband just could never get to sleep without it. Here. Fetinya! Come, rub and tickle the gentleman!

CHICHIKOV   No, thank you, sweet lady. I don't think I'll have my heels tickled tonight.

KOROBOCHKA   Some pancakes, good sir. Don't stand on ceremony, I pray you. Eat.

CHICHIKOV   Your pancakes, dear lady, are first rate. So is the fruit brandy. *(Drinks)*

KOROBOCHKA   And what might your own name be, sir? You talk a bit like a tax assessor. You're not a tax assessor, I hope?

CHICHIKOV   No, no, not a tax assessor, I certainly hope not. I'm on the road doing some private little business of my own.

KOROBOCHKA   Ah, so you're a dealer! What a pity that I sold my honey to those merchants, and so cheap! You, kind sir, I just know you'd have bought it all from me, wouldn't you?

CHICHIKOV   I'm afraid I'm not here to buy your honey.

KOROBOCHKA   Well, what then? What could you want from me? Maybe some hemp.

CHICHIKOV   No. My interests are special. Merchandise of a very special kind . . . Oh, tell me have your peasants been dying off?

KOROBOCHKA   Oh, oh, kind sir, eighteen of them. And the ones who died—such good workers! Just last week, my blacksmith caught fire. Such a clever blacksmith he was . . .

CHICHIKOV   Oh, you had a fire, poor thing?

KOROBOCHKA   God preserve us! I didn't have a fire, sir! The blacksmith had a fire; he burned up all by himself. Inside him something flared up, somehow, he must have had too much vodka, and little blue flames started coming out of him. Then he smouldered all over, poor thing, just smouldered and smouldered, and turned black as coal, and then he was ashes. Now, you see, I can't drive out at all, I have nobody to shoe the horses.

CHICHIKOV   It's all in God's hands, my dear. Against the wisdom of God there is nothing to be said . . . Madame Korobochka, may I ask your Christian name, and patronymic?

KOROBOCHKA   Nastasya Petrovna.

CHICHIKOV   Nastasya Petrovna. I had an aunt, my own mother's sister; she was Nastasya Petrovna, too. Lovely name. Nastasya Petrovna, couldn't you just let me have them?

KOROBOCHKA   What might you speak of, sir?

CHICHIKOV   Well, you know, all of those, who died.

KOROBOCHKA   But how can I let you have them?

CHICHIKOV   Well, just simply do it. Or, you might rather sell them. Eh? I'll give you money for them.

KOROBOCHKA   I'm too simple, sir. I can't figure the meaning in this. Do we have to dig them out of the ground?

CHICHIKOV   Ekh, dear lady, no . . . We write them out on paper, the name of each soul. That's all. Think how nice, not to pay those taxes on them. And I shall give you fifteen rubles in currency. So what do you think, little lady; do we have a deal?

KOROBOCHKA   To tell the truth, sir, I've never had the occasion before to sell the deceased, in any form. Now, live ones I've done; I let the parish priest have two little females at a hundred rubles apiece, and very happy he was with that deal.

CHICHIKOV   Well, we're not talking about live ones, dear. I'm asking for the dead.

KOROBOCHKA   Well, you see, that's the very thing that's stopping me, the fact that they're dead. You could possibly be deceiving me, sir, and they . . . I mean . . . What if they're worth more?

CHICHIKOV   Now you listen to me, you don't know what you're talking about! How much can they be worth? What are they? They're dust!

KOROBOCHKA   Well now, that's very true. They're of no use at all. But I'm afraid, you see. I'm such an inexperienced widow, I might somehow end up losing . . . It might be better, good sir, if I could wait a while, maybe some other dealers will come along and I can compare prices.

CHICHIKOV   Shame, shame! Oh, for shame! What are we talking about? Think! Who is going to buy them? What possible use could anyone find in them?

KOROBOCHKA   Well, could be, around the farm, somehow, in case of emergency?

CHICHIKOV   Dead men, around the farm? Ekh, little mother, where are we heading? Maybe, prop them up in your vegetable garden at night, scare the sparrows off?

KOROBOCHKA   Good Lord have mercy, what frightful things you say! *(Crosses herself)*

CHICHIKOV   Well, where else? Where else would you like to use them? —Anyway, remember: The bones and the graves—we'll leave all that with you. I just want a piece of paper! Well, what do you think? . . . Say something at least! *(A pause)* Nastasya Petrovna!

KOROBOCHKA   I think I'd better sell you some hemp instead.

CHICHIKOV   *(Banging his chair)* Go to the devil! . . .

KOROBOCHKA   Och, don't even mention his name, let him rest! Och! . . . Just two nights ago, I kept dreaming about the Evil One, he was so naughty looking and his horns were longer than my bull's!

CHICHIKOV   Well, he can have you! Out of plain Christian charity, I wanted to help . . . I see a poor widow, wearing herself out, suffering from real need, and I—Ah, the hell with you and your peasants and your village, may the whole damned estate slide into a dark hole!

KOROBOCHKA   But why do you get so angry at me? Your face gets so hot. If I had known earlier that you were such an angry one, I'd never have breathed a word back to you. If you will, sir, I'm ready to let you have them for fifteen rubles. Currency. But if you should be wanting some hemp, or lard, or buckwheat flour, now don't you forget me!

CHICHIKOV   *(Mopping his brow)* No, no, darling lady, how could I ever forget you? . . . I won't burden you now with a trip to town, but do you have a friend, or anyone there, who you would trust to sign the deed of purchase for you?

KOROBOCHKA   But of course, Father Kyril—our archpriest—his son works right in the law courts. A clerk, he is.

CHICHIKOV   Well, that's excellent. *(Writes)* Please, just sign here. *(Gives her the money)*

PETRUSKA's VOICE   The carriage is ready, sir.

KOROBOCHKA   And next time, you'll buy my hemp?

CHICHIKOV   Of course I will buy your hemp. *(Significant pause)* And your lard, too, my dear.

KOROBOCHKA   I'll have plenty of lard by Christmastime.

THEY *exchange the Russian triple cheek kiss.* CHICHIKOV *exits.*

CHICHIKOV   *(Offstage, triumphantly)* On the road, Petrushka!

PETRUSHKA   *(Offstage)* Gee-up! Hup, my lads! Fly . . .

KOROBOCHKA *is alone, agitated, pacing, crossing herself repeatedly.*

KOROBOCHKA   Oh my good Lord! Oh my good Lord! He got me so excited! My heart keeps pounding! Oh, I can't think straight, after that man's visit! How can I know? Oh, my heart! . . . Fifteen rubles. Currency. I'll have to get to town before he does! . . . I don't even know how much they're going for . . . I've made a terrible mistake! A widow's mistake! . . . Fetinya, get my things packed! We're going to town! . . . *I've sold too cheap!*

ACT II

Scene 1

Signing and Celebration Ball. Scene begins at the office of the PRESIDENT OF THE COURTS: *a long desk or table. The* PRESIDENT *is looking over several of* CHICHIKOV's *deeds of purchase.*

PRESIDENT OF THE COURTS Ah, Mr. Chichikov. Dear Pavel Ivanovich. You have acquired property, haven't you?
CHICHIKOV I have, sir. I have.
PRESIDENT OF THE COURTS A great deal of property! Well, well, well . . .

Enter MANILOV, *in gorgeous fur coat. Meeting* CHICHIKOV, HE *can only utter a cry of astonishment and joy.*

MANILOV Ah . . . !

HE smothers CHICHIKOV *with embraces, and* THEY *exchange kisses "so hard that their front teeth hurt for the rest of the day."* MANILOV *is so overjoyed that "his eyes disappear completely, leaving only his nose and lips still showing on his face."*

PRESIDENT OF THE COURTS Our dear guest, Mr. Chichikov, has become a man of property. Look here . . .

The PRESIDENT *wants to show the deeds, but* MANILOV *pulls out his own elaborate scroll, done up in pink ribbon, and hands it to* CHICHIKOV.

CHICHIKOV But what is this?
MANILOV Your peasants!

CHICHIKOV   AH!

PRESIDENT OF THE COURTS   More property! *(Comes closer to* CHI-CHIKOV, *trying to hug him, too, or to stroke his person, somehow)*

CHICHIKOV   *(Unrolls and glances over the deed)* It's so beautifully done! A work of art, not a deed of purchase! *(To* PRESIDENT) No need even to re-copy it! . . . And who made the lovely border, all around it? Flowers!

MANILOV   Oh, please don't ask.

CHICHIKOV   It was you!

MANILOV   No, my darling wife, Lizanka . . .

CHICHIKOV   It puts me to shame, that you've taken so much trouble over this!

MANILOV   Trouble? The very word does not exist in reference to Pavel Ivanovich Chichikov.

Enter SOBAKEVICH, *and also* FATHER KYRIL. SOBAKEVICH *shoves a detailed sheaf of papers at* CHICHIKOV, *without a word.*

CHICHIKOV   *(Looking over deed, impressed again)* How are you, old boy?

SOBAKEVICH   Can't complain, thanks to God.

PRESIDENT OF THE COURTS   Can't complain! Your good health is famous! *(To* CHICHIKOV) Just like his late father, another powerhouse.

SOBAKEVICH   Yes, my father used to go out after bear, using only his own two hands.

CHICHIKOV   I think you could bring a bear down, too. I mean, if the thought appealed to you.

SOBAKEVICH   No, I couldn't. My father was stronger . . . No, people aren't what they used to be.

SOBAKEVICH *sinks into melancholy, shaking his head. The* OTHERS *stare at him.*

FATHER KYRIL   I am here to sign the deed for dear widow Koroboch-ka. Her health, of course, is too fragile to allow the travel and emotional stress of such an event.

PRESIDENT OF THE COURTS   Yes, and I apparently am to sign for old Plyushkin. I didn't know he was still alive . . .

SOBAKEVICH   A dog! A scoundrel! Starves his peasants to death!

PRESIDENT OF THE COURTS   Yes, yes, yes. Ready, gentlemen?

The PRESIDENT OF THE COURTS, MANILOV, SOBAKEVICH, *and* FATHER KYRIL'S SON *all sign, with quills and whatever ceremony their temperaments allow—while the* FATHER *makes the sign of the cross over them.*

CHICHIKOV *races along the table, counter-signing with lightning speed.*

PRESIDENT OF THE COURTS   It's done!

CHICHIKOV   It's done!

PRESIDENT OF THE COURTS   A transfer of peasants, worth two hundred thousand rubles, in a single day! Wait till the town hears about this! Sasha! A message to my wife! You, *(To the* CLERK) go tell the Governor! Just say it's done! We can celebrate!

MANILOV   Ah!

PRESIDENT OF THE COURTS   A man of property!

CHICHIKOV   A man of property!

FATHER KYRIL   A man of property! *(Gives the blessing of the cross)*

Music starts up, and preparation for the Ball at Governor's Salon, as:

To one side of stage, CHICHIKOV *prepares himself for the ball, before a long mirror held by* PETRUSHKA, *and:*

To the other side, LADIES *begin to gather, dressed for the ball—in particular,* MANILOV'S WIFE, ANNA GRIGORYEVNA, *and* SOFYA IVANOVNA—*and* THEY *gossip.*

Notes from the novel: *"A whole hour was devoted solely to the examination of his face in the looking glass. He tried to assume a multitude of various expressions: One moment he tried to look grave and important, another moment respectful but with the ghost of a smile, then simply respectful without a smile; a number of bows were made to the looking glass, accompanied by inarticulate sounds resembling French, though Chichikov did not know French at all. He even gave himself a number of pleasant surprises, winking an eye and twitching a lip, and even did something with his tongue; in short, one is liable to do all sorts of odd things when left alone, feeling, moreover, that one is a handsome fellow . . .*

At last, he chucked himself slightly under the chin and said: 'Oh, you silly old face!' and began dressing. He felt perfectly happy and contented all the time he was dressing; pulling on his braces or trying his cravat, he bowed and scraped with particular adroitness, and though he had never danced in his life, he executed an entrechat. This entrechat produced a small and harmless effect: The chest of drawers shook and the brush fell from the table . . ."

CHICHIKOV   Silly old face!

The LADIES gossip about CHICHIKOV.

ANNA GRIGORYEVNA   Soit dit entre nous, cheri—I wonder why we didn't notice him more?

MANILOV'S WIFE   He had most agreeable manners, n'est ce pas?

SOFYA IVANOVNA   Bien sûr, but we never would have guessed that he was a millionaire!

ANNA GRIGORYEVNA   Of course, we are not really impressed with that!

MANILOV'S WIFE   Don't you think he has an unusually attractive nose?

SOFYA IVANOVNA   Such an interesting word: millionaire!

ANNA GRIGORYEVNA   Millionaire? A very attractive word!

SOFYA IVANOVNA   He has many qualities we didn't notice at first.

ANNA GRIGORYEVNA   Oh, I think qualities are such a nice thing for a millionaire to have!

CHICHIKOV arrives at the ball.

ALL   Here he is!

ALL move toward CHICHIKOV, but the high officials get him first—EACH ONE embracing him and handing him on to another, as in a dance.

GOVERNOR   Ah, Mr. Chichikov!

POSTMASTER   Our dear Mr. Chichikov!

PRESIDENT OF THE COURTS   Our dear, dear Mr. Chichikov!

POLICE CHIEF   Our most honorable Mr. Chichikov!

GOVERNOR'S WIFE   Do I get a kiss, too, Mr. Chichikov?

CHICHIKOV is now surrounded by the LADIES. With little mincing steps and happy bows to left and right, HE charms them all.

MANILOV'S WIFE   Oh, you charming Pavel Ivanovich!

SOFYA IVANOVNA   *Enchantée,* you fascinating Mr. Chichikov!

ANNA GRIGORYEVNA   Oh, Mr. Chichikov, Mr. Chichikov!

> *Garlands of flowers are pressed into* CHICHIKOV's *hands.* MU-SIC: *A waltz is struck up, and couples begin to dance.* CHICHIKOV *watches, beaming.*

GOVERNOR'S WIFE   And so, Mr. Chichikov, you have acquired property?

CHICHIKOV   I have, I have, Madam Excellency.

GOVERNOR'S WIFE   And a goodly thing it is to do. A goodly thing, indeed.

CHICHIKOV   Yes, yes, Madam Excellency, I have to admit, I myself cannot think of anything more . . . goodly. Say what you will, a man is not really a man until he finally stands on a foundation he has built for himself, instead of the free-thinking day-dreams of his youth . . .

> *But the* GOVERNOR *is no longer listening. In fact,* HE *begins to dance a waltz with his* DAUGHTER, *a fair and radiant 16 year old. Her white, simple dress stands out against the elaborate finery of the ladies.*
>
> CHICHIKOV *stares at her, astounded by her beauty.* HE *drops his flowers.*

GOVERNOR'S WIFE   Mr. Chichikov, you have not met our daughter? She is just home from boarding school; a fresh young flower.

CHICHIKOV   Yes, yes, Madam Excellency, I see what you mean.

> GOVERNOR'S WIFE *wanders off to join her* DAUGHTER. CHICHIKOV *strains his neck, to stare at the fresh young flower. His gaiety is gone;* HE *looks lost and distracted.*
>
> *The* LADIES *parade up to him to make arch comments, each* LADY *taking the occasion to flaunt before* CHICHIKOV *what* SHE *considers her best feature—whether a profile, or bosom, or lovely hair, or fantastic gown.*

SOFYA IVANOVNA   Oh, Mr. Chi-chi-kov. May we know the name of her . . .

ANNA GRIGORYEVNA   . . . who has plunged you so deep into this sweet valley of oblivion?

SOFYA IVANOVNA *pushes her dance card at him; a mazurka has begun. But* CHICHIKOV *looks past them trying to find the* GOVERNOR'S DAUGHTER. HE *sees her with a place free to sit next to her, and* HE *rudely walks away from the* LADIES, *even bumping one of the dancers out of the way.*
The LADIES *draw together, like avenging furies.*

SOFYA IVANOVNA   Oh!
ANNA GRIGORYEVNA   Well!
SOFYA IVANOVNA   He may be a millionaire, but he has absolutely no qualities.
ANNA GRIGORYEVNA   And look at that brazen little flirt just flinging herself at him!

In fact, the GOVERNOR'S DAUGHTER *only smiled sweetly when* CHICHIKOV *bowed and presented himself to her, and* SHE *is already bored to tears with his conversation.*

CHICHIKOV   *(To* GOVERNOR'S DAUGHTER*)* . . . Perhaps you would like to hear about the property I have acquired and my plans for ultimate settlement in Kherson Province? Or perhaps, being young, you would rather hear a terribly amusing story about something that happened to me once in Simbirsk Province, at Sofron Bespechny's when his daughter Adelaida was there and her three sisters-in-law, Maria, Alexandra, and Maklatura . . . or, was it at Fydor Perekroyev's in Pyazan Province, and it was his sister-in-law, Katerina . . .

GOVERNOR'S DAUGHTER *tries desperately to conceal her yawns. The* LADIES *glare at* CHICHIKOV.

SERVANT   *M'sieurs, dames:* Dinner is served!

MUSIC: A polonaise, and the GUESTS *promenade to the banquet table.*
NOTE: If time and mood allow, the platters of food could be labeled as they pass by. For example: White Sturgeon. Ordinary Sturgeon. Salmon. Pressed Caviar. Herrings. Stellated Sturgeon. Cheeses of All Sorts. Smoked Tongue. Dried Sturgeon. Sturgeon Pie. Mushroom Pie. Fried Pastries. Dumplings Cooked in Butter. Fruit Stewed in Honey.

ACT II

Scene 2

Banquet at the GOVERNOR's.

PRESIDENT OF THE COURTS Pavel Ivanovich, some of us have been wondering. How can you be buying so many peasants without land? Do you mean to resettle them?

CHICHIKOV I do! Definitely, resettlement.

GOVERNOR And where, may I ask?

CHICHIKOV To Kherson Province.

GOVERNOR Ah. Excellent land, in Kherson.

PRESIDENT OF THE COURTS Splendid! Grassland! . . . Isn't it?

POSTMASTER And can you really have enough land there?

CHICHIKOV The land I have there is . . . just enough for the peasants I have bought.

POLICE CHIEF Do you have a river?

POSTMASTER Or is it a pond? I've always wanted a pond.

CHICHIKOV A river. But then again, Mr. Postmaster, there's a pond, too. I'm thinking of various improvements . . . The system of crop rotation, you know . . .

SOBAKEVICH Mr. Chichikov. Why don't you tell the gathered gentlemen exactly what kind of property you did buy? At least, from me. What people! Pure gold! Why, I've even sold him my best carriage maker.

PRESIDENT OF THE COURTS Mikheyev! No! Not Mikheyev! I know Mikheyev: splendid carftsman. Fixed my coach for me. First-class! But, hold on, just a moment, I thought you told me he was dead.

SOBAKEVICH Mikheyev? Dead? No. That was his brother who died. Also named Mikheyev. No, no, he's very much alive, even enjoying a bit of a rebound in his health, you might say.

GOVERNOR Excellent craftsman, Mikheyev.

POLICE CHIEF All this chitchat is very well, Your Excellency. But isn't it likely that Mr. Chichikov's new peasants are a bunch of thieves and drunkards?

CHICHIKOV What are you saying? They are quiet, tranquil people.

SOBAKEVICH Very quiet. Very tranquil.

POLICE CHIEF Come, come. No landowner in his right mind will ever sell his good peasants. Why should he? No, these peasants Pavel Ivanovich has got hold of will get raving, stinking drunk the moment they get to Kherson Province and they'll start a mutiny. Burning down poor Chichikov's manor house, and—

SOBAKEVICH   What's that? My Mikheyev get stinking drunk? I'll stake my head on it, that Mikheyev will never ever get stinking drunk nor start a rebellion. Never!

POLICE CHIEF   We shall see . . . But I think His Excellency is willing to speak to us on this subject.

ALL   Yes, yes . . . Let's hear his Excellency . . . *(Etc., ad lib)*

GOVERNOR   Gentlemen! Let me resolve this little dispute . . . A true Russian is capable of anything, and he can adjust himself to any climate!

> *Murmur of approval, and the beginning of a toast, but the* PRESIDENT OF THE COURTS *shushes everyone down, for the* GOVERNOR *wishes to continue.*

GOVERNOR   *(Continued)* And so, so, I quite agree . . . Mr. Chichikov's new peasants are drunkards.

POLICE CHIEF   *(Gratified at corroboration from on high)* Hear, hear!

GOVERNOR   They are drunkards, but you must take into account that there is a moral to this story, and where there is a moral, are morals not also involved? The lands in the Kherson district are indeed good, and fertile. And therefore, I conclude, although the serfs of my good friend Pavel Ivanovich are at present entirely made up of the criminal element, the experience of resettlement on new land might yet transform them into model subjects. There are many instances of this in the world around us, and in history, too. Pavel Ivanovich Chichikov takes upon his shoulders today a sacred duty: He must become to his peasants a kind of father, the bearer of enlightenment and of—ah—educational reforms. It is in this spirit that I drink—to the health of our new Kherson landowner! . . . Hurrah!

ALL   Hurrah! Hurrah!

> CHICHIKOV *gets up to express his thanks with a deep bow.* HE *is clearly getting ready to go, while the going is good.*

PRESIDENT OF THE COURTS   No! Wait! To the health of the beautiful, future *bride* of our new Kherson landowner!

> *Applause and toasts.* CHICHIKOV *is embarrassed and still is edging to get away.*

CHICHIKOV   Well, perhaps there is no point in dragging my feet . . . Marriage, after all, is not the worst thing in the world . . . The only trouble is, you have to have a bride.

POSTMASTER   Of course you'll have a bride! We'll marry you off, off, off . . .

ALL   (Except SOFYA and ANNA) You'll have a bride! Of course you will! We'll find you one!

Chanting of "CHICHIKOV" *by* COMPANY.

Enter NOZDRYOV, *even drunker than usual, accompanied—a few steps behind—by* MIZHUYEV.

NOZDRYOV   Your Excellency! I am late! As usual! I beg forgiveness . . . My brother-in-law, Mizhuyev . . . *(Pause;* HE *looks about)*

CHICHIKOV *tries to slip away.*

NOZDRYOV   *(Continued)* Look! The Kherson landowner! Whoopee! The Kherson landowner! Well, say there, doing a brisk trade in dead souls? *(General silence)* But he probably forgot to mention, Your Excellency, he buys up dead souls, cross my heart and hope to die, that's what he does! *(Silence)* I swear to God! Listen, Chichi—I always used to call him that in school. Chichi, we're all chums here . . . And here's His Excellency! I'd string him up, Your Excellency, before it's too late, I'd just find a branch and . . . He tried to cheat, in checkers! Your Excellency! I was winning, you see . . . And when he says to me: "Sell me you dead peasants." I was afraid I'd split my sides! Your Excellency! You just have no idea how attached Chichi and I have always been to each other! I mean, how can I explain this? . . . Ah! Suppose you were to say—I mean, here I stand before you, and you were to say, "Nozdryov! Swear on the Bible! Who is more dear to you—your own father, blood of your blood, or Chichikov?" I'd say, "Chichi!" I swear to God, "Chichi!" . . . Here let me give you one little kiss . . . You won't withhold permission, Your Excellency, for me to give him a little kiss . . . Now, now, Chichi, no fighting back this time, let me press *un petit baiser* on thine snow-white cheek . . .

EVERYONE *recoils from* NOZDRYOV. CHICHIKOV *rises, his face in a fury, and hits* NOZDRYOV *in the chest as the latter tries to embrace him.* NOZDRYOV *goes flying back.*

NOZDRYOV   *(Continued) Un petit baiser!*
GOVERNOR'S DAUGHTER   Shriek!

NOZDRYOV *embraces the* GOVERNOR'S DAUGHTER *and kisses her, instead. The* DAUGHTER *shrieks like a banshee. Tumult. Everyone up.*

GOVERNOR   This time he's gone too far! Take him outside! We can also do without his brother-in-law, Mizhuyev.

SERVANTS *lead* NOZDRYOV *and* MIZHUYEV *out.*

NOZDRYOV   *(Off stage. Threatening)* That's my brother-in-law! Mizhuyev!

GOVERNOR *gives sign for more music. A Musical Flourish begins, but then stops, in confusion.*

GOVERNOR   *(To his* DAUGHTER, *mildly)* Pay no attention, he's a drunkard and a liar . . .

GOVERNOR, GOVERNOR'S WIFE, POSTMASTER: *Consoling lines to* CHICHIKOV.

During scene change:

KOROBOCHKA   *(Crosses)* Now, they're beginning to buy dead souls— Time to compare prices! Oh, I've sold too cheap!

ACT II

Scene 3

At the PRESIDENT OF THE COURTS'.
Sound of a bell. Pots of flowers.

ANNA GRIGORYEVNA—*"the lady agreeable in all respects"*—
races to greet SOFYA IVANOVNA—*"the merely agreeable lady"*—
who sweeps in, dressed in gay checked cotton outfit . . . THEY *clasp
each other by the hands, kiss, utter little screams, and kiss again.*

ANNA GRIGORYEVNA   Oh, I'm so glad it's you, my dear! I heard your
carriage drive up and guess who I thought it was? The Governor's wife!
I was about to tell my servant I wasn't at home!

SOFYA IVANOVNA   I hope I'm not too early! I couldn't *wait* to come
see you!

ANNA GRIGORYEVNA   Oh, what a cheerful little gingham check!

SOFYA IVANOVNA   It is cheerful, isn't it? But my cousin-in-law thinks
it would have been better in pale blue instead of brown, and narrow
little stripes, you see, with little spots and sprigs in between, spots and
sprigs all up and down, and festoons instead of frills—oh, I must tell
you, frills are out!

ANNA GRIGORYEVNA   Frills are out?

SOFYA IVANOVNA   Yes, frills are out, festoons are in: festoons on the
sleeves, little epaulettes made of festoons, festoons below, festoons
everywhere!

ANNA GRIGORYEVNA   But, my dear, that would be gaudy!

SOFYA IVANOVNA   Oh no, not gaudy at all!

ANNA GRIGORYEVNA   Yes! Gaudy!

SOFYA IVANOVNA   Oh, my. Do you think so?

ANNA GRIGORYEVNA   Whatever you say. You'll *never* find *me* following such a fashion!

SOFYA IVANOVNA   Nor I, either . . . Really! When you see what *gaudy*
extremes fashion will go to, it's just . . . fantastic! I asked my sister to
send me the pattern, just for fun, and my Melanya has started sewing
it up.

ANNA GRIGORYEVNA   You mean, you've really got the pattern?

SOFYA IVANOVNA   I told you, my sister sent it.

ANNA GRIGORYEVNA   Oh, my darling, I simply must have it next!

SOFYA IVANOVNA   Oh, but I gave my word to my cousin-in-law. You
can be next, after her.

ANNA GRIGORYEVNA   I, after your cousin?! No, Sofya Ivanovna, it's
just clear that you came here purposely to insult me. I can see that you're
tired of me, and that you want to bring our friendship to an end.

SOFYA IVANOVNA *looks woebegone, not knowing what to say.*

ANNA GRIGORYEVNA   . . . Well! And how is our charming *gentleman* today? Monsieur Chi-chi-kov?

SOFYA IVANOVNA   Oh dear, what am I doing, sitting here like a stick? That's what I came to tell you about!

ANNA GRIGORYEVNA   Oh, good! But no matter how you try to defend your Mr. Chichikov or praise him, I tell you and I'd tell *him* straight to his face, he's perfectly revolting! You can't imagine, my dear, how revolting I find him! He is unworthy, unfit, and his nose is a very . . . unattractive nose . . . his—

SOFYA IVANOVNA   You keep interrupting my story! It's quite scandalous, *c'est qu'on appelle une histoire.*

ANNA GRIGORYEVNA   What story?

SOFYA IVANOVNA   About him! The wife of our priest, Father Kyril, came to me, and what do you think? What do you think our millionaire's been up to, eh?

ANNA GRIGORYEVNA   You don't mean to say he's making love now to the priest's wife?

SOFYA IVANOVNA   Oh my dear, if that were all it is! Listen to what she told me. She said that Mrs. Korobochka, an estate owner, came to her as pale as death—and what a story she came with! At blackest midnight, a knocking at the gate, and there stands Chichikov—

ANNA GRIGORYEVNA   This Korobochka—is she young and good looking?

SOFYA IVANOVNA   No, no she's an old widow.

ANNA GRIGORYEVNA   Well, that *is* charming! Now he's trying to rape old widows in the middle of the night! Wait till I tell my husband about *this!* (SHE *starts to ring for her husband)*

SOFYA IVANOVNA   No, no, Anna Grigoryevna, it's not what you think, at all! He is armed, from head to foot, a real brigand, and he demands: "Sell me all your souls who are dead! Right now!"

ANNA GRIGORYEVNA   But what can those dead souls mean? That's not it, at all. Anyway, my husband says Nozdryov was lying through his teeth about that, as usual.

SOFYA IVANOVNA   What do you mean, lying? I'm telling you that Korobochka—

ANNA GRIGORYEVNA   *(Interrupting)* And I'm telling you, it's not a question of dead souls at all. There's something else behind it.

SOFYA IVANOVNA   What?

ANNA GRIGORYEVNA   The dead souls . . .

SOFYA IVANOVNA   What, what?

ANNA GRIGORYEVNA   The dead souls . . .

SOFYA IVANOVNA   Tell me, for heaven's sake!

ANNA GRIGORYEVNA   They are being used to cover up something else. And that something else is—the abduction of the Governor's daughter!

SOFYA IVANOVNA   Oh my God! I never would have suspected!

ANNA GRIGORYEVNA   And yet I realized what it was all about from the moment you opened your mouth!

Doorbell rings. Enter POSTMASTER: IVAN ANDREYEVICH.

POSTMASTER   Good morning, Anna Grigoryevna! Good morning, Sofya Ivanovna!

ANNA GROGORYEVNA   Ivan Andreyevich, you're all in a sweat.

POSTMASTER   What *is* all this nonsense about dead souls? The whole town is talking about nothing else!

SOFYA IVANOVNA   Not nonsense at all, Ivan Andreyevich, he has a plan to abduct the Governor's daughter.

POSTMASTER   Oi, oi, oi, God save us! But how can Chichikov—after all, he was just a traveler, passing through—how could he have come to such a daring—such an insolent—Somebody must be helping him!

ANNA GRIGORYEVNA   What about Nozdryov?

POSTMASTER   Nozdryov! *(Strikes himself on the forehead)* Of course!

SOFYA IVANOVNA   Nozdryov?

ANNA GRIGORYEVNA   Nozdryov! Nozdryov! It's just his sort of thing. You know, he once tried to sell his own father . . . or no, he lost him I think, at cards . . .

Sharp ring of bell.

POSTMASTER   Ah, I must go!

ANNA GRIGORYEVNA   You just got here.

POSTMASTER   Good morning, good ladies! (HE *bumps into the* PRESIDENT OF THE COURTS *in doorway)*

PRESIDENT OF THE COURTS   Ivan Andreyevich! We're supposed to be meeting!

POSTMASTER   There's a new . . . element. A new . . . factor. I have to see . . . I'll be back! *(Exits)*

PRESIDENT OF THE COURTS   Sofya Ivanovna . . . *(Kisses her hand)*

ANNA GRIGORYEVNA   Did you hear the latest? Did you hear?

PRESIDENT OF THE COURTS   What now, my little goldfinch?

ANNA GRIGORYEVNA   He wants to carry off the Governor's daughter.

PRESIDENT OF THE COURTS   Oh, Lord!

SOFYA IVANOVNA   Well, my darlingest, darlingest Anna Grigoryevna, I must fly off, I simply must!
ANNA GRIGORYEVNA   But where, where!
SOFYA IVANOVNA   To the Governor's wife.
ANNA GRIGORYEVNA   Oh good! I'll go too!
SOFYA IVANOVNA   And then to my cousin-in-law.
ANNA GRIGORYEVNA   I must go with you! I can't wait to see them, oh, I'm so horribly . . . excited!

> *Both* LADIES *leave. Their carriage can be heard, pulling away.*

PRESIDENT OF THE COURTS   Sasha! Sasha!
SASHA   *(Entering)* Yes, sir?
PRESIDENT OF THE COURTS   Tell them not to receive anybody . . . except the town officials. Understand? And if Chichikov comes, I'm not at home. Do you hear?
SASHA   I hear, Ivan Grigoryevich.
PRESIDENT OF THE COURTS   Wait a minute . . . Sasha! Prepare us a snack.
SASHA   A snack, sir?
PRESIDENT OF THE COURTS   A snack! A snack! A snack!
SASHA   Yes, sir.

> *Exits. The* POSTMASTER *enters, with the* GOVERNOR, *and the* POLICE CHIEF, *all talking at once. Another* POLICEMAN *stations himself outside the door. The* OFFICIALS *look worried and, somehow, thinner than* THEY *used to be.*

POLICE CHIEF   Ivan Grigoryevich!
GOVERNOR   My head is just going around in a whirl. I cannot make it out: Who or what, is this Chichikov? What about the dead souls? And now my daughter is involved and we've had to lock her in her room!
POSTMASTER   There, there, Your Excellency. We were all fooled by him, as a man, by his worldly gloss, his style . . .
GOVERNOR   Yes.
PRESIDENT OF THE COURTS   Now.
POLICE CHIEF   Yes.
PRESIDENT OF THE COURTS   *(To* POLICE CHIEF) You've been to Sobakevich?
POLICE CHIEF   Oh, yes.
PRESIDENT OF THE COURTS   And?
POLICE CHIEF   He says, he spits on the whole affair!

GOVERNOR   *What?*

POLICE CHIEF   Spits, Your Excellency. He says Chichikov is a good businessman and he sold him excellent peasants, alive in every sense of the word. But he could not answer for what might happen to them in transit, what with fevers and the hardships of the road. I said, as threatening as I could, that the town is full of rumors about this. He said, that's because the town is also full of idiots.

POLICEMAN *laughs.*

POLICE CHIEF   *(Continued)* And he went home.

PRESIDENT OF THE COURTS   What about Nozdryov? Is he coming in?

POLICE CHIEF   He was in a rage that I woke him up, and he told me to go to hell.

GOVERNOR   To hell?

POLICE CHIEF   To hell, Your Excellency. But I told him there'd be a game of cards, and something to eat, so he'll come.

GOVERNOR   Good work.

POLICE CHIEF   As you will, gentlemen, but we must get to the bottom of this, somehow. I must report that two communications came to the Governor . . . Your Excellency?

GOVERNOR *takes two papers and waves them about, futilely.*

POLICE CHIEF   *(Continued)* Thank you, sir. They state that there is a forger of false bank notes at large in our province, and also a highwayman wanted for armed robbery and murder, now a fugitive from the law. Now, either of those could be Chichikov. We have never seen his papers . . . Have we, sir?

GOVERNOR   He was so vague. I'm trying to remember. He said he had suffered in the cause of justice, and that he had many enemies.

POLICE CHIEF   Thank you, sir . . . Now, finally, I don't know whether I should mention this to you, but there are some who say that what Chichikov is—well, in brief, that he is really Napoleon. In disguise. We are checking on his height, at this moment.

GOVERNOR   Oh, Lord, Oh, Lord . . .

PRESIDENT OF THE COURTS   Well, gentlemen?

POLICE CHIEF   I say we should take decisive measures.

PRESIDENT OF THE COURTS   Decisive?

POLICE CHIEF   I say, arrest him, as an undesirable character.

PRESIDENT OF THE COURTS   And suppose he arrests us, as undesirable characters?

POLICE CHIEF   Arrest us?

PRESIDENT OF THE COURTS   Suppose he is here on *secret* papers. Hm?
From the Governor General? We know he came here from the capital.
Dead souls . . . I wonder . . . Maybe he has other dead ones in mind.
Hm? A few skeletons in our little closet? The hospital? The jail? You
follow my meaning, as executives of the law?

POSTMASTER   I just handle the mail.

PRESIDENT OF THE COURTS   Ivan Andreyevich. Is that all you have to
say?

POSTMASTER   No, I've been thinking. Gentlemen, what we need to do
is we should meet together.

> *Pause.*

POLICE CHIEF   We're already meeting.

POSTMASTER   Yes. But we must make a joint decision.

POLICE CHIEF   Your Excellency?

GOVERNOR   I heartily endorse the sense of the meeting. Thus far.

PRESIDENT OF THE COURTS   *(To* POLICE CHIEF) All right then. Have
you gone through Chichikov's papers?

POLICE CHIEF   No, Ivan Grigoryevich.

PRESIDENT OF THE COURTS   *(Angry)* Why not?

POLICE CHIEF   He was in the room with them. Gargling with a mixture
of milk and fig juice. We have to follow the next best tack. Petrushka!

> POLICEMAN *leads in* PETRUSHKA, *not sober, carrying his driv-
er's whip.*

POLICE CHIEF   *(Continued)* All right, good fellow. We just want you
to tell us a bit about your master.

PETRUSHKA   Yes, sir, that's right . . . He is.

POLICE CHIEF   What does that mean?

PETRUSHKA   Well, you know, sir. Masters. You can't tell one from
another.

POLICE CHIEF   What kind of people did he associate with?

PETRUSHKA   Classy types people, sir . . . I think one of 'em was named
Mr. Perekroyev.

POLICE CHIEF   Where did he work?

PETRUSHKA   Government, sir. In the Silver Service.

POLICE CHIEF   The Civil Service?

PETRUSHKA   The Silver Service, yes sir. Costumes Department, too.
And government buildings.

POLICE CHIEF   What buildings, specifically? Tell me.

PETRUSHKA   He has three horses, sir. Bought one three years ago. Then he traded in the grey mare for you know what? Another grey mare. *(Laughs)* Name's Kubari. Did you write that down, sir?

POLICE CHIEF   Just tell us, is this Chichikov really named Pavel Ivanovich?

PETRUSHKA   You got it, sir. Now, the Chairman horse, he pulls decent, I'd give the bay an extra cup of oats any time, he pulls decent. He pulls ... Tprrr ... Hey, my good lads! ... Hup, hup, hup! Tprrr ... *(Waves his whip as if already on the road)*

POSTMASTER   He's drunk as a shoemaker.

POLICE CHIEF   I'll have you flogged up and down.

PETRUSHKA   *(Opens his coat)* Whatever Your Lordship wants. If it's flogging Y'r Lordship wants, I say let's get on with it! *(Waves his whip in the air)*

POLICE CHIEF   Get out!

PETRUSHKA   *(Disappointed)* You're not going to flog me, sir?

POLICE CHIEF   *Out!*

PETRUSHKA   *(Exits) Tprrr* . . . hup, hup, hup . . . fly, lads, hup! . . .

Silence.

PRESIDENT OF THE COURTS   I suggest we interrogate those from whom he bought the peasants.

POLICE CHIEF   *(To* POLICEMAN*)* Did you bring Mrs. Korobochka? Ask her to step in here.

Enter KOROBOCHKA.

POLICE CHIEF   *(Continued, gruffly)* All right!

PRESIDENT OF THE COURTS   Allow me ... Now, dear lady, would you please tell the court whether or not a certain individual came to you at a nocturnal hour and whether or not he threatened you with bodily harm if you did not yield up to him certain of your serfs?

KOROBOCHKA   Put yourself in my shoes, good sir ... fifteen rubles, in currency ... I'm only a widow, an inexperienced person ...

PRESIDENT OF THE COURTS   Yes, of course. But we are interested in the facts, Madame. Facts, and circumstances. You see? Was he armed with pistols?

KOROBOCHKA   Oh no, God save me, I saw no pistols of any kind. But I'm only a widowed woman, sir, I wouldn't know much about pistols.

Will you help me, so at least I'll understand: What's the going price, sir?

PRESIDENT OF THE COURTS   Price? What price? My good woman, who's talking price?

KOROBOCHKA   Well, a dead soul, sir! What's he going at, today?

GOVERNOR   Oh, Lord . . .

KOROBOCHKA   Fifteen rubles, in currency . . . What was I to do? . . . Maybe they go at fifty . . . or even more! . . .

POLICE CHIEF   Show me that banknote! *(Threateningly)* I say, show-the-court-that-banknote! (HE *examines it)* Well . . . it's a banknote.

PRESIDENT OF THE COURTS   All right, Madame. Now simply tell us, how did he buy them from you, and just what did he buy? I can't get a clear idea here, of—

KOROBOCHKA   He bought! He bought! I've told you. But now you, sir, what reason could you have not to tell little old me, for what price can you get a dead peasant today, if he's in good condition?

PRESIDENT OF THE COURTS   But my poor, misguided woman, what are you talking about? Where have you ever seen people selling dead souls?

KOROBOCHKA   But why, why, why won't you tell me the price?

PRESIDENT OF THE COURTS   Price, price, price! What price!? There is no price! Just tell me, woman, in plain simple Russian: Did he threaten you, and if so, with what?

KOROBOCHKA   But I see what's going on! You're a dealer yourself! You want to—

PRESIDENT OF THE COURTS   My good woman, I am the President of the Courts!

KOROBOCHKA   Ah no, ah no, you're the little devil, you are . . . You're out to do me in, yourself. All the worse for you, sir. Although, I *could* sell you some nice pillow feathers . . .

PRESIDENT OF THE COURTS   No! No pillow feathers!

KOROBOCHKA   *(Led out, still grumbling and dissatisfied)* All right, Mister, I can see now what you want. You want to buy, and you want to undercut me. That's it, clear as the nose on my face.

POLICE CHIEF   Oof! What a case!

GOVERNOR   *(Weakly)* Gentlemen, we're not getting to the heart of our—

Enter NOZDRYOV, *followed by* MIZHUYEV.

NOZDRYOV   Ah, ah, ah, there you are! His Excellency, too! And the Judge!

POLICE CHIEF We don't need the brother-in-law.

MIZHUYEV *is led out.* SASHA *brings a tray of food, and wine.*

NOZDRYOV We don't need the brother-in-law . . . Ah, where the powers of government are, there's always a bite to eat. *(Pours a glass and drinks it down)* Who's got the cards?

POLICE CHIEF We'll get the cards. Just tell us, what the devil is going on, about these dead souls? Is it or is it not true that Chichikov is buying up dead people?

NOZDRYOV True. *(Drinks again)*

GOVERNOR But there is no logic to it!

NOZDRYOV Absolutely none. Hey, what is this? Where are the cards?

POLICE CHIEF Later, later . . . All right—begging your pardon, Excellency—how did the Governor's daughter get mixed up with Chichikov's dead souls?

NOZDRYOV He wanted to give them to her. *(Drinks)* As a present, you know.

GOVERNOR Dead souls? For my . . . daughter? (HE *seems to be growing more feeble, as the process goes on)*

PRESIDENT OF THE COURTS Is it possible that the man is actually investigating something about us? As a kind of spy?

NOZDRYOV He's a spy.

PRESIDENT OF THE COURTS He's really a spy?

NOZDRYOV Oh sure, way back in school—Did you know we went through school together?—We always called him "the sneak" and "Sneachikov," names like that. Caught him at it once, gave him such a pounding, they had to fix a hundred leeches to his temples alone.

PRESIDENT OF THE COURTS *(Writing down the testimony)* You said, "a hundred"?

NOZDRYOV A dozen.

POLICE CHIEF Is it possible that he is a forger of counterfeit banknotes?

NOZDRYOV He's a forger. *(Drinks)* These banknotes he's been passing around—what a joke! One day they found out he had two million in forged currency right in his own home, so of course they sealed off the house and—

POLICE CHIEF Look it will be best for you if you simply tell us straight: Was Chichikov, or was he not, plotting to abduct the Governor's daughter?

NOZDRYOV Of course he was. I was in on it. I'm telling you, without me the whole thing would never have gotten off the starting line.

PRESIDENT OF THE COURTS Were they supposed to get married?

The GOVERNOR *sighs, loudly.*

NOZDRYOV   Absolutely. In the village of Trakh-ma-cho-vka . . . Got that? Father Sidor, officiating: For a wedding he charges seventy-five rubles.

POSTMASTER   That's expensive.

NOZDRYOV   To you, everything is expensive. I scared him down on it anyway, since I knew he had married Mikhail—the corn chandler—to his god-sister while his first wife was still alive. You see? Then I gave him my little carriage to make up for it . . . and threw in a change of horses.

POLICE CHIEF   To whom? Who got the horses? The corn chandler, or the priest?

NOZDRYOV   None of your business, you filthy scandalmonger! Always mucking about in other people's business! . . . Time for cards! For this, you disrupted my poetic solitude? Oh. Chichikov. Right. So?

PRESIDENT OF THE COURTS   It's strange even to talk about this . . . but, do you have any idea how the rumor got started around town, that Chichikov really is, is . . . Napoleon?

NOZDRYOV   He is Napoleon.

PRESIDENT OF THE COURTS   He *is* Napoleon?

GOVERNOR   *(Total despair)* He's Napoleon . . .

NOZDRYOV   No question about it.

> *Confusion or alarm on the faces. Can* THEY *believe anything* NOZDRYOV *says? The* GOVERNOR *buries his head, this is all too much for him.*

PRESIDENT OF THE COURTS   But . . . what? How?

NOZDRYOV   In disguise. *(Drinks)* You know, wearing civies.

POLICE CHIEF   Look. There is no reason to believe anything that comes out of your mouth!

NOZDRYOV   *(Confidentially)* You see, they've got him on the long leash.

POLICE CHIEF   Who?

NOZDRYOV   The English . . . Never underestimate the British Lion! They've let him out of St. Helena's, you see, so that he can penetrate deep into Russia, disguised as Chichikov. But listen,

> THEY *all lean close;* HE *leans toward them.*

NOZDRYOV   *(Continued)* the fact is, he isn't Chichikov at all!

NOZDRYOV *is completely drunk again.* HE *puts the* POLICE CHIEF's *three-cornered hat on his own head, grins at them, and falls asleep.*
      POLICEMAN *hands a note to* POLICE CHIEF.

PRESIDENT OF THE COURTS   Gentlemen. Have we reached a conclusion?
POSTMASTER   I've got it! Gentlemen, I've got it! Do you know who this Chichikov really is?
ALL Who? Who is he?
POSTMASTER   This, gentlemen, my good sir—this is none other than the return of Captain Kopeikin!
PRESIDENT OF THE COURTS   And who, may we ask, is Captain Kopeikin?
POSTMASTER   Gentlemen, my good sir, you mean to say, you have never heard of Captain Kopeikin?
POLICE CHIEF   No.
POSTMASTER   (*Settles back with a pinch from his snuffbox, which* HE *does not offer around*) Captain Kopeikin, well, my good sir, he'd make quite a story for some writer. Could be an epic or, er . . . an epic.
POLICE CHIEF   So?
POSTMASTER   So, my good sir—I always say "good sir," but I really mean everybody present—'Twas after the Campaign of 1812. Among the wounded sent home was Captain Kopeikin. I regret to say, I forget whether at Krasnoye, or perchance, Leipzig, but keep in mind that he has some things blown off him—er, an arm, and a leg. Well, in those days, good sir, they had no instructions about . . . er, if you had a leg or an arm missing—or especially, both. What I mean to say is, the pension plan for the wounded was they should either find work or starve to death, that was the . . . er, plan, in those days.
      Well, Kopeikin, my good sir, I ask you to remember, has only one arm, and—ah, I forgot, it was his left one, with great effort he could blow his nose with it, let alone find work . . . So, he wants to see the Emperor to tell him he had, in a certain sense, as it were, spilled blood for the Fatherland, lost several parts of himself . . .
      So there he is, a one-legged freak, in the Capital, our Petersburg, than which there is no other, the like which, in a manner of speaking, you see, to compare with it in the whole world . . . a regular Scheherazade, every street with a different name, Nevsky Avenue and so forth, and those . . . er, spires sticking straight up and the bridges suspended up there in the air with no visible means of support . . . in a word, good sir, it all smells of money and Kopeikin doesn't have any.

He hobbles over to see the First Minister. The window panes were, if you believe it, ten feet of smooth, polished glass, so that everything inside the rooms, such as Chinese vases and the . . . er, doorknob, looked like it was outside. That was the kind of place where Kopeikin stands and waits for a period of not less than four and not more than seven hours. Out comes the Minister, everybody trembles like leaves in the . . . er, wind. "What do *you* want? What's *your* business?" Mostly, they all faint dead away, but Kopeikin, my good sir, begins his tale, this and that, lost some limbs for the Fatherland, can't find work, making bold, as it were, to ask His Majesty's favor in respect to this question of not starving to death . . .

"You'll have to wait!" booms the Minister. "The Emperor will return. A decree will be passed on the subject of the wounded." "Er . . . when, so to speak?" asks Kopeikin. "You will be told when the time comes." "What do I do now?" asks Kopeikin, "what with this nasty business of starving, and such . . ." "You'll have to find means of support! Get yourself a source of income! Next!"

The Minister, my good sir, had generals awaiting his decisions, important affairs of state, as they say, and here was this rather incomplete looking ex-Captain who wouldn't leave the . . . er, room. The Minister got quite annoyed, this I admit, and told Kopeikin to heave his carcass promptly out of there, whereupon Kopeikin, my good sir, just went for him, using whatever fist or foot he could muster up, just went off the deep end, as you can imagine . . .

"Corporal of the Guard, remove this person to his place of residence! At government expense, so to speak . . ." This Corporal, my good sir, six-foot-six, with fists like a dentist, he deposits the miserable sinner in a cab, keeps him company on the drive home.

"Free cab ride," says Kopeikin to himself, "at least that's a start. Never you worry, you lords and masters, I'll find myself a source of income!"

And then all news of our humble Captain was lost in the waters of . . . er, Lethe, as the poets like to say. Where did Kopeikin vanish to? What happened? No one knows. But . . . and here is the part of interest to us, my good sir . . . two months had not passed . . . actually, I think I should have begun the story right here . . . er, a band of fugitives and cutthroats pops up in the Ryazan Forests . . . *(Ominously)* armed robbery and murder, as Your Excellency's letter said. And the leader of that band, my good sir, was none other than—

CAPTAIN KOPEIKIN   *(Appearing in the doorway and announcing himself)* Captain Kopeikin . . .

GOVERNOR   A-ah! *(Falls and dies)*

PRESIDENT OF THE COURTS   *(Frightened)* What may we do for you?

CAPTAIN KOPEIKIN   I am Captain Kopeikin, of the Courier Service. Dispatches from St. Petersburg, sir. *(Coughs and retires)*

PRESIDENT OF THE COURTS   *(Opening dispatches and reading)* Congratulations, a Governor-General has been appointed to our province. He will shortly visit . . . for inspection . . .

POLICE CHIEF   *(To* POSTMASTER*)* Ivan Andreyevich! How could Chichikov ever have been Captain Kopeikin? You said yourself, Kopeikin lost an arm and a leg, whereas Chichikov—

POSTMASTER   *(Uttering a cry and slapping himself violently on the forehead)* Of course! I forgot that! Oi, what a piece of veal I turn out to be!

POLICE CHIEF   We shall arrest Chichikov, as an undesirable character!

PRESIDENT OF THE COURTS   Good God in heaven, what has happened to our Governor? Quick! Help! Water! Leeches! We have to let his blood! . . . Oh, Lord, His Excellency . . . he can't really be dead?

MIZHUYEV *appears in doorway, to help.*

NOZDRYOV   Did I miss something? . . .

ACT II

Scene 4

A room at the inn.
CHICHIKOV, *alone in his room, giving a last look at his deeds and property lists, while packing them away in his trusty strongbox.*
PETRUSHKA, *on tiptoe.*

CHICHIKOV   What do you want?

PETRUSHKA   I think we should go.

CHICHIKOV   Go? Where?

PETRUSHKA   On the road. *Tprrr* . . . hup, hup . . . hup.

CHICHIKOV   What have you done?

PETRUSHKA   Had a talk . . . It's a good kind of town to get out of, sir.

CHICHIKOV   With whom? Your talk?

PETRUSHKA   The police, sir. The army. And such like.

CHICHIKOV   And why were they interested in you? What have you done now?

PETRUSHKA   They're interested in you, sir. Very interested in you, sir. Wanted to know everything about you. The names of your horses. How much each one cost you, where you got it. Very personal questions, Your Honor.

CHICHIKOV   *(Eyeing him closely)* You may be right, for once. All right, then, harness up.

PETRUSHKA   Can't.

CHICHIKOV   *What?*

PETRUSHKA   Can't.

CHICHIKOV   Why not?

PETRUSHKA   Kubari needs shoes. The Chairman too.

CHICHIKOV   *You* just told *me* we should get out.

PETRUSHKA   Yes, Master.

CHICHIKOV   You idiot! Toadstool! Been sitting here a week, you know the horses needed shoeing, and you didn't do it!

PETRUSHKA   Didn't do it, Master. Knew, and didn't do it. Been sitting here a week, and didn't do it.

CHICHIKOV   You come here to tell me we ought to leave and . . . Yekh! What do we do now?

PETRUSHKA   I'd flog me, Master. It's the only way.

CHICHIKOV   Go-find-a-smith-and-get-those-horses-shod-and-if-they're-not-ready-in-two-hours-I'll-bend-you-double-and-tie-you-in-a-knot!

PETRUSHKA   Yes, Master. Flogging's the thing, though . . .

> PETRUSHKA *exits.*
> CHICHIKOV *sits down hurriedly to his papers again. Then,* HE *runs to the door and shouts.*
> CHICHIKOV *collides with* NOZDRYOV *and* MIZHUYEV, *coming in.*

NOZDRYOV   As the old proverb has it, I'd walk a mile for a friend! . . . Just passing by, saw the light in your window, I say to myself, why not drop in on old Chichi? Here, order your man to fill my pipe, will you? Where's yours?

CHICHIKOV   I have never smoked a pipe in my life.

NOZDRYOV   That's pure crap. I know you're a smoker, and you know I know. Hey, Vakhramey!

CHICHIKOV   He's not Vakhramey. Petrushka.

NOZDRYOV   Then why did you call him Vakhramey?

CHICHIKOV   Never. I never had a man named Vakhramey.

NOZDRYOV   You know, you're right? That was somebody else . . . Listen, you old pig's snout, you behaved very, very badly toward me. I think you should know that. Remember, the game of checkers? I had that game won, and you, you turned the board over on me! I love you madly, but . . . Oh, almost forgot, I had something to tell you—the whole town's against you now, they all think you're a counterfeiter. You know, forging fake banknotes? . . . They tried to break me down, but I stood by you, all the way, I'm a rock when it comes to loyalty . . . They're even trying to claim we went to school together, all kinds of—

CHICHIKOV   I—Chichikov—forge banknotes?

NOZDRYOV   Why'd you have to give them such a shake-up? No criticism, but they're small-town people, you've got them scared out of their skin! They're charging you with armed robbery and being a spy, and now the Governor's keeled over from fright, the funeral's tomorrow. And, oh, Chichi, Chichi, you should never play a long shot like that!

CHICHIKOV   What? What long shot?

NOZDRYOV   Thinking you could get away with the Governor's daughter. That's partly what killed him. I knew it, too. First time I saw the two of you jostling at the ball, I said to myself, "Keep your eye on Chichikov! He's got an eye for the virgins!"

CHICHIKOV   What? What? You're babbling! You're insane! The Governor's daughter? And now I'm the cause of his death?! *(Screams)*

Enter PETRUSHKA, *frightened. Noise of spurred boots nearby.* NOZDRYOV *vanishes through a window, followed by* MIZHUYEV.

Enter POLICE CHIEF *with* POLICEMAN. *Another is stationed at the door.*

POLICE CHIEF   Pavel Ivanovich Chichikov, you are hereby under arrest.

CHICHIKOV   Aleksei Ivanovich, what is this? . . . What for? . . . Without warning? . . . Prison!? . . . I'm a nobleman! . . .

POLICE CHIEF   Don't get hysterical, it's court orders.

POLICEMAN   Calm down.

POLICE CHIEF   Sit down.

CHICHIKOV   Aleksei Ivanovich, what on earth? . . . Is this you? . . . Well, you listen! My enemies, they slander me . . . I . . . By God's witness, it's all circumstantial evidence . . . it's coincidence, and . . .

POLICE CHIEF   Take his things.

> POLICEMAN *takes trunk.*

CHICHIKOV   No! Stop! Wait! . . . My things . . . my deeds! . . .

POLICE CHIEF   Just what we want.

CHICHIKOV   Everything in my world. All my property.

ACT II

Scene 5

Prison Cell.

CHICHIKOV   (*Alone: pacing his cell*) . . . Why am I in here when *they* are out there? What have I done? Where is my crime? . . . I am not fat enough! That is my only fault. Just take a look at them, and then look at me. To have a life full of comfort and luxuries, to put other people in jail and have your own coffers filled with the Lord's blessings, and a big house in town, and a bigger house in the country, and clothes from Paris for your wife and daughters, and soon an estate with orchards, and, and, fine glossy horses, and servants who dress better than you do, and to be honored and respected in a town like this and to leave a fortune for your children, you must be fat. The fat ones just sit down and their chairs creak and groan under them and they play cards with each other, and everything just drops into their laps, while we thin ones, we dash about here and there on our ridiculous errands, insecure and flighty, we're toothpicks, not men, we're like air, always on the rush, and everything slips through our fingers! . . . Oh, oh, this is my darkest hour, I thank the Lord for one thing; that my mother is no longer alive to see me here and that I have as yet no darling children to hide their faces in shame! *(Stops; feels his waist)* But wait; I'm not really so thin. *(Feels himself up and down)* I'm not fat, but I'm not so thin, either! I'm neither fat nor thin! I'm just right! I'm a better man than any of them. A more honest man! I deserve the fruits of my labors, and *they* will get it all! Why? Why? Why such a cruel blow? (HE *stops, hearing mournful Music and funeral chanting from without.* HE *watches through the window)* Ah, the Governor's funeral. *(Shakes fist at the window)* This whole town, I know them for what they are! A cult of swindlers! Judases, every one; sellers of Christ!

Enter the POLICE CHIEF and PRESIDENT OF THE COURTS.

CHICHIKOV   *(Continued)* My friends. My benefactors.

POLICE CHIEF   Benefactors? You're wasting your irony, Chichikov.

PRESIDENT OF THE COURTS   You have stained your name with an act so vile, so dishonorable, that I doubt any man before you has ever lowered his name into such filth! *(Takes out papers)* Carriage maker Mikheyev! Everyone of them, dead!

CHICHIKOV   Everyone! I confess it! I'll confess the whole truth to you . . . But I'm the victim of slander . . . I have enemies . . . Nozdryov!

POLICE CHIEF   You lie! *(Points to a huge portrait of Czar Nicholas I visible through the door)* This will reach the Emperor! This is theft, this is crime against the State, this is dishonoring the Christian dead! Look! That is Czar *Nicholas,* have you forgotten? That is the whip, that is Siberia!

CHICHIKOV   Oh, he'll slaughter me, he'll destroy me! I'll die naked in the ice! *(Throws himself upon them)* Save me! Benefactors, grant me a reprieve! I was tempted, I was wrong . . . but he showed me the way, how could I not listen?

PRESIDENT OF THE COURTS   Who? Who showed you the way?

CHICHIKOV   The Secretary of the State Mortgage Bank, he started me on this whole thing. I never would have known . . . listen to me, I'll testify in court!

PRESIDENT OF THE COURTS   The State Mortgage Bank? *(Suddenly sees the light; to POLICE CHIEF)* Aaah! *(To CHICHIKOV)* You were actually going to mortgage this whole list to the Government?

CHICHIKOV   Yes.

PRESIDENT OF THE COURTS   For cash?

CHICHIKOV   Yes. I'm guilty.

PRESIDENT OF THE COURTS   What makes you think you can get away with it?

CHICHIKOV   The Secretary told me. If they're still on the tax lists—

PRESIDENT OF THE COURTS   They're legally alive! They're mortgageable property, under the law!

POLICE CHIEF   But there will be another census in two or three years. The truth will come out! What will the Government do then?

CHICHIKOV   They'll foreclose.

PRESIDENT OF THE COURTS   On the dead? They'll get nothing!

CHICHIKOV   (Giggles)

PRESIDENT OF THE COURTS   The man is brilliant! I knew it, he's a genius!

POLICE CHIEF   But then, in two or three years, he'd be a criminal.

PRESIDENT OF THE COURTS   He could also be gone . . . the Riviera . . .

POLICE CHIEF   Baden-Baden . . .

PRESIDENT OF THE COURTS   Paris . . .

POLICE CHIEF   (Suddenly tough) How many deeds have you got there? (Taps the deed case)

CHICHIKOV   About a thousand.

PRESIDENT OF THE COURTS   How much will the Government bank give you?

CHICHIKOV   Two hundred rubles, per soul.

The POLICE CHIEF and PRESIDENT OF THE COURTS whisper together.

PRESIDENT OF THE COURTS   We'll hold a public trial.

CHICHIKOV   But I already confessed!

POLICE CHIEF   In St. Petersburg . . . (The POLICE CHIEF points to portrait of Czar Nicholas again)

CHICHIKOV   Save me! . . . I'm lost! I'll die alone, in rags.

PRESIDENT OF THE COURTS   You should have thought of that, before.

POLICE CHIEF takes a whole pile of deeds out of their case.

PRESIDENT OF THE COURTS   (Continued, waving bundle of deeds) Pavel Ivanovich, look here, just sign these over to us, and pay us ten thousand rubles to cover our office expenses.

CHICHIKOV   And I'll be free (Immediately plucks up courage) No more—? (Points to Czar Nicholas)

The POLICE CHIEF *closes the door on Czar Nicholas.*

PRESIDENT OF THE COURTS   No more Nicholas.

CHICHIKOV   Oh. Well. Listen, here's what we'll do. I shall pay you the ten thousand, of course, and we'll split the dead souls.

POLICE CHIEF   Oh you will, will you?

PRESIDENT OF THE COURTS   *(Amiable)* Look here, why don't we let you keep whatever you bought from old widow Korobochka? You must have worked hard for those . . . *(Sternly)* We are being exceedingly generous.

CHICHIKOV   *(Takes out his note case and hands over the bribe money, with the same words* HE *used in the Prologue:)* Well, if you'll be so kind, sir, as to allow me . . .

THEY *take the money and give him the Korobochka deed.*

POLICE CHIEF   Now get out! If you're not fifty miles out of here by nightfall, we'll lock you up for good.

Sound of horses without. PETRUSHKA *rushes in, confused and scared.*

PETRUSHKA   Master, they told me, be ready. (HE *sees* CHICHIKOV *drained and exhausted, and comforts him)* All harnessed up, Master. Shiny new shoes on Kubari and the Chairman, I swear to God . . . They'll pull decent, now . . . pull!

PETRUSHKA *and* CHICHIKOV *race out.*

POLICE CHIEF   Good-bye Chichikov. *(Starts counting up the deeds)*

PRESIDENT OF THE COURTS   *(Calling after)* Pavel Ivanovich! *Bon Voyage!*

PETRUSHKA   *(Off stage)* Tprr . . . Hup, hup . . . Fly, you lads . . . Fly!

POLICE CHIEF *and* PRESIDENT OF THE COURTS *look up at the huge portrait of Nicholas I, who smiles down at them and winks an eye.*

ACT II

Epilogue

On the road.
    CHICHIKOV *and* PETRUSHKA *dash about madly, with belongings, then,* THEY *reach their carriage and climb in.*
    Music of the Road comes up, and then builds, over the following, as THEY *drive.*

CHICHIKOV   Petrushka! Onward! Onward!
PETRUSHKA   Where, Master?
CHICHIKOV   What do you mean, where? You earmuff! You sea slug! Anywhere!
PETRUSHKA   Yes, Master. Anywhere it is!
CHICHIKOV   Russia is vast, Petrushka! I know where I went wrong! On now, to a new province! We'll start at the Governor's!
PETRUSHKA   Hup, hup . . . Fly, lads, fly!

FOB

by

David Henry Hwang

ABOUT
DAVID HENRY HWANG

David Henry Hwang was born in 1957 of immigrant Chinese American parents. He grew up in Los Angeles and received his B.A. in English from Stanford University. While there, he and Nancy Takahashi co-founded the Stanford Asian American Theatre Project, which first produced *FOB*. He has also attended the Yale School of Drama. Since *FOB*, David Hwang has written *The Dance and The Railroad* and *Family Devotions*. The former opened at the New Federal Theatre, then moved to the New York Shakespeare Festival, where it became an acclaimed long-running hit. The latter enjoyed a successful extended run at the New York Shakespeare Festival. He has directed at San Francisco's Asian American Theatre Company and leads playwriting workshops at Basement Workshop in New York's Chinatown. David Hwang is the recipient of a Dramalogue Playwriting Award and the 1981 Best Play Obie Award for *FOB*.

PRODUCTION HISTORY

FOB was nominated for the *Plays in Process* series by Gail Merrifield, director of Play Development at the New York Shakespeare Festival.

Joseph Papp produced *FOB* at the New York Shakespeare Festival's Public Theater, where it opened on June 8, 1980, directed by Mako; scenery by Akira Yoshimura; lighting by Victor En Yu Tan; costumes by Susan Hom; musical direction and original music by Lucia Hwong. The cast was as follows:

DALE .... Calvin Jung
GRACE .... Ginny Yang
STEVE.. John Lone
ON-STAGE MUSICIAN.. Lucia Hwong
ON-STAGE STAGE MANAGERS .... Tzi Ma
Willy Corpus

Production Note: The ON-STAGE MUSICIAN supplied traditional Chinese instrumental accompaniment for the mythological scenes and percussion for the battle scenes. In the New York Shakespeare Festival production the ON-STAGE STAGE MANAGERS were used in the manner of traditional Chinese opera and Japanese Kabuki.

FOB was first produced by Nancy Takahashi for the Stanford Asian American Theatre Project and Okada House on March 2, 1979. It was also part of the 1979 National Playwrights Conference at the O'Neill Theater Center in Waterford, Connecticut. Between October 16 and December 13, 1980, it was presented by the East West Players in Los Angeles. Between July 17 and August 30, 1981, it was produced by the Asian American Theatre Company, San Francisco.

PLAYWRIGHT'S NOTE

The roots of *FOB* are thoroughly American. The play began when a sketch I was writing about a limousine trip through Westwood, California, was invaded by two figures from American literature: Fa Mu Lan, the girl who takes her father's place in battle, from Maxine Hong Kingston's novel *The Woman Warrior,* and Gwan Gung, the adopted god of early Chinese Americans, from Frank Chin's play *Gee, Pop!*

FOB's sources testify to the existence of an Asian American literary and theatrical tradition. Chinese operas, many featuring Gwan Gung, have long been performed in Chinatowns. Theatres such as Los Angeles' East West Players, San Francisco's Asian American Theatre Company, New York's Pan-Asian Repertory, and Seattle's Asian Exclusion Act, have established themselves as centers for a body of new and exciting dramatic work.

The reader who enjoys *FOB,* and especially the one who does not, would do well to investigate the work of Wakako Yamauchi, Jessica Hagedorn, Frank Chin, Philip Gotanda, Winston Tong, Momoko Iko, and others.

Asian American theatre is not limited to any one content or form. To expect our work to deal solely with ethnic issues, for instance, is to imply that we have fewer concerns than Americans of Jewish, Italian, or WASP origin—that we are somehow less American and, by extension, less human.

Similarly, producers and directors who consider Asian American actors only to play coolies, foreigners, and "ethnic" roles deny the reality of our world. We live in a multi-ethnic society, and it is a measure of producers' reactionary tendencies that this mix is rarely reflected on our mainstream stages and screens.

In America, the term "ethnic theatre" is ultimately a misnomer. There are simply the ethnics that have had access to an audience and those that have not. As Asian American theatre artists, we are claiming our audience.

Definitions: chong you bing is a type of Chinese pancake, a Northern Chinese appetizer often made with dough and scallions, with a consistency similar to that of pita bread.

Gung Gung means "grandfather."

Mei Guo means "beautiful country," a Chinese term for America.

CHARACTERS

In order of appearance
DALE, an American of Chinese descent, second-generation
GRACE, his cousin, a first-generation Chinese American
STEVE, her friend, a Chinese newcomer

All the characters are in their early 20s.

TIME

Present. Act I, scene 1, takes place in the late afternoon. Act I, scene 2, is a few minutes later. Act II is after dinner.

PLACE

The back room of a small Chinese restaurant in Torrance, California.

THE PLAY

FOB

For the warriors of my family

PROLOGUE

Lights up on a blackboard. Enter DALE, *dressed preppie. The blackboard is the type which can flip around so both sides can be used.* HE *lectures like a university professor, using the board to illustrate his points.*

DALE F-O-B. Fresh Off the Boat. FOB. What words can you think of that characterize the FOB? Clumsy, ugly, greasy FOB. Loud, stupid, four-eyed FOB. Big feet. Horny. Like Lenny in "Of Mice and Men." Very good. A literary reference. High water pants. Floods, to be exact. Someone you wouldn't want your sister to marry. If you are a sister, someone you wouldn't want to marry. That assumes we're talking about boy FOBs, of course. But girl FOBs aren't really as . . . FOBish. Boy FOBs are the worst, the . . . pits. They are the sworn enemies of all

ABC—Oh, that's "American-Born Chinese"—Of all ABC girls. Before an ABC girl will be seen on Friday night with a boy FOB in Westwood, she would rather burn off her face. (HE *flips around the board. On the other side is written: "1. Where to find FOBs 2. How to spot a FOB")* FOBs can be found in great numbers almost anyplace you happen to be, but there are some locations where they cluster in particularly large swarms. Community colleges, Chinese-club discos, Asian sororities, Asian fraternities, Oriental churches, shopping malls, and, of course, Bee Gee concerts. How can you spot a FOB? Look out! If you can't answer that, you might be one. (HE *flips back the board, reviews)* F-O-B. Fresh Off the Boat. FOB. Clumsy, ugly, greasy FOB. Loud, stupid, four-eyed FOB. Big feet. Horny. Like Lenny in "Of Mice and Men." Floods. Like Lenny in "Of Mice and Men." F-O-B. Fresh Off the Boat. FOB.

Lights fade to black. We hear American pop music, preferably in the funk-R&B-disco area.

ACT I

Scene 1

The back room of a small Chinese restaurant in Torrance, California. Single table, with tablecloth; various chairs, supplies. One door leads outside, a back exit, another leads to the kitchen. Lights up on GRACE, at the table. The music is coming from a small radio. On the table is a small, partially wrapped box, and a huge blob of discarded scotch tape. As GRACE tries to wrap the box, we see what has been happening: The tape SHE's using is stuck; so, in order to pull it out, SHE must tug so hard that an unusable quantity of tape is dispensed. Enter STEVE, from the back door, unnoticed by

GRACE. HE *stands, waiting to catch her eye, tries to speak, but his voice is drowned out by the music.* HE *is dressed in a stylish summer outfit.*

GRACE   Aaaai-ya!
STEVE   Hey! *(No response;* HE *turns off the music)*
GRACE   Huh? Look. Out of tape.
STEVE   *(In Chinese)* Yeah.
GRACE   One whole roll. You know how much of it got on here? Look. That much. That's all.
STEVE   *(In Chinese)* Yeah. Do you serve chong you bing today?
GRACE   *(Picking up box)* Could've skipped the wrapping paper, just covered it with tape.
STEVE   *(Chinese)* Excuse me!
GRACE   Yeah? *(Pause)* You wouldn't have any on you, would ya?
STEVE   *(English from now onward)* Sorry? No. I don't have bing. I want to buy bing.
GRACE   Not bing! Tape. Have you got any tape?
STEVE   Tape? Of course I don't have tape.
GRACE   Just checking.
STEVE   Do you have bing?!

   Pause.

GRACE   Look, we're closed 'til five . . .
STEVE   Idiot girl.
GRACE   Why don't you take a menu?
STEVE   I want you to tell me!

   Pause.

GRACE   *(Ignoring* STEVE) Working in a Chinese restaurant, you learn to deal with obnoxious customers.
STEVE   Hey! You!
GRACE   If the customer's Chinese, you insult them by giving forks.
STEVE   I said I want you to tell me!
GRACE   If the customer's Anglo, you starve them by not giving forks.
STEVE   You serve bing or not?
GRACE   But it's always easy just to dump whatever happens to be in your hands at the moment. (SHE *sticks the tape blob on* STEVE's *face)*
STEVE   I suggest you answer my question at once!

GRACE   And I suggest you grab a menu and start doing things for yourself. Look, I'll get you one even: How's that?

STEVE   I want it from your mouth!

GRACE   Sorry. We don't keep 'em there.

STEVE   If I say they are there, they are there. (HE grabs her box)

GRACE   What—What're you doing? Give that back to me!

> THEY *parry around the table.*

STEVE   Aaaah! Now it's different, isn't it? Now you're listening to me.

GRACE   'Scuse me, but you really are an asshole, you know that? Who do you think you are?

STEVE   What are you asking me? Who I am?

GRACE   Yes. You take it easy with that, hear?

STEVE   You ask who *I* am?

GRACE   One more second and I'm gonna call the cops.

STEVE   Very well I will tell you.

> SHE *picks up the phone;* HE *slams it down.*

STEVE   *(Continued)* I said, I'll tell you.

GRACE   If this is how you go around meeting people, I think it's pretty screwed.

STEVE   Silence! I am Gwan Gung! God of warriors, writers, and prostitutes!

> *Pause.*

GRACE   Bullshit!

STEVE   What?

GRACE   Bullshit! Bull-shit! You are not Gwan Gung. And gimme back my box.

STEVE   I am Gwan Gung. Perhaps we should see what you have in here.

GRACE   Don't open that! *(Beat)* You don't look like Gwan Gung. Gwan Gung is a warrior.

STEVE   I am a warrior!

GRACE   Yeah? Why are you so scrawny, then? You wouldn't last a day in battle.

STEVE   My credit! Many a larger man has been humiliated by the strength in one of my size.

GRACE   Tell me, then. Tell me, if you are Gwan Gung. Tell me of your battles. Of one battle. Of Gwan Gung's favorite battle.

STEVE   Very well. Here is a living memory: One day, Gwan Gung woke up and saw the ring of fire around the sun and decided, "This is a good day to slay villagers." So he got up, washed himself, and looked over a map of the Three Kingdoms to decide where first to go. For those were days of rebellion and falling empires, so opportunity to slay was abundant. But planned slaughter required an order and restraint which soon became tedious. So Gwan Gung decided a change was in order. He called for his tailor, who he asked to make a beautiful blindfold of layered silk, fine enough to be weightless, yet thick enough to blind the wearer completely. The tailor complied, and soon produced a perfect piece of red silk, exactly suited to Gwan Gung's demands. In gratitude, Gwan Gung stayed the tailor's execution sentence. He then put on his blindfold, pulled out his sword, and began passing over the land, swiping at whatever got in his path. You see, Gwan Gung figured there was so much revenge and so much evil in those days that he could slay at random and still stand a good chance of fulfilling justice. This worked very well, until his sword, in its blind fury, hit upon an old and irritable atom bomb.

GRACE   (*Catches* STEVE, *takes back the box*) Ha! Some Gwan Gung you are! Some warrior you are! You can't even protect a tiny box from the grasp of a woman! How could you have shielded your big head in battle?

STEVE   Shield! Shield! I still go to battle!

GRACE   Only your head goes to battle, 'cause only your head is Gwan Gung.

Pause.

STEVE   You made me think of you as a quiet listener. A good trick. What is your name?

GRACE   You can call me, "The Woman Who Has Defeated Gwan Gung," if that's really who you are.

STEVE   Very well. But that name will change before long.

GRACE   That story you told—that wasn't a Gwan Gung story.

STEVE   What—you think you know all of my adventures through stories? All the books in the world couldn't record the life of one man, let alone a god. Now—do you serve bing?

GRACE   I won the battle; you go look yourself. There.

STEVE   You working here?

GRACE   Part time. It's my father's place. I'm also in school.

STEVE   School? University?

GRACE   Yeah. UCLA.

STEVE   Excellent. I have also come to America for school.

GRACE   Well, what use would Gwan Gung have for school?

STEVE   Wisdom. Wisdom makes a warrior stronger.

GRACE   Pretty good. If you are Gwan Gung, you're not the dumb jock I was expecting. Got a lot to learn about school, though.

STEVE   Expecting? You were expecting me?

GRACE   *(Quickly)* No, no. I meant, what I expected from the stories.

STEVE   Tell me, how do people think of Gwan Gung in America? Do they shout my name while rushing into battle or is it too sacred to be used in such ostentatious display?

GRACE   Uh, no.

STEVE   No—what? I didn't ask a "no" question.

GRACE   What I mean is, neither. They don't do either of those.

STEVE   Not good. The name of Gwan Gung has been restricted for the use of leaders only?

GRACE   Uh, no. I think you better sit down.

STEVE   This is very scandalous. How are the people to take my strength? Gwan Gung might as well not exist, for all they know.

GRACE   You got it.

STEVE   I got what? You seem to be having trouble making your answers fit my questions.

GRACE   No, I think you're having trouble making your questions fit my answers.

STEVE   What is this nonsense? Speak clearly, or don't speak at all.

GRACE   Speak clearly?

STEVE   Yes. Like a warrior.

GRACE   Well, you see, Gwan Gung, god of warriors, writers, and prostitutes, no one gives a wipe about you 'round here. You're dead.

Pause.

STEVE   You . . . you make me laugh.

GRACE   You died way back . . . hell, no one even noticed when you died—that's how bad off your PR was. You died and no one even missed a burp.

STEVE   You lie! The name of Gwan Gung must be feared around the world—you jeopardize your health with such remarks. *(Pause)* You—you have heard of me, I see. How can you say—?

GRACE   Oh, I just study it a lot—Chinese American history, I mean.

STEVE   Ah. In the schools, in the universities, where new leaders are born, they study my ways.

GRACE   Well, fifteen of us do.

STEVE   Fifteen. Fifteen of the brightest, of the most promising?

GRACE   One wants to be a dental technician.

STEVE   A man studies Gwan Gung in order to clean teeth?

GRACE   There's also a middle-aged woman that's kinda bored with her kids.

STEVE   I refuse—I don't believe you—your stories. You're just angry at me for treating you like a servant. You're trying to sap my faith. The people—the people outside—they know me—they know the deeds of Gwan Gung.

GRACE   Check it out yourself.

STEVE   Very well. You will learn—learn not to test the spirit of Gwan Gung.

STEVE *exits.* GRACE *picks up the box.* SHE *studies it.*

GRACE   Fa Mu Lan sits and waits. She learns to be still while the emperors, the dynasties, the foreign lands flow past, unaware of her slender form, thinking it a tree in the woods, a statue to a goddess long abandoned by her people. But Fa Mu Lan, the Woman Warrior, is not ashamed. She knows that the one who can exist without movement while the ages pass is the one to whom no victory can be denied. It is training, to wait. And Fa Mu Lan, the Woman Warrior, must train, for she is no goddess, but girl—girl who takes her father's place in battle. No goddess, but woman—warrior-woman and (SHE *breaks through the wrapping, reaches in, and pulls out another box, beautifully wrapped and ribboned)*—and ghost. (SHE *puts the new box on the shelf, goes to the phone, dials)* Hi, Dale? Hi, this is Grace . . . Pretty good. How 'bout you? . . . Good, good. Hey, listen, I'm sorry to ask you at the last minute and everything, but are you doing anything tonight? . . . Are you sure? . . . Oh, good. Would you like to go out with me and some of my friends? . . . Just out to dinner, then maybe we were thinking of going to a movie or something . . . Oh, good . . . Are you sure? . . . Yeah, okay. Um, we're all going to meet at the restaurant . . . No, *our* restaurant . . . right—as soon as possible. Okay, good . . . I'm really glad that you're coming. Sorry it's such short notice. Okay. Bye, now . . . Huh? Frank? Oh, okay. *(Pause)* Hi, Frank . . . Pretty good . . . Yeah? . . . No, I don't think so . . . Yeah . . . No, I'm sorry, I'd still rather not . . . I don't want to, okay? Do I have to be any clearer than that? . . . You are not! . . . You don't even know when they come—you'd have to lie on those tracks for hours . . . Forget it, okay? . . . Look, I'll get you a schedule so you can time it properly . . . It's not a favor, damn it. Now goodbye! (SHE *hangs up)* Jesus!

STEVE *enters.*

STEVE   Buncha' weak boys, what do they know? One man—Chinaman —wearing a leisure suit—green! I ask him, "You know Gwan Gung?" He says, "Hong Kong?" I say, "No, no. Gwan Gung." He says, "Yeah. They got 60,000 people living on four acres. Went there last year." I say, "No, no. Gwan Gung." He says "Ooooh! Gwan Gung?" I say, "Yes, yes, Gwan Gung." He says, "I never been there before."

GRACE   See? Even if you didn't die—who cares?

STEVE   Another kid—blue jeans and a T-shirt—I ask him, does he know Gwan Gung? He says, he doesn't need it, he knows Jesus Christ. What city is this now?

GRACE   Los Angeles.

STEVE   This isn't the only place where a new Chinaman can land, is it?

GRACE   I guess a lot go to San Francisco.

STEVE   Good. This place got a bunch of weirdos around here.

GRACE   Yeah.

STEVE   They could never be followers of Gwan Gung. All who follow me must be loyal and righteous.

GRACE   Maybe you should try some other state.

STEVE   Huh? What you say?

GRACE   Never mind. You'll get used to it—like the rest of us.

Pause; STEVE *begins laughing.*

STEVE   You are a very clever woman.

GRACE   Just average.

STEVE   No. You do a good job to make it seem like Gwan Gung has no followers here. At the university, what do you study?

GRACE   Journalism.

STEVE   Journalism—you are a writer, then?

GRACE   Of a sort.

STEVE   Very good. You are close to Gwan Gung's heart.

GRACE   As close as I'm gonna get.

STEVE   I would like to go out tonight with you.

GRACE   I knew it. Look, I've heard a lot of lines before, and yours is very creative, but . . .

STEVE   I will take you out.

GRACE   You will, huh?

STEVE   I do so because I find you worthy to be favored.

GRACE   You're starting to sound like any other guy now.

STEVE   I'm sorry?

GRACE Look—if you're going to have any kinds of relationships with women in this country, you better learn to give us some respect.

STEVE Respect? I give respect.

GRACE The pushy, aggressive type is out, understand?

STEVE Taking you out is among my highest tokens of respect.

GRACE Oh, c'mon—they don't even say that in Hong Kong.

STEVE You are being asked out by Gwan Gung!

GRACE I told you, you're too wimpy to be Gwan Gung. And, even if you were, you'd have to wait your turn in line.

STEVE What?

GRACE I already have something for tonight. My cousin and I are having dinner.

STEVE You would turn down Gwan Gung for your cousin?

GRACE Well, he has a X-1/9.

> *Pause.*

STEVE What has happened?

GRACE Look—I tell you what. If you take both of us out, then it'll be okay, all right?

STEVE I don't want to go out with your cousin!

GRACE Well, sorry. It's part of the deal.

STEVE Deal? What deals? Why am I made part of these deals?

GRACE 'Cause you're in the US in 1980, just like the rest of us. Now quit complaining. Will you take it or not?

> *Pause.*

STEVE Gwan Gung . . . bows to no one's terms but his own.

GRACE Fine. Why don't you go down the street to Imperial Dragon Restaurant and see if they have bing?

STEVE Do you have bing?

GRACE See for yourself.

> SHE *hands him a menu;* HE *exits;* GRACE *moves with the box.*

GRACE (*Continued*) Fa Mu Lan stood in the center of the village and turned round and round as the bits of fingers, the tips of tongues, the arms, the legs, the peeled skulls, the torn maidenheads, all whirled by. She pulled the loose gown closer to her body, stepped over the torsos, in search of the one of her family who might still be alive. Reaching the house that was once her home, crushing bones in her haste, only to find the doorway covered with the stretched and dried skin of that which was once her father. Climbing through an open window, noticing the shiny black thousand-day-old egg still floating in the shiny black sauce. Finding her sister tied spread-eagle on the mat, finding her mother in the basket in pieces, finding her brother nowhere. The Woman Warrior went to the mirror, which had stayed unbroken, and let her gown come loose and drop to the ground. She turned and studied the ideographs that had long ago been carved into the flesh of her young back . . . Carved by her mother, who lay carved in the basket.

DALE *enters, approaches* GRACE.

GRACE *(Continued)* She ran her fingers over the skin and felt the ridges where there had been pain.

DALE *is behind* GRACE.

GRACE *(Continued)* But now they were firm and hard.

DALE *touches* GRACE, *who reacts by swinging around and knocking him to the ground. Only after* HE *is down does* SHE *see his face.*

GRACE *(Continued)* Dale! Shit! I'm sorry. I didn't . . .!
DALE   *(Groggy)* Am I late?
GRACE   I didn't know it was you, Dale.
DALE   Yeah. Well, I didn't announce myself.
GRACE   You shouldn't just come in here like that.
DALE   You're right. Never again.
GRACE   I mean, you should've yelled from the dining room.
DALE   Dangerous neighborhood, huh?
GRACE   I'm so sorry. Really.
DALE   Yeah. Uh, where're your other friends? They on the floor around here too?
GRACE   No. Uh, this is really bad, Dale. I'm really sorry.
DALE   What?—you can't make it after all?
GRACE   No, I can make it. It's just that . . .
DALE   They can't make it? Okay, so it'll just be us. That's cool.
GRACE   Well, not quite us.
DALE   Oh.
GRACE   See, what happened is—You know my friend Judy?
DALE   Uh, no.

GRACE Well, she was gonna come with us—with me and this guy I know—his name is . . . Steve.

DALE Oh, he's with you, right?

GRACE Well, sort of. So since she was gonna come, I thought you should come too.

DALE To even out the couples?

GRACE But now my friend Judy, she decided she had too much work to do so . . . oh, it's all messed up.

DALE Well, that's okay. I can go home—or I can go with you, if this guy Steve doesn't mind. Where is he, anyway?

GRACE I guess he's late. You know, he just came to this country.

DALE Oh yeah? How'd you meet him?

GRACE At a Chinese dance at UCLA.

DALE Hmmmm. Some of those FOBs get moving pretty fast.

GRACE *glares.*

DALE *(Continued)* Oh. Is he . . . nice?

GRACE He's okay. I don't know him that well. You know, I'm really sorry.

DALE Hey, I said it was okay. Jesus, it's not like you hurt me or anything.

GRACE For that, too.

DALE Look—(HE *hits himself*) No pain!

GRACE What I meant was, I'm sorry tonight's got so messed up.

DALE Oh, it's okay. I wasn't doing anything anyway.

GRACE I know, but still . . .

Silence.

DALE Hey, that Frank is a joke, huh?

GRACE Yeah. He's kind of a pain.

DALE Yeah. What an asshole to call my friend.

GRACE Did you hear him on the phone?

DALE Yeah, all that railroad stuff?

GRACE It was real dumb.

DALE Dumb? He's dumb. He's doing it right now.

GRACE Huh? Are you serious?

DALE Yeah. I'm tempted to tie him down so for once in his life, he won't screw something up.

GRACE You're kidding!

DALE Huh? Yeah, sure I'm kidding. Who would I go bowling with?

GRACE   No, I mean about him actually going out there—is that true?

DALE   Yeah—he's lying there. You know, right on Torrance Boulevard?

GRACE   No!

DALE   Yeah!

GRACE   But what if a train really comes?

DALE   I dunno. I guess he'll get up.

GRACE   I don't believe it!

DALE   Unless he's fallen asleep by that time or something.

GRACE   He's crazy.

DALE   Which is a real possibility for Frank, he's such a bore anyway.

GRACE   He's weird.

DALE   No, he just thinks he's in love with you.

GRACE   Is he?

DALE   I dunno. We'll see when the train comes.

GRACE   Do you think we should do something?

DALE   What?—You're not gonna fall for the twirp, are you?

GRACE   Well, no, but . . .

DALE   He's stupid—and ugly to boot.

GRACE   . . . but staying on the tracks is kinda dangerous.

DALE   Let him. Teach him a lesson.

GRACE   You serious?

DALE   *(Moving closer to* GRACE*)* Not to fool with my cousin.

> HE *strokes her hair.* THEY *freeze in place, but his arm continues to stroke.* STEVE *enters, oblivious of* DALE *and* GRACE, *who do not respond to him.* HE *speaks to the audience as if it were a panel of judges.*

STEVE   No! Please! Listen to me! This is fifth time I come here. I tell you both my parents, I tell you their parents, I tell you their parents' parents and who was adopted great-granduncle. I tell you how many beggars in hometown and name of their blind dogs. I tell you number of steps from my front door to temple, to well, to governor house, to fields, to whorehouse, to fifth cousin inn, to eighth neighbor toilet—you ask only: What for am I in whorehouse? I tell north, south, northeast, southwest, west, east, north-northeast, south-southwest, east-eastsouth —Why will you not let me enter in America? I come here five times—I raise lifetime fortune five times. Five times, I first come here, you say to me I am illegal, you return me on boat to fathers and uncles with no gold, no treasure, no fortune, no rice. I only want to come to America—

come to "Mountain of Gold." And I hate Mountain and I hate America and I hate you! *(Pause)* But this year you call 1914—very bad for China.

> *Pause; light shift.* GRACE *and* DALE *become mobile and aware of* STEVE's *presence.*

GRACE   Oh! Steve, this is Dale, my cousin. Dale, Steve.
DALE   Hey, nice to meet . . .
STEVE   *(Now speaking with Chinese accent)* Hello. Thank you. I am fine.

> *Pause.*

DALE   Uh, yeah. Me too. So, you just got here, huh? What'cha think?

> STEVE *smiles and nods,* DALE *smiles and nods;* STEVE *laughs,* DALE *laughs;* STEVE *hits* DALE *on the shoulder.* THEY *laugh some more.* THEY *stop laughing.*

DALE   *(Continued)* Oh. Uh, good. *(Pause)* Well, it looks like it's just gonna be the three of us, right? *(To GRACE)* Where you wanna go?
GRACE   I think Steve's already taken care of that. Right, Steve?
STEVE   Excuse?
GRACE   You made reservations at a restaurant?
STEVE   Oh, reservations. Yes, yes.
DALE   Oh, okay. That limits the possibilities. Guess we're going to Chinatown or something, right?
GRACE   *(To STEVE)* Where is the restaurant?
STEVE   Oh. The restaurant is a French restaurant. Los Angeles downtown.
DALE   Oh, we're going to a Western place? *(To GRACE)* Are you sure he made reservations?
GRACE   We'll see.
DALE   Well, I'll get my car.
GRACE   Okay.
STEVE   No!
DALE   Huh?
STEVE   Please—allow me to provide car.
DALE   Oh. You wanna drive.
STEVE   Yes. I have car.
DALE   Look—why don't you let me drive? You've got enough to do

without worrying about—you know—how to get around LA, read the stop signs, all that.

STEVE   Please—allow me to provide car. No problem.

DALE   Well, let's ask Grace, okay? *(To* GRACE) Grace, who do you think should drive?

GRACE   I don't really care. Why don't you two figure it out? But let's hurry, okay? We open pretty soon.

DALE   *(To* STEVE) Look—you had to pick the restaurant we're going to, so the least I can do is drive.

STEVE   Uh, your car—how many people sit in it?

DALE   Well, it depends. Right now, none.

GRACE   *(To* DALE) He's got a point. Your car only seats two.

DALE   He can sit in the back. There's space there. I've fit luggage in it before.

GRACE   *(To* STEVE) You want to sit in back?

STEVE   I sit—where?

DALE   Really big suitcases.

GRACE   Back of his car.

STEVE   X-1/9? Aaaai-ya!

DALE   X-1/9?

STEVE   No deal!

DALE   How'd he know that? How'd he know what I drive?

STEVE   Please. Use my car. Is . . . big.

DALE   Yeah? Well, how much room you got? *(Pause; slower)* How-big-your-car-is?

STEVE   Huh?

DALE   Your car—how is big?

GRACE   How big is your car?

STEVE   Oh! You go see.

DALE   'Cause if it's, like, a Pinto or something it's not that much of a difference.

STEVE   Big and black. Outside.

GRACE   Let's hurry.

DALE   Sure, sure. *(Exits)*

GRACE   What you up to, anyway?

STEVE   *(Dropping accent)* Gwan Gung will not go into battle without equipment worthy of his position.

GRACE   Position? You came back, didn't you? What does that make you?

DALE   *(Entering)* Okay. There's only one black car out there—

STEVE   Black car is mine.

DALE   —and that's a Fleetwood limo. Now, you're not gonna tell me that's his.

STEVE   Cadillac. Cadillac is mine.

DALE   Limousine . . . Limousine is yours?

STEVE   Yes, yes. Limousine.

   Pause.

DALE   *(To* GRACE) You wanna ride in that black thing? People will think we're dead.

GRACE   It does have more room.

DALE   Well, it has to. It's built for passengers who can't bend.

GRACE   And the driver *is* expensive.

DALE   He could go home—save all that money.

GRACE   Well, I don't know. You decide.

DALE   *(To* STEVE) Look, we take my car, savvy?

STEVE   Please—drive my car.

DALE   I'm not trying to be unreasonable or anything.

STEVE   My car—just outside.

DALE   I know where it is, I just don't know why it is.

GRACE   Steve's father manufactures souvenirs in Hong Kong.

DALE   *(To* STEVE) Oh, and that's how you manage that out there, huh? —from thousands of aluminum Buddhas and striptease pens.

GRACE   Well, he can't drive and he has the money—

DALE   *(To* GRACE) I mean, wouldn't you just feel filthy?

GRACE   —so it's easier for him.

DALE   Getting out of a limo in the middle of Westwood? People staring, thinking we're from 'SC? Wouldn't you feel like dirt?

GRACE   It doesn't matter either way to me.

   Pause.

DALE   Where's your social conscience?

GRACE   Look—I have an idea. Why don't we just stay here.

STEVE   We stay here to eat?

GRACE   No one from the restaurant will bother us, and we can bring stuff in from the kitchen.

STEVE   I ask you to go out.

DALE   Look, Grace, I can't put ya out like that.

GRACE   *(To* DALE) It's no problem, really. It should be fun. *(To* STEVE) Since there are three of us—

DALE   Fun?

GRACE   *(To* STEVE)—it is easier to eat here.

DALE   How can it be fun? It's cheaper.

STEVE   Does not seem right.

GRACE   I mean, unless our restaurant isn't nice enough.

DALE   No, no—that's not it.

STEVE   *(Watching* DALE) No—this place, very nice.

GRACE   Are you sure?

DALE   Yeah. Sure.

STEVE   *(Ditto)* Yeah. Sure.

DALE   Do you have . . . uh, those burrito things?

GRACE   Moo-shoo?

DALE   Yeah, that.

GRACE   Yeah.

DALE   And black mushrooms.

GRACE   Sure.

DALE   And sea cucumber?

STEVE   Do you have bing?

Pause.

GRACE   Look, Dad and Russ and some of the others are gonna be setting up pretty soon, so let's get our place ready, okay?

DALE   Okay. Need any help?

GRACE   Well, yeah. That's what I just said.

DALE   Oh, right. I thought maybe you were just being polite.

GRACE   Yeah. Meet me in the kitchen.

DALE   Are you sure your Dad won't mind?

GRACE   What?

DALE   Cooking for us.

GRACE   Oh, it's okay. He'll cook for anybody.

Exits. Silence.

DALE   So, how do you like America?

STEVE   Very nice.

DALE   "Very nice." Good, colorful Hong Kong English. English—how much of it you got down, anyway?

STEVE   Please repeat?

DALE   English—you speak how much?

STEVE   Oh—very little.

DALE   Honest. *(Pause)* You feel like you're an American? Don't tell me. Lemme guess. Your father. (HE *switches into a mock Hong Kong accent)* Your Fad-dah tink he sending you here so you get yo' MBA, den go back and covuh da world wit' trinkets and beads. Diversify. Franchise. Sell, ah, Hong Kong X-Ray glasses at tourist shop at Buckingham Palace. You know—ah—"See da Queen?" *(Switches back)* He's hoping your American education's gonna create an empire of defective goods and breakable merchandise. Like those little cameras with the slides inside? I bought one at Disneyland once and it ended up having pictures of Hong Kong in it. You know how shitty it is to expect the Magic Kingdom and wind up with the skyline of Kowloon? Part of your Dad's plan, I'm sure. But you're gonna double-cross him. Coming to America, you're gonna jump the boat. You're gonna decide you like us. Yeah—you're gonna like having fifteen theatres in three blocks, you're gonna like West Hollywood and Newport Beach. You're gonna decide to become an American. Yeah, don't deny it—it happens to the best of us. You can't hold out—you're no different. You won't even know it's coming before it has you. Before you're trying real hard to be just like the rest of us—go dinner, go movie, go motel, bang-bang. And when your Father writes you that do-it-yourself acupuncture sales are down, you'll throw that letter in the basket and burn it in your brain. And you'll write that you're gonna live in Monterey Park a few years before going back home—and you'll get your green card—and you'll build up a nice little stockbroker's business and have a few American kids before your Dad realizes what's happened and dies, his hopes reduced to a few chattering teeth and a pack of pornographic playing cards. Yeah—great things come to the US out of Hong Kong.

STEVE   *(Lights a cigarette, blows smoke, stands)* Such as your parents?

STEVE *turns on the music, exits. Blackout.*

ACT I

Scene 2

Lights up on DALE *and* STEVE *eating. It is a few minutes later and food is on the table.* DALE *eats Chinese style, vigorously shoveling food into his mouth.* STEVE *picks.* GRACE *enters carrying a jar of hot sauce.* STEVE *sees her.*

STEVE   *(To* GRACE*)* After eating, you like to go dance?

DALE   *(Face in bowl)* No, thanks. I think we'd be conspicuous.

STEVE   *(To* GRACE*)* Like to go dance?

GRACE   Perhaps. We will see.

DALE   *(To* STEVE*)* Wait a minute. Hold on. How can you just . . .? I'm here, too, you know. Don't forget I exist just 'cuz you can't understand me.

STEVE   Please repeat?

DALE   I get better communication from my fish. Look, we go see movie. Three here. See? One, two, three. Three can see movie. Only two can dance.

STEVE   *(To* GRACE*)* I ask you to go dance.

GRACE   True, but . . .

DALE   *(To* GRACE*)* That would really be a screw, you know? You invite me down here, you don't have anyone for me to go out with, but you decide to go dancing.

GRACE   Dale, I understand.

DALE   Understand? That would really be a screw. *(To* STEVE*)* Look, if you wanna dance, go find yourself some nice FOB partner.

STEVE   "FOB?" Has what meaning?

GRACE   Dale . . .

DALE   F-O-B. Fresh Off the Boat. FOB.

GRACE   Dale, I agree.

DALE   See, we both agree. *(To* GRACE*)* He's a pretty prime example, isn't he? All those foreign students—

GRACE   I mean, I agree about going dancing.

DALE   —go swimming in their underwear and everything—What?

GRACE   *(To* STEVE*)* Please understand. This is not the right time for dancing.

STEVE   Okay.

DALE   "Okay." It's okay when *she* says it's okay.

STEVE   *(To* DALE*)* "Fresh Off Boat" has what meaning?

Pause.

DALE   (*To* GRACE) Did you ever hear about Dad his first year in the US?

GRACE   Dale, he wants to know . . .

DALE   Well, Gung Gung was pretty rich back then, so Dad must've been a pretty disgusting . . . one, too. You know, his first year here, he spent, like, $13,000. And that was back 'round 1950.

GRACE   Well, Mom never got anything.

STEVE   FOB means what?

DALE   That's probably 'cause women didn't get anything back then. Anyway, he bought himself a new car—all kinds of stuff, I guess. But then Gung Gung went bankrupt, so Dad had to work.

GRACE   And Mom starved.

DALE   Couldn't hold down a job. Wasn't used to taking orders from anyone.

GRACE   Mom was used to taking orders from everyone.

STEVE   Please explain this meaning.

DALE   Got fired from job after job. Something like fifteen in a year. He'd just walk in the front door and out the back, practically.

GRACE   Well, at least he had a choice of doors. At least he was educated.

STEVE   (*To* DALE) Excuse!

DALE   Huh?

GRACE   He was educated. Here. In America. When Mom came over, she couldn't quit just 'cuz she was mad at her employer. It was work or starve.

DALE   Well, Dad had some pretty lousy jobs, too.

STEVE   (*To* DALE) Explain, please!

GRACE   Do you know what it's like to work eighty hours a week just to feed yourself?

DALE   Do you?

STEVE   Dale!

DALE   (*To* STEVE) It means you. You know how, if you go to a fish store or something, they have the stuff that just came in that day? Well, so have you.

STEVE   I do not understand

DALE   Forget it. That's part of what makes you one.

Pause.

STEVE   (*Picking up hot sauce, to* DALE) Hot. You want some?

Pause.

DALE   Well, yeah. Okay. Sure.

STEVE *puts hot sauce on* DALE's *food.*

DALE   *(Continued)* Hey, isn't that kinda a lot?
GRACE   See, Steve's family comes from Shanghai.
DALE   Hmmmm. Well, I'll try it. (HE *takes a gulp, puts down his food)*
GRACE   I think perhaps that was too much for him.
DALE   No.
GRACE   Want some water?
DALE   Yes.

GRACE *exits.*

DALE   *(Continued)* You like hot sauce? You like your food hot? All right—here. (HE *dumps the contents of the jar on* STEVE's *plate, stirs)* Fucking savage. Don't you ever worry about your intestines falling out?

GRACE *enters, gives water to* DALE. STEVE *sits shocked.*

DALE   Thanks. FOBs can eat anything, huh? They're specially trained. Helps maintain the characteristic greasy look.

STEVE, *cautiously, begins to eat his food.*

DALE   *(Continued)* What—? Look, Grace, he's eating that! He's amazing! A freak! What a cannibal!
GRACE   *(Taking* DALE's *plate)* Want me to throw yours out?
DALE   *(Snatching it back)* Huh? No. No, I can eat it.

DALE and STEVE *stare at each other across the table. In unison,* THEY *pick up as large a glob of food as possible, stuff it into their mouths.* THEY *cough and choke.* THEY *rest, repeat the face-off a second time.* THEY *continue in silent pain.* GRACE, *who has been watching this, speaks to us.*

GRACE   Yeah. It's tough trying to live in Chinatown. But it's tough trying to live in Torrance, too. It's true. I don't like being alone. You know, when Mom could finally bring me to the US, I was already ten. But I never studied my English very hard in Taiwan, so I got moved back to the second grade. There were a few Chinese girls in the fourth grade, but they were American-born, so they wouldn't even talk to me. They'd just stay with themselves and compare how much clothes they all had, and make fun of the way we all talked. I figured I had a better chance of getting in with the white kids than with them, so in junior high I started bleaching my hair and hanging out at the beach—you know, Chinese hair looks pretty lousy when you bleach it. After a while, I knew what beach was gonna be good on any given day, and I could tell who was coming just by his van. But the American-born Chinese, it didn't matter to them. They just giggled and went to their own dances. Until my senior year in high school—that's how long it took for me to get over this whole thing. One night I took Dad's car and drove on Hollywood Boulevard, all the way from downtown to Beverly Hills, then back on Sunset. I was looking and listening—all the time with the window down, just so I'd feel like I was part of the city. And that Friday, it was—I guess—I said, "I'm lonely. And I don't like it. I don't like being alone." And that was all. As soon as I said it, I felt all of the breeze—it was really cool on my face—and I heard all of the radio—and the music sounded really good, you know? So I drove home.

Pause; DALE *bursts out coughing.*

GRACE   *(Continued)* Oh, I'm sorry. Want some more water, Dale?
DALE   It's okay. I'll get it myself. (HE *exits*)
STEVE   *(Looks at* GRACE) Good, huh?

STEVE *and* GRACE *stare at each other, as lights fade to black.*

ACT II

In blackout.

DALE   I am much better now. *(Single spot on* DALE*)* I go out now. Lots.
I can, anyway. Sometimes I don't ask anyone, so I don't go out. But I
could. *(Pause)* I am much better now. I have friends now. Lots. They
drive Porsche Carreras. Well, one does. He has a house up in the
Hollywood Hills where I can stand and look down on the lights of LA.
I guess I haven't really been there yet. But I could easily go. I'd just
have to ask. *(Pause)* My parents—They don't know nothing about the
world, about watching Benson at the Roxy, about ordering hors
d'oeuvres at Scandia's, downshifting onto the Ventura Freeway at midnight. They're yellow ghosts and they've tried to cage me up with
Chinese-ness when all the time we were in America. *(Pause)* So, I've
had to work real hard—real hard—to be myself. To not be a Chinese,
a yellow, a slant, a gook. To be just a human being, like everyone else.
(Pause) I've paid my dues. And that's why I am much better now. I'm
making it, you know? I'm making it in America.

> *A napkin is thrown in front of* DALE's *face from Right. As it
> passes, the lights go up. The napkin falls on what we recognize as
> the dinner table from the last scene. We are in the back room.
> Dinner is over.* STEVE *has thrown the napkin from where* HE *is
> sitting in his chair.* DALE *is standing Upstage of the table and had
> been talking to* STEVE.

DALE   *(Continued)* So, look, will you just not be so . . . Couldn't you
just be a little more . . .? I mean, we don't have to do all this . . . You
know what's gonna happen to us tomorrow morning? (HE *burps)* What
kinda diarrhea . . .? Look, maybe if you could just be a little more
. . . (HE *gropes)* normal. Here—stand up.

> STEVE *does.*

DALE   *(Continued)* Don't smile like that. Okay. You ever see "Saturday
Night Fever"?
STEVE   Oh. "Saturday . . ."
DALE   Yeah.
STEVE   Oh. "Saturday Night Fever." Disco.
DALE   That's it. Okay. You know . . .
STEVE   John Travolta.

DALE   Right. John Travolta. Now, maybe if you could be a little more like him.

STEVE   Uh, Bee Gees?

DALE   Yeah, right. Bee Gees. But what I mean is . . .

STEVE   You like Bee Gees?

DALE   I dunno. They're okay. Just stand a little more like him, you know, his walk? (DALE *tries to demonstrate*)

STEVE   I believe Bee Gees very good.

DALE   Yeah. Listen.

STEVE   You see movie name of . . .

DALE   Will you listen for a sec?

STEVE   . . . "Grease"?

DALE   Hold on!

STEVE   Also Bee Gees.

DALE   I'm trying to help you!

STEVE   Also John Travolta?

DALE   I'm trying to get you normal!

STEVE   And—Oliver John-Newton.

DALE   WILL YOU SHUT UP? I'M TRYING TO HELP YOU! I'M TRYING . . .

STEVE   Very good!

DALE   . . . TO MAKE YOU LIKE JOHN TRAVOLTA!

> DALE *grabs* STEVE *by the arm. Pause.* STEVE *coldly knocks* DALE's *hands away.* DALE *picks up the last of the dirty dishes on the table and backs into the kitchen.* GRACE *enters from the kitchen with the box she wrapped in Act I.* SHE *sits in a chair and goes over the wrapping, her back to* STEVE. HE *gets up and begins to go for the box, almost reaching her.* SHE *turns around suddenly, though, at which point* HE *drops to the ground and pretends to be looking for something.* SHE *then turns back front, and* HE *resumes his attempt. Just as* HE *reaches the kitchen door,* DALE *enters with a wet sponge.*

DALE   (*To* STEVE) Oh, you finally willing to help? I already brought in all the dishes, you know. Here—wipe the table.

> DALE *gives sponge to* STEVE, *returns to kitchen.* STEVE *throws the sponge on the ground, sits back at table.* GRACE *turns around, sees sponge on the floor, picks it up, and goes to wipe the table.* SHE *brings the box with her and holds it in one hand.*

GRACE   Look—you've been wanting this for some time now. Okay. Here. I'll give it to you. (SHE *puts it on the table*) A welcome to this country. You don't have to fight for it—I'll give it to you instead.

Pause; STEVE *pushes the box off the table.*

GRACE   *(Continued)* Okay. Your choice. (GRACE *wipes the table*)
DALE   *(Entering from kitchen, sees* GRACE) What—you doing this?
GRACE   Don't worry, Dale.
DALE   I asked him to do it.
GRACE   I'll do it.
DALE   I asked him to do it. He's useless! (DALE *takes the sponge*) Look, I don't know how much English you know, but look-ee! (HE *uses a mock Chinese accent*)
GRACE   Dale, don't do that.
DALE   *(Using sponge)* Look—makes table all clean, see?
GRACE   You have to understand . . .
DALE   Ooooh! Nice and clean!
GRACE   . . . he's not used to this.
DALE   "Look! I can see myself!"
GRACE   Look, I can do this. Really.
DALE   Here—now you do. (DALE *forces* STEVE's *hand onto the sponge*) Good. Very good. Now, move it around. (DALE *leads* STEVE's *hand*) Oh, you learn so fast. Get green card, no time flat, buddy.

DALE removes his hand, STEVE stops.

DALE   *(Continued)* Uh, uh, uh. You must do it yourself. Come. There—now doesn't that make you feel proud?

HE *takes his hand off,* STEVE *stops.* DALE *gives up, crosses Downstage.* STEVE *remains at the table, still.*

DALE   *(Continued)* Jesus! I'd trade him in for a vacuum cleaner any day.
GRACE   You shouldn't humiliate him like that.
DALE   What humiliate? I asked him to wipe the table, that's all.
GRACE   See, he's different. He probably has a lot of servants at home.
DALE   Big deal. He's in America, now. He'd better learn to work.
GRACE   He's rich, you know.
DALE   So what? They all are. Rich FOBs.
GRACE   Does that include me?
DALE   Huh?

GRACE   Does that include me? Am I one of your "rich FOBs"?

DALE   What? Grace, com'on, that's ridiculous. You're not rich. I mean, you're not poor, but you're not rich either. I mean, you're not a FOB. FOBs are different. You've been over here most of your life. You've had time to thaw out. You've thawed out really well, and, besides— you're my cousin.

> DALE *strokes* GRACE's *hair, and* THEY *freeze as before.* STEVE, *meanwhile, has almost imperceptibly begun to clean with his sponge.* HE *speaks to the audience as if speaking with his family.*

STEVE   Yes. I will go to America. "Mei Guo." *(Pause;* HE *begins working)* The white ghosts came into the harbor today. They promised that they would bring us to America, and that in America we would never want for anything. One white ghost told how the streets are paved with diamonds, how the land is so rich that pieces of gold lie on the road, and the worker devils consider them too insignificant even to bend down for. They told of a land where there are no storms, no snow, but sunshine and warmth all year round, where a man could live out in the open and feel not even discomfort from the nature around him—a worker's paradise. A land of gold, a mountain of wealth, a land in which a man can make his fortune and grow without wrinkles into an old age. And the white ghosts are providing free passage both ways. *(Pause)* All we need to do is sign a worker's contract. *(Pause)* Yes, I am going to America.

> At this point, GRACE *and* DALE *become mobile, but still fail to hear* STEVE. GRACE *picks up the box.*

DALE   What's that?

STEVE   *(His wiping becomes increasingly frenzied)* I am going to America because of its promises. I am going to follow the white ghosts because of their promises.

DALE   Is this for me?

STEVE   Because they promised! They promised! AND LOOK! YOU PROMISED! THIS IS SHIT! IT'S NOT TRUE.

DALE   *(Taking the box)* Let's see what's inside, is that okay?

STEVE   *(Shoves* DALE *to the ground and takes the box)* IT IS NOT! *(With accent)* THIS IS MINE!

DALE   Well, what kind of shit is that?

STEVE   She gave this to me.

DALE   What kind of . . . we're not at your place. We're not in Hong

Kong, you know. Look—look all around you—you see shit on the sidewalks?

STEVE   This is mine!

DALE   You see armies of rice bowl haircuts?

STEVE   She gave this to me!

DALE   People here have their flies zipped up—see?

STEVE   You should not look in it.

DALE   So we're not in Hong Kong. And I'm not one of your servant boys that you can knock around—that you got by trading in a pack of pornographic playing cards—that you probably deal out to your friends. You're in America, understand?

STEVE   Quiet! Do you know who I am?

DALE   Yeah—you're a FOB. You're a rich FOB in the US. But you better watch yourself. 'Cause you can be sent back.

STEVE   Shut up! Do you know who I am?

DALE   You can be sent back, you know—just like that. 'Cause you're a guest here, understand?

STEVE   *(To* GRACE) Tell him who I am.

DALE   I know who he is—heir to a fortune in junk merchandise. Big deal. Like being heir to Captain Crunch.

STEVE   Tell him!

Silence.

GRACE   You know it's not like that.

STEVE   Tell him!

DALE   Huh?

GRACE   Well, the sidewalks are a mess, I guess, but all the stuff about rice bowls and—zippers—have you ever been there, Dale?

DALE   Well, yeah. Once. When I was ten.

GRACE   Well, it's changed a lot.

DALE   Remember getting heat rashes.

GRACE   People are dressing really well now—and the whole place has become really stylish—well, certainly not everybody, but the people who are well-off enough to send their kids to American colleges— they're really kinda classy.

DALE   Yeah.

GRACE   Sort of.

DALE   You mean, like him. So what? It' easy to be classy when you're rich.

GRACE   All I'm saying is . . .

DALE   Hell, I could do that.

GRACE   Huh?

DALE   I could be classy, too, if I was rich.

GRACE   You *are* rich.

DALE   No. Just upper-middle. Maybe.

GRACE   Compared to us, you're rich.

DALE   No, not really. And especially not compared to him. Besides, when I was born we were still poor.

GRACE   Well, you're rich now.

DALE   Used to get one lifesaver a day.

GRACE   That's all? One lifesaver?

DALE   Well, I mean, that's not all I lived on. We got normal food, too.

GRACE   I know, but . . .

DALE   Not like we were living in cardboard boxes or anything.

GRACE   All I'm saying is that the people who are coming in now—a lot of them are different—they're already real Westernized. They don't act like they're fresh off the boat.

DALE   Maybe. But they're still FOBs.

STEVE   Tell him who I am!

DALE   Anyway, real nice dinner, Grace. I really enjoyed it.

GRACE   Thank you.

STEVE   Okay! I will tell myself.

DALE   Go tell yourself—just don't bother us.

GRACE   *(Standing; to* STEVE) What would you like to do now?

STEVE   Huh?

GRACE   You wanted to go out after dinner?

STEVE   Yes, yes. We go out.

DALE   I'll drive. You sent the hearse home.

STEVE   I tell driver—return car after dinner.

DALE   How could you . . .? What time did you . . .? When did you tell him to return? What time?

STEVE   *(Looks at his watch)* Seven-five.

DALE   No—not what time is it. What time you tell him to return?

STEVE   Seven-five. Go see.

DALE *exits through kitchen.*

STEVE   *(Continued, no accent)* Why wouldn't you tell him who I am?

GRACE   Can Gwan Gung die?

Pause.

STEVE   No warrior can defeat Gwan Gung.

GRACE   Does Gwan Gung fear ghosts?
STEVE   Gwan Gung fears no ghosts.
GRACE   Ghosts of warriors?
STEVE   No warrior ghosts.
GRACE   Ghosts that avenge?
STEVE   No avenging ghosts.
GRACE   Ghosts forced into exile?
STEVE   No exiled ghosts.
GRACE   Ghosts that wait?

    Pause.

STEVE   *(Quietly)* May I . . . take you out tonight? Maybe not tonight, but some other time? Another time? (HE *strokes her hair)* What has happened?
DALE   *(Entering)* I cannot believe it . . . (HE *sees them)* What do you think you're doing? (HE *grabs* STEVE's *hand. To* STEVE) What . . . I step out for one second and you just go and—hell, you FOBs are sneaky. No wonder they check you so close at immigration.
GRACE   Dale, I can really take care of myself.
DALE   Yeah? What was his hand doing, then?
GRACE   Stroking my hair.
DALE   Well, yeah. I could see that. I mean, what was it doing stroking your hair? *(Pause)* Uh, never mind. All I'm saying is . . . (HE *gropes)* Jesus! If you want to be alone, why don't you just say so, huh? If that's what you really want, just say it, okay?

    Pause.

DALE   *(Continued)* Okay. Time's up.
GRACE   Was the car out there?
DALE   Huh? Yeah. Yeah, it was. I could not believe it. I go outside and—thank God—there's no limousine. Just as I'm about to come back, I hear this sound like the roar of death and this big black shadow scrapes up beside me. I could not believe it!
STEVE   Car return—seven-five.
DALE   And when I asked him—I asked the driver, what time he'd been told to return. And he just looks at me and says, "Now."
STEVE   We go out?
DALE   What's going on here? What is this?
STEVE   Time to go.
DALE   No! Not 'til you explain what's going on.

STEVE   *(To* GRACE) You now want to dance?

DALE   *(To* GRACE) Do you understand this? Was this coincidence?

STEVE   *(Ditto)* I am told good things of American discos.

DALE   *(Ditto)* You and him just wanna go off by yourselves?

STEVE   I hear of Dillon's.

DALE   Is that it?

STEVE   You hear of Dillon's?

DALE   It's okay, you know.

STEVE   In Westwood.

DALE   I don't mind.

STEVE   Three—four stories.

DALE   Really.

STEVE   Live band.

DALE   Cousin.

STEVE   We go. (HE *takes* GRACE's *hand)*

DALE   He's just out to snake you, you know. *(HE takes the other hand)*

From this point on, almost unnoticeably, the lights begin to dim.

GRACE   Okay! That's enough! (SHE *pulls away)* That's enough! I have to make all the decisions around here, don't I? When I leave it up to you two, the only place we go is in circles.

DALE   Well . . .

STEVE   No, I am suggesting place to go.

GRACE   Look, Dale, when I asked you here, what did I say we were going to do?

DALE   Uh, dinner and a movie—or something. But it was a different "we," then.

GRACE   It doesn't matter. That's what we're going to do.

DALE   I'll drive.

STEVE   My car can take us to movie.

GRACE   I think we better not drive at all. We'll stay right here. (SHE *removes* STEVE's *tie)* Do you remember this?

DALE   What—you think I borrow his clothes or something? Hell, I don't even wear ties.

GRACE *takes the tie, wraps it around* DALE's *face like a blindfold.*

DALE   *(Continued)* Grace, what are you . . .?

GRACE   *(To* STEVE) Do you remember this?

DALE   I already told you. I don't need a closer look or nothing.

STEVE   Yes.

GRACE   *(Ties the blindfold, releases it)* Let's sit down.
DALE   Wait.
STEVE   You want me to sit here?
DALE   Grace, is he understanding you?
GRACE   Have you ever played Group Story?
STEVE   Yes, I have played that.
DALE   There—there he goes again! Grace, I'm gonna take . . . (HE *starts to remove the blindfold)*
GRACE   *(Stopping him)* Dale, listen or you won't understand.
DALE   But how come *he's* understanding?
GRACE   Because he's listening.
DALE   But . . .
GRACE   Now, let's play Group Story.
DALE   Not again. Grace, that's only good when you're stoned.
GRACE   Who wants to start? Steve, you know the rules?
STEVE   Yes—I understand.
DALE   See, we're talking normal speed—and he still understood.
GRACE   Dale, would you like to start?

    Pause.

DALE   All right.

    By this time, the lights have dimmed, throwing shadows on the stage. GRACE will strike two pots together to indicate each speaker change and the ritual will gradually take on elements of Chinese opera.

DALE   *(Continued)* Uh, once upon a time . . . there were . . . three bears—Grace, this is ridiculous!
GRACE   Tell a story.
DALE   . . .three bears and they each had . . . cancer of the lymph nodes. Uh, and they were very sad. So the baby bear said, "I'll go to the new Cedar Sinai Hospital, where they may have a cure for this fatal illness."
GRACE   But the new Cedar Sinai Hospital happened to be 2,000 miles away—across the ocean.
STEVE   *(Gradually losing his accent)* That is very far.
DALE   How did—? *(Sees GRACE)* So, the bear tried to swim over, but his leg got chewed off by alligators—are their alligators in the Pacific Ocean?—Oh, well. So he ended up having to go for a leg *and* a cure for malignant cancer of the lymph nodes.
GRACE   When he arrived there, he came face to face with—

STEVE   With Gwan Gung, god of warriors, writers and prostitutes.

DALE   And Gwan Gung looked at the bear and said . . .

GRACE   . . . strongly and with spirit . . .

STEVE   "One-legged bear, what are you doing on my land? You are from America, are you not?"

DALE   And the bear said, "Yes. Yes."

GRACE   And Gwan Gung replied . . .

STEVE   *(Getting up)* By stepping forward, sword drawn, ready to wound, not kill, not end it so soon. To draw it out, play it, taunt it, make it feel like a dog.

DALE   Which is probably rather closely related to the bear.

GRACE   Gwan Gung said,

STEVE   "When I came to America, did you lick my wounds? When I came to America, did you cure my sickness?"

DALE   And just as Gwan Gung was about to strike . . .

GRACE   There arrived Fa Mu Lan, the Woman Warrior. (SHE *stands, faces* STEVE)

From here on in, striking pots together is not needed.

GRACE   *(Continued)* "Gwan Gung."

STEVE   "What do you want? Don't interfere! Don't forget, I have gone before you into battle many times."

DALE   But Fa Mu Lan seemed not to hear Gwan Gung's warning. She stood between him and the bear, drawing out her own sword.

GRACE   "You will learn I cannot forget. I don't forget, Gwan Gung. Spare the bear and I will present gifts."

STEVE   "Very well. He is hardly worth killing."

DALE   And the bear hopped off. Fa Mu Lan pulled a parcel from beneath her gown.

SHE *mimes.*

DALE   *(Continued)* She pulled out two items.

GRACE   "This is for you."

STEVE   "What is that?"

GRACE *removes the tie from* DALE's *head, gives it to* STEVE.

DALE   She showed him a beautiful piece of red silk, thick enough to be opaque, yet so light, he barely felt it in his hands.

GRACE   "Do you remember this?"

STEVE   "Why, yes. I used this silk for sport one day. How did you get a hold of it?"

DALE   Then she presented him with a second item. It was a fabric—thick and dried and brittle.

GRACE   "Do you remember this?"

STEVE   *(Turning away)* "No, no. I've never seen this before in my life. This has nothing to do with me. What is it—a dragon skin?"

DALE   Fa Mu Lan handed it to Gwan Gung.

GRACE   "Never mind. Use it—as a tablecloth. As a favor to me."

STEVE   "It's much too hard and brittle. But, to show you my graciousness in receiving—I will use it tonight!"

DALE   That night, Gwan Gung had a large banquet, at which there was plenty, even for the slaves. But Fa Mu Lan ate nothing. She waited until midnight, 'til Gwan Gung and the gods were full of wine and empty of sense. Sneaking behind him, she pulled out the tablecoth, waving it above her head.

GRACE   *(Ripping the tablecloth from the table)* "Gwan Gung, you foolish boy. This thing you have used tonight as a tablecloth—it is the stretched and dried skins of my fathers. My fathers, whom you slew— for sport! And you have been eating their sins—you ate them!"

STEVE   No. I was blindfolded. I did not know.

DALE   Fa Mu Lan waved the skin before Gwan Gung's face. It smelled suddenly of death.

GRACE   "Remember the day you played? Remember? Well, eat that day, Gwan Gung."

STEVE   "I am not responsible. No. No."

> GRACE *throws one end of the tablecloth to* DALE, *who catches it. Together,* THEY *become like* STEVE's *parents.* THEY *chase him about the stage, waving the tablecloth like a net.*

DALE   Yes!

GRACE   Yes!

STEVE   No!

DALE   You must!

GRACE   Go!

STEVE   Where?

DALE   To America!

GRACE   To work!

STEVE   Why?

DALE   Because!

GRACE   We need!

STEVE   No!
DALE   Why?
GRACE   Go.
STEVE   Hard!
DALE   So?
GRACE   Need.
STEVE   Far!
DALE   So?
GRACE   Need!
STEVE   Safe!
DALE   Here?
GRACE   No!
STEVE   Why?
DALE   Them. *(Points)*
GRACE   Them. *(Points)*
STEVE   Won't!
DALE   Must!
GRACE   Must!
STEVE   Won't!
DALE   Go!
GRACE   Go!
STEVE   Won't!
DALE   Bye!
GRACE   Bye!
STEVE   Won't!
DALE   Fare!
GRACE   Well!

> DALE *and* GRACE *drop the tablecloth over* STEVE *who sinks to the ground.* GRACE *then moves Offstage, into the bathroom-storage room, while* DALE *goes Upstage and stands with his back to the audience. Silence.*

STEVE   *(Begins pounding the ground)* Noooo! (HE *throws off the table-cloth, standing up full. Lights up full, blindingly)* I am GWAN GUNG!
DALE   *(Turning Downstage suddenly)* What . . .?
STEVE   I HAVE COME TO THIS LAND TO STUDY!
DALE   Grace . . .
STEVE   TO STUDY THE ARTS OF WAR, OF LITERATURE, OF RIGHTEOUSNESS!
DALE   A movie's fine.
STEVE   I FOUGHT THE WARS OF THE THREE KINGDOMS!

DALE   An ordinary movie, let's go.

STEVE   I FOUGHT WITH THE FIRST PIONEERS, THE FIRST WARRIORS THAT CHOSE TO FOLLOW THE WHITE GHOSTS TO THIS LAND!

DALE   You can pick, okay?

STEVE   I WAS THEIR HERO, THEIR LEADER, THEIR FIRE!

DALE   I'll even let him drive, how's that?

STEVE   AND THIS LAND IS MINE! IT HAS NO RIGHT TO TREAT ME THIS WAY!

GRACE   No. Gwan Gung, *you* have no rights.

STEVE   Who's speaking?

GRACE   *(Enters with two long fighting poles)* It is Fa Mu Lan. You are in a new land, Gwan Gung.

STEVE   Not new—I have been here before, many times. This time, I said I will have it easy. I will come as no Chinaman before—on a plane, with money and rank.

GRACE   And?

STEVE   And—there is no change. I am still treated like this! This land . . . has no right. I AM GWAN GUNG!

GRACE   And I am Fa Mu Lan.

DALE   I'll be Chiang Kai-Shek, how's that?

STEVE   *(To* DALE) You! How can you—? I came over with your parents.

GRACE   *(Turning to* STEVE) We are in America. And we have a battle to fight.

SHE *tosses one pole to* STEVE. THEY *square off.*

STEVE   I don't want to fight you.

GRACE   You killed my family.

STEVE   You were revenged—I ate your father's sins.

GRACE   That's not revenge!

Poles strike.

GRACE   *(Continued)* That was only the tease.

Strike.

GRACE   *(Continued)* What's the point in dying if you don't know the cause of your death?

Series of strikes. STEVE *falls.*

DALE   *(Continued)* Okay! That's it!

> GRACE *stands over* STEVE, *her pole pointed at his heart like a sword.* DALE *snatches the pole from her hands;* SHE *does not move.*

DALE   *(Continued)* Jesus! Enough is enough!

> DALE *takes* STEVE's *pole;* HE *also does not react.*

DALE   *(Continued)* What the hell kind of movie was that?

> DALE *turns his back on the couple, heads for the bathroom-storage room.* GRACE *uses her now-invisible sword to thrust in and out of* STEVE's *heart once.*

DALE   That's it. Game's over. Now just sit down here. Breathe. One. Two. One. Two. Air. Good stuff. Glad they made it. Right, cousin?

> DALE *strokes* GRACE's *hair.* THEY *freeze.* STEVE *rises slowly to his knees and delivers a monologue to the audience.*

STEVE   Ssssh! Please, miss! Please—quiet! I will not hurt you, I promise. All I want is . . . food . . . anything. You look full of plenty. I have not eaten almost one week now, but four days past when I found one egg and I ate every piece of it—including shell. Every piece, I ate. Please. Don't you have anything extra? *(Pause)* I want to. Now. This land does not want us any more than China. But I cannot. All work was done, then the bosses said they could not send us back. And I am running, running from Eureka, running from San Francisco, running from Los Angeles. And I been eating very little. One egg, only. *(Pause)* All America wants Chinamen go home, but no one want it bad enough to pay our way. Now, please, can't you give even little? *(Pause)* I ask you, what you hate most? What work most awful for white woman? *(Pause)* Good. I will do that thing for you—you can give me food. *(Pause)* Think—you relax, you are given those things, clean, dry, press. No scrub, no dry. It is wonderful thing I offer you. *(Pause)* Good. Give me those and please bring food, or I be done before these things.

GRACE   *(Steps away from DALE with box)* Here—I've brought you something. (SHE *hands him the box*) Open it.

> HE *hesitates, then does, and takes out a small chong you bing.*

GRACE   *(Continued)* Eat it.

HE *does, slowly at first, then ravenously.*

GRACE   *(Continued)* Good. Eat it all down. It's just food. Really. Feel better now? Good. Eat the bing. Hold it in your hands. Your hands . . . are beautiful. Lift it to your mouth. Your mouth . . . is beautiful. Bite it with your teeth. Your teeth . . . are beautiful. Crush it with your tongue. Your tongue . . . is beautiful. Slide it down your throat. Your throat . . . is beautiful.
STEVE   Our hands are beautiful.

SHE *holds hers next to his.*

GRACE   What do you see?
STEVE   I see . . . I see the hands of warriors.
GRACE   Warriors? What of gods then?
STEVE   There are no gods that travel. Only warriors travel. *(Silence)* Would you like go dance?
GRACE   Yeah. Okay. Sure.

THEY *start to leave.* DALE *speaks softly.*

DALE   Well, if you want to be alone . . .
GRACE   I think we would, Dale. Is that okay? *(Pause)* Thanks for coming over. I'm sorry things got so screwed up.
DALE   Oh, uh, that's okay. The evening was real . . . different, anyway.
GRACE   Yeah. Maybe you can take Frank off the tracks now?
DALE   *(Laughing softly)* Yeah. Maybe I will.
STEVE   *(To* DALE*)* Very nice meeting you. *(Extends his hand)*
DALE   *(Does not take it)* Yeah. Same here.

STEVE *and* GRACE *start to leave.*

DALE   *(Continued)* You know . . . I think you picked up English faster than anyone I've ever met.

Pause.

STEVE   Thank you.
GRACE   See you.
STEVE   Goodbye.
DALE   Bye.

CODA

DALE *alone in the back room. HE examines the swords, the tablecloth, the box. HE sits down.*

DALE   F-O-B. Fresh Off the Boat. FOB. Clumsy, ugly, greasy FOB. Loud, stupid, four-eyed FOB. Big feet. Horny. Like Lenny in "Of Mice and Men." F-O-B. Fresh Off the Boat. FOB.

Slow fade to black.

STILL LIFE

A Documentary

by

Emily Mann

ABOUT EMILY MANN

Emily Mann was born in Boston, Massachusetts in 1952; she received a B.A. from Harvard and an M.F.A. from the University of Minnesota. She wrote and directed *Still Life* which premiered at the Goodman Studio Theatre in Chicago and was subsequently produced at the American Place Theatre in New York City. The latter production received Obie awards for playwriting and direction, for all three performances and for best production. Mann's first play *Annulla Allen: Autobiography of a Survivor* premiered at the Guthrie Theater's Guthrie 2 under her direction and was later produced at the Goodman Theatre. She redirected the play for the drama series *Earplay* for broadcast by National Public Radio both in the United States and abroad. Mann was associated with the BAM Theater Company for which she directed *He and She* and *Oedipus the King* and also assisted artistic director David Jones. She has served as resident director of the Guthrie Theater and associate director of Guthrie 2. At the Guthrie, she directed *The Glass Menagerie.* At Guthrie 2, she directed David Rudkin's *Ashes,* David Mamet's *Reunion,* Tankred Dorst's *On Mount Chimborazo* and Michael Casale's *Cold,* among others. Other directorial credits include productions at The Cincinnati Playhouse in the Park, the St. Nicholas Theater Company, Minneapolis' Theater in the Round, The Walker Art Center, and Oregon Contemporary Theater. Emily Mann also teaches acting and has acted professionally. She was actively involved in the development of new scripts at the Playwrights' Center in Minneapolis. Most recently, she directed the world premiere of Michael Weller's *Dwarfman: Master of a Million Shapes* at the Goodman Theatre.

PRODUCTION HISTORY

Still Life was nominated for the *Plays in Process* series by Julia Miles, associate director of the American Place Theatre in New York City. It was presented there from February 10 to March 22, 1981.

Emily Mann directed. The set and costumes were designed by Tom Lynch and the lighting by Annie Wrightson. The cast, in order of appearance, was as follows:

MARK.. John Spencer
CHERYL... Mary McDonnell
NADINE .... Timothy Near

Still Life premiered at the Goodman Studio Theatre in Chicago in October 1980 and played there through November. It was given a rehearsed staged reading as part of the American Place Theatre's Women's Project on February 2, 1981, and a full production at the same theatre shortly after. *Still Life* has also been produced at the Empty Space in Seattle, spring, 1981, and is being produced by the Eureka Theatre in San Francisco, March, 1982.

PLAYWRIGHT'S NOTE

Still Life is about three people I met in Minnesota during the summer of 1978. It is about violence in America. The Viet Nam War is the backdrop to the violence at home. The play is dedicated to the casualties of the war—all of them.

The play is a "documentary" because it is a distillation of interviews I conducted during that summer. I chose the documentary style to insure that the reality of the people and events described could not be denied. Perhaps one could argue about the accuracy of the people's interpretations of events, but one cannot deny that these are actual people describing actual events as they saw and understood them.

The play is also a personal document. A specialist in the brain and its perceptions said to me after seeing *Still Life* that the play is constructed as a traumatic memory. Each character struggles with his traumatic memory of events and the play as a whole is my traumatic memory of their accounts. The characters speak directly to the audience so that the audience can hear what I heard, experience what I experienced.

I have been obsessed with violence in our country since I came of age in the 1960s. I have no answer to the questions I raise in the play but I think the questions are worth asking. The play is a plea for examination and self-examination, an attempt at understanding our own violence and a hope that through understanding we can, as Nadine says, "come out on the other side."

Production Notes

The actors speak directly to the audience. The rhythms are of real people's speech, but may also at times have the sense of improvisation one finds with the best jazz musicians: the monologues should sometimes sound like extended riffs.

The play is written in three acts but this does not denote act breaks. Rather, the acts represent movements and the play should be performed without intermission. The ideal running time is one hour and 30 minutes.

For the New York production, three verses from the song, "No More Genocide" by Holly Near were played. If the director would like to use the song, contact Hereford Music, P.O. Box 996, Ukiah, California 95482 for written permission.

Lyrics for "No More Genocide" by Holly Near

Verse 1:
Why do we call them the enemy
This struggling nation that we're bombing 'cross the sea
we put in prison/now independent
Why do we want these people to die
Why do we say North and South
Oh why, Oh why, Oh why?

Chorus
Well, that's just a lie
One of the many and we've had plenty
I don't want more of the same
Genocide in my name
Genocide, no, no, no, no
No more genocide, no, no, no, no
No more genocide in my name.

Verse 2:
Why are our history books so full of lies
When no word is spoken of why the Indian dies
Or that the Chicano loves the California land
Do our books all say it was discovered by white man.

Chorus

Verse 3:
Why are the weapons of the war so young
Why are there only older men around when it's done
Why are so many of our soldiers black or brown
Do we say it's because they're good at cutting yellow people down.

Chorus

Verse 4:
Then came two men from the world of secrecy
They carried some secrets off and shared them with you and me
I read the Pentagon papers seeking truth in their history
But who says that we have been preserving a democracy.

Chorus

CHARACTERS

In order of appearance

MARK, an ex-marine, Viet Nam veteran, husband, artist, lover, father, 28 years old
CHERYL, his wife, mother of his children, also 28
NADINE, his friend, artist, mother of three, divorcee, a woman with many jobs and many lives, 43

TIME

The present

PLACE

The setting is a long table with ashtrays, water glasses, Mark's pictures and slides upon it. Behind it is a large screen for slide projection. The look is of a conference room or perhaps a trial room.

The director may also choose to place each character in a separate area, i.e. Cheryl in her living room (couch), Mark in his studio (framing table), Nadine at home or at a cafe table.

THE PLAY

STILL LIFE

ACT I

I

MARK   *(Snaps on slide of* CHERYL: *young, fragile, thin, hair flowing, quintessentially innocent)* This is a picture of my wife before.

Lights up on CHERYL. *Six months pregnant, heavy, rigid.*

MARK   *(Continued)* This is her now.

She's been through a lot. *(Snaps on photographic portrait of himself. Face gentle. Halo of light around head)* This is a portrait Nadine made of me.

> *Lights up on* NADINE.

MARK   *(Continued)* This is Nadine.

> *Lights out on* NADINE. *Snaps on slide of marine boot and leg just below the knee.*

MARK   *(Continued)* This is a picture of my foot.
  I wanted a picture of it because if I ever lost it,
  I wanted to remember what it looked like. (HE *laughs)*

> *Fade out.*

II

CHERYL   If I though about this too much I'd go crazy.
  So I don't think about it much.
  I'm not too good with the past.
  Now, Mark, he remembers.
  That's his problem.
  I don't know whether it's 1972 or 1981.
  Sometimes I think about divorce.
  God, I don't know.
  Divorce means a lot of nasty things
  like it's over.
  It says a lot like
  Oh yeah. I been there. I'm a divorcee . . . Geez.
  You could go on forever about that thing.

I gave up on it.
You know, I wasn't willing to give up on it,
and I should have,
for my own damn good.

You look:
It's all over now,
it's everywhere.
There are so many men like him now.

You don't have to look far to see how
sucked in you can get.

You got a fifty-fifty chance.

III

NADINE   When I first met Mark, it was the big stuff.
Loss of ego, we shared everything.

The first two hours I spent with him and what I thought
then is what I think now, and I know just about everything
there is to know, possibly.

He told me about it *all* the first week I met him.
We were discussing alcoholism.
I'm very close to that myself.
He said that one of his major projects
was to face all the relationships he'd been in
where he'd violated someone.
His wife is one.

He's so honest he doesn't hide anything.

He told me he beat her very badly.
He doesn't know if he can recover that relationship.

I've met his wife.
I don't know her.
I sometimes even forget . . .

He's the greatest man I've ever known.
I'm still watching him.

We're racing. It's very wild.
No one's gaming.
There are no expectations.
You have a foundation for a lifelong relationship.
He can't disappoint me.

Men have been wonderful to me,
but I've never been treated like this.
All these—yes, all these men—
businessmen, politicians, artists, patriarchs—none of
them, no one has ever demonstrated this to me.

He's beyond consideration.
I have him under a microscope.
I can't be fooled.
I know what natural means.
I know when somebody's studying.
I've been around a long time.
I'm forty-three years old.
I'm not used to being treated like this.

I don't know. I'm being honored, cherished, cared about.

Maybe this is how everybody's treated and I've missed out. *(Laughs)*

IV

MARK   My biggest question to myself all my life was

How I would act under combat?
That would be who I was as a man.

I read my Hemingway.
You know . . .

The point is,
you don't *need* to go through it.

I would break both my son's legs
before I let him go through it.

CHERYL   I'm telling you—
if I thought about this, I'd go crazy.
So I don't think about it.

MARK   *(To* CHERYL) I know I did things to you, Cheryl.
But you took it.
I'm sorry.
How many times can I say I'm sorry to you? *(To audience)* I've, uh,
I've, uh, hurt my wife.

NADINE   He is incredibly gentle. It's madness to be treated this way. I
don't need it. It's great without it.

CHERYL   He blames it all on the war . . . but I want to tell you . . . don't
let him.

MARK   My wife has come close to death a number of times, but
uh . . .

NADINE   Maybe he's in awe of me.

CHERYL   See, I read into things,
and I don't know if you're supposed to, but I do.
Maybe I'm too against his artist world,
but Mark just gets into trouble
when he's into that art world.

NADINE   *(Laughing)* Maybe he's this way to his mother.

CHERYL   One day I went into the basement
to take my clothes out of the washer,
Jesus I have to clean out that basement, and I came across this
jar . . .

NADINE   Especially from a guy who's done all these dastardly deeds.

CHERYL   He had a naked picture of me in there,

cut out to the form,
tied to a stake with a string.
And there was all this broken glass,
and I know Mark.
Broken glass is a symbol of fire. *(Thinking)* What else did he have at
the bottom?

NADINE   I accept everything he's done.

CHERYL   Yeah, there was a razor blade in there
and some old negatives of the blood stuff, I think.
I mean, that was so violent.
That jar to me, scared me.
That jar to me said:
Mark wants to kill me.
Literally kill me for what I've done.
He's burning me at the stake like Joan of Arc.
It just blew my mind.

NADINE   Those jars he makes are brilliant, humorous.
He's preserving the war.
I'm intrigued that people think he's violent.
I know all his stories.
He calls himself a time-bomb.
But so are you, aren't you?

MARK   I don't know what it would be for women.
What war is for men.
I've thought about it. A lot.
I saw women brutalized in the war.
I look at what I've done to my wife.

CHERYL   He keeps telling me: He's a murderer.
I gotta believe he can be a husband.

MARK   The truth of it is, it's different
from what we've heard about war before.

NADINE   He's just more angry than any of us.
He's been fighting for years.
Fighting the priests, fighting all of them.

MARK   I don't want this to come off as a combat story.

CHERYL   Well, a lot of things happened that I couldn't handle.

MARK   It's a tragedy is what it is. It happened to a lot of people.

CHERYL   But not too, you know, not anything
dangerous or anything like that—
just crazy things.

NADINE   I guess all my friends are angry.

CHERYL   But, uh, I don't know.

It's really hard for me to bring back those years.

NADINE   Mark's just been demonstrating it, by picking up weapons,
leading a group of men.

CHERYL   Really hard for me to bring back those years.

MARK   My brother . . .
He has a whole bunch of doubts now,
thinking, "Well I wonder what I'd do
if I were in a fight."
And you don't NEED to go through that shit.
It's BULLSHIT.
It just chews people up.

NADINE   Leading a whole group into group sex, vandalism, theft.
That's not uncommon in our culture.

MARK   You go into a VFW hall, that's all men talk about.
Their trips on the war.

NADINE   I don't know anyone who cares so much about his parents.
He's trying to save them.
Like he sent home this bone of a man he killed, from Nam.
It was this neat attempt to demand for them to listen,
about the war.

MARK   I can't talk to these guys.
There's just no communication.
But we just . . . know.
We look and we know.

NADINE   See, he's testing everyone all the time.
In very subtle ways.
He can't believe I'm not shocked.
I think that intrigues him.

CHERYL   Oh. I don't know.
I want it suppressed as fast as possible.

NADINE   He laughed at me once.
He'd just told a whole raft of stories.
He said: "Anyone who understands all this naughtiness
must have been pretty naughty themselves."
Which is a pretty simplistic way of saying we can all do it.

MARK   I thought:
If I gave *you* the information,
I couldn't wash my hands of the guilt,
because I did things over there.
We all did.

CHERYL   I would do anything to help suppress it.

MARK   *(Quietly to audience)* We all did.

V

NADINE   You know what war is for women?
  A friend of mine sent me this line:
  I'd rather go into battle three times than give birth once.
  She said Medea said that.
  I stuck it on my refrigerator.
  I showed it to Mark. He laughed for days.
MARK   When Cheryl, uh, my wife and I first met,
  I'd just come back from Nam.
  I was so frightened of her.
  She had this long hair and she was really thin.
  I just thought she was really, uh,
  really American.
NADINE   Do you know I never talked with my husband
  about being pregnant?
  For nine months there was something going on down there and we
  never mentioned it. Ever.
MARK   You know, it was like I couldn't talk to her.
  I didn't know how to respond.
NADINE   We completely ignored it.
  We were obsessed with names.
  We kept talking constantly about what we would name it.
  I gained fifty pounds. It was sheer ignorance.
  I was a good Catholic girl
  and no one talked about such things.
  I never knew what that part of my body was doing.
CHERYL   It was my naivety.
  I was so naive to the whole thing, that his craziness
  had anything to do with where he'd been.
  I mean, I was naive to the whole world
  let alone somebody
  who had just come back from there.
NADINE   When the labor started, we merrily got in the car
  and went to the hospital.
  They put me immediately into an operating room.
  I didn't even know what dilation meant.
  And I couldn't.
  I could not dilate.
CHERYL   See, I'd hear a lot from his family.
  I worked for his father as a dental assistant.

CHERYL   *(Continued)* And it was all they talked about—Mark—so I had
to meet the guy.

NADINE   I was in agony, they knocked me out.

CHERYL   And I saw, I mean, I'd open a drawer and I'd see these pictures—

NADINE   My lungs filled up with fluid.

CHERYL   . . . dead men. Men hanging. Things like that.
Pictures Mark had sent back.

MARK   Yeah. I kept sending everything back.

NADINE   They had to give me a tracheotomy.
My trachea was too small.
They went running out of the operating room to get
the right equipment.
Everyone thought I was going to die.

CHERYL   Once he sent back a bone of a man he killed. To his mother.

MARK   To my brother, not my mother.

CHERYL   Boy, did that lady freak.

NADINE   My husband saw them burst out of the room in a panic.
He thought I was gone.

CHERYL   Now it doesn't take much for that lady to freak.
Very hyper. I think I'd've gone nuts.
I think I'd wanna take it
and hit him over the head with it.
You just don't do those things.
WHAT THE HECK IS HAPPENING TO YOU? I'd say.
They never asked that though.
I don't think they wanted to know
and I think they were afraid to ask.

MARK   I know. I really wanted them to ask.

CHERYL   I think they felt the sooner forgotten, the better off you'd be.

NADINE   I remember leaving my body.

MARK   I'll never forget that.

CHERYL   They didn't want to bring up a bad subject.

MARK   I came home from a war, walked in the door,
they don't say anything.
I asked for a cup of coffee,
and my mother starts bitching at me about drinking coffee.

NADINE   I looked down at myself on that operating table and felt so
free.

CHERYL   Your mother couldn't deal with it.

NADINE   They gave me a C-section.
I don't remember anything else.

CHERYL   My memory's not as good as his.
  It's like I put bad things in one half
  and in time I erase them.
NADINE   I woke up in the hospital room with tubes in my throat,
  stitches in my belly. I could barely breathe.
  My husband was there. He said: Have you seen the baby?
  WHAT BABY, I said.

  Can you believe it?
CHERYL   That's why I say there's a lot of things, weird things,
  that happened to us, and I just generally put them
  under the title of weird things . . .
  and try to forget it.
  And to be specific, I'm real vague on a lot of things.
NADINE   I never knew they were in there
  and so I guess I didn't want them to come out.
CHERYL   I mean, my whole life has turned around since then.
  I mean, gosh, I got a kid and another one on the way.
  And I'm thinking of climbing the social ladder.
  I've got to start thinking about schools for them,
  and I *mean* this, it's a completely
  different life,
  and I've had to . . .
  I've WANTED to change anyway.

  It's really hard to bring these things back out.
NADINE   For my second child, the same thing happened.
  By the third time around
  they had to drag me out of the car.
  I thought they were taking me to my death for sure.
MARK   Cheryl is amazing.
  Cheryl has always been like chief surgeon.
  When the shrapnel came out of my head,
  she would be the one to take it out.
CHERYL   It's no big deal.
NADINE   So when people ask me about the birth of my children,
  I laugh.
MARK   Just like with Danny.
  She delivered Danny herself.
NADINE   My children were EXTRACTED from me.
CHERYL   It's no big deal. Just like pulling teeth.
  Once the head comes out, there's nothing to it.

VI

MARK   I want to tell you what a marine is.
                    (Alternate)

NADINE   I have so much to do.
Just to keep going.

Just to keep my kids going.

I don't sleep at all.

When my kids complain
about supper.

I just say:
I know it's crappy food.
Well, go upstairs
and throw it up.

I was in a cafe today.

I heard the funniest comment:

She must be married.
She spends so much money.

CHERYL   See, I got kids now.

I can't be looking into myself.

I've got to be looking *out.*

For the next five years at least.

When I'm ready to look in,
look out.

God, don't get into the kid rou-
tine. It'll do it to you every
time.

Because you're getting *their*
best interests mixed up with
your best interests. And they
don't go together.

They go together because it
should be your best interest,
and *then their* best interest. So
what are you gonna do to them
in the meantime?

You're talking head-trips.

VII

MARK   There was this whole trip that we were really special.
  And our training was really hard,
  like this whole Spartan attitude.
CHERYL   The war is the base of all our problems.
  He gets crazy talking about it
  and you can't get him to stop
  no matter what he's doing to the people around him.
MARK   And there was this whole thing too,
  I told Nadine about that really knocked me out.
  There was this whole ethic;
  You do not leave your man behind on the field.
  I love that.
CHERYL   Well, he's usually talking more than they can handle.
NADINE   You know, we had two months of foreplay.
MARK   I came to a point in there:
  Okay, you're here, there's no escape, you're going to get taken,
  it's all right to commit suicide.
  And it was as rational as that.

  We came across a hit at night, we got ambushed,
  it was a black guy walking point, and you know,
  bang, bang, bang.
  You walk into it. It was a surprise.

  Well, they got this black guy.
  And they took his body and we found him about a week later.
CHERYL   People start getting really uncomfortable,
  and you can see it in his eyes,
  the excitement.
NADINE   The first time I met Mark,
  I'd gone to his shop to buy supplies.
  I didn't think anything about him at first.
  (I've never been attracted to younger men.)
  But he seemed to know what he was doing.
CHERYL   It's almost like there's fire in his eyes.
MARK   And they had him tied to a palm tree,
  and his balls were in his mouth.
  They'd opened up his stomach and it had been pulled out.
  And I knew . . .
NADINE   I saw some of his work.

MARK   Nobody was going to do that to me.

NADINE   Some of the blood photography I think.

MARK   Better for me to rationalize suicide
  because I didn't want . . .
  that.
  I don't know.

CHERYL   It bothers me because it's better left forgotten.
  It's just stirring up clear water.

NADINE   We talked and I left. But I felt strange.

MARK   R.J. was my best friend over there.
  He and I got into a whole weird trip.
  We found ourselves competing against one another,
  setting up ambushes,
  getting people on *kills* and things,
  being the best at it we could.

NADINE   All of a sudden, he came out of the shop and said:
  "You want a cup of tea?"

  I was in a hurry,
  (I'm always in a hurry)
  but I said, "sure," and we went to a tea shop. *(Laughs)*

MARK   R.J. is dead.
  He got killed in a bank robbery in Chicago.
  (He was one of the few friends of mine who survived the war.)

NADINE   Two hours later, we got up from the table.
  I'm telling you, neither of us could stand up.
  We were gasping for breath.

MARK   See, I got all these people involved
  in a Far East smuggling scam when we got back,
  and then it all fell apart
  and we were waiting to get arrested.

  The smack got stashed in this car that was being held
  in a custody lot.
  Everyone was afraid to go get it.
  So I decided to get it.
  I did this whole trip Thanksgiving weekend.
  I crawled in there,
  stole the tires off the car
  that were loaded with the smack.
  I had R.J. help me.
  We were doing the war all over again.

That was the last time I saw him alive.

NADINE   We had said it *all* in two hours.
  What I thought then is what I think now
  and I think I know everything there is to know.

  We must have looked pretty funny staggering out of there.

MARK   I hear from another guy on a regular basis, maybe once a year.
  He was green to Viet Nam.
  We were getting into
  some real heavy contact that Christmas.
  It was late at night, the VC went to us
  while we were sleeping.
  They just threw grenades in on us.
  The explosion came, I threw this kid in a bush.
  All I did was grab him down,
  and he got a medical out of there.
  But he feels I saved his life.

NADINE   When we got out onto the street we said good-bye
  but we both knew that our whole lives had changed.

CHERYL   I know he has other women. I don't know who they are.
  At this point I don't really care.
  I have a child to think about
  and just getting by every day.

NADINE   We used to meet and talk.
  We'd meet in the plaza and talk.
  We'd go for rides in the car and talk.

CHERYL   See, lots of times people break up.
  And then the man goes on to the next one.
  And you hear the guy say:
  "Oh, my wife was crazy"; or something like that.
  "She couldn't take it."

NADINE   Sometimes we'd be driving,
  we'd have to stop the car and get our breaths.
  We were dizzy, we were gasping for breath,
  just from being together.

CHERYL   But the important question to ask is: WHY is she crazy?

MARK   So he wants to see me.
  I haven't been able to see him.

CHERYL   My brother is a prime example.
  He nearly killed his wife a number of times.
  She was a real high-strung person.
  She snapped.

The family keeps saying, oh, poor Marge, she was so crazy.
MARK   He was only in the bush maybe five, six weeks,
  but it did something to him.
He spent two years, he wrote me a letter,
in a mental institution.
I don't know.

I knew he knew what I knew.
CHERYL   My brother's now got one little girl
  that SAW her little brother
get shot in the head by his mother . . .
MARK   I know who's been there.
  And they know.
CHERYL   And then saw her mother come after her.
MARK   But in a sense we want to be as far away
  from each other as possible.
It's become a *personal* thing. The guilt.
There IS the guilt.
It's getting off on having all that power every day.
Because it was so nice.
I mean, it was power . . .
NADINE   You know they're doing surveys now, medical research on
  this.
MARK   I had the power of life and death.
NADINE   They think something actually changes
  in the blood or the lungs when you feel this way.
CHERYL   I'm sorry. They were married too long
  for it just to have been Marge.
MARK   I'm sitting here now deep down thinking about it . . .
NADINE   You watch. Soon there'll be a science of love, and there should
  be.
CHERYL   When someone goes so-called crazy in a marriage,
  I always think:
IT TAKES TWO.
MARK   It's like the best dope you've ever had, the best sex you've ever
  had.
NADINE   It was like dying,
  and it was the most beautiful feeling of my life.
CHERYL   My brother's on to a new woman now.
MARK   You never find anything better.
  And that's not something
you're supposed to feel good about.

CHERYL   If Mark and I split up, I pity the next one.
MARK   I haven't told you what a Marine is yet.
CHERYL   Women should warn each other. *(Pause)*
NADINE   Everything Mark did was justified.
  We've all done it.
  Murdered someone we loved, or ourselves.
MARK   I mean, we were trained to do one thing.
  That's the one thing about the Marines.
  We were trained to kill.
NADINE   This is hard to say.
  I have been in the jungle so long,
  that even with intimates, I protect myself.
  But I know that Mark felt good killing.
  When he told me that I didn't bat an eye.
  I understand.
CHERYL   Look,
  I think Mark and R.J. were close
  only because they both got off on the war.
  And I think they were the only two over there that did.
  Doesn't it kill you when they get into this men-talk?
  All men don't talk like that,
  when they get together to reminisce.
  They don't talk about getting laid and dope.
  Imagine getting together with your best girlfriend
  and talking about what it was like the night before in the sack.
  That grosses me out.
NADINE   I judge everyone so harshly
  that it is pretty ironic
  that I'm not moved by anything he tells me.
  I'm not changed. I'm not shocked.
  I'm not offended. And he must see that.
MARK   I had the power of life and death.
  I wrote home to my brother.
  I wrote him, I told him.
  I wrote:
  I dug it. I enjoyed it.
  I really enjoyed it.
NADINE   I understand because I'm *convinced*
  that I am even angrier than Mark.
  I went off in a different direction, that's all.
CHERYL   Now I don't think Mark and R.J. were rare.
  I think the DEGREE is rare.

I mean men would not be going on fighting like this
for centuries if there wasn't something besides
having to do it for their country.
It has to be something like Mark says.
I mean he said it was like orgasm.
He said it was the best sex he ever had.
You know where he can take that remark.
But what better explanation can you want?
And believe me, that is Mark's definition of glory.
Orgasm is GLORY to Mark.

MARK   I talked with R.J. about it.
He got into a hit once at about 8:30 at night.
And there was this "person" . . .
laying down, wounded,
holding onto a grenade.
(It was a high contact.)
We watched R.J. walk over and he just shot . . .
the person . . .
in the face.

He knew it.

As incredibly civilized as we are in this room, these things go on.

NADINE   Until you know a lot of Catholics
you can't understand what hate means.
I mean I'm a . . . I was a Catholic.
And Catholics have every right to hate like they do.
It requires a whole lifetime
to undo what that training does to them.

MARK   It's getting hard to talk.
Obviously, I need to tell it,
but I don't want to be seen as . . .
a monster.

NADINE   Just start talking to Catholics
who allow themselves to talk.
It's unspeakable what's been done to Catholic youths.
Every aspect of their life from their table manners
to their sexuality. It's just terrible.

MARK   I'm just moving through society now. *(Pause)*

VIII

NADINE   I mean my definition of sophistication
   is the inability to be surprised by anything.
MARK   I look at my face in a mirror,
   I look at my hand, and I cannot believe . . .
   I did these things.
CHERYL   Mark's hit me before.
MARK   See, I see the war now through my wife.
   She's a casualty too.
   She just doesn't get benefits for combat duties.
   The war busted me up, I busted up my wife . . .
CHERYL   He's hit me more than once.
MARK   I mean I've hit my wife.
NADINE   Have you ever been drunk for a long period of time?
MARK   But I was always drunk.
NADINE   Well, I have.
MARK   We were always drunk.
   It would boil out,
   the anger,
   when we were drunk.
NADINE   I used to drink a lot
   and did vicious things when I was drunk.
   And until you're there,
   you don't *know.*
MARK   When I was sober, I found out what I'd done to her.
   It was . . . I just couldn't stop.
CHERYL   I was really into speed—oh, how many years ago?
   I'm not good with the past.
   I mean Mark knows dates and years.
   God I don't know.
MARK   It's like . . .
   I feel terrible about it.
   The last time it happened
   it was about a year ago now.
   I made up my mind to quit drinking
   because drinking's what's brought it on.
CHERYL   We got into some kind of argument about speed.
   And he pushed me down the stairs.
   He hit me a couple of times.
NADINE   Yeah it's there and it takes years.
   My husband and I were

grooving on our fights.
I mean really creative.
And five years ago we got down to the count.
Where we were batting each other around.
Okay, I hit my husband. A lot.
See I'm capable of it.

MARK   I dropped out of AA.
I put the cork in the bottle myself.

NADINE   Okay—I was really drunk, really mad.
And I beat him up and do you know what he said to me?
He turned to me after he took it and he said:
I didn't know you cared that much.
It was the most incredible thing.
And he stood there and held his face
and took it
and turned around in a state of glory and said:
I didn't think you cared.
I'll never hit another person again.

CHERYL   I went to the hospital
cause my ribs . . .
I think, I don't know.
I don't remember it real clearly.
It had something to do with speed.
The fact that I wasn't, I was,
I wasn't rational.
No, I must have really tore into him.
I mean I can be nasty.
So anyway that was hard because I couldn't go to work
for a couple of weeks.

NADINE   And I see Mark.
The fact that he beat his wife.
I understand it.
I don't like it.
But I understand it.

MARK   I've been sober so long now, it's terrifying.
See, I really got into photography while I was drunk.
Got involved in the art program at the U.
I mean I could be fine
and then the wrong thing would come up
and it would shut me off.

NADINE   Don't distance yourself from Mark.

MARK   I'd space out and start talking about the war.

See, most of these people
didn't have to deal with it.
They all dealt with the other side.

NADINE   I was "anti-war," I marched, I was "non-violent." *(Laughs)*

MARK   I brought some photos.
This is a picture of some people who at one point in time
were in my unit. That is,
they were there at the time the photo was taken.
Some of them are dead, some of them made it home, *(Pause)* some of
them are dead now.

NADINE   But I'm capable of it.

MARK   After I was there, I could never move with people
who were against the war in a real way.
It took a part of our life.
I knew what it was and they didn't.

NADINE   We all are.

MARK   They could get as pissed off as they wanted to
I didn't fight with them.
I didn't bitch with them.
I just shut up. Excuse me.

Looks at audience. Sees or thinks HE *sees they're on the other
side. Moment of murderous anger.* MARK *shuts up and exits.*

IX

CHERYL   I'm scared knowing that I have to keep my mouth shut.
I don't know this for a fact, but I mean
I fantasize a lot.
I have to.
I've got nothing else to do.
See, I've got no real line of communication at all, on

this issue. If I ever told him I was scared for my life,
he'd freak out. If I ever said anything like that, how
would he react? Would he get angry?
What do you think? Do I want to take that chance?

I got too much to lose.
Before, you know, when we were just single together,
I had nothing to lose. I have a little boy up there.
And if I ever caught Mark hurting me
or that little boy again, I'd kill him.
And I don't wanna be up for manslaughter.

Danny means more to me than Mark does.
Only because of what Mark does to me.
He doesn't realize it maybe, but he squelches me.

God, I'm scared.
I don't wanna be alone for the rest of my life
with two kids. And I can't rob my children of what
little father they could have.
NADINE   I've always understood
how people could hurt each other
with weapons.

If you've been hurt to the quick,
and a weapon's around, WHAP.

I signed my divorce papers because
last time he came over, I knew if
there'd been a gun around, I'd've
killed him.

MARK *reenters.*

X

MARK   I'm sorry.
   I don't think you understand.

   Sure, I was pissed off at myself that I let myself go.
   Deep down inside I knew I could have stopped it.

   I could just have said:
   I won't do it.
   Go back in the rear, just not go out,
   let them put me in jail. I could have said:
   "I got a toothache," gotten out of it.
   They couldn't have forced me.
   But it was this duty thing.
   It was like:
   YOU'RE UNDER ORDERS.
   You have your orders, you have your job,
   you've got to DO it.

   Well, it was like crazy.
   At night, you could do anything . . .
   It was free fire zones. It was dark, then
   all of a sudden, everything would just burn loose.
   It was beautiful . . . You were given all this power to work outside the
   law.
   We all dug it.

   But I don't make any excuses for it.
   I may even be trying to do that now.
   I could have got out.
   Everybody could've.
   If EVERYBODY had said *no,*
   it couldn't have happened.
   There were times we'd say:
   Let's pack up and go, let's quit.
   But jokingly.
   We knew we were there.
   But I think I knew then
   we could have got out of it.
NADINE   Oh,
   I'm worried about men.

MARK   See, there was a point, definitely, when I was
  genuinely interested in trying to win the war.
  It was my own area.
  I wanted to do the best I could.
  I mean I could have played it really low-key.
  I could have avoided things, I could have made sure
  we didn't move where we could have contacts.
NADINE   I worry about them a lot.
MARK   And I watched the younger guys.
  Maybe for six weeks there was nothing.
  He'd drift in space wondering what he'd do under fire.
  It only takes once.
  That's all it takes . . .
  and then you dig it.
NADINE   Men are stripped.
MARK   It's shooting fireworks off, the Fourth of July.
NADINE   We took away all their toys . . . their armor.

  When I was younger, I'd see a man in uniform
  and I'd think:
  what a hunk.
  Something would thrill in me.
  Now we look at a man in uniform—
  a Green Beret, a Marine—
  and we're embarrassed somehow.
  We don't know who they are anymore.
  What's a man? Where's the model?

  All they had left was being Provider.
  And now with the economics, they're losing it all.
  My father is a farmer.
  This year, my mother learned to plow.
  I talked to my father on the phone the other night and I said:
  Hey, Dad, I hear Mom's learning how to plow.
  Well, sure, he said.
  She's been a farmer's wife for forty, fifty years.
  Yes. But she's just learning to plow now.
  And there was a silence
  and then he said:
  That's a feminist issue I'd rather not discuss
  at the moment.

So. We don't want them to be the Provider,
because we want to do that ourselves.
We don't want them to be heroes,
and we don't want them to be knights in shining armor, John Wayne—
so what's left for them to be, huh?

Oh, I'm worried about men.
They're not coming through.
(My husband)
How could I have ever gotten married?
They were programmed to fuck,
now they have to make love.
And they can't do it.
It all comes down to fucking versus loving.

We don't like them in the old way anymore.
And I don't think they like us, much.
Now that's a war, huh?

ACT II

I

MARK   This is the photo I showed you.
   Of some guys in my unit.

   We were south-southwest of Danang—
   we were in that whole triangle, not too far
   from where My Lai was.
   Near the mountains, near the coast.

   Everybody knew about My Lai.
   But it wasn't different from what was going on.
   I mean, the grunts did it all the time.

   This fellow up there, that's Michele.
   He ended up in the nuthouse,
   that's the fellow I pulled out of the bush.
   This is the machine gunner.
   The kid was so good
   he handled the gun like spraying paint.
   This kid was from down South.
   Smart kid.
   He got hit in the head, with grenade shrapnel.
   He's alive, but he got rapped in the head.
   That was the end of the war for him.
NADINE   I don't know what it is with Mark.
   I have a lot of charming friends
   that are very quiet, like him—
   but they don't have his power.

CHERYL   You know what Mark's power is:
He's got an imagination that just doesn't quit.
NADINE   It got to be coincidental when we'd been somewhere together
and someone said: You know your friend Mark,
I liked the way he was so quiet.
MARK   There were no two ways about it . . .
CHERYL   He's got an imagination that, that embarrasses me . . .
MARK   People who were into it really got a chance to know.
CHERYL   Because I am conservative.
MARK   You knew that you were killing something.
You actually knew it, you saw it, you had the body.
You didn't take wounded. That was it.
You just killed them.
And they did the same to you.
NADINE   *(Laughing)* I told him his face is a dangerous weapon.
He ought to be real responsible with it.
CHERYL   All his jars . . .
NADINE   I think we'd only known each other for a week and I said:
You should really have a license for that face.
MARK   (That's my friend, that's R.J.)
My friend R.J. used to carry a machete.
I don't know why he never did it.
But he always wanted to cut somebody's head off.
NADINE   You know why they went crazy out there?
It's that totally negative religion.
It makes you fit to kill.
Those commandments . . .
MARK   He wanted to put it on a stick and put it in a village.
NADINE   Every one of them
"thou shalt not."
MARK   It was an abuse of the dead.
We got very sacred about taking the dead.
NADINE   Take an infant and start him out on the whole world with
THOU SHALT NOT . . .
and you're perpetually in a state of guilt
or a state of revolt.
MARK   There's a whole Buddhist ceremony.
R.J., everybody—got pissed off.
He wanted to let them know.
CHERYL   But he's got an imagination . . .
MARK   I never saw our guys rape women. I heard about it.
CHERYL   And it's usually sexually orientated somehow.

MARK   But you never took prisoners, so you'd have to get
  involved with them while they were dying
  or you'd wait until they were dead.
CHERYL   Everything Mark does is sexually orientated.
MARK   The Vietnamese got into that.
  There was this one instance I told you about
  where R.J. shot the person in the face . . .
  it was a woman.
CHERYL   I don't know why we got together.
MARK   The Vietnamese carried that body back.
  It took them all night long to work that body over.
CHERYL   When I think back on it, he was weird, off the war.
MARK   It was their spoils.
  They could do what they wanted.
NADINE   So you send these guys out there
  all their lives they've been listening
  to nuns and priests
  and they start learning to kill.
MARK   *(Snaps on picture of him with medal. Full dress)* This is a picture
  of my first Purple Heart.
NADINE   Sure Mark felt great. I understand that.
  His senses were finally alive.
CHERYL   His Purple Hearts never got to me.
  I was never impressed with the fighting man,
  I don't think.
MARK   A lot of people bullshitted that war
  for a lot of Purple Hearts.
  I heard about a guy who was in the rear
  who went to a whorehouse.
  He got cut up or something like that.
  And he didn't want to pay the woman
  or something like that.
  He ended up with a Purple Heart.
CHERYL   Well, drugs helped, a lot.
  We didn't have much in common.
MARK   I don't know. We were out in the bush.
  To me, a Purple Heart meant it was something you got
  when you got wounded and you bled.
  You were hurt during a contact.
  I didn't feel anything getting it.
  But I wanted a picture of it.
CHERYL   I mean, I've got to get that basement cleaned out.

MARK   Actually, I was pissed off about getting that medal.

CHERYL   My little boy's getting curious.

MARK   There were South Vietnamese who were sent out with us, fought with us.

CHERYL   He goes down and sees some of that crap down there Mark's saved . . .

MARK   They didn't really give a shit.

CHERYL   Never throws anything away.

MARK   If things got too hot you could always
count on them running.
Jackasses.

CHERYL   Mark's a packrat . . .

MARK   *(Holds up a belt)* I'm a packrat. I never throw anything away.
This belt is an artifact.
I took it off of somebody I killed.
It's an NVA belt.
I sent it home. I think it was kind of a trophy.

This is the man's blood.
That's a bullet hole.
This particular fellow had a belt of grenades
that were strapped to his belt.
See where the rust marks are?

CHERYL   Everything he's done,
everything is sexually orientated in some way.
Whether it's nakedness or violence—it's all
sexually orientated.
And I don't know where this comes from.

> MARK *searches for more slides.*

CHERYL   *(Continued)* He can take those slides
and you know where he can put em.
Right up his butt.
I mean he's just,
he'll go down there
and dig up old slides.
I won't do that for him anymore.
I will not,
no way.

MARK   Here's a picture of me . . . *(Snaps on picture of him and some children)*

CHERYL   He asked if he can take pictures of Danny and I . . .
MARK   And some kids. God I LOVED those kids.
CHERYL   I think that's why I'm so against the artist world.
   I just can't handle his work a lot of it.
   It's because he's done that to me.
MARK   Everybody hated them.
   You couldn't trust em.

   The VC would send the kids in with a flag.
   I never saw this, I heard about it,
   the kid would come in asking for C-rations,
   try to be your friend, and they'd be maybe wired
   with explosives or something
   and the kid'd blow up.
   There was a whole lot of weirdness . . .
CHERYL   Mark's got this series of blood photographs.
   He made me pose for them.
   There's a kitchen knife sticking into me,
   but all you can see is reddish-purplish blood.
   It's about five feet high.
   He had it hanging in the shop! In the street!
   Boy, did I make him take it out of there.
MARK   I really dug kids. I don't know why. *(More pictures of kids)* I
   did a really bad number . . .
   It went contrary, I think,
   to everything I knew.
   I'm not ready to talk about that yet.
CHERYL   You just don't show people those things.
MARK   These are some pictures of more or less dead bodies and things.
   *(Snaps on pictures of mass graves, people half blown apart, gruesome
   pictures of this particular war)* I don't know if you want to see them.
   *(Five slides. Last picture comes on of a man, eyes towards us, the bones
   of his arm exposed, the flesh torn, eaten away. It is too horrible to look
   at.* MARK *looks at the audience, or hears them)* Oh, Jesus.
   Yeah . . .
   We have to be patient with each other. (HE *snaps the pictures off)*
CHERYL   You know. I don't think . . .
MARK   You know, I get panicky
   if there's any element of control taken away from me.
   (I don't like to be alone in the dark.
   I'm scared of it. I'm not armed.)

I don't like fireworks.
If I can control them fine.
I don't like them when I can't control them.

I've had bad dreams
when my wife's had to bring me back out.
Nothing like jumping her, though.
I've heard about vets killing their wives in their sleep.
But this is personal—for me,
the gun was always the instrument, or a grenade.
I never grabbed somebody and slowly killed them.
I've never choked them to death or anything.
I've never beaten anybody up, well . . .

I never killed
with my bare hands.

   Pause.

II

CHERYL   You know, I don't think that
   men ever really protected women
   other than war time.
NADINE   Listen, nobody can do it for you.
   Now maybe if I weren't cunning and conniving and
   manipulative and courageous, maybe I wouldn't be able
   to say that.
MARK   It's still an instinctive reaction to hit the ground.
NADINE   I'll do anything as the times change to protect my stake in life.
CHERYL   And war's the only time man really goes out and protects
   woman.

MARK   You know—when I got back, I said I'd never work again.

That's what I said constantly, that I'd never work again, for anyone.

NADINE   I have skills now.

I remember when I didn't have them.

I was still pretty mad, but I wasn't ready.

MARK   I was MAD.

I figured I was *owed* a living.

NADINE   I'm stepping out now, right?

CHERYL   I know my mother protected my father all through his
life. Held things from him, only because she knew it would hurt him.

MARK   And then I got in a position where I couldn't work because
after I got busted and went to prison, no one would hire me.

I did the whole drug thing from a real
thought-out point of view.

I was really highly decorated, awards,

I was wounded twice.

I really looked good.

CHERYL   That's where I get this blurting out when I'm drunk.

Because I'm like my mother—

That's the only time my mother would really let my
father know what's going on in this house.

(When he's not around seven days a week is when she's had a couple.)

Otherwise she was protecting him all the time.

Excuse me. I'm going to get another drink. (CHERYL *exits Off*)

MARK   I knew I could get away with a lot.

I knew I could probably walk down the streets
and kill somebody and I'd probably get off.

Simply because of the war.

I was convinced of it.

NADINE   I could have ended my relationship
with my husband years ago.

I sometimes wonder why I didn't.

And I don't want to think it was because of the support.

MARK   I thought about killing people when I got back.

NADINE   I've been pulling my own weight
for about eight years now.

Prior to that, I was doing a tremendous amount of work ·
that in our society is not measurable.

CHERYL   *(Angry. Reenters)* My house is not my home.

It's not mine.

NADINE   I kept a house.

I raised my children.

CHERYL   Now, if it were mine I'd be busy at work.

NADINE   I was a model mother.

CHERYL   I'd be painting the walls,
I would be wall-papering the bedroom.
I would be making improvements.
I would be . . . linoleum the floor.
I can't do it.
Because it's not mine.

MARK   I thought of killing people when I got back.
I went to a party with a lady, Cheryl, you know,
later we got married—
She was into seeing people who were into LSD.
And I had tried a little acid this night,
but I wasn't too fucked-up.
And we went to this party.

NADINE   I tried to explain to Mark that Cheryl may not
always want from him what she wants right now:
looking for him to provide, looking for status.

CHERYL   And Mark will never be ready to have the responsibility
of his own home. Never. Never.

MARK   And there was this big guy.
I was with a friend of mine who tried to rip him off,
or something like that.
He said, the big guy said:
Get the fuck out of here
or I'll take this fucking baseball bat
and split your head wide open.

CHERYL   And I'm being stupid to ever want it from Mark.

MARK   I started to size up what my options were . . .

NADINE   *(Shaking her head)* Looking for him to provide, looking for
status.

MARK   In a split second, I knew I could have him.
He had a baseball bat,
but there was one of these long glass coke bottles.
I knew . . . Okay, I grabbed that.
I moved toward him, to stick it in his face.
I mean, I killed him.
I mean in my mind.
I cut his throat and everything.

CHERYL   Because your own home means upkeep.
Means, if there's a drip in the ceiling

you gotta come home and take care of it.

NADINE   But between us, I can't understand why a woman her age,
an intelligent woman,
who's lived through the sixties and the seventies,
who's living now in a society where women have finally been given
permission
to drive and progress and do what they're entitled to do
. . . I mean, how can she think that way?

MARK   My wife saw this and grabbed me.
I couldn't talk to anybody the rest of the night.
I sat and retained the tension and said:
"I want to kill him."
They had to drive me home.
It was only the third time I'd been out with my wife.

CHERYL   That fucking dog in the backyard
—excuse my French—
That dog is so bad. I mean,
there are cow-pies like this out there. *(Demonstrates size)* And when
I was three months pregnant and alone here—
when Mark and I—
when I finally got Mark to get out of here—
I came back to live
because I just could not go on living at my girlfriend's,
eating their food and not having any money and
—and I came back here
and I had to clean up that yard.

MARK   It wasn't till the next day that I really got shook by it.
My wife said,
"Hey, cool your jets."
She'd say, "Hey, don't do things like that.
You're not over there anymore.
Settle down, it's alright."

CHERYL   I threw up in that backyard picking up dog piles.
That dog hasn't been bathed since I took her over to
this doggie place and paid twenty dollars
to have her bathed.
And that was six months ago. That dog has flies.

You open the back door
and, you always get one fly from the fricking dog.
She's like garbage. She . . . she . . .

MARK   I think my wife's scared of me.

I really do.
She'd had this really straight upbringing.
Catholic.
Never had much . . . you know.
Her father was an alcoholic and her mother was too.
I came along and offered her
a certain amount of excitement.

CHERYL   My backyard last year was so gorgeous.
I had flowers.
I had tomatoes.
I had a whole area garden.
That creeping vine stuff all over.
I had everything.
This year I could not do it with that dog back there.

MARK   Just after I got back, I took her up to these races.
I had all this camera equipment.
I started running out on the field.
I started photographing these cars zipping by at
ninety miles an hour.

NADINE   What's important to me is my work.
It's important to Mark too.

MARK   She'd just gotten out of high school.
She was just, you know, *at that point.*
She was amazed at how I moved through space.

NADINE   We talk for hours about our work.

MARK   Cuz I didn't take anybody with me.

NADINE   We understand each other's work.

MARK   I moved down everybody's throats verbally.
First of all it was a physical thing.
I was loud.
Then I'd do these trips to out-think people.

NADINE   His jars are amazingly original. Artifacts of the war.
Very honest.

MARK   I'd do these trips.

NADINE   You should see the portrait Mark did of himself.

MARK   I had a lot of power, drugs,
I was manipulating large sums of money.

NADINE   He has a halo around his head. *(Laughs)*

MARK   She became a real fan.

NADINE   And the face of a devil.

CHERYL   That dog grosses me out so bad.
That dog slimes all over the place.

My kid, I don't even let him out in the backyard.
He plays in the front.
That's why his bike's out front.
I'll take the chance of traffic before I'll let him out
to be slimed over by that dog.
NADINE She decided to have that child.
MARK Later on, it got into this whole thing.
We lived together and with this other couple.
NADINE It's madness.
Everyone was against it.
MARK It was a whole . . . I don't know whether I
directed it . . . but it became this *big* . . .
sexual thing . . . between us . . . between them . . .
between groups of other people . . .
It was really a fast kind of thing.
Because no one really gave a shit.
CHERYL Oh, shut up!
NADINE His theory is she's punishing him.
MARK I don't know why I was really into being a stud.
NADINE Now no man has ever been able to lead *me* into sexual abuse.
MARK I wasn't that way before I left, so I don't know. Maybe it was like
I was trying to be like all the other people.
NADINE See, she participated. She had the right to say no.
CHERYL That dog jumps the fence, takes off.
I have to pay twenty dollars
to get her out of the dog pound.
She is costin' me so damn much money that I hate her.
She eats better than we do.
She eats better than we do.
NADINE She must have thought it would be fun.
And wow! That was that whole decade where a whole population of
people that age thought that way.
CHERYL My Danny is getting to the age where there's gotta be food.
I mean he's three years old.
He goes to the freezer he wants ice cream there.
He goes in the icebox there's gotta be pop.
I mean it's not like he's an infant anymore.
NADINE Every foul thing I've ever done,
I'm not uncomfortable about it.
And I don't blame anyone in my life.
CHERLY These things have to be there.
And it's not there.

NADINE   I don't blame anyone.
   I'm sorry, maybe you have to be older
   to be able to look back and say that.
CHERYL   But there's always a bag of dogfood in the place.
   Anyways I run out of dogfood,
   Mark sends me right up to the store.
   But I run out of milk I can always give him Kool-Aid
   for two or three days.
   Yeah—that's the way it is though.
   We haven't been to the grocery store in six months
   for anything over ten dollars worth of groceries
   at a time. There is no money.

III

MARK   You'd really become an animal out there.
   R.J. and I knew what we were doing.

   That's why a lot of other kids really got into trouble.
   They didn't know what they were doing.

   We knew it, we dug it, we knew
   we were very good.

IV

CHERYL   I'd turn off to him.
  Because I knew that it was hard for me to accept—
  you know what he . . . what happened and all that.
  And it was hard for me to live with, and him being
  drunk and *spreading* it around to others. (*To* MARK) How long has it
  been since anything like that happened?
MARK   Well, last July I hurt you.
CHERYL   Yeah, but Danny was what a year and a half so everything was
  pretty . . .
MARK   He was exposed to it.
  My wife, uh, Cheryl, left one night.
CHERYL   Don't.
MARK   She left with, uh, she had a person come over and pick her up
  and take her away.
  I walked in on this.
  I was drunk. Danny was in her arms.
  I attacked this other man and . . .
  I did something to him.
  I don't know.
  What did I do to him?
  Something.
CHERYL   You smashed his car up with a sledge hammer.
MARK   I, uh, Dan saw all that.
CHERYL   He was only six months old though.
MARK   No. Dan I think he knows a lot more than we think.
  He saw me drunk and incapable of walking up the steps.
  Going to the bathroom
  half on the floor and half in the bowl.
  He's a sharp kid.
  Cheryl and I separated this spring.
  And he really knew what was going on.
NADINE   Christ, I hate this country.
  I hate all of it.
  I've never really said it before.
MARK   I come in and apologize when I think about the incidents
  that I've done in the past now that I'm sober,
  and I feel terribly guilty.
  I've exploited Cheryl as a person, sexually . . .
  it wasn't exactly rape, but . . .
CHERYL   I can't deal with *that* at all.

But I find that if I can at least put it out of my mind it's easier.

If I had to think about what he's done to me, I'd
have been gone a long time ago.
NADINE   I have yet to be out of this country, by the way.
   And I'm criticizing it as if I think it's better everywhere else.
MARK   See, I wanted to get back into the society and
   I wanted to live so much life, but I couldn't.
   I was constantly experimenting.
CHERYL   It was awful . . .
   He'd pick fights with people on the streets.
   Just about anyone. It was like a rage.
   He'd just whomp on the guy.
   Not physically but he would become very obstinate,
   very mean and cruel. In bars, handling people . . . *(To* MARK) You have
   to be *nice* to people to have them accept you.
MARK   I don't know.
   I was afraid.
   I thought people were . . . uh . . . I mean
   I was kind of paranoid.
   I thought everybody knew . . .
   I thought everybody knew what I did over there,
   and that they were against me.
   I was scared. I felt guilty and a sense of . . .
CHERYL   I can't talk to you.
NADINE   He's trying to judge himself.
   One time we were together after a
   long period of incredible, sharing times.
   I said: "You're so wonderful."
   And he started to cry.
MARK   *(To* NADINE) I've done terrible things.
NADINE   *(To* MARK) I know. *(Long pause)* Christ, I hate this country.

   I can remember everything
   back to being two years old,
   and all these terrible things they taught us.
   I can't believe we obeyed them *all.*
MARK   *(Very quiet)* I had two cousins who went through Viet Nam.
   One was a truck driver and got through it.
   My other cousin was in the army.
   His unit, about one hundred men were climbing up a hill.
   They were all killed except for him and another guy.

And they were lying there.
The VC were going around putting bullets
into people's heads.
Making sure they were dead.
And he had to lay there wounded faking he was dead.
He and I never talked.
Ever.
Someone else communicated his story to me,
and I know he knows my story.

   Pause.

V

CHERYL   I feel so sorry for Margie, my brother's wife.
   I told you about.
   You wonder why there's so much more lesbianism around now?
   Look at the men!
   You can see where that's turned a lot of women the other way.
NADINE   He possibly is overpowering.
   I don't know. She was proud to be his woman.
   So he said frog, and they all jumped.
   Well, that's terrific.
   It cost him a lot
   to have that power where he abused it.
CHERYL   Christ!
   Mark pushed me into that, once, too.
   We were doing this smack deal in Hong Kong.
   He brought this woman into our room.
   He wanted me to play with her.
   He wanted me to get it on with her, too.
   It just blew my mind.

I mean it just blew me away.
NADINE   I know, I know, I know . . .
   But I see when he talks about his wife,
   I feel encouraged that there are men that can be that way.
   He has never, ever said an unkind word about her.
   God, I mean it's incredibly civilized
   the way he talks about her.
   In fact, had he ever said anything foul about her,
   it would have grated on me.
   Maybe he just knows what I require.
   But I have yet to hear him say
   anything bad about anyone;
   even those terrible people he had to deal with
   in the jungle.
MARK   I saw my cousin at his Dad's funeral last December.
CHERYL   Now it's so complex
   everytime I look . . .
   Oh, God . . . everytime I look
   at a piece of furniture, it reminds
   me of something.
MARK   Wherever we moved,
   we knew where the other was.
   Something radiates between us.
NADINE   I think he's quite superior.
   I really do.
   I think he's got it all figured out.
MARK   Our eyes will meet, but we can't touch.
NADINE   I think he's gonna make it. *(Nervous)* I wonder how you
   perceive him.
MARK   There's no difference between this war and World War II.
   I'm convinced of that.

   Maybe it was different in that it was white man
   against white man. The race thing. *(Admitting)* We referred to them
   as zips, or dinks, or gooks.
   But I don't think I would have had any trouble shooting anything.

   We weren't freaks out there.
   Guys in World War II cracked up, too.

   We're their children.

I would like to play you a song.

Music: "No More Genocide" *by Holly Near.* MARK *turns on tape recorder. Use of music optional here.*

ACT III

I

MARK   *(Snaps on slide of him and R.J.)* This is a picture of me and R.J.
We look like a couple of bad-asses.
It was hot. Shit, I miss him.
We were so close.
We talked about everything.
We talked about how each of us lost our
virginity, we talked about girls.
CHERYL   *(Agitated)* My girlfriend across the street told me
how babies were made when I was ten years old.
I just got sick. I hated it.
MARK   We talked about fights, getting back on the street, drugs.
CHERYL   From that moment on,
I had a model:
I wanted kids . . .
MARK   We talked about getting laid . . .
CHERYL   But I didn't want the husband that went along with it.
I still feel that way.
MARK   We talked about how we would be inseparable
when we came home.
We never would have, even if he hadn't died.
We knew too much about each other.
CHERYL   And this spooks me because I said this
when I was ten years old.
MARK   *(New slide)* This is the place, the Alamo.
That's where the rocket came in and

killed a man . . . uh . . . *(Indicates in the picture)* We got hit one night.
Some several people were sleeping, this fellow . . . *(Picture of him)* A
rocket came in and blew his head off.

NADINE   I said to Mark:
"You're still pissed off because they let you go.
Even assholes stopped their kids from going.
Your good Catholic parents sent you to slaughter."

MARK   It was near dawn.
We moved his body out of there.
We put his body on a rice paddy dike.
I watched him. He was dead and he was
very close to me and I don't know.

NADINE   His parents pushed him into going.
They believed all those terrible cliches.

MARK   I didn't want him to lay in that place where he died.
I didn't want him laying in the mud.
And I think I was talking to him.
I was crying, I don't know.

NADINE   Do you know, to this day his father
will not say the word Viet Nam.

MARK   His dog came out and started . . .
The dog was eating him.
I just came out and fired at the dog.
I got him killed. *(Snaps picture)* Later, I took that picture.

NADINE   But his father talked to everyone but Mark about the war.
He's got his medals on his wall.

MARK   I don't know.
It became a sacred place. It was "the Alamo."
That's what we named it.
I shot the dog because it was desecrating.
The dog was eating our friend . . .
I would have done anything, if I could have,
if I could have kept flies off of him, even.

NADINE   His father's ashamed of himself.
When you let your son go to war
for all the wrong reasons,
you can't face your son.

MARK   *(Crying)* I just wanted him . . .
He coulda gone home the next day.
The war was over for him.
I wanted him to get home. *(Pause)*

II

CHERYL   I want to go home.
  To the church, to my family.
  The sixties are over.
NADINE   The sixties . . .
  You know, a lot of us went through that whole
  decade pretending to ourselves we were pacifists.
MARK   I wanted to get home so bad.
CHERYL   Well, I mean I'm gonna have another kid.
  I'm gonna have to take him to the Cathedral to be
  baptized 'cuz our wedding wasn't blessed.
  It wasn't in a church.
  We had to get married and we had to do it fast.
  In South Dakota.
  In the clothes we'd been in for three days.
NADINE   As if we didn't know what violence was.
MARK   You know, the biggest thing I had to adjust to
  coming home was I didn't have my gun.
CHERYL   My dad had just died so I didn't really care.
  My dad and I were really close.
  He was the only one who mattered . . .
MARK   I mean, that gun was mine.
CHERYL   I don't know why I'm remembering all this
  all of a sudden . . .
MARK   I knew every part of it.
NADINE   God, we hated those vets.
MARK   The barrel burned out of it.
  You know, I had a new barrel put in,
  but I mean that gun was mine.
  I took that gun everywhere I went.
  I just couldn't live without that gun.
NADINE   All that nonsense about long hair, flowers and love.
CHERYL   I mean, my family just dug my father's hole
  and put him right in there.
NADINE   And the women were exempt!
  They were all supposed to be Mother Earths making pots.
CHERYL   My brother's wife went nuts and shot her two-year-old son and
  killed him.
  I told you.
  I mean—all the things we did to him.
  He had to come and get me out of jail

at three in the morning and he's not—
he wasn't a strong man.
So my father just jumped into that bottle
and nobody could get him out of it.
NADINE I think I knew then what I know now.
MARK When I got on the plane coming home
I was so happy. I didn't miss my gun then.
It was my birthday.
NADINE I don't know.
MARK I turned twenty-one.
I did my birthday coming home.
NADINE Oh, Jesus.
MARK I did my birthday across the dateline.
I was incredibly happy.
We hit Okinawa.
R.J. was there.
We saw all these guys who were just going over.
NADINE I only hope I would have done exactly what Mark did.
MARK All these guys were asking us how it was.
We were really getting off on the fact
that we were done.
These guys were so green and fat.
We were brown, we were skinny.
We were animals.
NADINE I think he survived
because he became an animal.
I hope I would have wanted to live that bad.
CHERYL I used to stay up all night with my dad.
I was doing a lot of speed then
and I used to stay up all night with him and talk.
I'd be sewing or something like that at the kitchen table
and he'd be sittin' there drinking and bitching.
MARK I don't know why I couldn't talk to my parents when I got back.
NADINE We just can't face that in ourselves.
MARK I told my dad everything when I was over there.
CHERYL My dad was an intelligent, common sense type man.
He had no college education, but judging characters . . .
NADINE Oh, God.
CHERYL Oh, God.
MARK The only way I could cry was to write to my dad.
"God, Dad. I'm really scared. I'm really terrified."
CHERYL Oh, God. He could pick out people.

MARK   When I sent somebody out and they got killed, I could tell my
dad.

CHERYL   My dad told me: Stay away from Mark.

MARK   I got into L.A. . . ., called:
"Hey, I'm back. I'm back."
My dad said: "Oh, great. We're so relieved.
I'm so happy." My mother cried, she was happy.
I said: "I'm going to buy a hamburger."

CHERYL   He told me: Mark can't communicate, his style of dress is
weird, the war . . .

MARK   I just got on this stool going round and round.
"Hey, I'm back."
No one wanted anything to do with me.
Fuckin' yellow ribbons.
I thought I was tired.

NADINE   The problem now is knowing what to do with what we know.

CHERYL   My dad said:
I want you to forget him.
Just forget him.
Get out of this now, while you can.

MARK   I waited around until 3 a.m.,
caught a flight, got out here.
6:30 in the morning.
Beautiful, beautiful day.
Got my stuff, threw it over my shoulder,
and started walking.

CHERYL   I saw Mark occasionally, anyway.
Shortly after that, my dad had a stroke.
You know, my dad and I are identical.

MARK   I walked in the door and set everything down.
I was home.
My dad looked at me, my mom looked at me.
I sat down. Said:
Could I have some coffee?
That's when my mother started raggin' on me
about drinking coffee.
The whole thing broke down.

NADINE   Oh, God . . .

CHERYL   My sister had a baby when she was seventeen.
They put her in a home, you know, the whole route.
Shortly after that, I was five years younger than her,
I was just starting to date.

MARK   "Well," my mom said, "you better get some sleep.
   I've got a lot to do."
   I said: like I don't want to sleep.

   I got incredibly drunk.
CHERYL   I remember—I'd come home from a date.
   The only time I saw my father was late at night.
   He would take a look at me and say:
   Well, I hope you learned from your sister
   that the only way to stay out of trouble
   is to keep your legs crossed.
MARK   My mom and dad had to go out that night.
   I thought, well, I'd sit down
   and talk with them at dinner.
   They were gone.
CHERYL   End of conversation.
MARK   We didn't see each other that day.
   We never really did see each other.
CHERYL   I mean, he got his point across . . .
   more or less.
MARK   I had no idea what was going on.
   This was 1970.
   My hair was short.
   I got really crazed out on junk and stuff.
   Then when I was totally avoiding going home
   somewhere in that I wanted to . . .
   I really wanted bad to . . .
   communicate with a woman.
NADINE   You know, all Mark did was
   He brought the war back home
   and none of us could look at it.
MARK   I wanted to fuck my brains out.
CHERYL   God, I was naive.
   I was naive as they come.
   And to sit here and say that now knowing what I know
   and what I've been through
   just gives me the creeps.
MARK   No one wanted anything to do with me.
NADINE   We couldn't look at ourselves. We still can't.
CHERYL   Because I am so far from being naive.
   I mean, just the idea if I ever divorced Mark . . .
   I don't think I could ever find anyone who

could handle my past.
I mean, I have a hard time relating to it myself.

III

NADINE   Oh, God.
I'm worried about us.

I keep this quiet little knowledge with me everyday.
I don't tell my husband about it
I don't tell my kids,
or Mark.
Or anyone.
But something has fallen apart.
I'm having trouble being a mother.
How can you believe in sending your children to special classes
when you know it doesn't matter?
Oh,
I worry, I worry,
I worry one of my daughters
will be walking down the street
and get raped or mugged by someone who is angry or hungry.
I worry I have these three beautiful daughters (pieces of life)
who I have devoted my whole life to,
who I've put all my energy into—bringing up—raising—
and then somebody up there goes crazy one day
and pushes the "go" button and
phew! bang, finished, the end.
I worry that my daughters won't want to give birth
because of my bad birthing experience.
And I worry that they *will* want to give birth.

I worry that—
Well, one of my daughters does blame me
for the divorce
because I have protected them from knowing
what kind of man their father really is.

(I worry that I worry too much about all this
and I worry that I really don't worry enough about it all.)

I worry so much it makes me sick.
I work eighteen hours a day to pay the bills.
This year, I work on the feminist caucus,
I do my portraits, run my magazine, organize civic events.
I hold two jobs and more.
I invited my dear, sweet, ninety-one-year-old uncle
to come die at my house.

I go to recitals, shopping, graduation,
I don't go through the ritual
of getting undressed at night.
I sleep with my shoes on.
My husband's alcoholism has ruined us.
(Forty-five thousand dollars in debt.)

I don't dare get angry anymore.
Can you imagine what would happen,
if I got angry?
My children . . . *(Can't go on)*
MARK   My wife means so much to me.
I don't want to jeopardize what she's giving to me.
I don't want to jeopardize her.

It's like the Marine Corps.
Cheryl is like a comrade. She's walking wounded now.
You don't leave a comrade on the field.
NADINE   It's all out of control.
MARK   Sometimes I think Nadine loses sight of things.
Sometimes, I think she's way ahead of me.
NADINE   I don't know what I'm doing.
MARK   I can't talk to you about Nadine.
NADINE   Oh, men. I have to take care of them.
And they're all cripples.

It's so depressing.

MARK   It's like I know that I'm carrying a time bomb
and there are times that I just don't know
if I'll go off.
I don't know that in the end
I won't destroy myself.

NADINE   And yet, there's that little voice inside me
that reminds me that even though it's hopeless
I have little children that can't survive without me.

MARK   Maybe because I just can't comprehend war.
War that's political enough in terms of
what you have and what you get out of it.

NADINE   I guess I could possibly be the most
vulnerable person of all of us.
But I've also built up all these other devices
which will overrule that.

MARK   I need to tell you what I did.
My wife knows it.
She's come through times
when I got to the very edge of suicide.
She's helped me through a couple of times
that without her help . . .
I'd be dead.
Now, I've been very honest with Nadine
except when she asked me about suicide.
I couldn't tell her that.

NADINE   I couldn't even think about suicide.

IV
The Spaghetti Story

CHERYL   I hate to cook.
  Probably because he likes to cook.
  I hate to cook.
  I don't know how to cook,
  and I hate it.

  Mark does this spaghetti dinner once a year.
  Has he ever told you about that?
  Holy Christ!
MARK   Excuse me. *(Leaves)*
CHERYL   Every day before Thanksgiving
  Mark does a spaghetti dinner, and this
  is a traditional thing.
  This is the one traditional bone Mark has in his body,
  and I'd like to break it.

  He has 20-45 people come to this thing.
  He makes ravioli, lasagne, spaghetti, meatballs,
  three different kinds of spaghetti sauce:
  shrimp, plain, meat sauce.
  Oh, he makes gnocci! He makes his own noodles!
  And it's good.
  He's a damn good cook for Italian food.
  But you can imagine what I go through
  for three weeks for that party
  to feed forty people.
  Sit-down dinner.
  He insists it's a sit-down dinner.

  So here I am running around
  with no time to cook with him.
  I'm trying to get enough shit in my house
  to feed forty people sit-down dinner.
  We heated the porch last year
  because we did not have enough room to seat forty people.
  And I run around serving all these slobs,
  and this is the first year he's really charged anyone.
  And we lose on it every year.

I mean, we lose, first year we lost $300.
This dinner is a $500 deal.
I'm having a baby this November,
and if he thinks he's having
any kind of spaghetti dinner,
he can get his butt out of here.
I can't take it.

Pizzas! He makes homemade pizzas.
You should see my oven.
Oh my God! There's pizza-shit everywhere.
Baked on.
And when it's over with,
he just gets up·and walks out.
He's just done.
The cleanup is no big deal to him.
He won't even help.
He rolls up the carpets for this dinner.
People get smashed!
He's got wine everywhere, red wine.
It has to be red so if it gets on my rugs,
my rugs are ruined and my couch is ruined.
I've just said it so many times I hate it.
He knows I hate it.

My brother brought over some speed
to get me through that night.
My brother, Jack, who is a capitalist—
intelligent—makes me sick.
Never got into drugs. Was too old.
Missed that whole scene.
But he now has speed occasionally
on his bad day, you know, drink, two drinks one night,
speed to get him through the day.
Business man.

He brought me some speed to get me through the night
'cause he knew what a basket case I'd be.

And then Mark goes and invites my family.
And they're the last people I want to see at this.
Sure, they love it.

I mean, they all sit around and they
stuff themselves to death.
I'm not kidding!
It is one big stuffing feast.

The first time, the first spaghetti dinner we had was
right after Danny was born.
Danny's baby book got torn up.
I had to start a whole new one.
Mark's crazy friends.
Drunk.
Broken dishes everywhere.
I'm not kidding.
It's just a disaster.

Spaghetti on the walls.
Spaghetti pots dropped in the kitchen.
Spaghetti all over the sink.

That's why I ask him.
I go: "Why?"
"It's traditional. I have to do this every year."
It was three years ago he started.
Tradition, my ass.

I'm telling you.
I mean, he wonders why I can't sleep with him sometimes.
Because I just work up such a hate for him inside that . . .

    MARK *reenters.*

CHERYL   *(Continued)* I'm a perfectionist.
My house has to be this way,
and before I go to sleep,
I'll pick up after him.
I'm constantly picking up after him.
Christ Almighty!
In the morning, if he comes in late,
he's read the newspaper
and there's newspaper all over the room.
He *throws* it when he's done with it.
I've broken toes on his shoes.

I broke *this* toe on his shoe.
He always leaves his shoes right out in walking space.
Every morning I trip on
either his tennis or his good shoes.
Whichever pair he doesn't have on.
He's so inconsiderate of other people.
He's so selfish, he's so self-centered.
And this is what I tell him.
I'm just tired of it.
He's so selfish.
Because this spaghetti dinner just ruins me.
Baby or no baby,
it just completely ruins me.
And he's showing off his,
his wonderful cooking that he does once a year.
And I suppose this is why I hate cooking.

V

MARK   *(Shows us slide of wounded children)* This is a picture of some
   kids who were hurt.
   I used to take care of them,
   change their bandages and shit.
   I loved these kids.

   Oh, God . . .

VI

CHERYL What am I gonna do? I mean,
  someday Danny's gonna have to see Mark
  for what he is.
  And that just scares the piss right out of me.
NADINE How do you tell your children their father is an asshole?
CHERYL I don't wanna be here when Mark tells Danny
  about the war.
  I don't trust him.
NADINE How could I tell my children that their father is
  in town and hasn't called?
CHERYL I don't trust what he's gonna tell the kid.
  And the way I wanna bring the kid up,
  you can't tell him anything.
NADINE You can't tell your kids
  they can't have something they want
  because their father has squandered their money.
CHERYL You're just better off not saying anything.
NADINE What'm I going to do,
  tell them he's off somewhere getting drunk
  and has forgotten all about them?
CHERYL I'm just, you know,
  when that sort of thing comes along,
  I live from day to day.
NADINE The counselors tell me and my lawyers tell me
  that I should stop protecting them from him.
  But it's hard enough, don't you think?
  They hurt enough already.
CHERYL Later on, you know—
  there might not be a war going on.
  I might not have to deal with that.
  And maybe someday *I* can explain to him.
NADINE One time I told them he was in town
  because I couldn't find a way
  to cover up the fact that I knew.
  They were depressed for weeks.
  I have to protect them.
CHERYL *(Angry)* See, why do I have to do all this????
  And I do.
  I find myself doing everything.
  Covering for him . . .

NADINE   I don't protect Mark.
  He doesn't need it.
  He judges himself all the time,
  he's devoted to his son.
CHERYL   Sure Mark plays with him.
  But when it comes to discipline,
  that kid's a little brat,
  I mean he is.
  And Mark's never around when it comes to discipline.
NADINE   He works hard at his shop. He is supporting his family.
CHERYL   He's never around.
NADINE   He is working his way back into society.
  (He's an artist.)
  He's beginning to believe in himself
  and do his work.
CHERYL   I'm past the sixties.
  I want to go back to the Church.
  And Mark just will not understand the importance of this for me.
  I mean, when there's no father around,
  the Church shows some order, you know.
NADINE   He told me he's discovering
  who he always thought he was.
  I think of him as an artist
  and a lifelong friend.

VII

MARK   *(Holding the picture* HE *has framed of the children)* I'm ter-
  rified . . .
  I have a son . . .
  There's another child on the way . . .
  I'm terrified for what I did now . . .

CHERYL   The war is the base of all our problems.
MARK   It's guilt . . .
it's a dumb thing . . .
it makes no sense logically . . .
but I'm afraid there's this karma I built up
of hurting . . .
there are children involved . . .
like it's all going to balance out
at the expense of my kids.
CHERYL   I get so scared when he says that.
I mean, I never did anything.
MARK   There's no logic to it but it's there.
I try . . .
I'm really intense with my boy.

I think what we're beginning to see here is
that it was a different world I was in.
I'd like to be real academic about this . . .
closed case . . .
but this is an ongoing struggle.
NADINE   Mark!
MARK   I don't know.
I just don't know.
Sometimes I look at a news story.
I look at something someone goes to prison for here,
I think about it.
There's no difference.
It's just a different place.
This country had all these rules and regulations
and then all of a sudden they removed these things.

Then you came back and try to make your life
in that society where you had to deal with them.
You find that if you violate them,
which I found,
you go to jail,
which I did.
I sit back here sometimes and watch the news,
watch my mother,
watch my father.
My parents watch the news and say:
"Oh my God somebody did that!

Somebody went in there . . . and started shooting . . .
and killed all those people.
They ought to execute him."
I look at them.
I want to say,
"Hell, what the fuck,
why didn't you ever listen . . .
You want to hear what I did?"
It's real confusion.
I'm guilty and I'm not guilty.
I still want to tell my folks.
I need to tell them what I did.

VIII

CHERYL   There was a time when a man would confess to me,
"I'm a jerk,"
at a private moment
and I would smile
sweetly
and try to comfort him.

Now I believe him.

IX
The Confession

MARK   I . . . I killed three children, a mother and father in cold blood.
  (Crying)
CHERYL   Don't.
MARK   I killed three children, a mother and father . . . *(Long pause)*
NADINE   Mark.
MARK   I killed them with a pistol in front of a lot of people.

I demanded something from the parents and then
systematically destroyed them.
And that's . . .
that's the heaviest part of what I'm carrying around.
You know about it now, a few other people know about it,
my wife knows about it, Nadine knows about it,
and nobody else knows about it.
For the rest of my life . . .

I have a son . . .
He's going to die for what I've done.
This is what I'm carrying around;
that's what this logic is about with my children.

A friend hit a booby-trap.
And these people knew about it.
I knew they knew.
I knew that they were working with the VC infrastructure.
I demanded that they tell me.
They wouldn't say anything.
I just wanted them to confess before I killed them.
And they wouldn't.
So I killed their children
and then I killed them.

I was angry.
I was angry with all the power I had.
I couldn't beat them.
They beat me. *(Crying)* I lost friends in my unit . . .
I did wrong.
People in the unit watched me kill them.

Some of them tried to stop me.
I don't know.
I can't . . . Oh, God . . .

A certain amount of stink
went all the way back to the rear.
I almost got into a certain amount of trouble.

It was all rationalized,
that there was a logic behind it.
But they knew.
And everybody who knew had a part in it.
There was enough evidence,
but it wasn't a very good image to put out
in terms of . . .
the Marines overseas, so nothing happened.

I have a child . . .
a child who passed through the age
that the little child was.
My son . . . my son
wouldn't know the difference between a VC and a Marine.

The children were so little.

I suppose I could find a rationalization.

All that a person can do is try and find words
to try and excuse me,
but I know it's the same damn thing
as lining Jews up.
It's no different
than what the Nazis did.
It's the same thing.

I know that I'm not alone.
I know that other people did it, too.
More people went through more hell than I did . . .
but they didn't do this.

I don't know . . .
I don't know . . .

if it's a terrible flaw of *mine,*
then I guess deep down I'm just everything that's bad.

I guess there is a rationale that says
anyone who wants to live that bad
and gets in that situation . . . *(Long pause)* but I should have done better.
I mean, I really strove to be good.
I had a whole set of values.
I had 'em and I didn't.
I don't know.

I want to come to the point
where I tell myself that I've punished myself enough.
In spite of it all,
I don't want to punish myself anymore.
I knew I would want to censor myself for you.

I didn't want you to say:
What kind of a nut, what kind of a bad person is he?
And yet, it's alright.
I'm not gonna lie.

My wife tries to censor me . . .
from people, from certain things.
I can't watch war shows.
I can't drive.
Certain things I can't deal with.
She has to deal with the situation,
us sitting around, a car backfires,
and I hit the deck.

She knows about the graveyards, and R.J. and the woman.
She lives with all this still hanging out.
I'm shell shocked.

X

NADINE   Well, I'm going to look forward to the rest of my life
because of what I know.
I can't wait to test myself.
See, I guess I've known what it is to feel hopeless
politically.
And I've known what it is to plunge
personally.
But Mark has become a conscience for me.
Through him—I've come to understand the violence
in myself . . . and in him, and in all of us.
And I think if we can stay aware of that,
hold on to that knowledge,
maybe we can protect ourselves
and come out on the other side.
MARK   (*Mumbling*) I'm just a regular guy.
A lot of guys saw worse.
NADINE   If anything I'm on a continuum now.
MARK   See, I didn't want to see people
going through another era of
being so ignorant of the fact that war kills people.
NADINE   And I don't know if it's cynicism or just experience,
but I'm sure I'm never gonna plunge
in the old way again.
I'm not saying that trying to sound tough.
I know about that. I know all about that.
MARK   I feel protective of our children.
Once you're out there, you know there is no justice.
I don't want the children to die.
NADINE   But I have no old expectations anymore.
And when you have none,
you're really free.
And you don't ever plunge.
What do you plunge for?
MARK   It will happen again.
NADINE   I'm just going to work so hard because of what I know.
I do every day.
Did I tell you about not going to sleep at night
because I can't bear to stop thinking about it all?
I'm just going to be so busy for whatever's left.
(But I'm not mad at anyone.)

I don't blame anyone.
I've forgiven everyone.
God, I feel my house is in order at last.
MARK   I DEDICATE . . . this evening to my friends . . .
I'd like a roll call for my friends who died.
NADINE   There's one other thing.
When we all sit around together
with our friends
and we tell women
that no man can do it for you,
we all know it's true,
but I guess for some of us
it never works that way.
At this point in my life,
this curtain has dropped.
MARK   Anderson, Robert.
NADINE   And we see . . .
MARK   Dafoe, Mark.
NADINE   We need them—to be here, questioning themselves
and judging themselves—and us—like Mark.
MARK   Dawson, Mark.
NADINE   I love Mark.
MARK   Fogel, Barry.
NADINE   Well, . . . so . . .
The material has been turning over and over.
MARK   Grant, Tommy.
NADINE   Where is it at now?
MARK   Gunther, Bobby.
NADINE   You see.
MARK   Heinz, Jerry.
NADINE   What do you see, just a cast of characters?
MARK   Jastrow, Alan.

Lawrence, Gordon

Mullen, Clifford

> *Roll call continues through* CHERYL's *speech, ending with a conscious decision on* MARK's *part to name R.J. among the casualties of Viet Nam.*

XI

CHERYL   The men have it all.

MARK   Nelson, Raymond.

CHERYL   They've had it for the longest time.

MARK   Nedelski, Michael.

CHERYL   There's another thing I believe.
There's a lot more people
that are messed up because of the way we were brought up.

MARK   Nevin, Daniel.

CHERYL   Not brought up, but the things we've been through
since we were brought up.

MARK   O'Brien, Stephen.

CHERYL   So I think our generation,

MARK   Rosiello, Daniel.

CHERYL   the hippie generation, shortly before and after,
are gonna be the ones that suffer.

MARK   Rogers, John.

CHERYL   Because 90 percent of the men never straightened out.

MARK   Ryan, John.

CHERYL   But what I also believe
is that for every woman that has her beliefs,
there's a man that matches.

MARK   Sawyer, Steven.

CHERYL   Whether you find him or not,
is, is like finding a needle in a haystack.
With our population,
I mean, that's the odds you have.

MARK   Simon, Jimmy.

CHERYL   And there's the Women's Libs.
And there's a man for them too.

MARK   Skanolon, John.

CHERYL   See, what we're doing is crossing.
We're meeting the men
that should be with the other ones.
And I truly believe that,
that there is an equal balance.
Even though our group is so fucked-up.
And we are.

MARK   Spaulding, Henry.

CHERYL   You'll look, you'll go in college campuses now
and it's completely back the way it was . . .

and it should stay there.

MARK   Stanton, Ray.

CHERYL   I don't wanna see that shit come back.

I didn't even get that involved in it.

I got involved in it in my own little niche.

But I didn't, you know, get into it

in the school matter.

I went two years and I had it up to here.

And sure I would like to have gone on to school,

but I was competing with Mark.

And I'm not,

I do not like competing with someone.

MARK   Vechhio, Michael.

CHERYL   I'm a happy go lucky person.

I used to be anyway, before I met Mark,

where you couldn't depress me on the worst day.

And I had a good day every day of my life.

MARK   Walker *(Pause)*

CHERYL   And that is the way life was gonna be for me.

MARK   R.J.

Pause.

XII

MARK   *(Points to his photograph of two grapefruits, an orange, a broken egg, with a grenade in the center on a dark background. Also some fresh bread, a fly on the fruit. From far away it looks like an ordinary still life)*

My unit got blown up.

It was a high contact.

We got hit very, very hard.

The Marine Corps sends you

this extra food, fresh fruit, bread,
a reward
when you've had a heavy loss.

What can I say?
I am still alive—my friends aren't.
It's a still life.
I didn't know what I was doing.

   The WOMEN's *eyes meet for the first time as lights go down.*

THE RESURRECTION OF LADY LESTER

A Poetic Mood Song
Based on the Legend of Lester Young

by

OyamO

ABOUT OYAMO

OyamO (Charles F. Gordon) was born in Lorain, Ohio, in 1943; he has a B.A. from the College of New Rochelle, New York (1979), and an M.F.A. from the Yale School of Drama (1981). He has been published in magazines, anthologies, and *Hillbilly Liberation* (1976), a self-published book containing plays, essays and poems. He has received Rockefeller, Guggenheim, and Creative Artists Public Service program grants, and has had three plays selected for the Eugene O'Neill Theater Center's National Playwrights Conference.

OyamO was a founding member of the Black Theatre Workshop in Harlem (an arm of the now-defunct New Lafayette Theatre). *His First Step,* a one-act, was produced at the New York Shakespeare Festival in 1972. For Sidney Poitier and Harry Belafonte's Verdon/Cedric Productions, he wrote the screenplay *Three Red Falcons* in 1973. At the Yale School of Drama, he received the Molly Kazan Playwriting Award in 1980. His productions at Yale have included the first two parts of his family trilogy: *Mary Goldstein and the Author,* a one-woman piece, and *The Place of the Spirit Dance,* a one-man piece. At the Yale Cabaret, he has been represented by an earlier version of *The Resurrection of Lady Lester* in 1979, and *No Haven Dragtime* in 1981.

A production of *Lady Lester* is planned for CBS Cable TV's cultural channel in 1982. OyamO is currently working on a musical about an international religious movement headed by a panda bear, a futuristic drama about obsolete humanity and assorted animated organic creatures, and a film about a camp of runaway American slaves in an inaccessible Southern swamp.

PRODUCTION HISTORY

The Resurrection of Lady Lester was nominated for the *Plays in Process* series by Lloyd Richards, artistic director of the Yale Repertory Theatre in New Haven. It was presented there as part of the new play festival, "Winterfest," from January 21 until February 21, 1981.

James A. Simpson directed. The set was designed by Michael H. Yeargan and Kevin Rupnik, costumes by Dunya Ramicova and Douglas Stein, and lighting by Michael H. Baumgarten. Music for the Yale production was composed and arranged by Dwight Andrews, who also directed a musical band consisting of himself, Paul Sullivan, Mario Pavone and Pheeroan Aklaff. The cast, in order of appearance, was as follows:

WOMAN IN BLACK, WHITE MARIE .... Cecilia Rubino
LESTER YOUNG.. Darryl Croxton
SARAH, TUTA, AGATHA .... Zakiah Barksdale Hakim
VOICE, GRAND MARSHALL,
SWOOP, MOUSE.. Scott Rickey Wheeler
BOOBOO, TWEED, SLUMP, SERGEANT..............David Alan Grier
MISS LADY, LADY DAY .... Isabell Monk
POOKY, LINCOLN.. Reg E. Cathey
EXHORTER, DR. TRAMB, MANAGER, MAJOR .. Clarence Felder

An earlier version of *Lady Lester* was performed at the Yale Cabaret in 1979. The play was subsequently produced in its present form at the Yale Repertory Theatre and then at the Manhattan Theatre Club from October 22 to November 22, 1981.

PLAYWRIGHT'S NOTE

I call this piece "a poetic mood song based on the legend of Lester Young" because it does not attempt to present Lester Young's life as chronological biography or as factual "docudrama." This piece is not a schoolroom lesson on an eccentric American genius. Just as Lester used the standard notes of a given melody to create a hundred new melodies and just as he used the words and grammar of English to create his own poetic language, so too have I used the "*legend* of Lester Young" to create a universal story of an American musical hero. I sought his essence, not his obituary. This play is intended for a general theatre audience as opposed to the specialized audience of jazz cultist-"Lestorians."

The structure of the piece is informed by Young's musical style which broke most conventions in an easy, laid-back virtuosity that used rhythm but was not dominated by it, and the mysterious nature of memories which are not bound by traditional dramaturgical considerations. The entire piece is designed to flow like music across the stage, but it is not to be simply another black musical revue.

The casting arrangement itself makes a statement. Each actor has to play several characters in Lester's life and the several roles that an actor plays may themselves be subtly interrelated; however, each role is separate and requires distinct character work.

The language of this play is an extension, of sorts, of Lester's linguistic inventions, but actors should not get hung up on attempting to recite "poetry." They should simply speak the words with the passion of ordinary dialogue. If the character is achieved, the words will speak for themselves. There is much intended humor in this piece which should be consciously played to balance against the tragic aspects of Young's brief life. A lexicon of jazz argot could be helpful for those words which might not be understood in context.

The play moves in time. It begins near his death, backs up a year, leaps back to his childhood, comes forward to his incipient manhood, leaps ahead to the year before his death, leaps back to his peak years in the thirties and early forties, and finally leaps ahead to where the play begins. So Lester's age, health and mental attitudes change several times in the course of the play's movement.

The staging should be clean and simple. It should keep the action moving forward crisply. The stage should not be encumbered with too much set or set pieces. Lighting is most important to create mood, change scenes, and give the feeling of actual physical movement where appropriate. Characters should "appear" and "disappear" with proper lighting techniques. The playing area should be fairly large. Running time with intermission should not exceed two hours.

I would naturally expect some of the music that goes with the piece to differ in each production because of the nature of jazz itself; it is improvisational, and since the piece requires a live band, the musical director and some of the music and many of the musical arrangements will change with each production. With the exceptions of "Goodbye Porkpie Hat," "Come and Go To That Land," "Old Black Joe," "Dixie," "Curse of Mora," "D.B. Blues", "Darn That Dream," "Strange Fruit," "Dried Up Corncob Blues," "Three Little Words" and "Ain't No Place Like the Open Road," the specific tunes suggested in the script can be replaced depending on the nature of the production. Limited rights to use the music are available from various owners for small fees. For convenience, a list of songs that have been used in one or more of the three productions this play has had so far is appended.

Most important, it is crucial that the director of this piece be reasonably comfortable with or be willing to work toward its nontraditional form.

ABOUT LESTER YOUNG

Lester Willis Young died on March 15, 1959, after a lifetime devoted to music. Born in Mississippi in 1909, Young was the son of a musician who had studied at the Tuskegee Institute and who performed in a travelling carnival band. Young learned how to play many musical instruments (including alto sax), but first worked in the family band as a drummer. At 18, he left his family to join Art Bronson's Bostonians, a Kansas jazz band that switched him from alto to tenor sax. In the early thirties, Young played with a number of groups in the Midwest, at one point leaving Count Basie to replace Coleman Hawkins, reigning king of the tenor, in the Fletcher Henderson band. Disinclined to imitate Hawkins' bold and breathy style, Young resigned and soon became part of Basie's Reno Club combo. From 1936 to 1940, he was one of Basie's star soloists. Young often recorded with Billie Holiday, with whom he formed a close personal and professional relationship; in return for dubbing her "Lady Day," Holiday nicknamed him "Prez"—the president of all saxophonists. After leading a number of small groups of his own—largely unsuccessful ventures—Young rejoined Basie in 1943. In 1944, he was drafted into the U.S. Army, which soon imprisoned him for drug possession (a photograph of Young's white second wife seems the more probable cause). After a dishonorable discharge, Young returned to jazz, but was overwhelmed by the new generation of tenors imitating his style. Both critics and fellow musicians derided him as a parody of his former self. Despite a moment of calm provided by a third marriage which produced two children, Young soon drank himself into bad health. He spent the last years of his life in a seedy hotel overlooking Birdland, a New York jazz club, attended by a girlfriend and a sympathetic doctor. In early 1959 he played an engagement in Paris; less than 24 hours after returning to his New York hotel room, he died.

MUSIC FOR THE PLAY

Production of the play requires five musicians: a pianist, a bassist, a drummer, and two multi-instrumentalists on reeds and winds.

Traditional songs (public domain):
1. "The Curse of Mora," arranged by William Arms Fisher, available in William Arms Fisher, ed., *Sixty Irish Songs* (Boston: Oliver Ditson, 1915).
2. "Old Black Joe"
3. "Dixie"

Music credits (in alphabetical order):
1. "Ain't No Place Like The Open Road" by Dwight Andrews & OyamO, Black Angel Music
2. "Birdland Jam" by Dwight Andrews, Black Angel Music
3. "Come And Go To That Land" by Sam Cook, used by permission of Venice Music
4. "Darn That Dream" by James Van Heusen & Edward Delange, used by permission of Lewis Music and Scarsdale Music Corporation
5. "Detention Barrack Blues" by Sydney Shemel, Unart Music Corp.
6. "Dried-Up Corn Cob Blues" by Dwight Andrews & OyamO, Black Angel Music
7. "Flying Home" by Buddy Robbins, Regent Music Corp.
8. "Goodbye Porkpie Hat" by Charles Mingus, used by permission of Jazz Workshop, Inc.
9. "Lester Leaps In" by Lester Young, used by permission of Bregman Vocco & Conn, Inc.
10. "Lester's Death Music" by Dwight Andrews, Black Angel Music
11. "Lush Life" by Billy Strayhorn, used by permission of Tempo Music, Inc.
12. "Miss Lady Ballad" by Dwight Andrews, Black Angel Music
13. "Three Little Words" by Bert Kalmar & Harry Ruby, used by permission of Warner Brothers Music

Original music (from Yale production):
1. "Corn Cob Blues"
2. "Jam Session"
3. "Scat"
4. Arrangements of traditional and protected songs

5. Incidental music in all scenes, including a quotation of "Three Little Words." For all of the above, contact: Dwight Andrews, 94 Lake Place, New Haven, Connecticut 06511.

Sound cue:
1. Original recording of a song sung by Billie Holiday (Second Movement, p. 273 ff.)

CHARACTERS

In order of appearance

WOMAN IN BLACK, WHITE MARIE, a white actress
LESTER YOUNG, a black actor
SARAH, TUTA, AGATHA, a black actress
VOICE, GRAND MARSHALL, SWOOP, MOUSE, a black actor
BOOBOO, TWEED, SERGEANT, a black actor
MISS LADY, LADY DAY, a black actress
POOKY, SLUMP, LINCOLN, a black actor
EXHORTER, DR. TRAMB, MANAGER, MAJOR, a white actor

The play requires eight actors, seven of whom must play multiple roles.

THE PLAY

THE RESURRECTION OF LADY LESTER

FIRST MOVEMENT

The MUSICIANS *ethereally improvise upon Mingus'* "Goodbye Porkpie Hat." *A veiled* WOMAN IN BLACK *helps* LESTER *enter into what we'll come to understand as a "hotel room." This "hotel room" is a surrealistic suggestion that exists in a defined patch of light. The space must be flexible enough to transform itself through shifts in lighting into various suggestions of other spaces that exist in the illusions of the "real world" of which the audience think they are.* HE *carries his horn case and* SHE *both supports him and carries his small suitcase.* SHE *is so completely clothed in black that we cannot discern her race or nationality.* HE *is sick and stumbling and coughing blood.* SHE*'s very careful and gentle, but anxious.* SHE *helps him sit down; takes off his long black cape, his jacket, porkpie hat and pants; unbuttons his shirt. A bottle of gin falls out of his*

jacket pocket. SHE doesn't try to retrieve it. The bass line of the
music lingers beneath their voices.

WOMAN IN BLACK   You should have seen a doctor before you left
Paris.

LESTER   But, Lady, I was at the airport fixin' to climb on a bird.

WOMAN IN BLACK   Orly is an international airport; they have doctors
on call.

LESTER   You're the only doctor I trust, Miss Lady.

WOMAN IN BLACK   But I'm not a doctor, Les.

LESTER   You care about me and it's better to be near you now. I need
to be home, Lady.

WOMAN IN BLACK   Home? The Alvin Hotel on fifty-second street in
New York City? This is no place to come and be sick, baby.

LESTER   It's the home of the brave; it's where the music left me. I
couldn't run from this monster all my life; I couldn't understand in
Paris.

WOMAN IN BLACK   Couldn't understand what?

LESTER   What I been feelin' all these years.

   LESTER *coughs violently. Blood spurts onto the handkerchief.*

WOMAN IN BLACK   Lie down, Lester. It'll be easier to breathe. Please,
Lester let me call an ambulance. There's too much blood.

LESTER   Don't call no ambulance! Just let me work with my bruises
before this jam blows away.

WOMAN IN BLACK   Jam? What? Lester, I'm going to go call Dr. Tramb.
I've got to do that much! It'll be alright, baby. Lie still; wait for me.

   SHE *exits. The bass line flows into another tune emanating from*
   the Birdland. LESTER *struggles up at the sound of the music.* HE *sits*
   for a moment gathering his strength and listening. HE *sees the gin*
   bottle and goes over to it, opens it, pours a small libation and drinks
   deeply which causes him to cough heavily for a moment. HE *re-*
   trieves his porkpie hat and his horn and walks over to glare through
   the "window pane." HE *tries to blow a note or two but always ends*
   up coughing and drinking more gin to relieve the coughing. HE
   begins to pace and mumble unintelligibly to himself about "repeater
   pencils," "machine guns," "jive, half-ass musicians" and the like. HE
   fingers ghost notes on the tenor sax and frequently wipes his mouth
   with the handkerchief. The music fades out. HE *begins singing in a*

common blues pattern. His feeling is 100 percent but his voice is sick and incompetent.

LESTER   UM JUST A DRIED-UP CORN COB
SINGING IN THE SWEET HOT SUN
UM JUST A DRIED-UP CORN COB . . . *(Talking)* What's wrong?
You don't think I can sing? I can carry a melody at least and when I drop
this lip extension *(Indicating his horn)* in my chops, I blow soft little
stories that make you cry they sound so true.

Singing again but with musical accompaniment.

LESTER   *(Continued)* UM JUST A DRIED-UP CORN COB
DUSTY IN THE SWEET HOT SUN
UM JUST A DRIED-UP CORN COB
DUSTY IN THE SWEET HOT SUN
MY BLOOD IS FLYIN' AWAY
I GUESS MY TRIP IS ALMOST DONE

Talking blues. Stop time.

LESTER   *(Continued)* I HAD ALL THE WOMEN
DRANK DOWN ALL THE WINE
BLUE UP ALL THE NOTES
RAN A MILLION STOP SIGNS

Talking again, with music under.

How yaw feelin'?
How yaw feelin' peekin' at a phony ghost?
The Prez, Mr. Lester Young, President—
I was president when presidents were good men and bop was in—
I know yaw out there listening;
I may be sick, crazy, talk to myself, drink gin like a dog, and black,
But I ain't no communist;
I'm just yo' typical, innocent unamerican—*(Pointing to his head)*
Everybody I want to say anything to is right here, you dig?
They can't be no other place now,
But somebody up here knows something,
Something that I have to know now.
I have been resurrected from the Land of the True Living Harmony
Where God sings in everybody's soul

And we all got it made—
I came here in the first beat to live,
You dig?
I came to hear a vision of simple love,
Fresh love, you dig?
I wanted to serve the Music
And smile bravely in its light
Because I had to—
I had to feel my way in the music—
I was a dumb child
And the music led me to secrets
Hidden in my own heart,
Secrets about what really matters
When you know you're a human person
And not a human monkey.
I came here to jam with my fellow sounds,
To help weave a cloth of light, soft harmony,
So my family,
None of you,
Don't have to be naked
In this drafty-ass world of the intelligent beast—
But there was something I didn't see—
There was something I never found—

HE *takes a drink. A late fifties rendition of* LESTER's "Red Boy Blues" *abruptly evolves from the previous blues. It is an imitation of his style.* HE *listens for a moment, grows immensely agitated, and says derisively:*

You hear *that* music?
That's Birdland—
I once blew a hole in the roof over there
And went through to Mars—
Them gentlemen there;
Listen to 'em;
They all had the same music teacher at Juilliard,
But tryin' to repeat after me—I should go show them where it's at—
I'll go show them how to feel free at the soul's bottom,
Where easy mellow breeze flows through silver lips
And THE MUSIC IS THE ENTIRE CREATION—

HE *retrieves his pants, but before* HE *can put them on:*

VOICE   Sarah! Yoohoo, Sarah!

> LESTER *tries to ignore the male* VOICE, *but stops trying to put on his pants. The* VOICE *is literally singing the initial salutations.*

VOICE   (Continued) Sarah! Sarah! Yoohoo, baby!

> LESTER *throws his pants down and shouts at the* VOICE *in his head as if through the "window."*

LESTER   Scratch the racket, Bohannon. Whas happnin'?

VOICE   *(Mocking incredulity)* Prez?! Prez! Yo Prez, is that sho nuff you?

LESTER   Who the hell you think it is?

VOICE   Damn Prez, I ain't seen you in three years, since 1955. I thought you was dead.

LESTER   Ding dong! You thought *I* was dead? Man, I'm probably more alive than you ever been! And I'm fixin' ta come out back there and jam.

VOICE   Jam what, poppa? I could sneeze into my tenor sax and blow you off the bandstand.

LESTER   Drag yo' young rusty tail to the Birdland and wait.

VOICE   I know you don't mean *the* Birdland. We hurt old cats like you over there; we'll cut you up till you look like used chitlins.

LESTER   They can't cut a knife sharpener. I keep them chumps sharp.

VOICE   Awww Prez, back off; I'm feelin' too good for all that bullshit. I came to check out Sarah.

LESTER   I ain't her salesman, you dig?

VOICE   Look, tell Sarah I'm playin' 'cross the street at the Birdland.

LESTER   Do you know who you talkin' to?

VOICE   I'm talking to somebody who used to be the president, but right now you just another old, sick, no playing, tired ass gin head!

> LESTER's *reply is a long, mean burst from his horn that ends in a coughing fit and a hearty swallow of gin. HE softly blows the first three notes of* "Three Little Words" *and repeats it twice. His mind summons* SARAH *to the space and* SHE *"appears." It is apparent that* SHE *has just finished giving herself a fix.* SHE *wears a flimsy, sexy dress, has streaked hair and a business-like manner.*

SARAH   *(Putting away her dope-taking tools)* I feel like a whipped fish already and I still got six more hours to work.

LESTER   I hear that.

SARAH   My legs. My legs ache so much.

LESTER *comes to her, pushes aside his horn, kneels before her, begins massaging her calves.*

LESTER   Concrete is hard on the soul. Relax yo' legs.

SARAH   *(Giggling)* Your fingers feel like you playing a solo on my leg, and it tickles.

LESTER   You got some pretty sounds laughing in this leg, baby. Why don't you take the night off?

SARAH   *(Stiffening)* Take the night off what?

LESTER   Take the night off your legs.

SARAH   *(Snatching her legs away)* But this hotel room is off my legs that brings in money every night so we can have some place to sleep, eat and act like normal people during the day.

LESTER   Normal peoples died out wayback yonda. Just they ghosts left out here now.

Pause.

SARAH   Les, you shouldn't stay up here all by yourself so much. People say you be up here talking to yourself in different voices. Go to the Birdland and play music or get something to eat.

LESTER   I ain't into no grit.

SARAH   Lester, you need to eat some food to soak up that liquor so your guts don't rot. *(Offering him money)* Take this and get you something to eat.

LESTER   My teeth ain't ready for no grit.

SARAH   Cut the food up good so you don't have to chew it, or order some soup.

LESTER   Scratch the grit, Sarah; I'd rather have a drink.

SARAH   My prize buffalo always say, "The sauce will cook you."

LESTER   I'm alright, Sarah. I don't need no advice from your buffalo.

SARAH   You won't be alright for long if you keep drinking and not eating. At least you oughtta take them vitamins that Dr. Tramb left for you.

LESTER   Them pills taste horrible with gin. Besides, they ain't no more.

SARAH   No more? All them pills gone that quick. What you do with them?

LESTER   I didn't do shit with 'em. They disappeared some way.

SARAH   *(Reoffering the money)* Take this down to the drugstore on Forty-second Street and git some more.

LESTER   My eyes ain't bulging for no vitamin pills.

SARAH   Lester, this is stupid; you got to take something besides wine and gin. I wish I had me somebody like Dr. Tramb looking out for me. That be just what I need to git my singin' career goin', a rich white doctor who'll take care of me and help me git famous.

LESTER   The white doctor can't do much for a black ghost.

SARAH *leaps up.*

SARAH   Stop it, Lester! I can't stand no more! I work till my tongue hang out to keep some food and liquor and pay the rent and all you can do is sit up here on your tired black behind, sucking on that horn and that bottle and talking that stupid boogeyman crap! You gonna git sicker and sicker and then you gonna die if you don't change your ways.

LESTER   Is that a wish?

SARAH   That's a warning and you better listen if you think living is worthwhile.

LESTER *laughs, coughs, drinks deeply.* SARAH *glowers in silence.*

SARAH   *(Continued)* Look, Lester, I'm gonna need this room tonight. You gonna have to put on your pants and go hang some place else, just for tonight, at least.

LESTER   No lady would sell her box in her own home; even ghosts know better than that.

SARAH   I'm not talking about ghosts; I'm talking about buffaloes. I need to have a convenient place to take care of my customers.

LESTER   Try the White House.

SARAH   Why I gotta support the White House Hotel? When you doin' bidness in America, baby, you got to keep your expenses down; otherwise the communists liable to start a war.

LESTER   (Screaming at her) DON'T TELL ME ABOUT NO WAR! I DON'T GIVE A DAMN ABOUT NO WAR!

SARAH   Lester, I'm fixin' to bring my buffaloes up here anyhow, so get lost for awhile!

LESTER   I am lost, but I know this is my squat, my place in the real world, if there is one. I created this place and it creates me over and over.

SARAH   Your place, huh? This is my place. I took you in, remember? You got another place too, don't you? You got that bitch and her babies stuck up in a nice house in Queens! You kin go lay up there. Yeah, they living good; they must be gittin' all the money from yo' records.

LESTER   Money? What money I done made? Go find it for me. Bring it here; let me feel it. I'll even tell you where it's at. Go to my scumbutt manager. Go to every greasy, crooked joint that put my name on they billboard. Go to the record companies, the radio stations and the publishing houses. Go tell them that *I*, the Prez,—me, you undastan—tell them I said to give *you* all *my* money so you kin bring it back here and let me wallow in it.

SARAH   That's just what I'm sayin'. You ain't got no money. I got to make the money, and I can't make no money with yo' black butt layin' around here messin' up my bidness.

LESTER   Yo' bidness? What is yo' bidness? When we first got together, you was a singer, or suppose to be. We was gon' make a world of music together, remember? But running after that stupid white dust cut through all the melodies and put you on the stroll. Bidness? You a little two dolla hoe; in Europe that's a bidness; in New York City it's what *they* call a social disease. That's when people done lost they self-respect.

SARAH   That's a funky lie! I do what I do and I respect myself too, understand? And it don't cost me nothin', Lester, *(Starts crying but continues ranting)* a few moans and groans, lots of petting and cooing of soft, withered egos, sweet lies and fragrant laughter. I give them chumps a bargain that benefits me. At least I still got something to sell and gon' have it for awhile.

SHE *buries her sobbing face in her hands.* LESTER *blows the first four notes from* "Three Little Words" *on his horn, walks over to her, touches her wet face, speaks slowly, tenderly.*

LESTER   I don't have nothin' to sell; I got plenty love to give you and nothing else. I got to keep on till it's over—I need plenty space to blow this horn and I can't breathe in Queens, you dig? It's not the ole lady and my children; it's not really Queens; it's the music; the music is out here. This room is the open road; it's a habit and I live in the habit. *(Pause as* HE *looks deeply into her eyes, sighs heavily)* Go back to work; when the stampede is done, you come home. I'll sing to you, wash the mud off your soul, make you pure again.

SARAH   Pure? I don't need to be pure again. Right now I need to make me some money, baby, and I want you to carry your tired, no playing black ass outta here.

LESTER *leaps up, angry, grabs his pants and violently dons them.*

LESTER   SHEEEET! Ding Dong!

HE *drives her from his consciousness with a violent motion of his hand and* SHE *"disappears," reenters the cosmic harmony.*

LESTER   *(Continued)*You think I can't play, bitch?
You too?
The problem is you can't hear;
I plays MUSIC, pure MUSIC—
I didn't start here in *this* crippled family;
I had more than you and this marketplace—
I came from a place where they needed me
'Cause I belonged to the Music.
We used to speed the Music down the road;
We wasn't no turkey minstrels;
We was musicians;
We traveled in America
But we had a home too,
Where we had steaming mouthwatering melodies
And nice, clean, warm toilets—
NEW ORLEANS . . . !

We immediately hear the sound of a small New Orleans marching band, circa 1919, and we see a BASS DRUMMER, HORN PLAYER and the GRAND MARSHALL enter strutting and dancing ebulliently. As THEY march past LESTER, HE gleefully falls into step. TUTA, his distressed sister, follows LESTER at a safe distance. The GRAND MARSHALL continues with his fancy dancing and strutting as HE answers the CHILD LESTER's questions.

LESTER   *(Continued)* What club you all fixin' to play at? Huh?
GRAND MARSHALL   We ain't fixin' to play at no club, boy!
LESTER   Oh, you wit the carnival, sho nuff? Give me a ticket, I'll pass out handbills for you. Where the carnival gon' be?
GRAND MARSHALL   What carnival?
LESTER   The one that yaw announcin'.
GRAND MARSHALL   We ain't wit da carny folks.
LESTER   Why you playin' music?
GRAND MARSHALL   We celebrating.
LESTER   Why?
GRAND MARSHALL   We done just buried my oldest son, one of the finest musicians New Orleans ever seed.
LESTER   *(Incredulous, wide-eyed, HE stops marching, but continues walking)* What?
GRAND MARSHALL   *(Laughing)* Got smashed by a truck, brains spread all over the street, but he resting; he happy now!
LESTER   He is?

GRAND MARSHALL   Oh yeah, he at peace with God; he got everything he ever needed; he got life everlasting.

> *The* MUSICIANS *and the* GRAND MARSHALL *march off.* LESTER *stops and watches them disappear.* TUTA, *careful to see that the* MARCHERS *are gone, approaches* LESTER, *grabs him and hustles him toward home.*

TUTA   This is the worse neighborhood in New Orleans! What if Booboo and Miss Lady find out we been here? With all these loud, lewd, honky-tonk darkies?
LESTER   You gon' tattle?
TUTA   No, not if you come home with me right now.
LESTER   Um comin', but don't tattle like you promised, alright?

> *Lights cut to area where* BOOBOO *is pacing furiously before* MISS LADY *and* POOKY, *seated.* TUTA *and* LESTER, *concealed, fearfully peek in at their father's rage.* BOOBOO *pulls a watch from his vest pocket, looks at it and explodes in a brief fit of shouting at no one in particular.*

BOOBOO   THIS IS THE LAST TIME THEY'LL DO THIS! I KNOW WHAT THEY NEED! YESSUH!
MISS LADY   (*Very calmly, evenly as counterpoint*) They probably forgot, dear, but they'll be . . .
BOOBOO   (*Interrupting*) I swear before my Lord Savior in Heaven I told them childrens to be at home by six for rehearsal because we due at prayer meeting by eight o'clock. We can't be excusing them all the time.
MISS LADY   But, Booboo, sometimes children will forget and . . .
BOOBOO   This band liable to fall apart if you keep singin' lullabies to they heads instead of swinging a strap on they behinds. Pooky's a child too, but Pooky's always on time; he's learning his musical discipline.
POOKY   (*Basking*) I sure am.
BOOBOO   Shut up! What time is it now?

> *As* HE *fumbles for his pocket watch, enter* TUTA *and* LESTER *timidly.* THEY *quickly take their seats.*

TUTA   (*Shaking nervously, talking rapidly under* BOOBOO's *merciless glare*) Booboo, I was coming back here with Lester so I could be here on time and then we saw this man whose brains got smashed out by a truck they was marching back from his funeral but Lester thought it was a carnival and went chasing and I ran after him and fell down and hurt my kneeeeeee and some old men was staring and staring at my ankles and I cried, but Lester kept running and I . . .

BOOBOO *(Interrupting but talking directly to* LESTER) The first thing you got to learn in a carnival band is how to be on time! The midway do not wait on some gunsel sittin' on his butt in the doniker. You supposed to be a professional musician, not a common gazoonie.

TUTA But, Booboo, we was . . .

BOOBOO *(Now directly at her, but with a faint conciliatory tone)* And Tuta, you know that you know better. I depend on you. You the oldest; you shoulda seen to it that yaw got here on time. This season you sit in on the drums.

> HE *turns back to* LESTER. TUTA *is visibly disappointed behind* BOOBOO's *back.*

BOOBOO *(Continued)* Lester, what instruments have I taught you so far?

LESTER Drums.

BOOBOO And . . .

LESTER Saxophone.

BOOBOO Not saxophone! I taught you reed instruments. Reeds! I just started you with the saxophone, remember?

LESTER Yes, Booboo, and I been practicing real hard; listen to this:

> LESTER *picks up his sax, but* BOOBOO *takes it away from him.*

BOOBOO I heard you slurring over the scale, but did you practice your singing?

LESTER *(Lying)* Yessir!

BOOBOO Are you sure?

LESTER Yessir, I practiced; you kin ask Pooky.

BOOBOO I don't have to ask Pooky. Let me hear you sing that song I taught you at yestiddy's rehearsal. Go 'head.

LESTER Uh . . . ain't the band gon' play?

BOOBOO *(A trifle irritated)* You don't need no band to sing. I want to hear it without accompaniment, a capella, understand? A capella. Miss Lady, give him a send off.

> After MISS LADY's *mimed introduction which is actually done by the pianist,* HE *very self-consciously clears his throat and starts to sing his own hip version of Stephen Foster's "Old Black Joe."*

LESTER GONE ARE THE DAYS WHEN MY HEART WAS
YOUNG AND GAY,
GONE ARE MY FRIENDS FROM . . .

BOOBOO *(Interrupting)* No boy, I know I didn't teach you to sound like
that. Look at me, Lester! The power comes from here. *(Indicating his
diaphragm)* You use all this *(Indicating vocal apparatus)* to shape the
power into what you want it to do and then it's easier to stay in tune,
understand?

LESTER Yes, Booboo.

BOOBOO Now listen while I go through it one time. And listen carefully. The rest of y'all sing the chorus.

> BOOBOO *correctly renders the following with chorus accompani-
> ment.*

GONE ARE THE DAYS WHEN MY HEART WAS YOUNG AND
GAY,
GONE ARE MY FRIENDS FROM THE COTTON FIELDS AWAY,
GONE FROM THE EARTH TO A BETTER LAND I KNOW.

Chorus

I HEAR THEIR GENTLE VOICES CALLING, "OLD BLACK JOE."
I'M COMING, I'M COMING, FOR MY HEAD IS BENDING LOW;
I HEAR THOSE GENTLE VOICES CALLING, "OLD BLACK JOE."

BOOBOO Alright, Lester, hit it again and remember what I say.

LESTER *(Clears throat and begins singing as before)* GONE ARE THE
DAYS WHEN MY HEART WAS YOUNG AND GAY,
GONE FROM . . .

BOOBOO *(Interrupting in a burst)* Lester, this ain't no plantation show
this season. We ain't working for poor jigs like us no more. We going
on the road with the Velare Brothers. Them ginnies don't want no jig
band that ain't got class. You got to practice them songs. For right now,
Tuta, take this banjo, I'll sing and, Lester, you play the drums again.

LESTER *(Whining loudly, miserably as places are exchanged)*
Awwwww, Booboo, you said I don't hafta carry them things no more;
my back still hurt every morning and . . .

BOOBOO SHUT UP THAT WHINING! Don't whine, boy. Say what

you got to say or shut up! No, that's right you too lazy to carry the drums, that's what! You think you ain't pretty enough with them drums.

LESTER   But I'm supposed to play the saxophone 'cause the doctor said I bent a rib from carrying them drums.

BOOBOO   *(Intimidated by his tone and responding with anger)* You 'bout to git yo' lips bent from carryin' that tone.

MISS LADY   *(Answering BOOBOO but directing it to LESTER)* It was a bruised rib, Lester, not a bent rib. Bruised badly too.

BOOBOO   *(Angrily to MISS LADY)* If he hadn't been so anxious to chase them nappy-head country girls, he wouldn't have hurt himself in the first place. *(To TUTA)* Tuta, I guess you have to go back to the drums.

TUTA   *(Quietly, sweetly)* Booboo, I don't mind playin' them drums, but I really need to practice on the banjo like you was showin' me yestiddy.

BOOBOO   *(Slightly calmed)* Alright, baby, take the banjo. *(Looks around at POOKY who is obviously trying to make himself inconspicuous)* Pooky!

POOKY *jumps.*

POOKY   Yes, Booboo?

BOOBOO   Take the drums.

POOKY   *(Trying TUTA's method)* But, Booboo, you said we gotta have a trumpet this season and I been practicing real hard just like you taught me.

BOOBOO   *(Whacking POOKY across the rear)* Don't give me no lip! Do what I say! I'll take the trumpet and sing too.

POOKY *moves toward the drums as HE malevolently glares at* LESTER *who keeps his head down to avoid POOKY's silent wrath.*

BOOBOO   *(Continued)* Miss Lady, you gon' have to write a few different arrangements for us now.

MISS LADY   I'll bring the new ones to rehearsal tomorrow, Booboo.

BOOBOO   *(Almost normal now)* Thank you, darlin'. Alright, we got just enough time to practice one song before prayer meeting. Can we get some work done now? Let's do that new arrangement of Dixie. Lester and Tuta play through your parts first. You can share the music stand.

LESTER *and* TUTA *begin to play in pantomime while* MUSI-CIANS, *Off, play the music.* TUTA *plays her part precisely;* LESTER *plays beautifully around what SHE plays.* TUTA *reaches the end of the page and stops playing to turn the page, but* LESTER *continues on, which doesn't escape* BOOBOO's *instant attention. When* TUTA *begins playing again,* LESTER *adjusts and begins playing around her once more.*

BOOBOO   *(Continued)* Hold it!

THEY *stop playing.*

BOOBOO   *(Continued)* Lester, you playing some of everybody's part; just play your part. Lester, turn the page back and play your part by yourself.
LESTER   *(Shaking)* Yes, Booboo. (LESTER *puts the horn to his mouth as* HE *frantically tries to figure out what his part is from the notes before him.* HE *starts to blow a note once or twice, stops, clears his throat, coughs)* Uh . . . I . . . uh . . . I forgot how it start.

BOOBOO's *frustrated anger returns;* HE *approaches* LESTER *who cringes slightly.* BOOBOO *points to the sheet music.*

BOOBOO   What do you mean, you forgot how it start? *(Stabbing at the notes)* All you got to do is read this part right here. Hum it to me, Lester, while I point to the notes. Start here. Okay, go 'head.

LESTER *is silent.* BOOBOO *explodes.*

BOOBOO   *(Continued)* You can't read, is that what you saying? What have I been teaching you and the other childrens to do the last six months? You mean I done wasted all that time on a glooming geek? You want to be the scum that lays in the wheel ruts? Answer me one question, Lester. CAN YOU READ THE MUSIC?
LESTER   *(In tears)* I don't know how, Booboo!
BOOBOO   *(Incredulous, angry, wildly gesticulating)* You don't know how? You don't know how? You don't know how?

As HE *says the previous,* HE *raises his arms in frustrated anger, and is about to bring them down on* LESTER *when* MISS LADY *speaks calmly but quickly.*

MISS LADY   It's almost prayer meeting time.

BOOBOO *halts with his arms in midair over* LESTER, *but* HE *blasts his words at* LESTER.

BOOBOO   Gimme that horn!

> LESTER *jumps at the task.*

BOOBOO   *(Continued)* You don't belong in a house of music! Get out! You're fired!

LESTER   *(Through sobs)* But I don't wanna go, Booboo.

BOOBOO   *(Shouting)* SHUT UP THAT WHEEZING! You can't read, you can't stay. *(As* HE *shoves* LESTER *away)* Get yo' butt out my face now! Everybody get ready for prayer meeting.

> ALL, *except* MISS LADY *and* LESTER, *disappear.* SHE *gets up and comes to* LESTER *who falls on his knees and clutches the hem of her dress.*

LESTER   Why can't I just play from the inside out, Miss Lady, huh? Why can't I just play inside out? I be so busy reading, I can't hear what I'm playing.

MISS LADY   Booboo won't let you come back to us unless you learn to read sheet music.

LESTER   They look like white tombstones with secret writing.

MISS LADY   Les, in this world you've got to be always on the lookout for secrets, just to survive, but still all the music comes from inside out. It all comes from God.

LESTER   I bet God don't read no tombstones.

MISS LADY   He doesn't have to because God made all music so we could better appreciate being alive.

LESTER   Yes, Miss Lady, but it seems like music 'sposed to be alive too.

MISS LADY   *(A bit flustered)* Look, Lester, music is alive because live people play it, and you got to have faith that God put Booboo here to bring you up proper. Now stop acting like somebody done chopped off your arms and legs. It's not difficult to read. Tuta and me will help you. And you know Pooky always helps you when you're in trouble.

LESTER   Pooky say he gon' kill me!

MISS LADY   I'll talk to Pooky; you just attend to the tombstone secrets. Make haste now! We got to get ready for prayer meeting.

LESTER   Wait, please, Miss Lady.

MISS LADY   *(A trifle irritated and concerned about* BOOBOO*)* What is it, Lester? Say it quickly!

LESTER   *(Speaking rapidly)* You think maybe Booboo could let us stay in New Orleans longer so we don't have to be traveling all the time?

MISS LADY   I thought you liked traveling with the carnival.

LESTER   I do, but . . . I miss the times when we used to make up songs together, in front of the fireplace and eat pan bread with molasses. We ain't done that since we started traveling. Do you remember how good it used to feel?

MISS LADY   Yes, I remember, but Lester, if Booboo say we travel, then we all got to travel. *(Bitterly)* Nothing I say can make him change his mind; nothing I ever say makes him change his mind, you understand?

LESTER   But please, Miss Lady; you can at least ask him. Please!

MISS LADY   *(Wearily)* Alright, I'll talk to him. *(Seeing LESTER brighten and wishing to deflate his hopes)* I ain't promising nothing, Lester, but I'll talk to him.

LESTER   *(Hugging her tightly)* I love you, Miss Lady.

BOOBOO   *(Offstage)* Miss Lady, we fixin' to leave.

MISS LADY   I'm coming! Let's hurry before he starts fussin' again.

THEY *move off. The colorfully dressed* EXHORTER *appears looking just like a carnival grinder and* HE *immediately begins his ballyhoo which is directed to the audience. Carnival midway music and attendant midway sounds are heard simultaneously. The lights themselves revolve and move as if on an actual midway.* LESTER, *alone, wanders in and watches with what becomes the youthful disdain of a cynical 18-year-old.*

EXHORTER   HURRAY HURRAY HURRAY the back-end is colossal, stupendous; we got the hottest pig iron this side of Attica, Anywhere; get on Mangel's Whip, leaves your knees trembling and the Witches Waves hustles you through mysterious sights in the black underworld; we got attractions for every taste and lack of taste; there's a wild man chained to an iron bar in that tent to your left; his name is Cronus; eats nothing but mud and pussywillows; found him wandering naked in Southern California; looks like a gorilla, but has the heart of an old darkie; pay your two bits and you'll see the most amazing wonders of the world. HURRAY HURRAY HURRAY; we got the only man in the world who had a baby; we got Ethiopian minstrels; we got pet bugs for enterprising youngsters of science; we got genuine dancing and singing jigs fresh from the plantation; this is your chance of a lifetime to see pickled punks, two headed fetuses, twenty toed babies and the happiest and hottest darky band this side of the Rockies; HURRAY HURRAY HURRAY; don't miss the most exciting events in this world

By this time LESTER *has become visibly agitated and eventually disgusted with the grotesque Americana of the proceedings.*

LESTER *(shouting)* SCRATCH SHEET!

The EXHORTER *disappears. Lights cut to another space.* BOO-BOO, TUTA *and* POOKY *simultaneously begin singing.* LESTER *shortly joins them and after a brief, silent admonishment about punctuality from* BOOBOO, *begins to sullenly sing. The* FAMILY *sits in what is understood to be the back of the church. The* EXHORTER, *now a rural evangelist, enters and stands at the front. The song is an old American spiritual, "Come And Go To That Land." It is enthusiastically and soulfully rendered by* ALL *except* LESTER. *The* EXHORTER's *accent is distinctly rural South of the 1920s.*

EXHORTER AND FAMILY   COME AND GO TO THAT LAND
COME AND GO TO THAT LAND
COME AND GO TO THAT LAND WHERE I'M BOUND
PEACE AND HAPPINESS IN THAT LAND
PEACE AND HAPPINESS IN THAT LAND
PEACE AND HAPPINESS IN THAT LAND WHERE I'M BOUND
I GOT A SAVIOR IN THAT LAND
I GOT A SAVIOR IN THAT LAND
I GOT A SAVIOR IN THAT LAND WHERE I'M BOUND

The singing ends but the CONGREGATION *hums the tune as the* EXHORTER *fervently attempts to seriously convert audience members.*

EXHORTER   Yes, come and go to that land which is the Kingdom of Heaven, but "Except ye be born again, ye cannot," I repeat, "cannot enter the Kingdom of Heaven." I want you to remember that Christ died for your sins; He died for sins of all mankind. He was brave enough to walk the stony path of life alone, to tread up Calvary Mountain and die just so you and me and everybody that ever walked this earth could live. Praise His Holy Name. And you know, He didn't ask for much in return. The only thing you got to do is die . . . and be born again in the blood of Christ. Praise His Holy Name. Jesus was a man who preached and acted a very simple philosophy. He went about the land doing unto others as He would have them do unto Him. He was such a Good Samaritan that when He found He could save humanity from the hell of confusion and pain only by giving up His own life, He willingly gave His life so that humanity, all of us, could live forever in harmony with the will of God. Praise His Holy Name. Let the wonderful message of Jesus enter your heart. Raise your voices in praise of His Holy Name.

> *The humming swings into the previous song once more. The* EXHORTER *beckons to the* CONGREGATION. LESTER, *who has been visibly moved by the vision of Jesus, rises of his own volition and proceeds to the front as the* EXHORTER *continues his spiel.*

EXHORTER   *(Continued)* Come renounce your confusion and pain before the Lord. Show Him that you want to pay your debt. He doesn't ask much; join Him; join Him; join Him.

> LESTER *starts to kneel at the front when the* EXHORTER *firmly takes hold of* LESTER, *gently helps him up and lovingly guides him back to the colored section.*

EXHORTER   *(Continued)* And I'm happy to say that in our church we have a special place for our nigra brethren before the Lord.

> LESTER, *stunned, looks at the* EXHORTER *and* BOOBOO, *and then angrily stomps out of the church.* BOOBOO *runs after him. The* OTHERS *continuing humming the previous song.* BOOBOO *catches* LESTER *some short distance from the church. The lights fade up on* BOOBOO *and* LESTER *and fade down on the church.*

BOOBOO   The Lord is too big, Les; you can't run away from Him.

LESTER   It ain't Him I'm runnin' from.

BOOBOO   Use your head, boy. We got to worship the Lord someplace. This is the only church in town. Ain't none of us here. You got to go along with the custom.

LESTER   That was the last go along for me.

BOOBOO   The Lord don't care what bench you kneel at, son.

LESTER   That's cause the Lord ain't no nigga.

BOOBOO   Thou shalt not take the Lord thy God's name in vain. It's evil to turn your back on someone who loves you totally.

LESTER   Then dig my mother you scratched way back there in New Orleans. She love you, but I guess you dig Jesus more.

BOOBOO   *(Hurt, defensive)* Oh, you done gone and got hep on me, talk that jive, huh? But look at you! Eighteen years old and still crying for your mama.

LESTER   Miss Lady love all of us. She sang sweet, pretty lullabies to us, made us dream music. Now she's just another misty face in the past 'cause you split us and broke the harmony that made everything feel alright!

BOOBOO   Miss Lady got tired of the road, but the carnival is where we earn our living. These last ten years on the road is where you mastered your rudiments and became a professional musician, one of the best, I might add. Sometimes your music can be more important than anything else, even Miss Lady.

LESTER   Horseshi . . .

BOOBOO   *(Interrupting menacingly)* Don't you dare say it; don't you dare talk to me like that. The music got between me and Miss Lady.

LESTER   Music? What music? You mean them minstrel minuets we be playin'?

BOOBOO   What you tryin' to say, boy? You don't like the music?

LESTER   I don't like grinnin' and shufflin' and tremblin' everytime one of them crackers belch in my face.

BOOBOO   Shut up, Lester, and listen. There's some things about this world that you still don't understand.

LESTER   I understand how to stand up straight.

BOOBOO   So does a oak tree, but when a hurricane come, the oak tree bends and sways so it don't get broke in half. Yeah, I grin in the crackers' faces. I play music, any music, Dixieland too. I go along with some of their stupid, evil ways, but the music gets me what *I* want. Look at your feet; I put shoes on your feet. Feel your stomach; it ain't never been empty. Talk about dreaming; you children always slept in good feather beds. Think about your heart; I taught you to open your heart to the peace that Jesus offers. I may bend and sway, but I ain't never been broken.

LESTER   Oak trees make good coffins too.

BOOBOO   What does that mean, Lester?

LESTER   It mean I'm tired of being afraid to live like a man; I'm tired of playing music that I hate for people who hate me.

BOOBOO   *(Misunderstanding)* Ooooooh, I understand now. One of these days you gon' learn to stop talking in riddles. You can lead the band; I'll give you a chance. Next season we going to make some quick jumps along the grits and chittlin' circuit. You can act as band leader and choose the music. How's that sound?

LESTER   It sound like shit to me!

BOOBOO *slaps* LESTER *swiftly upon that remark.* LESTER *staggers back, holds his face, glares at* BOOBOO.

LESTER *(Continued)* The grits and chittlin' circuit. Alabama, Mississippi, Georgia—Jesus own a plantation down there, don't He? Ain't that where they roast darkies in the daylight? Ain't that where the grits is dry stones and the chittlins come from inside you? There ain't nothin' left here for me.

LESTER *walks away.* BOOBOO *shouts after him.*

BOOBOO Go 'head! Leave! Don't come back! Keep running, keep running. You can't outrun Jesus, Lester. No, you can't. You gon' be running for the rest of your life, ungrateful, black, low-life scoundrel!

BOOBOO *and the* OTHERS *disappear.* LESTER's *mind returns to the "hotel room" where* HE *paces angrily.*

LESTER The Music had gone—
There was a empty shell,
But it wasn't no family;
We just tripped over tombstones together—
I wanted to follow the music,
Um gone!

DR. TRAMB *appears.*

DR. TRAMB Follow the music to where?
LESTER I followed the music to find my family, you dig, Dr. T.? 'Cause I knew when I found my family, I wouldn't have to be afraid no more.
DR. TRAMB Frightened of what?
LESTER Of God, freaks, hatred, the South. I didn't ever wanna swing through the South again. I hated it. Do you know what that kind of hatred is, Dr. T.?
DR. TRAMB Everyone seems to have his own giant rock to push uphill over and over.
LESTER What's your rock?
DR. TRAMB As you know I have two I labor at: medicine and psychology.
LESTER Dr. Tramb, dispenser of modern drugs and hoodoo rap to wasted natives.
DR. TRAMB There's nothing modern or mysterious about vitamins and human fellowship, actually. And, speaking of vitamins, I saw your friend Sarah and she says you don't take the pills I leave for you.
LESTER Doc, I been out on this road a long time, and I done seen a

whole lotta people start taking drugs from the pusher or the doctor and they end up gittin' chained to a mountain. I don't need no strawboss walking around with my feelings in his pocket, you dig, brotha Docta?

DR. TRAMB   I am not trying to control you, Lester. If I said you should try potatoes instead of gin sometime, you'd accuse me of gastro-imperialism, I suppose.

LESTER   Run it straight.

DR. TRAMB   If you take the white man's vitamins, stop taking the white man's alcohol and begin eating whoever's food, you can keep your black body alive and well, and I can continue to listen to your live music.

LESTER   Sheeet! Half the cats out there playing *my* live music. What in hell is so damn special about me playing *my* live music nowadays.

DR. TRAMB   Listen to me! It's that music I used to hear you play in the clubs and at the jam sessions I hunted down. It's the music you played a couple years ago at the Philharmonic concerts. That music is alive because *you* are. It makes even me want to believe that perhaps the human spirit has some creative potential after all. But, Prez, in today's world the art assassins will poison you with despair and bitterness if you let them, and they'll be especially brutal if your music is original. Only you can do what you do, and I'm here to help you because I need to keep hearing your live music.

LESTER   Why don't you git hip and make yo' own music?

DR. TRAMB   I can. Would you like to hear it?

LESTER   (*Mockingly*) Yeah, let me hear you blow some stomp down blues. I need to hear some of your live music for a change. Go 'head!

With a modest flourish, DR. TRAMB *begins to sing* "The Curse Of Mora," *a tune of 19th-century Irish mysticism.*

DR. TRAMB   THE FRETTED FIRES OF MORA
   BLEW O'ER HIM IN THE NIGHT,
   HE THRILLS NO MORE AT LOVING,
   NOR WEEPS FOR LOST DELIGHT . . .
   AROUND HIS PATH THE SHADOWS
   STALK EVER GRIM AND HIGH:
   SPEARS FLASH IN HANDS LONG WITHERE'D,
   AND DENTED SHIELDS GIVE CRY;
   OR MISTY WOMAN FACES
   LAUGH OUT AND PASS HIM BY,
   OR MISTY WOMAN FACES
   LAUGH OUT AND PASS HIM BY,
   HE HEARS THE WILD GREEN HARPER

CHANT SWEET A FAIRY RUNE,
AND THROUGH THE SLEEPING SILENCE,
HIS FEET MUST TRACK THE TUNE
WHEN THE WORLD IS BARR'D AND SPECKLED
WITH SILVER OF THE MOON
WHEN THE WORLD IS BARR'D AND SPECKLED
WITH SILVER OF THE MOON . . .

> LESTER, *both amused and moved, looks silently at* DR. TRAMB, *who smiles broadly, nervously but quickly and returns* LESTER's *look.*

LESTER   Them was some mean blues.

DR. TRAMB   Irish, man. I was singing Irish blues.

LESTER   *(Offering him a drink)* So you a Irish mu'fucka, eh?

DR. TRAMB   *(Accepting the drink)* I have some Indian blood, quite a bit, as a matter of fact.

LESTER   Oh, a Irish-Indian-American?

DR. TRAMB   My father was simply an Irishman who I never saw, except when I looked at my skin. My mother withered up like her people's ancient customs and died when I was a child. So, I eventually created myself a white American doctor to dull the pain of cosmopolitan living, and I sing a few random blues. It works. (DR. TRAMB *consumes the remainder of his drink in one gulp)*

LESTER   It sound good, but it don't work on my pain.

DR. TRAMB   It works on mine. In a world of no purpose it makes good sense to acquire a secure position from which one may dispense gifts of golden sympathy, a kind of personal foreign aid, you see?

LESTER   So America is your Great White Father now, eh?

DR. TRAMB   We're all the children of America, you know? All of us are here in assorted patterns of proud flotsam; bits of bloodstained driftwood, chunks of salty egalitarian notions, and wave after wave of wandering ghosts, tribal outcasts and such. We have a *collective* monopoly on computers and Los Angeles, you know.

LESTER   But this is the real life we're living, ain't it?

DR. TRAMB   Most assuredly.

LESTER   Well, they been callin' me Prez all these years, but now when I go to play, I sound like everybody else 'cause they sound like me, but I can barely earn my carfare now and my name is hanging on the bottom of the board. What kind of feelin' is this, Dr. T., where what's happening ain't really happening, except in my own head that I'm always fighting to git straight?

DR. TRAMB   That question describes a condition of human life to which one adjusts. Flexibility. You have to sort of improvise your own life around our conditions. Get a fresh perspective on things; take a tour of Europe; they respect Negro musicians over there.

LESTER   I was thinking of taking another touring gig over there, maybe in '59, but . . .

DR. TRAMB   *(Interrupting)* Take it now, Lester! Don't wait until next year. And take the pills! For Chrissake, you have a gift. It's criminal to destroy the body that bears the gift. You have everything you need to control the world. Others have imitated you; so what? That's a tribute, not a curse, even if they do earn more money. But you can earn money too! Stop drinking, get a good agent, work on the circuit again, stop staying by yourself so much, talk to people more, swing in the wind.

LESTER   Swing in the wind? Like strange fruit hanging from a poplar tree on Sunday?

DR. TRAMB   All of that is gone, Lester! It's over. The world has more than hypocritical Christians in it.

LESTER   What else do it have, Dr. Livingstone, I presume?

DR. TRAMB   For Chrissake, take your frightened ass out there and find out!

LESTER   *(Leaping and shouting)* SCRATCH SHEET!

> DR. TRAMB *visually disappears from* LESTER's *mind as* LESTER *speaks to "himself," directly to the audience.*

LESTER   *(Continued)* I had enough of that. It's too drafty out there now, you understand? You and Sarah are full of different answers, but we was just thrown together in the cities, a fellowship of confusion. You think I'm afraid? Ivey divey. But I remember when I ran for president; I had to fight all the way to the top, and in the battle, what I thought I had lost, I found. I found me some family. I wasn't afraid when I had to lock horns with Swoop in a mean cutting session in Kansas City! I wasn't afraid at all!

> *We hear an almost sinister 4/4 feeling with cymbal and brushes as the lights begin to revolve and undulate in his mind's recesses.* LESTER *begins to walk around the playing area.* HE *strolls very slowly, very hiply.* HE *does the profile of the coolest hipster, circa early 1930s. His left arm is held out from his body and swings back and forth. His shoulders swing from side to side, while his right arm hangs straight down his right side. Lights rise to illuminate a portion of his mind in which* SWOOP *and his sycophants await him.* SWOOP,

attired in a style which reflects his personal flamboyancy, sits on a high chair of sorts flanked by AGATHA and SLUMP who both preen him, and ingratiate themselves before him.

OTHERS *in the club are loose and eager for the cutting session.* THEY *will encourage the contestants and dance to the music. Their dance will be a gutsy stylization of 1930s popular dances.* SWOOP *reposes in absolute self-confidence.* HE *regards* LESTER's *approach with a kind of high style of hubristic condescension.* LESTER *reaches the "bandstand" and stops opposite at a distance from* SWOOP. LESTER *mimes removing a long cape and straightening his fine "clothes."* HE *then stands confidently facing* SWOOP.

SWOOP   Look at you, young cat, pretty and coming pretty late; umo have to swat you quick so I can make my Chicago date.

LESTER   To put it straight I just got out my bed; I didn't think you'd be here; matta fact I thought you was dead.

SWOOP   And now I see red, but you done forgot my name; they calls me Swoop 'cause I swoops all over a lame like you.

LESTER   Fortune and face, you got 'em, Lady Swoop, but I knows my thang will sing mighty swing and make you wear out three, four pair of wings tryin' to fly in my sky, you dig?

SWOOP   Yo' mouth may be greasy and yo' lips may be fat, but um fixin' ta let yo' young black butt know where you at.

LESTER   So jam!

SWOOP *mimes a chorus on his tenor as an offstage* MUSICIAN *plays a variation of the Hawkins style that is organic to* LESTER's *voice and the words of the first half of the following monologue. The music must be based on an early 30s Kansas City jam piece.* LES-TER's *word sounds have a distinct singing quality, as if broken swing incantation of the hip Afro griot. As* SWOOP *finishes his first chorus,* HE *decreases his volume while* LESTER *continues speaking.*

LESTER   *(Continued)* So he jumped off his throne
  And we came at each other in the middle of Creation—
  The Swoop was bad; that cat could play—
  He came in swinging low
  Walking a steady rumble—
  I leaped back, squeezed my axe,
  And got ready for a sho 'nuff tumble—

SWOOP *wails another chorus and then* LESTER *continues, the music underneath.*

LESTER   *(Continued)* He came crashing through the sound barrier,
Blew everything down to the ground,
And stomped off,
Swinging and thundering
Rollin', chargin'
Shoutin' and hollerin'
In tune to everybody's heart—

SWOOP *wails another chorus and then* LESTER *continues.*

LESTER   *(Continued)* And just when he thought he cut me clean
I rolled over and cooked some mighty beans.

LESTER *leaps into the fray and* HE *and* SWOOP *exchange furious riffs for two choruses.* SWOOP *backs off after the second chorus and* LESTER *continues his solo for two more choruses. As* HE *solos, the* OTHERS, *including* SWOOP *gradually disappear. When* LESTER *speaks again, the offstage* TENOR *continues beneath his voice but in an ethereal stylism of the original Lester Young.*

LESTER   *(Continued)* That whole night was homecooked sounds for me;
All I heard was new different;
Every chorus was "in the beginning,"
You dig?
Moments of highness,
Drifting through the silence of God,
You dig?
Floating ribbons of soft color sounds
Stretched out forever,
Traveling through everything alive and dead
And loving us into One Holiness.
I was swaying and rocking with stars I passed
And the longer I blew the bigger my heart got.
It kept growing and knowing with each beat
And I blew till my blood flowed through the horn
And turned the whole creation red
And yellow roses in sweet green dresses
With brown sound faces and blue hurt sighs
And hot white tears

Flowing down my black,
Rolling 'cross my blazing thighs,
Burning orange between night and day,
You dig, ladies?
Sun
Sunlight
I was Sun.
He was The Inventor and The King.
But I took his crown with his own Invention
And my sweet, mellow feelings.
Kin any of you ladies

LINCOLN, MOUSE *and* TWEED *appear.*

LESTER   *(Continued)* Dig what I'm blowin?

THEY *all laugh and indulge in good-natured ridicule.*

LINCOLN   This is what happens when you let them people be free.
TWEED   Why don't you climb down off yo' ass and join the race.
MOUSE   If now, at least order some drinks.
LESTER   *(Shouting to an imaginary waiter)* A round of drinks for my
friends.
LINCOLN   *(At the same waiter)* And tell the manager to bring us the
paychecks!
LESTER   *(Peering into the audience)* You know we gon' git the bread,
and it's got to be long with this many people squeezed up in this joint.
LINCOLN   Amen.
MOUSE   We oughtta celebrate by lettin' Lincoln buy us a second round.
TWEED.   Amen.
LINCOLN   Celebrate what?
TWEED   Even though we done seen each other around and listened to
each other, this is the first time we ever all played on the same bandstand
together.
MOUSE   And wasn't we mean as a frigid queen?
LINCOLN   We oughtta form a band and stay together.

The MANAGER *appears.*

LINCOLN   *(Continued)* Greetings, Mr. Manager, and please don't give
us nothing that stretches.
MANAGER   Unfortunately, I can't write you a check.

MOUSE   We ain't too hincty to take cash.

MANAGER   You can't be paid because you weren't officially scheduled to appear.

> *The background music fades out.*

LINCOLN   What kinda shit is this? We played music, didn't we?

LESTER   The cash register ain't stopped ringin', did it?

TWEED   We was called and told to be here tonight.

LESTER   You called yourself.

MANAGER   My secretary called and asked you boys if you wanted to be on standby. You came and played on your own accord.

LESTER   I know this ofay chump not serious.

MANAGER   I'm dead serious and I'm sorry, but that's the way it is. Look, I'll take care of your drinks and we'll call it square.

LESTER   Ding Dong!

> *On the "Dong," LESTER takes a wild swing at the MANAGER who ducks and incapacitates LESTER with a lethal blow to the gut. General mayhem breaks out: screaming, glass breaking, a drunken brawl in sound and light. LINCOLN tosses MOUSE some car keys and jumps on the MANAGER. As MOUSE exits to set up the "car," LINCOLN is quickly trapped in the MANAGER's arms. TWEED, who has been standing off, pretending not to be involved, hits the MANAGER from behind with a blackjack. The MANAGER, unconscious, falls. LINCOLN extricates himself and helps LESTER up. TWEED goes through the MANAGER's pockets.*

LESTER   *(Continued)* Miss Lincoln, I think we better split 'fore Bob Crosby show and put all these folks in the penitentiary. Is the royal carriage prepared?

LINCOLN   Brother Mouse got the elephant saddled and ready to shake.

> *LESTER, TWEED and LINCOLN run to another emerging area at the sound of a police siren. The sounds of the brawl fade out as THEY enter the "car," four chairs in two rows facing the audience.*

MOUSE   Where to, Mr. Young?

LESTER   Lady Mouse, since I'm the King, take me to my throne and please feed this elephant to death.

> *THEY all laugh as the engine roars them off. MOUSE mimes*

driving and breaks into a spontaneously improvised song in which eventually the OTHERS *join with further embellishment.* LESTER *passes a pint bottle of gin and* TWEED *lights up a stick of herb.*

MOUSE   AIN'T NO PLACE LIKE THE OPEN ROAD
SINGING, SWINGING ALL THE WAY
AIN'T NO PLACE LIKE THE OPEN ROAD
LEAVE YOUR BLUES TO YESTERDAY

ALL   AIN'T NO PLACE LIKE THE OPEN ROAD
SINGING, SWINGING ALL THE WAY
AIN'T NO PLACE LIKE THE OPEN ROAD
LEAVE YOUR BLUES TO YESTERDAY.

THEY *all begin doing an embellished "head" scatting of the melodic line, each in the range of his particular instrument. Though* EACH VOICE *embellishes distinctively, the* FOUR VOICES *remain in perfect harmony and basic rhythm. During the scatting, the lights fade to black.*

SECOND MOVEMENT

The car. In the following car riffs LESTER *and the* OTHERS *may sound verbally hostile to each other but their verbal jibes, no matter how harsh sounding, are generally "macho" expressions of genuine mutual affection and respect.* MOUSE *sings happily while* HE *drives. The* OTHERS *are asleep.* LESTER *stirs and wakes.*

LESTER   Where we at?

MOUSE   *(Stoically)* We lost.

LESTER   *(Starting and waking the* OTHERS*)* LOST! DAMN! Wake up yaw!

TWEED   What! What! What!

LINCOLN   What's the problem?

LESTER   We lost.

LINCOLN   *(Irritated)* Don't say that; we ain't lost yet.

LESTER   If Mouse don't know where we at, we must be lost! We lost.

TWEED   *(To* MOUSE *in jesting derision)* Blind turkey butt, why don't you look at the map.

MOUSE   'Cause you 'sposed to be reading the map.

TWEED   You know damn well I can't read.

LINCOLN   Yaw just watch the road signs; look for Cincy. I ain't never seen such blind niggas in all my life. It's a wonder yaw find yo' way to the bandstand.

LESTER   You can always tell where the bandstand at 'cause it stay surrounded with sweet smelling, pretty dark chocolate women.

TWEED   If you like dark chocolate so much, why you nibblin' on white chocolate in the Big Apple?

LINCOLN   Git to that!

LESTER   There's dark chocolate and light chocolate, and if you in Africa or Europe and you jumps in the ocean, it's the same ocean, but if you don't swim like Tarzan, you'll drown no matter where the chick come from. Git to that!

ALL *laugh, except* LINCOLN.

LINCOLN   I don't really want to. I'd rather git to our bidness! You still owe me $287.

LESTER   You mean $237; that's what I remember.

LINCOLN   The crap game in Topeka, remember?

LESTER   Oh yeah, sweet music didn't come through in Topeka.

LINCOLN   But I did, and I lent you another $50 after you lost everything again!

LESTER   Hey, I lost, I lost; no big thang. Life is a gamble they say.

MOUSE   Lincoln, you know darn well Lester always lose.

LESTER   No, I do not.

TWEED   Most of the time.

LESTER   And that ain't no big thang, um tryin' to tell you.

LINCOLN   We in the middle of the Depression; $287 is a big big thang!

LESTER   Yeah, but it ain't no big thang between brothers, 'cause you know I got it covered. We sound beautiful together, remember? What about when we traveled in Europe together? Remember Paris, Vienna, Stockholm, Geneva? You gon' git your money.

LINCOLN   You been saying that since Tulsa! I wanna know *when* I'm gon' git my money!

LESTER   *(Genuinely irritated)* What's a few dollars between brothers?

LINCOLN   *(Philosophically intended)* A head beating—that's what it is.

LESTER   Don't make no difference to me. Stop the elephant; we fixin' to take this to the pavement.

TWEED   Hold tight, fools! Yaw been like brothers for too long for this simple shit to happen.

MOUSE   Amen. Cool out, Lester. How you sound. Yaw both sound like fools.

LINCOLN   He's the one talking 'bout "taking it to the pavement."

LESTER   That's where they "beat heads," ain't it?

TWEED   Why don't yaw just cool out?

Pause.

LESTER   *(Introspectively)* This thing called life is gittin' stranger and stranger. All I want is a simple harmony and I got to go through all this bullshit again.

LINCOLN   What bullshit again?

LESTER   Reading tombstones for suckers on the midway.

TWEED   Run it straight, please?

LESTER   If I have some money and any of yaw need some of that money, we work it back and forth; then we straight, like good music, you dig?

LINCOLN   No, I don't dig. You be out there rappin' ballyhoo to the fine chicks while I'm behind the bandstand scufflin' with cats who want they money. If we working it back and forth, why I always be the one carryin' everything?

LESTER   You ain't carryin' doodlysquat! I bring the people in, you dig, Lincoln?

LINCOLN   You simple fathead bitch!

TWEED   *(Shouting)* Amen!

MOUSE   *(Shouting)* If yaw don't stop this mess right now, ah swear umo make this elephant stumble in the ditch.

> *Pause.*

LINCOLN   Pass me the gin and some of that reefer too. Since I got to pay for it, I might as well enjoy it.

LESTER   *(Passing the stuff)* Yeah, you might as well. Be my honored guest, Lady Lincoln.

> *Pause.*

MOUSE   *(Turning on the radio to some mellow blues sounds, late Thirties)* I need to hear me some music.

TWEED   *(Curling up, putting on his stocking cap and pushing his hat over his eyes)* I need to cop me some Z's.

> *Pause during which* LESTER *and* LINCOLN *share a joint and the bottle.*

LESTER   Dig Mr. Chops on the radio.

LINCOLN   Yeah, he know his blues; sound real good.

LESTER   He sound alright, but his right people keep stepping on everybody. Gittin' in the way, you dig? He need to work more with his left people.

LINCOLN   You think a pianist is supposed to be a drummer or something? Just play the rhythm, right?

LESTER   No, but I can't stand too much racket back there when I hit the first chorus. I want it light, quick, smooth, steady—not loud, not filled up till there ain't no room to fly.

LINCOLN   *(Jesting)* Nigga is you a musician or a pilot?

LESTER   *(Laughing)* Maybe I'm just a nigga; I don't know sometimes.

LINCOLN   Me neither, but you sho got a lotta stuff with you. Calling the man's hands "left people" and "right people." If I didn't know you, I wouldn't understand a damn word you was saying. *(Mimicking a white, Southern drawl)* What is yo' problem, boy?

THEY *both laugh, pass the gin.*

LESTER   Lincoln, I think the real problem is we need to ease out this life.
LINCOLN   You mean die? For what?
LESTER   I mean this life of a sad nomad. We jam; we have a ball and then we move on to the next place; the only home we seem to have is in the next place. Don't you ever think about that?
LINCOLN   My home is in my pocket, my brother. If you thinking about a home, save yo' money and buy one—after you pay me back—then stick you a wife and kids in it so you'll always have you some place to go back to. You know I'll be yo' best man—as many times as you want.
LESTER   But the "home" I want, money won't buy. Money just won't take care of the problem. I need . . .
LINCOLN   *(Interrupting)* Is you crazy? Money take care of anything; it definitely take care of me. If you ain't got no money in this place, you might as well be dead!
MOUSE   Amen!
LINCOLN   Check this out: My daddy was dead for ten years before he finally died from a serious lack of money. In Georgia, a sharecropper with nine crummies in a two room shack. Daddy didn't drink his miseries away 'cause he couldn't afford to drink. He used to come home all bent over every evening, wash up, eat some corn meal mush or grits with fatback bacon or collards and okra with fatback or fatback with turnips and cornbread. That's why I don't eat no pork. Then, after he'd eat and maybe grunt at his family, he'd take his raggedy harmonica and go sit under a tree just down the road from the shack, and he'd watch the road and the cotton fields and play the meanest blues I ever heard until it was time for him to go to bed. He did that every day, all year, year in and year out, good weather and bad. Hardly ever spoke a word. He started wasting away from the inside, and, even if we could have afforded to call a doctor, I don't think it would have done any good. Money, homey. When he died, I got on that same road he used to dream about and I ain't never looked back to Georgia or poverty ever since. I didn't make the laws of this land, but the law says that money keeps you alive, well and looking good. That's the secret of why I stay so pretty.
LESTER   And drunk.

LINCOLN   What you mean, Lester?

LESTER   I mean you stay drunk so you can forgit you living all cramped up in yo' pocket. People wasn't made to live in pockets. I'm one of the people, not a piece of small change.

LINCOLN   You sound like a piece of shit to me.

MOUSE   *(Turning off the radio)* Oh no, not again!

LESTER   You sound jealous to me; like you don't want me to git what I'm supposed to git.

LINCOLN   And what in the hell are you supposed to git?

LESTER   My throne, baby; that's what I'm supposed to git. I was on my way to the throne when we formed this combo, any-Goddamn-way. And I'm ready to split now.

LINCOLN   Oh shit, here's that problem again.

LINCOLN *shakes* TWEED *who wakes in a wild start.*

TWEED   WHAT! WHAT! WHAT!

LINCOLN   Lester wants to split, right, Mouse?

MOUSE   He done got tired of us again.

LESTER   I just need to grow some.

TWEED   Grow some what?

LESTER   I don't feel legit wit yaw; that's the problem.

TWEED   You done become a hincty nigga; that's the problem.

LESTER   Ding Dong! Here it go again. Brother Mouse, are we anywhere near my throne?

MOUSE   Another bar or two, I guess.

LESTER   It's time I went to sit in with a real band, 'cause these sounds in here is gittin' funky. I can't stand this whispering. Stop the elephant!

LINCOLN   Stop it! Stop the elephant, Mouse. Let this nigga out.

MOUSE   Whoa, elephant!

LESTER *climbs out.*

LINCOLN   Lester, you great but sometimes you ain't good. You need some whispering to blow away some of that weirdness you carry around.

MOUSE   Good luck, brother Lester.

TWEED   We leaving you in peace.

LINCOLN   All the memories ain't bad, homeboy.

LESTER   Hey, yaw the finest bitches I ever played with; but I need to be with people who can appreciate the music of my spirit.

TWEED   We'll catch you at the next junction, probably.

LINCOLN   Jam strong but when you need help, call.

LESTER   *(Chuckling disdainfully)* Thank you, but I don't think I'll ever be needing your help again.

> *The elephant and its* OCCUPANTS *disappear.* LESTER *hums a familiar song off-key as* HE *walks toward a combination chair and music stand understood as the metaphorical "throne." To the throne is attached a prominent placard on which is flamboyantly printed the name "SWOOP."* LESTER *smilingly removes the placard, rips it in half, takes a seat and continues humming. Enter* AGATHA, *carrying an album, and* SLUMP *who both surround* LESTER. AGATHA's *voice is high and piercing.* SLUMP *is a hip-walking, well-dressed chronic stutterer.*

AGATHA   Good morning, Lester. Slump and I brought a few records for you to listen to before the orchestra starts rehearsing for tonight's dance.

SLUMP   Since you takin' Swoop's place, me and Agatha wanna make certain you kin fill it.

LESTER   *(Very uncomfortably and suspiciously)* Oh yeah? Well, I been playin' a few months with yaw. We been gittin' along.

AGATHA   Lester, oh how I wish that were true. Now please listen carefully, Lester. When the boss hired you to take Swoop's place, we knew you couldn't fill his shoes overnight; it takes a great deal of time and effort to master standard musical technique, but we think we've just about run out of time.

LESTER   Run it straight.

AGATHA   *(Signaling* SLUMP *to start the "turntable")* We're a family here; everyone has an equal place. We want you to listen to Swoop's old solos and learn how to play with us.

> SLUMP *gives* LESTER's *chair a shove which starts it revolving as if on a turntable.* LESTER *holds desperately to the chair. The music heard is a loud, scratchy, nightmarish sound, a deliberately distorted improvisation distantly based upon the early 1930s Coleman Hawkins solos.*

SLUMP   You playing for a big, legitimate dance band now, not some dittybop jam combo.

AGATHA   See how *strong* Swoop's sense of rhythm is?

SLUMP   The Swoop cooked 'em, didn't he?

AGATHA   Imitation, that's how great art is made!

SLUMP   If you in a horse race, you should have you a horse.

> LESTER *begins repeating the word "no" more to himself than to his tormentors.* AGATHA *and* SLUMP *become more overtly aggressive, hostile.*

AGATHA   You play all outside the rhythm!
SLUMP   And you sound like a damn alto, not a tenor!
AGATHA   Your little ditties throw off the entire orchestra!
SLUMP   You play like a fat lady skating on thin ice!
AGATHA   I tried to warn them about you, but they hired you anyway.
SLUMP   Aw-w-w-w-nigga, you can't play for shit!
AGATHA   You should beat your horn into a plowshare, LADY LESTER!

> LESTER *leaps up and almost screams.*

LESTER   DING DONG!

> AGATHA *and* SLUMP *recoil slightly and look at each other.*

AGATHA   Is there some slight problem?
LESTER   *(Overtly calm and polite)* Where's the toilet at, please?
SLUMP   End of the hall to your right.

> LESTER *strolls away rapidly as the* TWO OTHERS *stand exchanging looks with each other about* LESTER. LESTER *reaches the end of the "hall" and turns left instead of right.* SLUMP *shouts.*

SLUMP   *(Continued)* I said turn right, not left. Damn, can't you do nothing like you told?

> LESTER *ignores him and heads to the "street." When* HE *gets to the street,* HE *cups his hands to his mouth and begins to loudly, clearly scat in the direction that* MOUSE, TWEED *and* LINCOLN *had once disappeared. It is the same scat which* THEY *had shared previously.* AGATHA *and* SLUMP *disappear. The elephant with the* THREE OCCUPANTS *appears.*

MOUSE   We was damn near in Chicago when you caught us!
TWEED   There's plenty bread for a musician in Chicago. You wanna hang with us this time?
LESTER   Let's go to Chicago!

HE *starts to get into the car but is stopped by* LINCOLN.

LINCOLN   *(Somewhat good-naturedly but firm and serious)* Hole tight, turkey; I don't wanna hear nothin' from you, homey. Even though it's been eight months since you left us, you come back here and expect to ease in like you just coming back from lunch.

LESTER   Awwwwwwwman, dig . . .

TWEED   DIG DOG DUDU!

MOUSE   You stepped in it, brother, and you got to wipe yo' feet at the door.

LESTER   I thought it would be different when . . .

LINCOLN   It is different! We know how to git along without yo' ass!

LESTER   Yaw found another tenor player!

TWEED   Uh huh, nigga scared now!

LINCOLN   Shut up, Tweed! Lester, we had made some plans together.

LESTER   *(Contritely)* That didn't include me?

TWEED   YOU!? WHY YOU, RUNAWAY NIGGA?

LESTER   *(Truly reduced)* Awwwwwman, I can't see straight sometimes, but I . . .

LINCOLN   Look, Lester, we on the way to Chicago and figuring to collect a few more cats and form a big band.

LESTER   I'd like to try out for the band—if nobody got any objections.

LINCOLN   When we heard you needed a gig, we saved a spot for you.

LESTER   *(Genuinely brightening)* You did? I knew my brothers would look out for me!

LINCOLN   *(Tongue-in-cheek)* You gon' be our drummer.

LESTER *misunderstands and explodes.*

LESTER   What!? TRAPS? IS YOU CRAZY, BITCH? *(Hearing their laughter)* Awwwww man, yaw gon' give somebody a heart attack behind some simple ass joke.

TWEED   Uh huh, but now you a happy nappy to be back here, ain't you?

LESTER   Pass the gin.

LINCOLN   Not till we arrive at a final understandin'.

Pause.

LESTER   To tell the truth, I'm sorry I ever left you rusty nomads. Now will you pass the gin, Miss Lincoln?

LINCOLN   *(Passing the gin)* With great pleasure.

Pause as LESTER *drinks deeply.*

MOUSE   What's happenin' at the throne?

LESTER   You mean the electric chair?

LINCOLN   We tried to tell you, homey!

LESTER   *(Angry, intense in an extremely hip, laid back way and sound-ing ironically incredulous for humorous effect)* Oh, it was drafty whis-pers every day;
Buns stayed tight
Tryin' ta keep up off that hot plate.
I'm lookin' for space to stretch out
Or lay out if I feel like it, but
They gon' make me a geek freak on the midway;
THE WILE MAN WHO EATS HIS AXE WHILE HE PLAYING IT,
You dig?
Um tryin' ta lay back and sing new songs;
Them turkeys lookin' for a repeater pencil,
Like a machine gun;
The bread's long,
But the bombs is a monster,
And I'm tired of hincty black circus tubs anyway,
You dig?
Um gone!

LINCOLN   Amen!

TWEED   But why didn't you just lay at home with us?

MOUSE   Yeah, we even got a new radio—check it out.

> *Turns on the radio. We hear a* LADY DAY *side,* "Darn That Dream."

LESTER   *(Enraptured by her voice, midspeech)* Home is beautiful, but you can't stay there all the time . . . especially if something is missing.

MOUSE   If something was missin'? What was missin'?

LESTER   Listen real good now, yaw.

> HE *takes a deep swig from the bottle as the* OTHERS *mistakenly wait for him to speak again.*

TWEED   Well, we listening, homey; run it. Tell us what was missing.

LESTER   I know you got to peep it by now.

LINCOLN   He probably mean he was missin' us.

TWEED   Naw, he think we missed him.

MOUSE   I'm missing everything.

LESTER   Wrong. All yaw dummies is wrong. You ain't listening. Listen!

Pause during which THEY ALL *listen to voice on the radio.*

LESTER   *(Continued)* Can you dig Miss Lady?

LINCOLN   She's the best vocalist Grand Walker ever had.

TWEED   Ah, she sound like warm molasses and fresh butter!

MOUSE   *(Raising his hands from the steering wheel)* Ah sing it, Miss Mama!

TWEED   *(Panicking)* Keep your goddamn hands on the wheel, fool!

LESTER   But that tenor stabbin' Miss Lady in the back.

LINCOLN   Her name is Billie Holiday.

LESTER   I just named her Miss Lady.

TWEED   You know Lester ain't got no respect for people names.

LESTER   Where's the show comin' from?

MOUSE   New York.

LESTER   Point the elephant to New York and put it in gallop.

LINCOLN   New York? Just like that? And you just coming back? Is you boxed behind that gin?

LESTER   But I know what's missin'.

MOUSE   Missin' from what?

LESTER   Poppa Walker and Lady Day missin' us, you dig? And we missin' them. Listen to the lady! She's giving birth to all the sounds we ever thought we played. Listen to that! *(Pause)* Can't no decent human being turn they back on her. We need to git inside that lady's soul and ride to the sun. Fellas, I scratched yaw and I got burnt. I learned my lesson about tape recorder bands, circus freaks and loneliness. We was runnin' off-key; that's why we was buzzin' on each other over nothin'. We need the music of her spirit to give us balance. This may be our last chance to git it. We listening to the most eloquent lady alive, you dig?

LINCOLN   *(Perfunctorily contrary)* Sound like you wanna split on us again.

LESTER   NO! Never again! I ain't goin' nowhere without yaw, ever again, even if we do blow the chance of a lifetime and don't go to New York to sit at the feet of this beautiful lady.

TWEED   I think this turkey is right.

MOUSE   I wish I had somebody like that to sing me bedtime lullabies.

Pause.

LINCOLN   Point the elephant to New York, but put it on cruise, not gallop. Ain't no need to hurry.

LESTER   That's right because we on the way to the top now; we kin cruise free in the jet stream. When I git to New York, I'm gon' call my mama and tell her what's happenin'. I'm gon' tell her that she don't have to worry about being alone or needing anything when she git old. No suh, not now, not with her son playing the big time in the big apple. In a little while we gon' be happenin' all over the country and Europe too.

> *Lights crossfade to reveal* LADY DAY *in a single spotlight. The previous song has blended into a melody of her most memorable songs ending with "Strange Fruit." After a few moments into the melody* LESTER *appears in a lone spotlight to the side and Upstage of her.* HE *accompanies her on his tenor and takes appropriate mini-solos. The offstage* MUSICIANS, *of course, accompany them both. At the end of* "Strange Fruit" *there is applause;* LESTER *and* BILLIE *bow and step out of the spotlights which crossfade with another area Downstage to be understood as the "backstage" of a nightclub.* LESTER *packs his horn.* BILLIE *fidgets with her gardenia and stares vacantly.*

LESTER   Baby, you could make a stone bleed if you wanted. They loved you.

LADY DAY   Thanks, Prez, but lately I been feeling like a second hand plastic tomato.

LESTER   Aw baby, what kinda crazy talk is that? You sounded beautiful.

LADY DAY   I'm talking about how I feel, and you, of all people, know what I mean.

LESTER   That's true, Lady, but let's not get off into that tonight. Let's go to Minton's and jam. We'll talk some more about that stuff later.

LADY DAY   There's nothing else to talk about, Prez. I finally made up my mind. As of tonight I'm officially on my own.

LESTER   Lady Day, I don't see where you got reason to have so many funky thoughts blowing around yo' brain. I'm doing everything I can to make you happy. You invite me to move in with you and yo' mama so you can show me New York and we could spend time together; I moves in. You invite me to move out; I moves out. You ask me to stay friends with you, I say of course. You always ask for me and the other fellas when you record; we drop everything and come running. Now, as soon as we make it to the big time, you wanna quit Grand Walker's band and go running off on your own.

LADY DAY   But Prez, I need to feel free.

LESTER   Free? We're free artists who find new sounds to tell old stories. We ain't slaves. I don't see no goddamn chains on you, woman. You must be dreaming.

LADY DAY   The chains on me ain't got nothing to do with dreaming. Prez, it's hard for me to explain things; that's why I sing, I guess. But something happened to me once that I'll never forget. When they locked me up in that girls' reform school, my first cellmate was this girl named Emma, a tall, black skin country girl, and she was a mean, vicious bitch and damn near strong as a man. They put her there for castratin' one of her uncles with a butcher knife. Soon as I step in the door, she jumped up and smacked me and told me how she hated my guts and I better do everything she said or she'd cut off my titties. Prez, I swear before my Saviour, I peed in my bloomers. I was so afraid I didn't move even when the water was running down my leg. I just stood there crying and trembling for a long time, afraid to move unless she said move. When I looked up at her, she was sitting back all cool, smiling. Then she got polite, even nice, let me sit down, gave me a chocolate bar, talked about herself and where she came from. She sounded so nice and was treating me so good, that I didn't think it would be no problem if I got up and changed my bloomers. Soon as I stood up, she punched me in the stomach, knocked me over the bed. I learned quick. As long as I did what pleased her, she was polite, gentle, loving, fun even. But if I did anything, even something accidental, that displeased her, she'd beat the living daylights out me or she'd starve me, or she'd make me stand alone in a corner during recreation periods, or something. Prez, this world ain't never let me forget what that feels like. I mean, I named you Prez because you're the best, just like Roosevelt, but you still colored and no matter how great you blow that tenor, if you don't do what ole marsa "ask" you to do in this place, you liable to be hung out to dry. You all tell me I'm a great singer, but no matter how good I sing, I'm still locked up in a small corner of everybody's mind, regardless to who marsa is.

LESTER   You got messed over, but, the past is ivey divey, Miss Lady. This is 1944; ole marsa must be dead by now. We playin' with the top band; we eatin' good; we sleepin' good; we workin' and playin' together regular; we all at peace in the music; ain't nothin' to be afraid of; ain't nothin' missin' from this tribe now.

LADY DAY   But I think I'm missin'.

LESTER   You? How?

LADY DAY   I just stopped feeling a part of what's happening because I know I can do better if I had my own small combo.

LESTER   You gittin' top pay now with Grand Walker. How can you do better than that?

LADY DAY   It's not money! I have songs I want to sing that can't work with a big band.

LESTER   You could ask Grand Walker to let . . .

LADY DAY   I can't ask Grand Walker nothing, Prez! That's his band. He plays what he wants and you all play what he wants too. Half the time I get drowned out with all that racket anyway.

LESTER   But you could ask them to play softer or get a better mike, or you could ask for a small combo when you do your numbers. You don't have to split; we can always write new arrangements of the music.

LADY DAY   No, *we* can't make enough arrangements to suit me. *I* want to have my own arrangements written under my supervision and sing 'em according to how I'm feeling, where I want to and when I want to. I don't wanna be suffocated up under Grand Walker's wing forever.

LESTER   Who's suffocating you? We doing everything to show you off. Wherever we gig we put you up front.

LADY DAY   Yeah, I'm the pretty high yellow bitch who stands out front and draws the suckers in.

LESTER   Awwww mama, what is you talkin' 'bout?

LADY DAY   A showpiece is empty and alone no matter where you put it.

LESTER   Empty? Alone? You the head lady of a full tribe, baby. We all singing with you, unnastan? Just relax and try to feel good like the rest of us.

LADY DAY   *(Angry)* Feel good about what?

LESTER   Feel good about how I feel when I play with you. Sometimes, Lady, I hear your exact mood in my horn.

LADY DAY   And sometimes, lots of times, I feel what I hear in your horn, and I just go there full of blind love, but not thinking. When I open my eyes, I'm standing at the edge of a cliff.

LESTER   Baby, you got to get them ugly pictures out yo' head.

LADY DAY   Like this picture of you and your sad-looking wife? (SHE *hands him a large photograph of him and a white woman cheek to cheek)*

LESTER   Where'd you git that?

LADY DAY   You forgot this when you moved out last week.

LESTER   *(Misunderstanding)* Is this it? Is this the problem?

LADY DAY   You are her problem, not mine.

LESTER   But I told you I'm gittin' a divorce . . .

LADY DAY   Les . . .

LESTER   But I can't git it till my deferment come through and I git them draft board people off my tail; she ain't . . .

LADY DAY   SHE AIN'T GOT NOTHIN' TO DO WITH NOTHIN' is what I'm tryin' to tell you. I feel sorry for the bitch 'cause I know she tryin' to git the same thing I am, freedom. Freedom from you, Grand Walker, Mouse, Lincoln and that sneaky Tweed. I'm either a sister, a mother or a lover, but I ain't never what I want to be. Everybody's kind and polite to me as if I'm important; they call me a star, but I ain't got nothin' to say with what goes down in that band. All I hear is Billie, do this or do that; or Billie, sing this or sing that; or Billie, go here or go there. I'm always serving or being served up to somebody. There's nothing left here for me. I done had enough of being trampled on along the road. Yaw kin move on without me.

    LADY DAY *removes some works from her purse and prepares to shoot up. At the sight of the works* LESTER *leaps up.*

LESTER   Check this out, mama; let's ease up to Minton's and blow some of this funky air away. Grand Walker and all them gon' be up there. It'll make you feel better.

LADY DAY   Goddammit, Prez! I feel like being alone! Okay?

LESTER   Why? So you kin sit up here dreamin' about pain and rememberin' stupid hatred?

LADY DAY   Prez, I don't wanna remember nothin'; I wanna forgit, and I can forgit better by myself. Besides I'm on my own now. It wouldn't feel the same.

LESTER   Why do you want to leave yourself behind like this?

LADY DAY   I ain't leavin' myself nowhere but where I wanna be, and Prez, even though we still friends, it ain't nobody's business what I do, you dig?

LESTER   Ain't got no choice.

    LADY DAY *lays aside her works, goes to* LESTER, *and embraces him.* HE *is limp.*

LADY DAY   Look, dahlin', I might stop by Minton's if I'm feelin' better. You just go there and jam strong for me, but watch out for alligators.

LESTER   Let the alligator git to Zanzy if it can. I'll jam for you until you come jam *with* us. I hope I see you later, Miss Lady.

LADY DAY   I hope so too.

    HE *kisses her hand and* SHE *disappears. As soon as* SHE *does, we*

*hear the explosive finale of "Flying Home" and then the laughing
voices of* LINCOLN, TWEED, *and* MOUSE *who appear fresh from a
jam, presumably at Minton's.* LESTER *arrives from the bandstand
and* THEY ALL *pack their instruments;* THEY *exude a slightly
drunken gaiety. A bottle of gin is passed.*

LINCOLN   After what you done tonight they might send yo' black butt
back to Firewood, Mississippi.
LESTER   Woodville, Mississippi, Woodville.
TWEED   Same difference; they both burn.
MOUSE   So did Prez.
LESTER   The dancers, homey, the dancers was doin' all the pushin'.
MOUSE AND TWEED   Amen!

THEY ALL *laugh.*

LINCOLN   I wish Lady Day coulda been here; it woulda made this ses-
sion perfect. Wasn't she supposed to come with you, Prez?
LESTER   I don't know what to do about Miss Lady.
TWEED   It's too late to do anything about her.
MOUSE   She gone, homey. It's over.
LINCOLN   We all tried to talk to her, but she wouldn't give up no light.
TWEED   I say forgit about her.
LESTER   I can't. Pass the gin. I need me a good stiff drink bad!
LINCOLN   *(Passing him an empty gin bottle)* You gon' have to forget
about her, homey.
TWEED   She the one leaving us; why should you be gloomy? Let her
simple black ass go; maybe she want to be a junkie whore.

LESTER *violently pushes* TWEED *who falls against* MOUSE.

LESTER   Don't put no bad mouth on the lady; she was good for us; she
brought us here together, didn't she?
TWEED   No, you brought us here, sucker! And I'm fixin' to put you
there.

Pointing to the floor, TWEED *goes after* LESTER *who grabs the
gin bottle.* MOUSE *and* LINCOLN *step between them.*

LINCOLN   That's enough!
MOUSE   Man, yaw stop this stupid mess!

TWEED   Naw, this nigga wanna break my chest. I want a piece of this nigga tonight.

LESTER   You gon' git five pieces of knuckle in yo' mouth.

LINCOLN   I said stop it, Lester!

MOUSE   (*Who holds* TWEED) Lay off, Tweed. Da nigga ain't worth it!

LESTER   Not worth it! I'll kick yo' simple ass too, blind buzzard.

> TWEED *shakes off* MOUSE *so violently that* MOUSE *falls to the floor.*

TWEED   Git the hell off me, Mouse.

> TWEED *pulls a blackjack and goes after* LESTER. LINCOLN *pushes* LESTER *out of the way and pulls a very long knife which stops* TWEED *from coming any closer.* MOUSE *gets up and roars at all of them.*

MOUSE   YOU SIMPLE MUTHAFUCKAS! I HAD ENOUGH! THAT'S IT! I'm finished with trying to hold nothin' together. We ain't nothin' but funky whispers banging up against each other in the dark. (HE *picks up his horn and says as* HE *departs:*) I got to git out this cave so I can see what I'm doing. BYE!

LINCOLN   What it is, brother Tweed?

> *Pause.* TWEED *finally picks up his instrument.*

TWEED   Prez, one day you gon' git caught without your cabinet.

LESTER   I don't need no cabinet, Tweed.

TWEED   There's more than one way to skin a groundhog.

> HE *departs.* LINCOLN *puts his knife away.* LESTER *retrieves the bottle and looks at its emptiness.*

LESTER   Sometimes I feel like a two-dollar whore. Now what, Lady Lincoln?

LINCOLN   It's been writ, homey.

LESTER   Just like that?

LINCOLN   Just like that.

LESTER   Where do we go?

LINCOLN   We keep going forward. I got a pocket fulla money; we don't need them.

LESTER   What will we do?

LINCOLN   Tonight?

LESTER   Forever.

LINCOLN   I ain't thought about forever, but tonight, tonight I'm gon' party and so are you. (LINCOLN *pulls out a wad of bills and forcefully hands a passive* LESTER *several of them*) Now look, I got me a sweet mama waitin' for me, and ain't Marie out there waiting for you?

LESTER   *(Numbly staring at the money)* Yeah.

LINCOLN   Well, stop walking on yo' bottom lip. They gone, they gone! Huh? A melody comes; you play it; it goes on. Ain't no road blocks up ahead, homey. Come out of it. Go have a good time with Marie! Party, party, party, till it's all a vague memory!

LESTER   *(Brightening)* Why not, Brother Lincoln.

LINCOLN   That's it, homey. Don't come down now. Stay up. Don't let nothin' bring you down, understand?

LESTER   *(Not entirely convinced)* I'm alright, Lincoln.

LINCOLN   I'm gone; I'll see you tomorrow at China House.

LINCOLN *departs. The lights go to black for a few moments and in the darkness we hear voices and laughter. One voice belongs to* LESTER, *the other to* WHITE MARIE *whose accent is hip Afro street feeling.*

LESTER   I thought that old ginnie would bust a nut when he saw us.

WHITE MARIE   Law, I thought I'd die laughin' when he poured salt in his wine. He was one lame turkey.

LESTER   Ain't that the truth.

WHITE MARIE   Damn, I can't find the keyhole.

LESTER   Let me try to find the hole.

WHITE MARIE   *(Giggling)* Oh, Lester, stop now. You know I don't be playin' that in the hallway. You crazy, man.

LESTER   Open the door and turn on the lights, baby.

WHITE MARIE   Okay, just hole tight, poppa.

Lights snap on. We see WHITE MARIE *and* LESTER. WHITE MARIE *is an attractive white woman, about 32, well-dressed. During the ensuing scene,* LESTER, *among other things, attempts to take her to bed, but* SHE *constantly thwarts him for her own reasons.*

WHITE MARIE   *(Continued, still with the black accent)* We home now, baby; you kin res' yo' axe.

LESTER *sets down his instrument and goes to her.*

LESTER   Marie, you know you was raised to talk different than that. Don't be gittin' colored on me now. I'm just gittin' used to you bein' white.

WHITE MARIE   *(Moving away as* SHE *chuckles)* No, sweetie, I don't think you'll ever get used to that, not in this place. We naturally attract attention because our simple appearance conjures ugly assumptions. But then it doesn't really matter, does it?

LESTER   *(Removing his top coat and hat)* What you sayin'? What don't really matter?

WHITE MARIE   Color.

LESTER   *(Going to her again)* I wouldn't say that, but I know what you mean.

WHITE MARIE   *(Moving away)* What do you think I mean?

LESTER   *(Following her)* You must mean that all people is just people, and I agree, but that ain't got nothin' to do with reality.

WHITE MARIE   Reality has nothing to do with reality.

LESTER   *(Stopping)* Ding Dong! Say what?

WHITE MARIE   Prez, I make my living being the mistress of several wealthy, powerful men. In other words, I sell my box, discreetly, to moral gentlemen of impeccable taste.

LESTER   I understand that, but that ain't got nothin' to . . .

WHITE MARIE   *(Interrupting)* Listen, sweetheart, several of my clients usually ask me to pretend I'm a Negro.

   Pause.

LESTER   You mean a Negro man or a Negro woman?

WHITE MARIE   A Negro woman, of course. You know what I have to do?

LESTER   What do you do?

WHITE MARIE   *(Seriously and skillfully acting out a certain image)* Yo Poppa, whas to it? I got the oven if you wanna bake a cake. How much money you got, daddy goodness? Come on, pink poppa, suck off this sweet black titty. And I go on and on and I get paid very well.

   Pause.

LESTER   You don't sound like no Negro woman to me.

WHITE MARIE   That's because I'm not and because you don't want to pretend reality is something other than what it is.

LESTER   I don't need to pretend.

WHITE MARIE   No, you don't *want* to pretend I'm a colored woman, but you still need to pretend.
LESTER   Pretend what?
WHITE MARIE   Pretend that I'm a white woman.

> *Pause.*

LESTER   Well, what the hell are you? And what's on your mind anyway? We came here to party, party, party, remember?
WHITE MARIE   Lester, this afternoon I read that you're getting married, again.
LESTER   *(Avoiding the issue)* Baby, if you can't sing 'em, don't ever believe no words you read about me. Can't no writer separate my life into a bunch of black marks on paper, and so what if I'm gittin' married?
WHITE MARIE   As long as we've been together, as many soft moments that we've shared, you could have told me.
LESTER   That ain't no big thing. You sleep with married men every day. That's reality too.
WHITE MARIE   Does that make a real difference to you?

> *Pause.*

LESTER   I think it does.
WHITE MARIE   And what about you? You're preparing to divorce one woman, hanging out with a second, me, and planning to marry a third, some poor Negro woman in Queens.
LESTER   Baby, what *is* the real problem?

> *Pause.*

WHITE MARIE   Satisfying *your* needs apparently.
LESTER   Needs? What am I supposed to need?
WHITE MARIE   I don't know; I'm a prostitute, not a witch doctor, but I know that there've been lots of women in your life and that you exist some place alone; everyone else is a misty face that you keep hovering around your private space. I mean, I wonder if women mean anything to you.
LESTER   *(Begins easing toward her again)* Women? Women are the closest thing to music I know on this planet. Sweet smellin', pretty music. Soft music like the clothes she wear on her body and the powder she sprinkles on her thighs. But funky too, like the music that oozes out of her body after she been dancing to my love melodies and swinging

on the end of my heavy rhythms. I like the songs I hear laughing in a woman's soul. Each of the musicians I play with is either a lady or he's not, you dig? Anybody who got a song in his soul is a lady.

WHITE MARIE *(Weakly pushing him away)* That's fine, but you're singing more than one song at the same time and they all sound weak.

LESTER Awwwww Marie, why you put me through all this? You know what's happnin'.

   Pause.

WHITE MARIE *(Sighing)* I guess you're right. *(Cheering up)* Look, I should be happy for you. Is the date set yet?

LESTER It depend on what the draft board do. You know them Germans is still kicking ass.

WHITE MARIE Oh, Germans schmermans; it's all about stone age politics and greed. My box is more important than that war, and I don't truly care about your wives, but, Prez, tell me just one thing: What have I meant to you? You can tell me now.

LESTER You taught me that I don't have to be afraid.

WHITE MARIE *(Incredulous)* Afraid? Afraid of what?

LESTER Of me.

WHITE MARIE What on earth does that mean, Prez?

LESTER Listen, Marie, this reality that don't look like reality in America still cause me pain, but because of you I ain't afraid of it no more. The music is the only reality I know and it was my music that touched you. The reality we share is bigger than them ugly assumptions you was talkin' 'bout.

MARIE Thanks, Prez, but I think my illusions have been bigger than reality, because the music alone isn't enough for me. Look, we had a wonderful beginning; it's been really terrific, but I think our relationship is about to end, don't you?

LESTER You like the moon, baby. You glow in the dark. Night and moon go together forever.

WHITE MARIE And in the daylight the moon disappears, is that it?

LESTER I'm not afraid to be seen with you night or day.

WHITE MARIE But still the moon only happens at night?

LESTER *(Angry)* So what are you sayin', White Marie?

WHITE MARIE I'm saying that my name is White Marie and I'm proud of it and I intend to keep on being proud of it, but I'd rather not be *your* midnight ghost too.

LESTER *(Angrily offering her coat)* Well, baby, I kin dig where you comin' from.

WHITE MARIE   *(Falling into exaggerated but convincing black street hipness of manner and accent as* SHE *begins to slowly remove her clothes)* Then don't worry 'bout how I sound poppa. Pull off your shirt and take off them shoes 'cause you fixin' to pay some sho' nuff heavy dues tonight.

LESTER   *(Smiles, shakes his head from side to side as* HE *strips down to his boxer shorts and tee shirt)* Lawd, Lawd, Lawd.

WHITE MARIE   Yes, call on Him, 'cause He loved us whores too. Can you swim, Mr. Man?

LESTER   *(Doing a mock swimming stroke)* Kin birds fly?

WHITE MARIE   Some can.

LESTER   Do a seahorse gallop?

WHITE MARIE   *(Down to her slip)* The beach is now officially open, and it ain't got no teeth, for the very last time.

SHE *turns off the lights. Pause. Then we hear the* SERGEANT'S VOICE *shouting cadence and marching feet.*

SERGEANT'S VOICE   Yo lep two three fo'
Yo lep two three fo'
Yo lep two three fo'
Yo lep two three fo'

The lights come up on LESTER *marching frantically, somewhat out of step, confused and trying not to show his genuine terror.*

SERGEANT   *(Continued)* Company halt! Private third class Lester Young, front and center, on the double; let's move it, boy!

LESTER *stumbles forward.*

SERGEANT   *(Continued)* Boy, yer ta reeport inside ta thuh Majur fer processing. You understand, soldier?

LESTER   Yeah.

SERGEANT   Sergeant. Yes, SERGEANT!

LESTER   Yes, Sergeant.

SERGEANT   *(Marching off with his invisible troop)* Company, forward, march!
Yo lep two three fo'
Yo lep two three fo'
Yo lep two three fo'
Yo lep two three fo'

LESTER *steps inside.* HE *assumes an at ease position. The* MAJOR *appears, seats himself before* LESTER *and proceeds to conduct the following interview at a rapid, computer-like pace and rhythm. The* MAJOR *constantly scribbles on official forms.*

MAJOR   Okay, boy, let me make perfectly clear what's happening. The medical records show that you've completely recovered from your surgical operation; therefore, you are being released from this hospital and being returned to drill training, understand? Fine. I have to verify the data in your personnel file by asking you a few simple questions that you must answer correctly and quickly. If you have any problems understanding, do not hesitate to ask for an explanation. Let me warn you that you must answer truthfully. Now then, let us begin.

The previous has been said so rapidly that LESTER *barely has had time to even hear most of it.* HE's *nervous, scared, restless, keeps twiddling his fingers as if fingering a horn.* LESTER *will have absolutely no time to answer most of the following questions put to him;* HE *will only stutter and stammer and grow increasingly depressed as* HE *witnesses his total helplessness. The* MAJOR *grows progressively hostile as* HE *has prejudged* LESTER *and seeks only confirmation—a robotized ritual* HE *conducts. The* MAJOR *scribbles on his forms as if recording answers.*

MAJOR   *(Continued)* Name? Rank? Serial Number? Place of birth? Mother's name? Father's name? Brother's name? Sister's name? Where did you grow up? Where did you attend school? Why do you have only a third grade education? What size jock strap did your grandfather wear? Have you ever smoked marijuana?

LESTER   Yeah, for 11 years.

MAJOR   Of course. Yes. This Eleanora Gough McKay, what was her daily habit like?

LESTER   Lady Day has a habit of singing her deepest feelings. She sing so pretty she make a man pee on hisself!

MAJOR   *(Scribbling the previous statement)* You and she shacked up for a long while, correct?

LESTER   We loved and now we have mellow memories.

MAJOR   Why did you move in with her and her mother? Why didn't you take her to your own house? You're a man, aren't you? When did she throw you out? Did you use up all the drugs this hospital gave you for post-operative treatment? How long have you been distilling the drugs with wine? How long did you think you could avoid the draft? Do you know how the army caught up with you?

LESTER   You tracked me, but I wasn't running. I thought newly married men were cool.

MAJOR   We'll get to your marriage later. Finding you turned out to be quite easy after your patriotic friend called us.

LESTER   What patriotic friend?

MAJOR   Francis Bartholomew, better known as Tweed.

LESTER   That bullshit mutha . . .

MAJOR   *(Interrupting)* Never mind him. Who was Harry Lincoln?

LESTER   Lady Lincoln. He's my friend, my sho nuff spiritual pardna. Is Lincoln here?

MAJOR   Do you believe in ghosts?

LESTER   What?

MAJOR   Your "sho nuff spiritual pardna" dropped dead three months ago; too much booze and narcotics.

LESTER   Dead? Lady Lincoln? Naw, I know didn't die on me. *(Beginning to cry)* But I love Lincoln; he can't be dead. Not Lincoln; not my homey. Dead? I still owe that bitch $75. How could that sweet lady just die on me?

MAJOR   You and he had something going, eh?

LESTER   *(Breaking stance)* Are you crazy?

MAJOR   You'll find out how crazy I am in a minute. At ease, soldier!

LESTER, *dazed, reassumes at ease position.*

MAJOR   *(Continued)* Is the following your footlocker number? 1909–P?

LESTER   Yeah.

The MAJOR *angrily pulls out a large photograph of* LESTER *and a white woman cheek to cheek.*

MAJOR   What are you doing with this shit in your footlocker?

LESTER   That's a picture of me and my wife.

MAJOR   Due to violations of the uniform military code, I'm recommending you be held for court martial.

LESTER   *(Angry but terrified)* Court martial? Me? What for? Tell me that! What for?

MAJOR   That's up to the prosecutor to decide from the available evidence.

LESTER   What evidence?

MAJOR   Everything you've admitted to in this interview which is over right now. You will be held in the detention barracks until court martial proceedings can be instituted. In the meantime I'll make a few arrangements to see that you get your share of our Georgia hospitality. We got to teach you what you forgot up there in New York City. SERGEANT!

LESTER   What about my horn? Where's my horn?

MAJOR   Your horn is in your footlocker which has been confiscated.

LESTER   But I need my horn for band practice.

MAJOR   Band practice? I don't have any record of your being in the band.

LESTER   But I tried out; I know I musta made it. You kin check with Sergeant Willis.

MAJOR   Sergeant Willis says you don't know your rudiments.

LESTER   I don't know my rudiments? Is he crazy?

MAJOR   *Him* crazy? He taught high school bands for ten years in Albany, Georgia. He should know if you know your rudiments, and he says you don't know yours. Your request to join the band is denied. Case closed, soldier!

LESTER   But I wanna take my horn with me anyway.

        The SERGEANT *arrives.*

MAJOR   Git it through that thick monkey's skull that your horn is being held for evidence. Understand, spook?

LESTER   I ain't going nowhere without that horn!

MAJOR   *You're telling me* what you're *not* going to do?

LESTER   The horn goes with me!

MAJOR   *(To the* SERGEANT) Remove this soldier immediately!

        The SERGEANT *grabs* LESTER *and begins beating him. The moment* HE *grabs* LESTER *the lights dim and blink with a strobe-like effect. The* MAJOR *has exited, leaving* LESTER's *body jerking to the* SERGEANT's *stiff punches.* LESTER *is screaming, grunting and trying to fight back, but is no match and is finally subdued, utterly spent. The lights shift to complete blackness, except for a relatively small, square patch of light, harsh yellow light. The light itself is a tiny prison cell. The* SERGEANT *roughly hustles* LESTER *over to the patch of light.* HE *opens the door and we hear the loud clank of steel against steel. The* SERGEANT *shoves* LESTER *into the cell and closes the door.* HE *walks away.* MUSIC *fades up slowly. The music is at first an ethereal rendering of* "D.B. Blues" *in the Lester Young style.* LESTER, *on his haunches with one arm shakily supporting his body, cries softly, coughs frequently and stares abjectly into space. After several moments of this, the lighted space expands to reveal the original hotel room concept into which rushes the* WOMAN IN BLACK, *breathlessly.*

WOMAN IN BLACK   Lester, I couldn't reach Dr. Tramb, but . . . *(Sees and rushes to* LESTER) Lester, what are you doing on the floor? Did you fall? Are you alright? *(Sees the empty gin bottle)* Lester, you drank the gin. You know what that's going to do. I called an ambulance; it'll be here any minute. *(Looking into his eyes and becoming truly alarmed at what* SHE *discovers)* Lester, LESTER, LESTER, speak to me; don't just stare like that. Speak to me! Speak to me, Lester! (SHE *shakes him)* LESTER!

LESTER   Listen, Miss Lady. Listen.

WOMAN IN BLACK   I'm listening, Prez; talk to me.

LESTER   Listen to the music. Can you hear it?

WOMAN IN BLACK   That's from the Birdland. Do you like it, Les? Do like the music? Talk to me about the music.

LESTER   It's funny, Lady, ain't it funny? That's my song. "Detention Barracks Blues." I made that song way back in 1945. And listen to them play it. They all sound just like me.

WOMAN IN BLACK   They sound like you because you sound the best.

LESTER   *(Trying to raise himself)* But when I try to play, I sound just like them. Who am I? Where am I going? I don't even know what I sound like anymore, and I can't hardly breathe out here.

WOMAN IN BLACK   Lester, please don't try to move; just talk to me.

LESTER   Repeater pencils, Lady. There ain't no more space out here; just repeater pencils jammed uptight, marching on my back, and . . . and . . . spittin' on me.

WOMAN IN BLACK   No one could spit on you, Lester. No one.

LESTER   Oh yes, they can, Miss Lady, but maybe that's the way it's supposed to be; I done some spittin' too. You hear that music, Miss Lady?

WOMAN IN BLACK   Yes, I hear it, baby.

LESTER   I love music and the music love me; we are love, but I can't hardly make it last past the bandstand, like church always end and the people go home and take up hatin' where they left off, and me too. I only know how to love music because people always seem temporary, even my family in Queens. I play from my soul, Lady, but I can't live with it in this drafty world. I think my soul is bigger than me, and I never could carry it all, so I always left a little piece behind. I was always missing from whatever I found; most of me got lost along the road. But my life ain't nothin' but a beat anyway, when a little melody comes together and then eases off into another feeling; only thing left is memory. And it's alright, Lady.

WOMAN IN BLACK   I know, Lester. I know it's alright.

LESTER   I ain't sad, Lady, I ain't sad 'cause the music is beautiful. *(Laughing)* You listening to me? You hearing me? *(As if seeing a fantastic sight)* Look, Lady, look. Oh, how wonderful it sounds. Ding Dong, Lady, DING DONG, DING DONG!

With one last heave of his chest HE *dies.* SHE *gently folds his hands across his chest and drapes his jacket over his face. An ambulance siren mixes in with the* "D.B. Blues." *Lights fade up to an intense glow and the sounds rise to a crescendo simultaneously. Lights and sound cut out.*

Curtain.

Recessional Music: "Goodbye Porkpie Hat" *by Charles Mingus.*

WINTERPLAY

A Hyperreal Comedy
In Two Acts

by

Adele Edling Shank

ABOUT
ADELE EDLING SHANK

Born in Minnesota, Adele Edling Shank
has lived in California since 1954. She has an M.A. in Playwriting from
the University of California, Davis, and she teaches playwriting there. Her
Sunset/Sunrise was a co-winner of the Great American Play Contest sponsored by the Actors Theatre of Louisville, Kentucky. It was presented
there as part of the 1980 New Play Festival and was published with an
interview with the author in the November 1979 volume of *West Coast
Plays* (No. 4). The American Theatre Critics Association selected it as one
of the 10 best plays to open outside New York during the 1979-80 season.
She received a Rockefeller Foundation Playwright-in-Residence grant for
1981 and a National Endowment for the Arts Playwriting Fellowship for
1981-82.

Winterplay, Sunset/Sunrise, Stuck and the more recent *Sand Castles* are
parts of a series of hyperreal comedies—a style which Adele Shank helped
to pioneer. They all deal with different aspects of California suburban life.
Adele Shank is also the author of *Fox & Co.,* a contemporary version of
Ben Jonson's *Volpone,* and, with Everard d'Harnoncourt, the translator
of Fernando Arrabal's *The Architect And The Emperor Of Assyria*
(Grove Press). Her articles on the theatre have appeared in *The Drama
Review,* the *Oxford Companion to the Theatre, Teatro Del Novecento*
and several European journals.

PRODUCTION HISTORY

Winterplay was nominated for the *Plays in Process* series by John Lion, general director of the Magic Theatre, San Francisco, California. It was presented there from October 1 through November 16, 1980.

Theodore Shank directed. The set was designed by John Ammirati, costumes by Phyllis Kress and sound by Terry Hunter. The cast was as follows:

LOUISE.. Stephanie Smith
JAMES... Arthur Holden
JOSH.. Daniel Press
ANNE... Kathleen Becket
GEM .... Sue Murphy
JONATHAN... Michael Tulin
MICHAEL... Bret Kuhne
JENNY .... Francine Lembi

Prior to the Magic Theatre production, *Winterplay* received a staged reading at the American Place Theatre, New York City, during February 1980.

PLAYWRIGHT'S NOTE

I wrote my first play 22 years ago. It was a kind of cross between Giraudoux and Pinter, although no one in the United States (including me) had heard of Pinter at the time. I wrote four more plays, and the Giraudouxesque part fell out and the Pinterish part got stronger. And then suddenly I no longer knew what I was doing. I had finished the first draft of a full-length play which, while it had some good things going for it, simply didn't work for me. It was 1966 and theatre felt irrelevant, at least the kind of theatre I could write. I kept thinking that one should be able to make an explosion on stage, a theatrical event so extraordinary that it would shake all of the world's idiocy and cruelty into common sense and compassion. Needless to say, I wasn't quite up to that task, so I stopped writing.

For the next 10 years, I did some work in theatre collectives and travelled a lot seeing other people's work. I learned more from other people's mistakes than I would have from my own because I was able to see a lot more theatre than I could make. Then, nearly as suddenly as I had stopped, I found myself ready to start again. I began to see a way of shaping a play, and of handling character, plot and visuals which I felt comfortable with and which would be fresh for the audience. Much of this came out of what I had learned from other theatre makers—Richard Foreman, Robert Wilson, and John Fox as well as Bertolt Brecht and Anton Chekhov. But the final catalyst came from the visual arts.

All I knew was that I was going to write a play set in the backyard of a suburban California home that included a swimming pool, barbecue, patio, etc., and that the play would deal with the family who lived there and their neighbors. My husband Ted Shank and I had been interested in the hyperreal painters since the late sixties, and Ted suggested looking at hyperrealism for the style of the play. The relationship between the hyperreal style and the setting for the play which became *Sunset/Sunrise* was so obvious that we began studying the painting style and thinking about what the theatrical equivalent would be. We were not, of course, trying to do the same thing. You can't duplicate one medium in another, and theatrical hyperrealism would be as different from hyperrealism in painting as theatrical expressionism is from expressionism in painting. But from studying the paintings we did draw some ideas. My notes from this period include these statements:

> *No exposition. What you see is what there is.*
>
> *Focus on the surface, don't let the audience project themselves into the situation; no emotional involvement.*
>
> *Treating details that are usually ignored creates a kind of barrier which does not let the audience go below the surface. They will notice what they usually don't see.*
>
> *Deal with mundane, everyday situations and people as the paintings deal with car bumpers and diners. When they leave this material and deal with the victim of a motorcycle accident (Duane Hansen's work) they let in emotion.*

We've learned a lot since then, but these basic principles are still part of my work. We have developed writing, directing, and acting techniques to make it happen on stage. The result is a somewhat distanced audience perspective. The audience tends to view the events on stage as if looking at them through a window or a hole in a fence. This voyeuristic attitude allows the audience to project onto the characters and events. In this way the "meaning" comes to the audience with the joy of discovery.

Winterplay is the second in a series of several plays. The first was *Sunset/Sunrise* which is set inside the same house where *Winterplay* takes place, and many of the characters are in both plays. *Stuck* carries over one character from *Winterplay,* Jenny, and is set on a freeway during a traffic jam. The fourth play, *Sand Castles,* is set on a beach where two characters from *Stuck* are vacationing with their families. All of the plays deal with various aspects of suburban California life and they are all in the hyperreal style. All combine the traditional elements of character and plot with the visual-arts focus. That these traditional elements are used somewhat differently is not of much importance, any more than is our theoretical interest in hyperrealism. They are only tools for making a kind of theatre which satisfies us.

Reprinted in part from "Theatrical Hyperrealism," first published in *Callboard,* (Vol. 5, No. 11, November 1980) the monthly newsletter of the Theatre Communications Center of the Bay Area, 1182 Market Street, San Francisco, California 94102.

CHARACTERS

In order of appearance

LOUISE, wife of James, mother of Jonathan, Josh and Anne. A 47-year-old housewife.

JAMES, husband of Louise, father of Jonathan, Josh, and Anne, brother of Gem. A 48-year-old lawyer.

JOSH, middle child of Louise and James, brother of Jonathan and Anne. A 20-year-old student.

ANNE, daughter of Louise and James, sister of Jonathan and Josh. A 17-year-old recluse.

GEM, sister of James, in the process of being divorced for the third time and newly in love. A 47-year-old business woman.

JONATHAN, oldest son of James and Louise, older brother of Josh and Anne, lover of Michael. 28 years old.

MICHAEL, Jonathan's lover. 24 years old.

JENNY, Jonathan's high school sweetheart, she grew up in the house across the street. A 28-year-old merchandising executive.

TIME

Last Christmas

PLACE

Suburban California

THE PLAY

WINTERPLAY

For Ted, without whom there is nothing

ACT I

    The sun is shining on the palm tree outside the family room sliding glass door. LOUISE *is in the kitchen.* SHE *has just finished stuffing the turkey and* SHE *washes her hands at the sink. The red light is on on the electric percolator.* SHE *pours herself a mug of coffee and leans against the counter drinking coffee and staring at the small uncooked turkey in a roasting pan.* JAMES *comes in from the master bedroom wearing a bathrobe.* HE *has a medium grade hangover.* HE *sits on a stool at the kitchen counter.* LOUISE *hands him a mug of coffee with a sympathetic smile.*

JAMES   Thanks.
LOUISE   Sleep well?
JAMES   It's late.

LOUISE   There's plenty of time.

> *Pause.* HE *doesn't open the morning paper which lies on the counter.*

JAMES   I hate the mirror in our bathroom.
LOUISE   Oh?
JAMES   Every morning I look like I died in the middle of the night.
LOUISE   You look fine.
JAMES   It must be the mirror.
LOUISE   Do you want something to eat?
JAMES   No.
LOUISE   Sure? We've already had lunch.
JAMES   Good. Have they called this morning?
LOUISE   Not yet. Maybe I should call.
JAMES   They'll phone if there's any change.
LOUISE   I suppose. I should have gotten a bigger turkey.
JAMES   Where's Josh?
LOUISE   Outside.
JAMES   They used to jump on us at five A.M.
LOUISE   I should have gotten a bigger one. But you don't like left over turkey.
JAMES   I don't?
LOUISE   But I didn't think, maybe Jonathan would have liked to take some back with them.
JAMES   He's a big boy. He can get his own turkey.
LOUISE   I never know whether to start it at 425 degrees for half an hour or whether to cook it at 325 degrees the whole time. It doesn't seem to matter, it's always dry anyway. Marian cooks hers in a paper bag but I don't like the idea.
JAMES   Oyster or cornbread?
LOUISE   My mother's.
JAMES   Oh.
LOUISE   I know you don't like it. I . . . I just wanted to.

> LOUISE *is covering the turkey with cheesecloth.* JAMES *goes to* LOUISE *and hugs her as* SHE *works.*

JAMES   It's OK. But we aren't having brussels sprouts are we?
LOUISE   Of course not. You'd better get dressed. They'll be here soon.

JOSH *enters from the backyard.* HE *is rubbing his greasy hands with a cloth.* JAMES *has moved into the family room.*

JOSH   Merry Christmas, Pop.

JAMES   Merry Christmas, Josh.

JOSH   Thanks again for the wrenches. I already took the carburetor apart. I've got a real strong feeling it's the carburetor. I'll have her on the road by New Year's.

LOUISE   You'd better get cleaned up Josh they'll be here soon.

JOSH *starts to go to his room.*

JAMES   Oh say Josh, hang on a minute. I uh, I just wanted to have a word with you. Uh . . . look, when Jonathan and Michael get here . . .

LOUISE   James!

JAMES   Louise, I've got to say something. Now look, Josh, if Michael behaves . . . well if he seems unusual in any way, just try to pretend you don't notice.

JOSH   Don't notice what, Dad?

LOUISE   Josh, go and wash up.

JOSH   Don't worry Dad. If he's weird I'll be cool. (JOSH *goes to his room*)

JAMES   Louise, I wish you wouldn't do that.

LOUISE   I thought we decided not to say anything about it to Josh! Anyway, he might not even notice.

JAMES   I wish I could believe that.

LOUISE   Do you think he knows?

JAMES   Hard to say. They did share a bedroom for what, fifteen years? Boys are, well, boys.

LOUISE   Mm.

JAMES   But Josh is all right. He and Christina seem to have something going.

LOUISE   Do you think so?

JAMES   When she gets back we should sort of encourage that.

LOUISE   How?

JAMES   Make sure they have the time and the place.

LOUISE   He's got his car.

JAMES   Which doesn't run. Will never run. And it's parked five feet from our bedroom window.

LOUISE *puts the turkey in the oven.*

LOUISE Josh will find a way.
JAMES I don't know. He's a little . . . well, slow.
LOUISE You'd better get dressed. They'll be here any minute.

> JOSH *comes into the family room and sits down on the sofa and reads the paper.* HE *has changed his shirt.*

JAMES What should I wear?
LOUISE I laid it out on the chair.
JAMES OK.

> JAMES *goes into the master bedroom.* LOUISE *is cleaning up the kitchen counter.* JOSH *speaks after a long pause.*

JOSH Mom, what's Anne doing?
LOUISE I haven't seen her this morning.
JOSH I heard her TV when I went out to work on the car. Church of the Air.
LOUISE Oh. Yes, of course. (LOUISE, *drying her hands on a towel, comes from the kitchen into the family room)* Josh?
JOSH *(Face in paper)* Yeah Mom.
LOUISE The turkey's in the oven.
JOSH Something wrong Mom?
LOUISE No. Not really. I guess I'm just sort of . . .
JOSH Grandma?
LOUISE When I was a little girl she was always so . . . so busy. She worked for weeks baking, sewing, decorating, to make Christmas really special. And now she's . . . I wonder if I've started it too late.
JOSH (HE *has returned to the newspaper)* What?
LOUISE The turkey.

> ANNE's *face appears on the TV monitor.*

ANNE Mom?

> LOUISE *moves toward the monitor and speaks at the microphone which is mounted next to the video camera on top of the monitor.*

LOUISE Good morning, dear. Merry Christmas.
ANNE Merry Christmas, Mom. It's time to feed Simon Peter.
LOUISE All right. What does he get today?
ANNE Hamster Chow and a carrot stick.

LOUISE *gets the food out of the kitchen cupboard and refrigerator.* JOSH *shouts toward the microphone from the sofa.*

JOSH   Morning Annie!
ANNE   Hi Josh. Merry Christmas!
JOSH   Same to you.
ANNE   Is it a beautiful day?

JOSH *looks at the palm tree outside.*

JOSH   Yeah. I guess so. Sun's shining.
ANNE   Good.

LOUISE *moves the hamster cage to sit in front of the video camera. As* ANNE *talks to the hamster* LOUISE *feeds it.*

ANNE   *(Continued)* Here we are Simon Peter. Are you a hungry little hamster? Yes, here's some nice food. And a special Christmas treat for Simey. There you are. Oh, you like that do you? Yes, sure you do. Thanks Mom.
LOUISE   You're welcome, Anne. Well, I've got work to do.
ANNE   OK. Will you put a book on for me?
LOUISE   Of course. What would you like.
ANNE   I want to finish *Can God Be Trusted?*

JOSH *speaks quietly so* ANNE *doesn't hear him.*

JOSH   Search me.
LOUISE   Josh!

ANNE *turns herself off and the monitor goes dark. The doorbell rings and almost immediately the front door opens and* GEM *enters carrying a casserole and two shopping bags full of presents.*

GEM   Hello hello! Merry Christmas!
LOUISE   Merry Christmas, Gem.

LOUISE *goes to help unload her.* THEY *hug.* GEM *sniffs the air.*

GEM   Not yet.
LOUISE   What?
GEM   I don't smell the turkey.

LOUISE   It hasn't been in long.
JOSH   Hi Aunt Gem.
GEM   Merry Christmas Josho! How goes it?
JOSH   Not bad.
GEM   Where is everyone?
LOUISE   Jonathan and Michael are due any minute. Jenny will be over later.
JOSH   Mom, you want me to put on Anne's book?
LOUISE   Thanks Josh.

> JOSH *goes out down the hallway toward* ANNE's *room.* GEM *gives* LOUISE *a covered casserole.*

GEM   This is the sweet potato thing. At least Jimmy will love it, it's loaded with bourbon.

> LOUISE *laughs.*

GEM   Anyway, this I have faith in. (SHE *produces two bottles of French champagne)*
LOUISE   Oh Gem, how lovely.
GEM   I thought we should celebrate. Welcome the lovebirds into the family circle, all that.
LOUISE   Gem.
GEM   Sorry. Don't worry, Louise, I'll behave myself.

> LOUISE *puts the champagne in the refrigerator and* GEM *puts her packages under the Christmas tree.*

LOUISE   I just don't want them to be uncomfortable.
GEM   I'm afraid that's pretty much inevitable.

> JAMES *comes out of the master bedroom.*

GEM   *(Continued)* Hello Jimmy. Merry Christmas.

> THEY *hug and kiss.*

JAMES   Merry Christmas.
GEM   Hey, you look awful.
JAMES   Thanks. You look great.
GEM   Thanks.

JAMES   It's a nice change. Last year you were so gloomy I thought your chin was going to droop into your mashed potatoes.

> GEM *laughs.*

GEM   Basically I hate Christmas. Always reminds me of what isn't there anymore. But this year seems different.

> JOSH *enters. HE is thinking, as HE does from time to time, about his grandmother and HE sits down by himself.*

GEM   What's the matter with Scrooge here, eh?
JAMES   I think he's missing his girl friend.

> JOSH *is annoyed at being teased like a kid.*

JOSH   Oh, Dad. God.
GEM   Who's the favored lady?
JAMES   Christina. You know, next door. Charles and Diane's daughter.
GEM   Sure.
JAMES   She's gone for Christmas.
JOSH   Big deal.

> *The doorbell rings.* JOSH *jumps up quickly.*

JOSH   *(Continued)* I'll get it.
JAMES   I need a drink.
LOUISE   In a minute.

> JOSH *opens the front door and greets* JONATHAN *and* MICHAEL *enthusiastically.* JONATHAN *and* MICHAEL *enter carrying packages.* LOUISE *comes forward and kisses* JONATHAN. *There is forced cheerfulness covering the tension.*

JONATHAN   Hi Mom. Merry Christmas.
LOUISE   Merry Christmas, Jonathan.

> JAMES *comes forward and stretches out his arm to shake hands.*

JAMES   Well. Glad you two could make it.

> *Instead of shaking hands* JONATHAN *hugs his father.*

JONATHAN   Thanks Dad.

JAMES   Made pretty good time did you?

JONATHAN   Traffic wasn't bad.

JAMES   Yeah. I guess it was probably worse last night.

JONATHAN   Probably. Dad . . . (JONATHAN *reaches behind him and pulls* MICHAEL *around)* This is Michael.

> JAMES *and* MICHAEL *shake hands.* JONATHAN *goes to* GEM *with a greeting and hugs her.* THEY *are fond of one another.* THEY *have a brief out-of-focus conversation while the major focus stays on* JAMES *and* MICHAEL.

> *NOTE: When a conversation is indicated as being out-of-focus the audience should be able to hear realistic conversation. Stage whispering or other "cheating" should not be used, but focus should be controlled by volume and positioning. The content should be improvised in rehearsal but precisely set before performance.*

JAMES   Michael.

MICHAEL   How do you do, sir.

> JAMES *starts to put a hand on* MICHAEL's *shoulder, doesn't.*

JAMES   Oh please, everyone calls me Jimmy. Well, except Louise, she likes to call me James. But most people call me Jimmy. Not Jim. Well. (HE *calls for help)* Louise?

> JONATHAN *carries his presents to the Christmas tree.* LOUISE *is shaking hands with* MICHAEL.

LOUISE   Hello, Michael. I'm very glad to meet you.

MICHAEL   Thank you. I'm . . . same here.

JONATHAN   Hey, what happened to the Christmas tree?

JOSH   It shrunk.

LOUISE   It's Anne's idea. She said we absolutely mustn't kill a tree for Christ.

JONATHAN   Good grief.

LOUISE   We'll plant it in front. Let me help you with those Michael.

> LOUISE *eases his package burden.* JONATHAN *puts his packages under the tree.*

MICHAEL   Thanks. Uh, I guess that one's no secret. It's for you.

LOUISE *looks at the large houseplant which is partially wrapped.*

LOUISE   Why thank you Michael.
MICHAEL   I got Jonathan's advice on it.
LOUISE   It's a *dieffenbachaia.*
MICHAEL   Oh. Oh, yes! So it is.
LOUISE   It's lovely. Thank you.

JONATHAN *comes forward with* GEM.

JONATHAN   Michael, this is my Gem of an Aunt.

JOSH *groans as* GEM *and* MICHAEL *shake hands.*

JOSH   Hasn't changed a bit.

The telephone rings. JAMES *watches* LOUISE *as* SHE *hurriedly goes to answer it.* JONATHAN *puts a red envelope in the tree.*

GEM   Hello, Michael. Good to meet you.
MICHAEL   Thank you. Jonathan's talked a lot about you.
LOUISE   *(On the phone)* Hello?
GEM   Ah, yes, I'll bet. Scandalous tales of the wicked divorcee no doubt.
MICHAEL   Well not exactly.

GEM *takes* MICHAEL's *and* JONATHAN's *coats and puts them in the guest room.*

LOUISE   *(On the phone)* Yes.
JAMES   Well. We need some drinks here. And Josh, go on out to Jonathan's car and bring in the rest of their things, eh?
JONATHAN   This is it Dad.
JAMES   No suitcases?
JONATHAN   We . . . I think we'd better go back tonight.
JAMES   We thought you'd stay over.
LOUISE   *(On the phone)* No, no of course not.
JONATHAN   It seemed better to go back tonight.
JAMES   I don't know. Weather man said there might be fog.
JONATHAN   Oh.
JAMES   You're welcome to stay you know. Plenty of room. Josh can take

the bed in the guest room and you and Michael can have the bunk beds in your old room.

JONATHAN   I see.

LOUISE   *(On the phone)* Yes, I understand, but I really didn't expect you.

JAMES   But of course you do as you like.

LOUISE   *(On the phone)* All right. See you next week. Bye.

JONATHAN   We'll wait and see how bad it gets, Dad.

THEY *look at each other.* GEM *has returned.* LOUISE *hangs up the phone and turns to go into the kitchen.*

JAMES   Who was it, Louise?

LOUISE   May Ling. She wanted to know if she was supposed to come to clean today.

JAMES   Doesn't she know it's Christmas?

LOUISE   Yes. But she didn't know if she was supposed to work or not.

GEM   Who's May Ling?

LOUISE   My cleaning girl. From Vietnam. I didn't want a cleaning girl, but James insisted.

JAMES   You shouldn't be scrubbing floors. You need time to do things you want to do.

LOUISE   There's nothing I want to do.

SHE *goes into the kitchen.* GEM *speaks privately to* JONATHAN.

GEM   Is everything set?

JONATHAN   You bet. How about your end?

GEM   All arranged.

JONATHAN   Ata girl.

JAMES   Louise, what's our schedule?

LOUISE   Dinner late this afternoon. If anyone's hungry they can have a snack now. Jonathan? Michael?

MICHAEL   No thanks. We had a huge breakfast.

LOUISE   I thought we'd have the rest of the presents before dinner. With our champagne.

JONATHAN   Champagne!

LOUISE   Gem thought we should celebrate.

JOSH   Ata girl, Aunt Gem!

JAMES *finds himself standing beside* MICHAEL *and rambles on in embarrassment.*

JAMES Louise's family always opened their presents on Christmas Eve, and my family opened them on Christmas morning. So we take turns every other year. We had most of our presents last night, but you know it never seems right on Christmas Eve. But that's how it goes, compromise is the essence of marriage.

MICHAEL Yes sir. Of any committed relationship.

JAMES Uh . . . yes. Yeah sure. How about a drink, Michael?

MICHAEL Is there any coffee?

JAMES Coffee. Sure. Louise is a big coffee drinker. Louise, Michael'd like a cup of coffee.

> MICHAEL *goes to* LOUISE *and* SHE *pours him a mug of coffee.* JONATHAN's *eyes follow* MICHAEL *to the kitchen and* HE *calls to* LOUISE.

JONATHAN Is it just the family for dinner?

LOUISE Jenny's coming over.

JONATHAN What's she doing here?

LOUISE She just got transferred to this branch. I think it's a promotion. She's living at home again. It's only temporary, until she finds a place of her own I guess. Anyway, her parents are in Hawaii so we invited her for dinner. I hope you don't mind.

JONATHAN Of course not. Why should I mind? It'll be great to see her.

> JAMES *explains to* MICHAEL *who is returning with his coffee.*

JAMES Jenny's Jonathan's old flame. High school sweethearts, weren't you Jonathan.

JOSH Jeez Dad.

> JAMES *realizes* HE *is being tactless.*

JAMES But that was years ago, eh?

JONATHAN (Smiling) Yes. A long time ago.

MICHAEL I remember the name.

> MICHAEL *does not sit down next to* JONATHAN *where* HE *is invited to sit.* JOSH, MICHAEL, *and* JONATHAN *talk out-of-focus.*

JAMES How about it Gem. Drink?

GEM Sure.

JAMES Louise, what are we supposed to be drinking?

LOUISE   Bloody mary, tequila sunrise, or white wine.
JAMES   What'll it be Gem?
GEM   Vino blanco, por favor.

LOUISE *takes a bottle from the refrigerator and pours a glass of wine.*

JAMES   I'll have a bloody mary. Easy on the blood. Anyone else? Jonathan?
JONATHAN   No thanks, Dad.

JAMES *takes the glass of wine to* GEM *as* LOUISE *makes* JAMES' *bloody mary.*

JAMES   Have you done something to yourself?
GEM   No.
JAMES   Something's different.
GEM   Probably.
JAMES   What is it?
GEM   I'm happy.
JAMES   Well well well. What brought this about?
GEM   Secret.

JAMES *starts to say something but* GEM *cuts him off by calling to* LOUISE.

GEM   *(Continued)* Anything I can do, Louise?
LOUISE   Not at the moment. I did the creamed onions yesterday. (SHE *brings* JAMES *his drink)*
JAMES   Thanks.
LOUISE   Everything's done except the green beans. We can do those later. (LOUISE *returns to the kitchen)*
GEM   She makes you turn each bean one quarter turn and slice it on the diagonal. It's tricky, but I've got it down.

JAMES *and* GEM's *conversation goes out-of-focus and we hear* JOSH *speak to* JONATHAN.

JOSH   Annie's dying to see you. She's got about a thousand questions. About you and Michael.
JONATHAN   I'll bet she has. I'd better say hello. Come on, Michael, it's time to meet my little sister.

JOSH   Hang on, I want to talk to you first. I'm worried about her.

JONATHAN   Are her allergy problems worse?

JOSH   How could they be worse?

MICHAEL   I don't understand. Is she really allergic to everything or does she only think she is?

JOSH   Who knows. But it amounts to the same thing either way. The only thing she can tolerate is plastic.

JONATHAN   Last I heard Charles thought there would be an improvement when she got through puberty.

JOSH   Yeah. Doctors. As far as I can see the problem's in her head not her ovaries. Anyway, it's not the allergies I'm worried about. It's the religion.

JONATHAN   What's the matter?

JOSH   She's getting worse. She scared me the other night.

JONATHAN   What happened?

JOSH   I got up in the middle of the night to take a pee and I heard this sound coming from her room. So I go in to see what's wrong. It's pretty strange. She's sitting in the middle of her plexiglass floor, stark naked and crying.

JONATHAN   I thought she had a special suit she wore.

JOSH   Only when she comes out, which is almost never. Anyway, when she saw me she yelled, "Get out of here, you're letting the dust in!" And she started sneezing. She was yelling and crying and sneezing. It was a real mess. I finally went out and talked to her on the monitor.

JONATHAN   What was the problem?

JOSH   Turns out she couldn't sleep because she was worried about all of us. She thinks we're all going to go to hell and she doesn't want to go to heaven by herself. She managed to get herself really worked up over it. It sounds dumb, but she's really worried about us.

JONATHAN   Me especially huh?

JOSH   Well, yeah.

JONATHAN   Maybe I can uh . . . make use of that. You didn't tell Mom about it did you?

JOSH   She made me promise not to. Oh by the way, she's got a terrific body.

JONATHAN   What?

JOSH   Annie. She looks great.

JONATHAN   Oh.

JOSH   Nice boobs.

JONATHAN   Josh.

The telephone rings. LOUISE *answers it.*

LOUISE   *(On the phone)* Hello. *(Pause)* Hello? Hello? (LOUISE *puts the receiver down.* SHE *looks at* JAMES) They hung up.
JAMES   What do you mean?
LOUISE   There was someone there, but when I answered she hung up.
JAMES   Must have been a wrong number.

> LOUISE *gives him a look of contempt and returns to the kitchen.*

JONATHAN   Ready Michael?
MICHAEL   As I'll ever be.
JONATHAN   Mom, we're going to say hello to Anne, OK?
LOUISE   Of course. She's looking forward to seeing you and to meeting your friend. We told her you were bringing a *friend* home for Christmas.
JONATHAN   I got it Mom. *(To* MICHAEL) Come on, friend.

> MICHAEL *and* JONATHAN *move to the TV monitor and* GEM *joins them there.* JAMES *quietly goes into the master bedroom.*

GEM   Let me say hello first, OK?
JONATHAN   Sure.

> GEM *turns on the microphone on top of the video monitor.* SHE *moves the video camera to focus on herself instead of the hamster.*

GEM   Anne?

> ANNE's *face appears on the monitor, a look of happy recognition.*

ANNE   Oh Aunt Gem. I didn't know you'd come.
GEM   Yup. It's me.
ANNE   Happy Christ's birthday.
GEM   Thanks. Same to you. Someone else wants to see you.
ANNE   Has Jonathan come?
JONATHAN   Right here Annabelle.

> GEM *joins* LOUISE *in the kitchen as* JONATHAN *moves in front of the video camera.*

GEM   So where are my green beans?
LOUISE   Let me give you an apron.

LOUISE *and* GEM *talk out-of-focus as* LOUISE *gets* GEM *an apron and gets the green beans out of the refrigerator.* GEM *snips the ends off the green beans, then slices them.*

ANNE   Hello Jonathan.

JONATHAN   How are you doing?

ANNE   I'm so glad to see you.

JONATHAN   Me too. I miss you.

ANNE   You do?

JONATHAN   Of course.

ANNE   Oh Jonathan. Ever since Josh told me, I've been so worried.

JONATHAN   Why?

LOUISE *goes out down the hallway leading to the kids' bedroom.*

ANNE   First Corinthians, chapter six, verse nine.

JONATHAN   Uh . . . what's that?

ANNE   "Do you not know that the unrighteous will not inherit the Kingdom of God? Do not be deceived; neither the immoral, nor idolaters, nor adulterers, nor homosexuals, nor thieves, nor the greedy, nor drunkards, nor revilers, nor robbers will inherit the Kingdom of God." That's why!

MICHAEL   *(Ironically to* JOSH*)* Wonderful company I keep.

JONATHAN   Do you think I belong with idolaters and thieves?

ANNE   No. But it says in the Bible!

JONATHAN   Anne, I've got someone for you to meet.

ANNE   Michael?

JONATHAN   Yes. My friend Michael. (JONATHAN *gestures to* MICHAEL *to join him at the video camera)*

MICHAEL   Hello there . . . uh . . . Hi.

ANNE   Hello. Come closer please, I can't see you very well.

MICHAEL *moves closer to the video camera.*

MICHAEL   How's that?

ANNE   Thank you. (ANNE *studies* MICHAEL. HE *is very uncomfortable)* How tall are you, Michael?

MICHAEL   *(Actor states his height)*

ANNE   Please smile.

MICHAEL *smiles.*

JONATHAN   Well? What's the verdict?

ANNE   He doesn't look like I thought he would.

JONATHAN   How's that?

ANNE   He looks . . . normal.

JONATHAN   Not what you expected huh?

ANNE   Well, I've never seen one before.

JONATHAN   You've seen me.

ANNE   That's different. You're my brother. You were my brother before you were anything else. (ANNE *looks thoughtful*) Does he have a small penis?

> JOSH *cracks up.* MICHAEL *collapses next to him, embarrassed but laughing.*

JONATHAN   Where'd you pick up that idea?

ANNE   In a book. I sent away for it.

JOSH   *(To* MICHAEL) You're lucky she didn't ask to see for herself. She has a very scientific mind.

JONATHAN   I hope the other information is more reliable.

> LOUISE *crosses through on her way to the master bedroom.* JONATHAN *is concerned that* SHE *might hear their conversation.*

JONATHAN   *(Continued)* Look Annabelle, I'll talk to you later about this, OK?

ANNE   But I need to know if . . .

JONATHAN   Anne! Not now.

ANNE   Oh all right. Can someone come and put my Bible on?

JOSH   I'll do it Annie.

ANNE   Thanks.

> ANNE *turns herself off and the monitor goes dark.* JOSH *starts toward* ANNE's *room.*

JONATHAN   Josh, is that football still around somewhere?

JOSH   Yeah. Want to toss a few?

JONATHAN   Sure. How about it, Mike?

MICHAEL   Might as well. I forgot my knitting.

JOSH   I'll be right back.

> JOSH *goes out.* LOUISE *comes in from the master bedroom.*

LOUISE   Have you seen James?

JONATHAN   I thought he went in your room.

LOUISE   He isn't there now.

> JAMES *is seen outside on the patio approaching from the Left.* HE *comes into the family room through the sliding glass door.* LOUISE *stares at him.*

JAMES   Gosh it's a beautiful day. Warm as April.

> JONATHAN *and* MICHAEL *move toward the front door.*

JONATHAN   Tell Josh we're out in front.

> MICHAEL *and* JONATHAN *go out.* JAMES *would like to join them but doesn't.*

LOUISE   Oh James.

JAMES   What have I done?

LOUISE   You couldn't even get through the afternoon without phoning her.

JAMES   Who?

LOUISE   You know who.

JAMES   Louise, I haven't, I didn't, honestly I didn't.

LOUISE   Disappearing. Nobody knows where you are. It's embarrassing.

> JOSH *comes into the family room with the football.* LOUISE *and* JAMES *drop their quarrel when* JOSH *appears.*

JOSH   Did they go out?

LOUISE   In front.

> JOSH *goes out. The quarrel continues.*

JAMES   Louise! I only called Howard to wish him Merry Christmas.

LOUISE   You played golf with him yesterday, wasn't that good enough?

> GEM *has overheard the argument and now coughs to call attention to her presence, then turns on the portable radio to drown them out.* JAMES *lowers his voice.*

JAMES   He's alone and I wanted to, well you know.

LOUISE   Why didn't you use this phone?
JAMES   I didn't want to disturb things.
LOUISE   I would have said hello.
JAMES   Why? You don't like the man, you never have.

> LOUISE *goes tight-lipped into the kitchen.* JAMES *looks around at the empty room and sighs.* GEM *has finished cutting the green beans.*

GEM   These are done. Now what?
LOUISE   Cook them.
GEM   Right. What's the recipe?
LOUISE   Boil some water, add salt, add the beans, cook two minutes, drain them, saute slivered almonds in butter and add the beans. We'll reheat them just before we eat.
GEM   Boil some water.

> GEM *fills a large cooking pot with water and sets it on the stove.* JAMES *comes into the kitchen.*

JAMES   How about a refill? (LOUISE *silently takes his glass*) Can I have a bloody mary with vermouth instead of tomato juice?
LOUISE   Gem? Wine?
GEM   Yup. A person can work up a thirst at this business.

> *The telephone rings.* LOUISE *moves quickly to answer it.* GEM *pours her own wine and then starts but doesn't finish making* JAMES' *drink. The doorbell rings.*

LOUISE   *(On the phone)* Hello.

> *The front door opens and* JENNY *calls.*

JENNY   Hello! It's me. (JENNY *enters carrying a present*)
JAMES   Jenny! Come on in.
LOUISE   *(On the phone)* Yes, she's here. Just a minute.
JAMES   Merry Christmas. (JAMES *kisses* JENNY *hello*)
LOUISE   Gem?

> GEM *stops drinking in mid-sip.*

GEM   Mmm?

JENNY   Merry Christmas.
LOUISE   It's for you.
JENNY   Should I put this under the tree?
GEM   Who is it?
JAMES   Sure.
LOUISE   A young man. He said Danny.

LOUISE *is holding out the receiver to* GEM. JENNY *goes to the Christmas tree and puts a package under it.*

LOUISE   *(Continued)* Well? Don't you want to talk to him?
GEM   Uh. Oh, yes. Of course. But . . . uh . . . can I take it in your room?
LOUISE   Of course.

GEM *passes* JENNY *as* SHE *moves hurriedly to the master bedroom.*

JENNY   Hi Gem.
GEM   Hello Jenny.
LOUISE   *(On the phone)* She'll be right here.
JAMES   What's that all about?
LOUISE   I don't know. A call for Gem. Someone named Danny.

LOUISE *hangs up the phone and goes to* JENNY. JENNY's *cheerfulness is a little forced.*

LOUISE   *(Continued)* Hello Jenny. It's nice to see you.
JENNY   It's good to be here. It's been a little spooky in that house alone. Too many childhood Christmases rattling around in the memory bank I guess.

LOUISE *finishes making* JAMES' *vodka martini.*

LOUISE   Have you heard from your folks?
JENNY   They phoned last night from Maui. They're having a wonderful time.
JAMES   Wish you were there eh?
JENNY   No. They need to be alone. It's hard on them having me around the house.
LOUISE   Nonsense, I'm sure they're delighted to have you home again.
JENNY   We're all adjusting.
LOUISE   Can I get you something Jenny?

JENNY   A glass of wine, thanks.

LOUISE *gets the wine.*

JENNY   *(Continued)* Anything I can do, Louise?
LOUISE   No, thank you, dear. Everything's under control.
JENNY   I brought something for Anne. Should I give it to her now or later?
LOUISE   Later I think. But you didn't have to do that.
JENNY   I wanted to.

LOUISE *brings* JAMES *and* JENNY *their drinks, then picks up* JENNY's *coat which* JAMES *has put on a chair.*

JENNY   *(Continued)* Thank you. How is she?
LOUISE   The same.
JENNY   Jonathan looks wonderful.
LOUISE   He does, doesn't he?

LOUISE *has taken* JENNY's *coat to the guest room. When* SHE *returns to the kitchen* SHE *salts the water and adds the green beans to the "boiling" water. The radio music continues.* JAMES *and* JENNY *sit down in the family room.*

JAMES   Well, how are things in the merchandising world?
JENNY   Oh fine.
JAMES   Interesting work?
JENNY   I wouldn't go that far. But it will do for now. The rewards are tangible. All questions are answered by the cash register.
JAMES   I wish Jonathan saw things like that.
JENNY   He doesn't?
JAMES   I ask him how his business is doing and he talks a lot about clients and not at all about money. It's not as if it were none of my business. I loaned him the money to start it.
JENNY   Maybe things aren't as straight forward in the travel agency game.
JAMES   Maybe. Jonathan and Jenny. Those were good days.
JENNY   You used to say I belonged in the family. Jonathan, Jenny, and Josh. You have a thing about Js don't you?
JAMES   Oh, it's sort of sentimental really. I wanted there to be, I don't know, some kind of connection. You never saw me did you?
JENNY   Saw you?

JAMES *makes a joke of it.*

JAMES Watching you . . . with lust in my heart.

JENNY Oh.

JAMES You were very . . . Well, you still are. Very.

JENNY Is Jonathan happy do you think?

JAMES I don't know. I hope so.

JENNY What do you think of Michael?

JAMES Have you met him?

JENNY Just now, out in front.

JAMES You know don't you?

JENNY Yes.

JAMES Maybe you were the first to know.

JENNY What do you mean?

JAMES You and Jonathan. When you were in high school. Drive-in movies, lovers' lanes, car-seat lovemaking.

JENNY Ah yes. Those romantic days. Coitus interrupted by the highway patrol spot light.

JAMES (*Chooses his words carefully*) Jenny, I know it's none of my business, but I'd like to try to understand what happened. I mean, tell me, was he . . . Did he seem . . . enthusiastic?

JENNY (*Decides not to be annoyed*) Neither of us knew what we were doing. It was all pretty tense and unsatisfying.

JAMES There must have been nights up at Folsom Dam. On a blanket under the stars.

JENNY No. I was always afraid of rattlesnakes in the grass. On the whole you could say we were enthusiastic amateurs.

LOUISE *leaves the green beans to drain in a colander in the sink and joins* JAMES *and* JENNY. SHE *is drinking a glass of white wine.*

LOUISE Amateur what?

JENNY Lovers.

LOUISE Oh.

JENNY Ancient history. I've lost my amateur standing.

LOUISE Jenny.

JENNY Sorry.

JAMES Gem is having quite a yak in there. Who is this fellow?

LOUISE She hasn't mentioned him.

JAMES It's not that guy, oh what's his name, the one she left Bill for?

LOUISE That was over months ago. He might be the one she . . .

JONATHAN, JOSH, *and* MICHAEL *come in laughing, full of energy, and a bit breathless.* JOSH *puts the football down on the dining table and heads for the refrigerator.*

JOSH   Michael throws a pretty fair pass, but this creep, my God, it's embarrassing.
JONATHAN   Fortunately the neighbors weren't watching.
JOSH   Anybody else want a beer?
MICHAEL   Sounds good.

JONATHAN *goes to the refrigerator and* HE *and* JOSH *get three beers and joke out-of-focus.*

JAMES   Are you, uh, interested in sports Michael?
MICHAEL   Not at all. (HE *realizes that an interest in sports would be desirable*) But I ran track in high school. Jon's been trying to get me to start jogging with him.
JAMES   Still jogging are you, Jonathan?

JONATHAN *brings* MICHAEL *a beer.*

JONATHAN   Yeah.
JAMES   What's your distance?
JONATHAN   Four miles five times a week. How about you, Dad? A man your age should get some exercise.
JAMES   I figure jogging adds what, at the most maybe two years to your life?
JONATHAN   Something like that.
JAMES   And I would spend damn near that much time jogging. You don't come out ahead. Besides, I'm not enough of a masochist.
JONATHAN   *(Defensively)* What's that supposed to mean?
JAMES   *(Innocently)* Nothing. I didn't mean . . .
JONATHAN   Forget it. Anyway, you're looking good, Dad.

LOUISE *has gone into the kitchen.* JOSH *has his head in the oven checking the turkey.* JONATHAN *crosses to* JENNY *and* THEY *talk out-of-focus.*

JONATHAN   *(Continued)* How's it going Jenny?
LOUISE   *(To* JOSH) How's it look?
JOSH   What's that funny looking cloth on it?
LOUISE   Cheesecloth. Supposed to keep it moist. Close the door Josh.

LOUISE *puts small plastic containers on a plastic tray.* JAMES *feels* HE *should talk to* MICHAEL, *but doesn't know what to say. The feeling is mutual.*

JAMES   Well, Michael. How long have you been working for Jonathan?
MICHAEL   Almost a year. But I don't exactly work for him. I work with him.
JAMES   Oh?
MICHAEL   He specializes in international travel, I handle the domestic business.
JAMES   I see.
LOUISE   Josh, I've got a lot to do before dinner. Would you mind feeding Anne?
JOSH   Sure Mom. No problem. (JOSH *takes the tray from her and starts toward* ANNE's *room.* HE *looks at the sealed containers of food)* Yuck.

GEM *comes out of the master bedroom looking very happy and a little embarrassed.* JAMES *is relieved to have a distraction.* JONA-THAN *and* JENNY *stop talking and look up as* GEM *enters.* SHE *can't control her smile.* LOUISE *is putting butter and slivered almonds in a frying pan, then adds the drained green beans.*

JAMES   There you are.
GEM   Here I am.
JAMES   Tell me, who is the man who makes you smile like that?
GEM   Don't be silly James.
JAMES   *(To* JONATHAN) What do you make of that?
JONATHAN   Out of character.
JAMES   Definitely.
GEM   *(To* LOUISE) So where was I?
LOUISE   I'm doing the beans. You could set the table.

LOUISE *opens the oven door and bastes the turkey, then makes another pot of coffee.* GEM *takes silverware to the dining table.*

MICHAEL   *(To* JONATHAN *and* JENNY) How long's it been since you two have seen each other?
JENNY   Years. You were home for the summer after your sophomore year at college.
JONATHAN   No, after that. The next Christmas.
JENNY   We were strangers by then.

The JONATHAN-JENNY-MICHAEL *conversation continues out-of-focus and* THEY *deliberately leave the past and talk about their present lives.* THEY *laugh occasionally.* JAMES *joins* GEM *at the dining table.* GEM *tosses the football to* JAMES *who does—or does not—catch it.*

GEM   Josh would be ashamed of you (or proud of you).

GEM *sets the table as* JAMES *follows her.*

JAMES   Fess up.
GEM   What?
JAMES   Who's the guy?
GEM   He's . . . he's just a friend.
JAMES   Gem you don't have friends.
GEM   He can't be anything else.
JAMES   Why not?
GEM   It's . . . impossible.
JAMES   He's married isn't he?
GEM   *(Laughs)* No.
JAMES   Gem, look at me. Are you in love with this guy?

There is a pause, then a sigh of surrender.

GEM   Yes.
JAMES   Oh, Gem! Already?!
GEM   James, I can't fall in love according to a socially acceptable time schedule! When it happens, it happens.
JAMES   Here we go again! Gem, as your lawyer I must . . .
GEM   Relax James. There is no question of marriage.
JAMES   Well good. You've finally learned you don't have to marry every man you go to bed with.
GEM   Don't tell me how to handle my sex life! You've got enough problems of your own!

JAMES *looks with alarm toward* LOUISE *who has turned around and is glaring at* GEM. JONATHAN, JENNY, *and* MICHAEL *have stopped talking and are watching.* JOSH *has come in and stands watching with detached interest.* GEM's *anger melts.*

GEM   *(Continued)* I'm sorry. But I didn't ask for your advice.
JOSH   That's good. He charges seventy-five dollars an hour.

JAMES *and* GEM *laugh, glad for an excuse to ease the tension.*

GEM   Your rates have gone up. It used to be free.
JAMES   And that's about what it's worth. Well, Louise. Is it time?
LOUISE   Yes.
JAMES   OK. If you'll all excuse me then, we'll get this party rolling in a minute.

JAMES *goes into the master bedroom.* JOSH *goes into the kitchen and looks hungrily at the turkey.* JONATHAN, JENNY *and* MICHAEL *are silent.* GEM *finishes setting the silverware then sets up the sideboard with serving spoons, forks, and hot pads.* LOUISE *takes seven champagne glasses out of the cupboard, puts them on a tray and then into the freezer.*

LOUISE   Close the door, Josh.

JOSH *closes the oven door.*

JOSH   I'm starving.
LOUISE   It won't be long.
GEM   Should I put the plates on?
LOUISE   No, I'll warm them later. Wine glasses.

GEM *gets red wine glasses down from the cupboard and puts them on the table.* JOSH *has his head in the refrigerator.*

JOSH   Can I have some cheese?
LOUISE   Of course.

JOSH *takes a piece of cheese out of the refrigerator and crackers out of the cupboard and stands in the kitchen eating.* JENNY *turns to* JONATHAN. SHE *has a habit of using her personal emotional life as anecdotal material to entertain, it is her form of wit.*

JENNY   Speaking of divorces, I assume you heard about mine.
JONATHAN   You're all right are you?
JENNY   What do you think?
JONATHAN   I'd say the wounds had pretty well healed.
JENNY   True.
JONATHAN   Any scar tissue?
JENNY   Minimal.

JONATHAN   It doesn't show.

JENNY   I don't really understand why I did it. Probably never will. It's as if a stranger had done it.

MICHAEL   What did you do?

JENNY   Got married.

MICHAEL   That is hard to understand.

JENNY   And two months later I split for Mexico City with our dentist.

MICHAEL   Interesting.

JENNY   Nuts. Poor Dad spent $4,812 on the prettiest wedding he could buy and eight weeks later I'm on the road with a creep I didn't even like much and Mom is stuck returning the wedding gifts. I didn't think that was absolutely necessary but Ann Landers did. So everything went back, except the wedding dress, that was used. Like me.

JONATHAN   And here you are, a beautiful and independent woman with a brilliant career in merchandising.

JENNY   I have to do something.

MICHAEL   You're good at it?

JENNY   Yup.

JONATHAN   And you've given up men?

JENNY   God no! I'm thinking of taking them up seriously. I'm just not having much luck at the moment.

JONATHAN   No current flames?

JENNY *makes light of something which isn't.*

JENNY   Now there's a sad tale.

JONATHAN   What happened?

JENNY   I wish I knew. I seem to have no talent for permanent relationships. There's a trick to it.

JONATHAN   What's that?

JENNY   Wanting what you've got. Oh well. Never mind. It's back to the body bars.

JONATHAN   Really?

JENNY   Sure. You've got to start somewhere. It beats masturbating in front of the soap operas.

JONATHAN   I wouldn't have thought . . . Are you likely to meet someone in a body bar with whom you can have a serious relationship?

JENNY   Who wants serious?

MICHAEL   Jonathan? What would you call the place where we met?

JONATHAN   Well yes, but that's . . . different.

THEY *all laugh.* LOUISE *and* GEM *are talking out-of-focus in the kitchen.* JOSH *has finished his cheese and crackers and has gone outside onto the patio.* HE *stretches in the fresh air and the late afternoon sunlight, then moves out of sight Left.* MICHAEL *watches him disappear.*

MICHAEL   How old is Josh?
JONATHAN   Twenty. He's got another year of college after this.
MICHAEL   What's he going to do?
JONATHAN   Who knows. Josh isn't big on plans. He just . . . floats.
MICHAEL   It's hard.
JONATHAN   I know. He'd love to show you his car.
MICHAEL   What kind of car has he got?
JONATHAN   Chevy. It doesn't run. Dad wants to buy him one that does, but Josh says no, no, I'll get her going. How about a tour?
MICHAEL   Sure.
JONATHAN   He's really got it fixed up. Rigged the seats to make into a full-size bed. (JONATHAN *opens the sliding glass door)* It's around the other side of the house.

MICHAEL *goes out,* JONATHAN *turns before going out.*

JONATHAN   *(Continued)* You want to come, Jenny?
JENNY   *(Stands up but shakes her head)* No. I hate cars. Maybe that's why I ran off with the dentist. He had a motorcycle.
JONATHAN   See you later.

JONATHAN *and* MICHAEL *go out of sight Left.* JENNY *watches them for a moment then, realizing* SHE *is left with the company of* LOUISE *and* GEM, SHE *goes outside onto the patio.* SHE *looks at the palm tree, absentmindedly fingering a frond, and then walks around in the yard.* LOUISE *and* GEM *bring salt and pepper shakers and candle holders to the table.* LOUISE *gets a dish of cranberry sauce out of the refrigerator and puts it on the table as* GEM *starts folding the cloth napkins and putting them around.*

LOUISE   OK. I think that's everything for now. When we have the champagne I'll put the sweet potatoes and creamed onions in the oven.
GEM   How's the turkey coming?
LOUISE   I just wiggled a leg. It didn't wiggle much. When it's done I'll heat the beans and scoop out the stuffing while you carve the turkey.
GEM   You mean hack it apart. It sure would be nice to have a carver in the family.

LOUISE   I sharpened the knives.

GEM   It won't help.

LOUISE   Michael's very nice don't you think?

GEM   How can you tell? He doesn't talk.

LOUISE   He's just quiet.

GEM   Scared to death. It's hard to meet your lover's family for the first time.

LOUISE   Gem.

GEM   You're not his family?

LOUISE   You know what I mean.

GEM   What do you want me to call them? Husband and husband? But actually, I'm a little disappointed in him.

LOUISE   What did you expect?

GEM   Lipstick and taffeta would have been rather fun.

LOUISE *does not respond.*

GEM   *(Continued)* Louise. You haven't really accepted it have you?

LOUISE   Yes. I have. I'm glad he's happy. I'm glad he's himself and not pretending. I'm glad he told us.

GEM   But.

LOUISE   It's just that I keep wondering. What is it that will keep them together?

GEM   When the first bloom fades?

LOUISE   With no children, no . . . obligations.

GEM   No legal entanglements. Maybe they don't think of permanence as a great virtue.

LOUISE   I can't imagine it. To me life is working at what you've got, knowing it isn't perfect but it never is. So you accept that and live with it. But if there's no commitment, then you just give up when things get rough. Just start again with someone else. A line of failures. And you end up old and alone.

GEM   So that's where I'm headed?

LOUISE   You know I didn't mean . . .

GEM   I know you didn't mean.

LOUISE   Anyway, you have a family. You have Gideon.

GEM   *(A sardonic laugh)* My devoted son didn't even send a card this year.

LOUISE   Gem, I just want him to be happy, to be settled.

GEM   You know there is something to be said for us love questers. It's an exciting life. Trekking through the fern bar jungles, paddling up rivers of booze, through the marijuana mists. *(Seriously)* Oh look,

Louise. Be grateful. Jonathan is in love and out of all that. At least for now.

LOUISE It's harder for James really. He can't understand what a life with no children means. He's proud of where he's come from, how your father did without so James could become a lawyer. And your father never resented that.

GEM No, he didn't. But I did.

LOUISE What?

GEM James went to college. I got pregnant.

LOUISE *is too self-absorbed to respond and follows her own thoughts.*

LOUISE We've never had to make any sacrifices of course, but James has always been proud that he could give the kids things that he didn't have. It's why he makes money. If there aren't any children then there's no point to anything. Do you see what I mean? There's no chain of progress. James thinks Jonathan has broken the chain, and he doesn't understand why.

GEM No. He wouldn't. Do you?

LOUISE *(Hates to admit it)* No.

The timing buzzer on the oven buzzes. LOUISE *goes into the kitchen, turns on the light, and shuts off the buzzer.* SHE *opens the oven and wiggles a turkey leg.*

GEM Louise, it isn't something he decided to do you know. It's just what he is.

LOUISE What?

GEM It isn't a conscious rejection.

LOUISE It's almost done.

JAMES *dramatically opens the master bedroom door.* HE *is dressed in a full Santa Claus costume complete with a sack over his back.*

JAMES Ho ho ho! Meeerreeeeee Christmasssssss . . . (JAMES *is astonished to find no audience)* Hey, where is everyone?!

LOUISE *and* GEM *laugh affectionately.* LOUISE *goes to him and hugs him.*

LOUISE I'm sorry James. They're out at Josh's car.

JAMES I thought it was time.

LOUISE It is. I'll tell you what. Why don't you go back in the bedroom and I'll call them in and you can make another entrance.

JAMES I don't know. Maybe we should forget it.

LOUISE You look wonderful.

JAMES Are you sure this is still a good idea?

LOUISE Now don't fuss. You know the kids love it.

JAMES OK. If you say so. But hurry up. It's hot in this thing.

> JAMES *goes back into the bedroom and closes the door.* GEM *chuckles sympathetically.* LOUISE *goes to the sliding glass door and opens it.*

GEM Poor James.

LOUISE Josh!

JOSH *(Calling from Off Left)* Yeah?

LOUISE Everybody come in. Champagne time!

JOSH Coming.

> LOUISE *and* GEM *go into the kitchen.*

LOUISE Will you take care of the champagne?

GEM You bet. Louise?

LOUISE Ummm?

GEM There's always Josh you know. To put some new leaves on the family tree.

LOUISE Yes. There's some salted nuts in the cupboard.

GEM OK.

> As THEY *talk* LOUISE *puts the sweet potato casserole and the creamed onions in the oven.* GEM *gets a large white napkin out of a drawer and puts it on a tray, then takes a champagne bottle out of the refrigerator.* LOUISE *hesitates, then decides now is as good a time as any.*

LOUISE Gem. Gideon phoned yesterday.

GEM He did?

LOUISE To say Merry Christmas. And to tell me his good news.

GEM Is he finally going to marry that girl?

LOUISE No. Gem, they're going to have a baby.

GEM What!

LOUISE   In April.

GEM   Oh my God!

LOUISE   He said they're very happy about it.

GEM   Did he ask you to tell me?

LOUISE   No. But he must have known that you'd be here today and I would tell you.

GEM   They aren't going to get married?

LOUISE   No. He says he doesn't believe in marriage.

GEM   This is ridiculous. I'm going to be a grandmother!

LOUISE   Oh don't worry. No one would guess.

GEM   *(Starts to laugh, not with mirth but with a touch of hysteria)* What timing!

JENNY   *(Comes in from the back yard)* Your daffodils are starting to come up.

LOUISE   Oh? I should have replaced some of those bulbs. They've been in too long. Gem? Are you all right?

GEM   Oh yes, fine. (GEM *gives the can of salted nuts to* JENNY *and points to a small bowl)* Here. Put those in there.

> JENNY *follows instructions as* GEM *takes the tray of champagne glasses out of the freezer. The shadows are long in the back yard, dusk is beginning.* JOSH, JONATHAN, *and* MICHAEL *come into the family room.*

MICHAEL   That's really something. You could live in that car!

JONATHAN   Now if you could just get it going.

JOSH   I'll get her going, don't you worry about that. I've got this real strong feeling it's the distributor. Once I get that taken care of, off she'll go.

> GEM *carries the bottle of champagne and glasses to the coffee table in the family room.* LOUISE *takes off her apron and goes to the TV monitor.* JENNY *brings in the dish of nuts.*

JONATHAN   Well, well, French yet.

GEM   Nothing but the best *(Sotto voce)* Where is it?

JONATHAN   In the tree. Shall I give it to her last?

GEM   Good idea.

> LOUISE *turns on the microphone on top of the monitor.* MICHAEL *has taken a nut from the dish and is about to put it in his mouth.*

JOSH   Hey, I'll bet that's the only pecan in the bunch!

MICHAEL   You're probably right. (MICHAEL *eats it*)

LOUISE   Anne? Anne, dear?

JONATHAN   (*To* JOSH) Where's Dad?

JOSH   (*Indicates the door to the master bedroom with a jerk of his thumb*) Ho ho ho.

LOUISE   (*Into microphone*) Anne?

JONATHAN   Oh no!

JOSH   I'll bet ya.

ANNE   Yes?

LOUISE   Time for champagne and presents. We'd like you to join us.

ANNE   Oh good. I'd love to. (ANNE's *face appears on the screen*) Hi everybody.

> JOSH, JENNY, JONATHAN *and* MICHAEL *say hello.* LOUISE *turns on the Christmas tree lights, then scurries into the master bedroom.*

ANNE   (*Continued*) Is that Jenny?

JENNY   Hi Anne. How are you?

ANNE   I've been reading. Jonathan I'm worried about something. Can you tell me . . .

JONATHAN   Later Anne.

> GEM *gives the champagne bottle wrapped in the white napkin to* JONATHAN.

GEM   Here, you pop it.

JONATHAN   OK. Big pop or little pop.

JOSH   Just don't waste any.

> LOUISE *gleefully returns, joins the others to enjoy the traditional moment. The champagne cork pops as* JAMES *opens the door, peeks out to make sure the audience is assembled, then throws open the door and calls heartily.*

JAMES   Ho ho ho! Merrrrryyeeeeeee Christmassssssssss!

> JAMES *enters and sets down his sack as the others respond with as much enthusiasm as* THEY *can manage.* THEY *do quite well.* JONATHAN *pours champagne.*

JOSH (*To* MICHAEL) Funny thing about Santa Claus. His stomach gets jollier every year.

JAMES Careful young man. You'll end up holding an empty sock.

JONATHAN *and* GEM *are handing around glasses of champagne.* SANTA *speaks with mock intimacy to* JENNY.

JAMES (*Continued*) And have you been a good little girl, young lady?

JENNY Well I've been trying very hard not to be.

JAMES Oh ho ho. Ho ho.

GEM As provider of the champagne it is my privilege, and honor, to propose a toast. Welcome Michael!

JONATHAN I'll drink to that!

JONATHAN *and* MICHAEL *touch glasses.* MICHAEL *is somewhat embarrassed but very pleased.* JAMES *and* LOUISE *raise their glasses with the others and* ALL *drink.*

JOSH Hear, hear.

ANNE Bottoms up.

JOSH Great stuff, Aunt Gem.

JENNY Ummm, lovely.

JAMES Very fine.

JONATHAN One more toast. To Santa Claus.

The toast is endorsed and ALL *raise their glasses.* JAMES *pats his Santa's stomach.*

JAMES Ho ho ho.

ANNE Mom?

LOUISE Yes dear?

ANNE I would like to say a prayer.

LOUISE Oh not now dear.

ANNE But I'm worried and I thought it would help if we could all pray together.

LOUISE A silent prayer will have to do.

ANNE But Mom I . . .

LOUISE Anne!

ANNE Yes, all right.

ANNE *closes her eyes and prays silently. Her expression is earnest and beseeching. The others find this somewhat disconcerting. GEM pours more champagne. JAMES has opened his Santa's sack.*

JAMES   Well let's get down to the nitty gritty here and see what Santa's got in the sack.

JAMES pulls out Christmas stockings. Those for JOSH, JONA-THAN, GEM and ANNE have names stitched on the top, those for JENNY and MICHAEL do not. HE passes them out with appropriate comments. Except for ANNE's stocking—which contains only things made of plastic—each has an orange and a roll of lifesavers. Throughout this scene there is general out-of-focus conversation with the focus going to the scripted lines at the appropriate times. Things are happening simultaneously. As the presents are un-wrapped, the room is transformed into a cluttered mess with piles of unneeded merchandise. JAMES goes to the monitor with ANNE's stocking but notices that SHE is still praying. HE looks at LOUISE.

JAMES   *(Continued)* I guess this had better wait huh?
LOUISE   She'll be finished soon.
JOSH   Huh! She can go on for hours.

At different moments the stocking openers reach their presents and thank MR. and MRS. CLAUS. MICHAEL has received a large bottle of Brut After Shave Lotion. JOSH now has his own member-ship in Triple A, and JONATHAN has a season ticket to his city's National or American league baseball team. When HE opens it JAMES says:

JAMES   We weren't sure if you . . . you do still like baseball, don't you?
JONATHAN   You bet I do. So does Michael. Thanks a lot, this is great.

At the bottom of JOSH, JONATHAN, and ANNE's stockings are checks for 50 dollars.

JOSH   Geez, fifty bucks!
JONATHAN   I remember when it used to be five.
JAMES   Inflation.
JENNY   *(Has received a wallet from JAMES and LOUISE)* Ah, just the thing. Thank you, Louise.

GEM has caviar and ballet tickets, JOSH a set of spark plugs,

JENNY *cologne.* ANNE *has finished praying, but from the looks of it, it has not been a satisfactory session.*

ANNE   Jonathan?
JONATHAN   Yes Anne?
ANNE   Jonathan, I need to know if you and . . .
JONATHAN   *(Gently but firmly)* Not now, Anne. It will have to wait. Come on, cheer up, Santa's brought you goodies. (HE *goes to the monitor and holds* ANNE's *stocking up to the video camera)*
ANNE   All right. What's in it?

JONATHAN *unwraps her presents for her and holds them up where* SHE *can see them.*

JAMES   Let's see now. We've got here some packages for folks who weren't here last night. This seems to be for you Michael.

JAMES *hands* MICHAEL *a present as* JOSH *suddenly stands up and goes out down the hallway to his room.*

JOSH   Oh yeah. I forgot.

JAMES *looks at* LOUISE *and* THEY *laugh.*

JAMES   *Semper paratus.*
LOUISE   I think he has made something. He spent most of yesterday afternoon in his room.

GEM *opens the second bottle of champagne and pours.* MICHAEL *unwraps and thanks* LOUISE *and* JAMES *for the necktie* THEY *have given him.* JONATHAN *has unwrapped a small toy.*

ANNE   What is it?
JONATHAN   Hey, Mom. What's this?
LOUISE   It's a toy for Simon Peter.
ANNE   Oh! Thanks. Put it in his cage, huh Jonathan?
JONATHAN   OK. (JONATHAN *puts the toy inside the cage.* MICHAEL *has put on the necktie)*
MICHAEL   Terrific.
JAMES   Here you go Jonathan. Annie, this is for you.

JAMES *hands around the presents.* JONATHAN *has finished with* ANNE's *stocking.* JENNY *crosses to him.*

JENNY   I'll do Anne's.
JONATHAN   (*Pats the top of the monitor affectionately*) Over to Jenny. See you later Annabelle.
ANNE   Does he like it?

JONATHAN *sits beside* MICHAEL *and notices the necktie.*

JONATHAN   You're a new man.
JENNY   Are you ready for this Anne?
ANNE   Who's it from?
JENNY   Me.

JAMES *has unwrapped a book.*

LOUISE   What's that, James?
JAMES   From Jonathan. "The Liberated Man." Well, thank you, Jonathan. Is this ah . . . a book about uh . . .
JONATHAN   No Dad. It's about men, all men.
JAMES   Oh I see. Liberated huh? Well that's me. Louise, is there any more of that champagne?

LOUISE *refills* JAMES' *glass.* JENNY *has unwrapped the record* SHE *has given* ANNE *and* JONATHAN *is exclaiming over his dark blue classic V-neck cashmere sweater.* JOSH *returns carrying five plain white envelopes with a name on each.* HE *passes them out to* JAMES, LOUISE, JONATHAN, GEM, *and takes one to the monitor.*

JAMES   (*Continued*) Well, what's this Josh?
JOSH   From me.

GEM *has passed out packages to* JONATHAN, MICHAEL, ANNE, JAMES *and* LOUISE. SHE *now hands one to* JOSH *as* HE *hands her an envelope.*

GEM   Trade ya.
JOSH   Right.
LOUISE   (*Has opened her envelope*) Oh Josh, that's very sweet.
JAMES   What is it?
LOUISE   It's a promissory note. "I will stay with Anne every Saturday

afternoon for the next six months." Josh, that's very nice, but it isn't necessary.

JOSH   Dad says you need to get out more.

JONATHAN   Hear hear!

GEM   It's certainly turning into a get-Louise-out-of-the-house Christmas.

JONATHAN   Shhh.

JAMES   Very nice Josh.

LOUISE   It's a conspiracy.

JONATHAN   *(Has opened his present from GEM: an English cap, matching scarf, and walking stick. JONATHAN laughs with delight)* Fantastic! Aunt Gem, that's marvelous. Look at this! (HE *tries on the cap and scarf and poses with the stick)*

MICHAEL   *(Has unwrapped a similar cap and scarf in a different color. HE uses an English accent)* I say! This is a bit of all right! (HE *also puts his on)* Tally ho old bean, shall we have a little stroll together. (HE *sings, music-hall style, as* THEY *perform)*

MICHAEL   *(Continued)* AS I TAKE MY MORNING PROMENADE SUCH A FASHION CARD ON THE PROMENADE.

> MICHAEL is suddenly self-conscious. JONATHAN *laughs.*

JONATHAN   Right you are.

MICHAEL   Thank you, Gem, very much.

GEM   Welcome. My pleasure. You both look terrific.

> JENNY *has opened* ANNE's *envelope and* SHE *reads the promissory note.* JAMES *has opened his envelope from* JOSH. HE *looks at* JOSH *and smiles.*

JAMES   This I have to see!

> JOSH *grins back at him.* MICHAEL *gets a package from under the tree and gives it to* JAMES. JOSH *is opening his package from* GEM: *a motoring cap and driving gloves.* HE *puts them on.*

JOSH   Oh wow!

GEM   I figured if you never get the car going, you can always wear them when you ride your bicycle.

> JONATHAN *goes to the tree for a present.* JAMES *has opened his present from* MICHAEL: *a very expensive, very good bottle of cognac.*

JAMES Oh well now. That really is just what I needed! Thank you, Michael.

JOSH *(To* GEM) I'll get her going. I got a feeling new points will do it.

JONATHAN Maybe this will help.

> JONATHAN *gives* JOSH *a present, returns to the tree and takes another package to* JENNY *who just opened* ANNE's *present from* GEM: *six large jigsaw puzzles.*

GEM I figure that's about a year's supply.

ANNE But Aunt Gem I'm allergic . . .

GEM The pieces are all plastic dear.

ANNE Oh great!

GEM I put some money in your savings account too.

ANNE Thank you.

> JOSH *has opened his present from* JONATHAN: *a mechanics manual for his Chevy.*

JOSH Fantastic!

JONATHAN I thought you could use a little professional help.

> JOSH *starts studying.* JONATHAN *gives* GEM *a present from under the tree which* SHE *opens out-of-focus—an art book from him.* JENNY *opens* ANNE's *present from* JONATHAN: *a book on homosexuality.* ANNE *and* JENNY *discuss the book out-of-focus.* LOUISE *is opening her package from* GEM: *a large floppy sun hat and a bright beach robe.* SHE *puts them on.*

LOUISE Oh Gem! Oh pretty!

ANNE Will you put the book on the machine for me Jenny?

ANNE Yes, all right.

GEM I thought it just might come in handy.

LOUISE What do you mean?

GEM *(Smiles with the air of knowing a secret)* Oh nothing.

JENNY Louise, Anne wants me to put on her new book.

> JENNY *goes to put* ANNE's *book on.* JONATHAN *has opened his envelope from* JOSH. HE *laughs.*

JONATHAN Thanks a lot Josh.

LOUISE Oh Anne! You're not going to read now are you?

JAMES   What's yours say?

ANNE   I'll stay on, but I can read too.

LOUISE   Oh, all right.

> LOUISE *gives* GEM *a present which* SHE *opens: a small but good piece of jewelry.* THEY *talk out-of-focus.*

JONATHAN   "Dear Jonathan and Michael, I will wash your car once a month for the next year. Josh." That's great Josh, but my car will be in the city.

JOSH   Yeah. Well, I thought maybe I could come and spend the weekend.

JONATHAN   Aren't you forgetting something?

JOSH   What's that?

JONATHAN   You just promised Mom you'd stay with Anne every Saturday.

JOSH   Oh. Well, she'll let me off. OK.

JONATHAN   Sure. We'd love to have you.

JAMES   Ah . . . I don't know if that's such a good idea.

JOSH   Why not Dad?

JAMES   Well. You don't want to impose on Jonathan and Michael, they have their own life.

JONATHAN   It's OK, Dad. We've got plenty of room.

> JAMES *has to remain silent.* JENNY *returns.* MICHAEL *has given* JOSH *a small package which* HE *opens. It is a knob.* JOSH *tosses it in the air.*

JOSH   Great! Uh . . . what is it?

MICHAEL   It's a necker's knob. You put it on the rim of the steering wheel and you can steer with one hand. (HE *pantomimes holding the knob and turning the wheel with his left hand while his right arm is around an imaginary person on his right)*

JAMES   I used to have one of those. Great invention! Remember, Louise?

> JAMES *and* LOUISE *talk out-of-focus.*

JOSH   That's great! Hey, you're all right Michael.

> MICHAEL *speaks quietly but good-naturedly to* JOSH. THEY *are*

near the TV monitor and MICHAEL *forgets that* ANNE *is present and can hear.*

MICHAEL   Hey tell me, Josh. What did you expect?

JOSH   What do you mean?

MICHAEL   You keep saying I'm all right. As if it were a relief and a surprise.

JOSH   Oh.

MICHAEL   What did you think I'd be a flaming faggot with red fingernail polish?

ANNE's *voice cuts through the other conversations.*

ANNE   Homosexuals are called faggots because during the medieval period heretics and homosexuals were burned at the stake. The pieces of wood used to burn them were called faggots.

There is silence.

GEM   Interesting bit of history, Anne.

ANNE   I can't understand why the church would do such a horrible thing. It's also true that queers . . .

LOUISE   Anne!

ANNE   What's the matter?

GEM   The subject is not appropriate Anne.

ANNE   *(Surprised)* Oh? I thought it was. I'm sorry.

GEM   It's OK.

MICHAEL   *(Speaks sotto voce to* JOSH) I'm sorry. I forgot she was there. I mean I forgot she could hear.

JOSH   I know.

GEM   *(To* JONATHAN) Now?

JONATHAN   Now.

GEM *and* MICHAEL *hum a Mexican tune as* JONATHAN *takes a large red envelope from the Christmas tree and gives it to* LOUISE.

JONATHAN   *(Continued)* For you.

LOUISE   Oh. Who's it from?

JONATHAN   Me.

LOUISE   Oh.

EVERYONE *watches as* SHE *opens the envelope. Inside is a travel brochure and a ticket.*

LOUISE   *(Continued)* I don't understand.
JAMES   What is it, Louise?
LOUISE   It's a brochure. For a ten day cruise to Mexico. And a ticket. But I don't understand. There's only one ticket. In my name.
JONATHAN   For you.
LOUISE   Me?
JAMES   I don't understand.

Blackout.

ACT II

When the lights come up EVERYONE *is in exactly the same position as at the end of* ACT I. THEY *carry forward whatever movement was frozen by the blackout.* MICHAEL *does a quick Mexican hat dance.*

MICHAEL   Ole!

LOUISE   I'm supposed to go on a ten-day cruise to Mexico by myself?

JONATHAN   That's the idea.

LOUISE   But I can't go!

JONATHAN   Yes you can.

LOUISE   I can't leave Anne.

GEM   All taken care of. I've hired a nurse's aide for the whole ten days.

LOUISE   But Gem you . . .

GEM   Jimmy's going to pay. Right, Jimmy?

JAMES   *(Thinking fast. It has just dawned on him that this would mean ten days of unrestricted freedom)* Oh . . . ah, sure. Sure!

LOUISE   But there's Josh. And James and . . .

JONATHAN   Mom, don't you want to go?

LOUISE   Of course. Jonathan, it's a lovely present, really. A very nice thought, but I've got responsibilities. I've got people to take care of.

GEM   They'll be all right. For heaven's sakes, they can get along for ten days without you.

JOSH   Sure Mom. With a little help from the Colonel.

JAMES   Sure. Heck, what's ten days. I'll work late at the office, eat out a lot.

LOUISE   *(Looks hard at JAMES, slowly shakes her head)* I can't go.

JONATHAN   *(Speaks very seriously, confident that HE knows what's best)* Of course you can. You need time on your own, Mom. You need to get away from all this work, to be alone. To find yourself.

LOUISE   Jonathan. I am not lost. And I am not like my mother, not yet.

I am still needed around here. (LOUISE *puts down the brochure and ticket*)

JONATHAN   Mom . . .

LOUISE   Now I'll just check the turkey, it should be done.

> LOUISE *goes into the kitchen and opens the oven door.* SHE *puts her hand in and wiggles a turkey leg to test for doneness.* JONATHAN *shrugs his shoulders helplessly, flops on the sofa in disappointment. Without anyone noticing* ANNE *has turned herself off.*

JENNY   It's a great idea, Jonathan.

JONATHAN   Yeah, I thought so.

JAMES   (*Thinking more of himself than* LOUISE) She'd have a wonderful time. All that . . . freedom. Don't worry, Jonathan, we'll talk her into it.

JOSH   Sure. We can always tie her up and carry her onto the boat.

> *There is mild amusement. The telephone rings.* LOUISE *turns off the oven and leaving the door ajar* SHE *goes to the telephone and picks up the receiver.*

LOUISE   Hello? (LOUISE *stiffens. On the phone*) Yes, this is she. *(Pause)* Yes. I see. *(Pause)* Is she . . . has she regained consciousness at all? *(Pause)* You're sure? *(Pause)* All right. *(Pause)* Yes, I understand. *(Pause)* Of course. No, of course, I understand. Thank you very much for calling. *(Pause)* You'll call if there's . . . when . . . *(Pause)* Yes, all right. Thank you. Goodbye.

> SHE *puts down the receiver and stands looking at it. Her thoughts are all internal,* SHE *does not appear upset, only tense and self-absorbed.* EVERYONE *is silent.*

JAMES   (*Goes to* LOUISE *and puts his hand on her shoulder*) Louise?

LOUISE   (*Goes to the refrigerator, takes out a dish of celery sticks and takes it to the table*) I'm all right James.

JAMES   Is she worse?

> LOUISE *nods. Then* SHE *sighs, realizing* SHE *has to give the information. Her attitude is matter-of-fact.* JOSH *escapes into the kitchen.*

LOUISE   Yes. Her "condition has deteriorated."

JAMES   How long . . .

LOUISE   They don't know. It could be hours, maybe days.

> GEM *has moved to* JAMES *and* LOUISE.

GEM   Louise, if you want to go I can take care of things here.

LOUISE   *(Shakes her head firmly)* No. Dinner's . . . almost . . . I've got
to . . .

GEM   We can manage. Jenny and I can get dinner on.

JENNY   Sure.

LOUISE   No! Thank you, Gem, I can't go. I mean, there's no reason for
me to go. She isn't conscious. She wouldn't even know I was there.
(LOUISE *turns abruptly to the rest of the group and speaks tensely)* OK.
Now. I haven't heard the magic words yet and you aren't going to get
any dinner until I do.

> *There is a confused silence.*

JONATHAN   What do you mean, Mom?

JOSH   *(From the kitchen)* It sure smells good in here, Mom.

LOUISE   There we are! Open sesame. Dinner in three minutes.

> GEM *has gone into the kitchen and is tying on an apron.*

LOUISE   *(Continued)* Josh, clean up the papers and straighten up. Jonathan, open the red wine on the sideboard. Michael, do you carve?

MICHAEL   I beg your pardon?

LOUISE   Turkeys. Do you know how to carve a turkey?

MICHAEL   Oh. Yes. Sure.

GEM   Hallelujah!

> LOUISE *and* MICHAEL *go into the kitchen.* SHE *puts on an apron
> and gives him a towel to tie around his waist.* EVERYONE *has a job
> except* JAMES *who sits, an island of inactivity.* JOSH *is cleaning up
> in the family room, piling presents under the tree and crumpling
> wrapping paper. It is almost dark and* HE *turns on a light.* HE *hands*
> JAMES *the book* JONATHAN *gave him.*

JOSH   Here you go, Dad. Required reading.

JAMES   Why's that?

JOSH   With Mom gone, you gotta learn to take care of yourself.

JAMES   Oh. I think I'll go put on a shirt.

JAMES *goes into the master bedroom.* LOUISE *has taken the turkey out of the oven and set it on the counter. During the intermission a cooked turkey has been substituted for the raw one in the oven.* LOUISE, MICHAEL *and* GEM *talk out-of-focus.* GEM *puts the dinner plates in the oven to warm and takes out the two casseroles and puts them on hotpads on the sideboard.* LOUISE *scoops stuffing into a bowl as* MICHAEL *prepares to carve.* GEM *puts the stuffing and green beans on the sideboard while* MICHAEL *carves the turkey. Except for the occupied* JOSH, JONATHAN *and* JENNY *are alone in the family room.* THEY *look at each other in silence.*

JONATHAN   Well, I guess I'd better get that wine open.

JENNY *straightens up presents that are near her.* JOSH *has found his necker's knob.*

JOSH   Hey. Did you ever have one of these?

JONATHAN *looks at* JENNY *without smiling.*

JONATHAN   No. We didn't.

JONATHAN *goes into the dining area and opens two bottles of red wine which are waiting on the sideboard.* JENNY *watches* JONATHAN *walk away and then turns suddenly and goes to* JOSH *who is sitting on a sofa.*

JENNY   Want to practice?
JOSH   What?
JENNY   Like this. (SHE *takes his right arm and puts it around her shoulders, rests her head on his shoulder)* Works pretty well, huh?
JOSH   Great.

JENNY *kisses* JOSH *hard on the mouth.*

JENNY   Sorry Josh.
JOSH   Geez, don't be sorry!
JENNY   *(Smiling)* I'm not. (JENNY *goes toward the kitchen leaving an amazed* JOSH *staring after her)* Anything I can do?
LOUISE   You can light the candles.

JENNY *gets matches from the kitchen.* JAMES *comes in from the master bedroom.*

JAMES   What's the matter, Josh?
JOSH   *(Starts guiltily)* Nothing Pop.

JOSH *puts presents under the tree and gathers up papers.* HE *takes his load outside onto the patio and around to the Left out of sight.* JAMES *goes to* JENNY.

JAMES   Hey, Jenny Wren. How about fixing me a short one. Just pour some vodka over a couple of ice cubes?
JENNY   Sure.

JENNY *does as* SHE *is asked.* JONATHAN *is opening the second bottle of wine.*

JAMES   We used to drink white wine with turkey, but Louise says red is better.
JONATHAN   A matter of individual taste.
JAMES   Say Jonathan. I wonder if I could have a word with you.
JONATHAN   Sure Dad. What's on your mind?
JAMES   Well, actually it's something I should have discussed with you before now, but I . . . well . . . there never seemed to be . . . (HE *breaks off as* JENNY *brings him his drink)* Thanks.

HE *leads* JONATHAN *into the empty family room.* JENNY *lights the candles on the table and sideboard.*

JAMES   *(Continued)* I don't want you to think I'm prying into your personal life. But there's a matter I'd like to discuss with you.
JONATHAN   Got it.
JAMES   Well. I know that you and Michael think of yourselves as being . . . that you consider your relationship to be a permanent one.
JONATHAN   Yes. Very much so.
JAMES   I'll be blunt if I may.
JONATHAN   Shoot.
JAMES   You haven't made any financial commitments to Michael have you?
JONATHAN   What?!
JAMES   The business. It's still in your name?
JONATHAN   Of course!

JAMES   You haven't made any promises have you? Nothing like, "I'll share what I have with you" or "I'll take care of you?"

JONATHAN   I don't think so. What are you getting at?

JAMES   Well, it's just that . . .

JENNY *calls into the kitchen.*

JENNY   Louise, should I pour the wine now?

LOUISE   No. Just let it breathe.

JAMES   *(Resumes with increased confidentiality)* There have been several cases recently involving the promissory obligations of lovers. Now these of course have been between a man and a woman, but it's only a matter of time before . . .

JONATHAN   Oh Dad! Michael's not going to sue me for support!

JAMES   Don't be offended. I'm only thinking of your financial future. I don't want you to think it's because you're a . . . I'd have exactly the same concern if Michael were a girl.

JONATHAN   I'll bet.

JAMES   It's just that right now this is a gray area. Legally, I only want to warn you.

JONATHAN   Got it. (JONATHAN *shakes his head in amazement and affection)* Dad. You're too much.

JAMES *looks at his empty glass.*

JONATHAN   *(Continued)* You need a refill.

JONATHAN *stands up and takes* JAMES' *glass.* JOSH *has come in from the back yard.* JONATHAN *goes toward the kitchen and meets* LOUISE *who is carrying the platter of sliced turkey to the sideboard.* GEM *has taken the heated plates out of the oven and put them on the sideboard.*

LOUISE   Not now Jonathan. We're going to eat. Dinner's ready everyone. Come and help yourselves. Somebody start. Jenny.

JOSH   I'll get Anne.

As LOUISE, GEM *and* MICHAEL *take off their aprons,* JOSH *goes to the TV monitor on its rolling cart and moves it to the table so that it takes the same position as a chair would. When the monitor is in place at the table* JOSH *turns on the microphone and calls.*

JOSH   *(Continued)* Anne?

> *We hear* ANNE's *voice but the monitor stays dark.*

ANNE   Yes?
JOSH   Turn yourself on. It's dinner time.
ANNE   OK.

> *It is almost dark.* LOUISE *turns off the overhead lights and the room is lit only by the candles and tree lights.* JENNY *and* JAMES *have taken plates and helped themselves to food and are now followed by* JONATHAN *and* MICHAEL, *then* GEM *and* JOSH.

LOUISE   As my Swedish grandmother used to say, eat now folks, there's plenty you know.
JONATHAN   It looks like plenty had turned into too much.
JENNY   It looks wonderful Louise.
MICHAEL   I'll say.
LOUISE   *(Is checking the table and sees that* ANNE *is not on)* Where's Anne?
JOSH   I called her. She's probably having a quick one before joining us heathens.

> JAMES *and* JENNY *now have full plates,* JONATHAN *and* MICHAEL *are almost finished serving themselves.*

JENNY   Where would you like us, Louise?
LOUISE   Oh. Jonathan, why don't you sit here next to Anne. Michael next to Jonathan. Jenny. No James, over here. Josh next to Jenny, then Gem. And please start.

> JAMES *abandons his hope of sitting next to* JENNY *and goes to his seat on* LOUISE's *right—the TV monitor is on* LOUISE's *left.* LOUISE *helps herself to food.* SHE *does not take much.* JONATHAN *moves around the table pouring wine.*

GEM   The sweet potatoes are specially for you, James. Loaded with bourbon.
JAMES   *(Comically slurs his words)* Honestly officer, I haven't been drinking. I've been eating.

> *Laughter.*

JOSH   Where am I?
JENNY   Here.

JOSH *sits down happily next to* JENNY.

JENNY   *(Continued)* Everything's absolutely delicious, Louise.
MICHAEL   Positively scrumptious. (HE *regrets his word choice)*
JAMES   Great, Lo.
JENNY   The stuffing. Is it sage?
LOUISE   Yes. And poultry seasoning.
JONATHAN   What's in poultry seasoning?
LOUISE   Heavens knows.
GEM   Conjures up disgusting images.
JAMES   It does?
GEM   It doesn't?
JONATHAN   Absolutely.
JAMES   Well, Jonathan. You must have had a good year.
JONATHAN   *(Smiles at* MICHAEL) It's been a great year.
JAMES   Good profit margin?
JONATHAN   Oh that. We're doing all right. Is something worrying you?
JAMES   I just wondered . . . that's an expensive present you gave your
   mother.
JONATHAN   I get a discount.
JAMES   Oh. I see.
JONATHAN   Speaking of which . . .
LOUISE   We'll talk about it later Jonathan.
JONATHAN   Will we?

There is silence. ANNE *comes out from the hallway leading to her
room.* SHE *is completely encased in a blue suit made of a plasticized
material and wears a gas mask. When* SHE *speaks her voice comes
out of a small speaker on the front of her suit.* MICHAEL, *who is
sitting across from where* ANNE *is standing and can see her, happens
to look up. His eyes bulge in amazement. A forkful of food freezes
on its way to his open mouth.* LOUISE *looks up from her plate and
notices his behavior.*

LOUISE   Michael? Is something wrong?
MICHAEL   Uh . . . is that . . . uh . . .

LOUISE *gets up and goes to* ANNE.

LOUISE   Anne! What a nice surprise.
JOSH   Hi Annie.

> LOUISE *puts her arm around* ANNE's *shoulders and leads her toward the table. Whenever* SHE *speaks* EVERYONE *gives her complete undivided attention.*

JAMES   Well, look who's here!
ANNE   Hi Daddy.
LOUISE   Don't you look pretty in your new suit.
ANNE   I thought I'd try it out.
JOSH   Hey Annie. You forgot your flippers. *(From the speaker on her shoulder comes a tinny sound)*
ANNE   Ha ha ha.
LOUISE   Michael, here's our Anne in person.
MICHAEL   *(Clears his throat)* Hi there.
ANNE   Hello, Michael.

> MICHAEL *clears his throat again.* HE *feels* HE *should say something else, but can't think of a single appropriate thing.*

GEM   I haven't seen you for a long time dear. It must be what . . . well months.
ANNE   The old suit was very uncomfortable. And I couldn't talk.
GEM   This is an improvement, eh?
ANNE   I think so.
JENNY   Pretty color.
ANNE   I like blue.
LOUISE   Well honey, maybe we'll see more of you now.

> JOSH *has moved the monitor and replaced it with a regular dining chair for* ANNE. HE *taps her on the shoulder from behind to let her know it's there.*

JOSH   Here you go Annie.
ANNE   Thanks.

> ANNE *sits down and* JOSH *returns to his seat.* ANNE *has a disturbing effect on the* OTHERS *at the table as* SHE *sits, not eating, and looking with innocence and curiosity from one to the other. It is as if someone from outer space had just joined the Christmas dinner.*

THEY *continue eating, trying to act as if there were nothing bizarre in this at all.*

ANNE *(Continued)* It took me longer than I thought to get ready. I wanted to come out in time to say grace.
JAMES Uh . . . we're past that point, Annie. Maybe next year. *(Pause)*
GEM Everything's great Louise, as usual.

The quality of the food is endorsed enthusiastically by OTHERS.

JENNY Is this homemade cranberry sauce?
LOUISE Yes.
MICHAEL I thought it grew in cans.

THEY *give him the courtesy laugh due a comparative stranger, silence.*

ANNE Jonathan, I'm worried about . . .
JONATHAN *(Horrified that* SHE *is going to come out with one of her devastating questions, interrupts)* Not now Anne.
ANNE But I need to know if it's true that . . .
JONATHAN This is a great turkey, Mom. Is it one of those butterball things?
LOUISE Of course not.
JONATHAN Still go out to the turkey farm for fresh birds huh?
ANNE The thing is that if they don't stop . . .
JONATHAN Dad, how about some more wine?
JAMES Yes, Jonathan, thanks. And now be quiet, huh, so your sister can talk?

JONATHAN *looks both ashamed and helpless as* HE *pours wine.*

ANNE I just wanted to know if you think that the oil shortage will have an effect on the availability of plastic. It seems to me that if they keep raising the price of oil I'm going to be in big trouble.
JAMES You're not the only one, honey. But don't worry. If it comes to that we'll get your name put on an emergency medical quota or something.
LOUISE Michael. Tell us about your family.
MICHAEL *(Surprised)* Did Jonathan tell you?
JONATHAN No Michael, I didn't.

MICHAEL   Oh. You mean my parents. Brothers, sisters, that sort of thing.

LOUISE   Yes.

MICHAEL   My Mom and Dad live in Arizona.

LOUISE   Is that where you grew up?

MICHAEL   No, they moved there a few years ago.

JAMES   What kind of work does your father do?

MICHAEL   Some kind of engineering. Metal stress.

JONATHAN   His folks have been married thirty-five years.

GEM   My God!

LOUISE   You have brothers and sisters?

MICHAEL   Six.

GEM   Incredible.

MICHAEL   My folks are very regular people. They got married, two years later came my sister, two years after that my brother, two more years and another boy, etc. I'm the youngest. I think they're finished.

JOSH   Mom and Dad had regular habits too. Jonathan's pre-law school, I'm post-law school. Anne's an afterthought.

LOUISE   Josh!

JOSH   What's the matter?

LOUISE   That's no way to talk about your sister.

JOSH   Well it's true isn't it? I mean you didn't plan to have Anne.

JAMES   That's enough Josh.

ANNE   It's true. I wasn't suposed to be born at all. I mean because you were using birth control techniques.

LOUISE   Anne!

JAMES   Your pre-conceptual knowledge is amazing.

ANNE   When we were little Josh found Mom's diaphragm in the medicine chest. What's the jelly for?

LOUISE   Anne for heavens sake be quiet.

ANNE   I don't understand.

JONATHAN   She's only exercising her curiosity, Mom.

LOUISE   If there is one thing in this house that does not need exercise, it is Anne's curiosity! Isn't it possible to have any privacy in this house?!

JONATHAN   We're just having a little honest talk.

JOSH   What's the big deal anyway?

LOUISE   Why does being honest about something always involve an unpleasant conversation?!

JONATHAN   Why is this unpleasant?!

JAMES   Maybe it's because you're shouting at each other.

There is silence.

ANNE   Mom, I'm sorry. I didn't mean . . .

LOUISE   No, Anne, I'm sorry. It's my fault. I'm . . . a little tense.

GEM   Vino! More vino pronto quicko!

MICHAEL   *(Jumps at the opportunity for action)* I'll get it.

> As the OTHERS *take up the awkward silence by focusing on their food,* MICHAEL *goes to the sideboard where the corkscrew lies beside the bottle of wine. When* HE *sees the corkscrew a conceptual joke bursts in his mind.*

MICHAEL   *(Continued)* Hey, Jonathan. An addition to our collection of urban comedies.

> Using *the corkscrew as a hypodermic syringe* HE *pantomimes shooting up. When* HE *finishes the performance* HE *discovers his* AUDIENCE *staring at him in uncomprehending silence.*

JONATHAN   You clown.

> JOSH, JONATHAN *and* GEM *laugh uncomfortably.* MICHAEL *brings the wine to the table and moves around pouring.*

JAMES   I think you're in the wrong business Michael. You're quite a comedian.

ANNE   Drug addiction is a very serious problem, I believe, even in our public school system.

JONATHAN   Actually he does perform. Not comedy, but he plays guitar at a club in the city.

ANNE   Is it one of the gay clubs?

JONATHAN   Yes.

JAMES   Where does she get all this stuff?!

> MOST PEOPLE *have finished eating and have pushed back their chairs and are lingering contentedly over their wine.*

LOUISE   Please, help yourselves to more food.

JENNY   Not another bite. I'm stuffed.

LOUISE   How about you, Michael?

MICHAEL   I really couldn't.

> GEM *is staring into space, her mind elsewhere.*

JAMES   Geemmmm? Oh Gem, Gem?

GEM   What?! What's the matter for Christ's sake? Oh, sorry Anne.

JAMES   The body is here but the mind is absent.

LOUISE   James what are you talking about?

GEM   Nothing. He's had too many sweet potatoes.

LOUISE   Pie now or later?

There are full stomach groans and calls for later.

LOUISE   *(Continued)* We'll just have coffee now then and the pie later.

LOUISE *is standing up and starts stacking plates.* GEM *and* JENNY *get up and help her.*

JENNY   I can hardly move.

JENNY *and* GEM *carry dirty dishes and glasses and the remaining food into the kitchen.* MICHAEL, JONATHAN, *and* JOSH *take loads in as well.* GEM *is unusually quiet.*

LOUISE   How many coffees?

GEM, JAMES, *and* MICHAEL *want coffee.*

JAMES   Really great dinner, Lo.

OTHERS *agree.*

LOUISE   Thank you. I'm glad you enjoyed it.

JAMES   Even the stuffing.

LOUISE   Thank you James.

LOUISE *goes into the kitchen, puts down a load of dishes, unplugs the coffee pot and puts it on the tray with the preset cups, saucers, sugar and cream.* MICHAEL *and* JOSH *put plates in the dishwasher.* JENNY *puts the leftover food in the refrigerator.*

ANNE   Jonathan?

JONATHAN   *(Answers from the kitchen)* Yes Annabelle?

ANNE   Can I talk to you now?

JONATHAN   Sure.

JAMES   Louise, get some brandy snifters. We'll give this cognac here a taste test.

GEM   Ouuuuweeeee! Where'd you get that?

JAMES   Michael.

GEM   (*Standing near* JAMES *at the Christmas tree*) James. You're doing fine. In fact I'm proud of you.

JAMES   I don't have much choice, do I?

GEM   No. But you're pulling it off well.

JAMES   Thanks. He's not exactly what I would have chosen for a daughter-in-law, but at least he knows his brandy.

JONATHAN   (*Goes to* ANNE *who is sitting alone at the dining table*) Would you like to take a walk?

ANNE   No.

JAMES   Why didn't you bring along your latest. It seems to be a day for introductions.

JONATHAN   (*To* ANNE) Why not?

GEM   (*To* JAMES) He's in Oregon with his family.

ANNE   (*To* JONATHAN) Someone might see me.

JAMES   (*To* GEM) Are his parents living?

JONATHAN   (*To* ANNE) Would that be so terrible?

GEM   (*To* JAMES) Oh yes.

ANNE   (*To* JONATHAN) I feel like a fool in this thing.

GEM   (*To* JAMES) You want to hear a joke?

JAMES   Sure.

JONATHAN   (*To* ANNE) Let's go in the back yard. We can walk around the swimming pool.

ANNE   OK.

GEM   (*To* JAMES) His mother's only three years older than I am.

JAMES   What?!

LOUISE   (*Calls from the kitchen*) Gem?

GEM   Yes?

LOUISE   Would you light the fire?

GEM   Sure.

GEM *goes to the fireplace and turns on the gas jet.* MICHAEL *takes the coffee tray into the family room for* LOUISE *and puts it on the coffee table.* LOUISE *brings brandy snifters.* JONATHAN *and* ANNE *start out the sliding glass door.*

LOUISE   Where are you going?

JONATHAN   We're just going to get a little air.

LOUISE   Won't you be cold?

JONATHAN   What would I do without you? (HE *finds his new sweater
under the tree and puts it on*)
LOUISE   Jenny? Join us. I'll do that later.
JENNY   I'll be right there.
LOUISE   Gem? Brandy?
GEM   Yes please.

> *It is dark out and JONATHAN turns on a patio light. The room
> inside is lit by a kitchen light, the fireplace, the Christmas tree lights
> and one low lamp in the family room. JONATHAN and ANNE go
> out onto the patio and walk out of sight. From time to time THEY
> are seen walking past the sliding glass door. Conversation at the
> coffee table goes out-of-focus as MICHAEL pours coffee and LOUISE
> pours brandy. In the kitchen JENNY catches JOSH looking at her.*

JENNY   Josh. I didn't mean anything you know.
JOSH   Oh yeah! Sure. I know.
JENNY   We're like brother and sister right?
JOSH   Oh sure.
JENNY   That's a thought. Incest might be fun. (SHE *laughs*. JOSH *moves
closer to her*)
JOSH   Well, it's not exactly, but we could pretend.
JAMES   *(Raises his brandy snifter)* A merry Christmas everyone.
MICHAEL   Cheers.

> THEY *drink.*

JAMES   Ahhhhhh. Now that's superb!

> JOSH *says something which we don't hear to JENNY. SHE laughs
> and gives him a hug and a sisterly kiss on the cheek.*

JAMES   *(Continued)* Hey Josh!
JOSH   Yeah?
JAMES   Get that guitar of yours huh? Maybe we can talk Michael into
playing for us.
JOSH   OK.

> JOSH goes to his room. The telephone rings. JENNY is very close
> to the phone.

JENNY   Should I get it?

LOUISE Please.

JENNY Hello? *(Pause)* Yes, this is the . . . (JENNY *looks at* LOUISE *and firmly shakes her head, indicating that it is not the hospital. On the phone)* Yes, she's here. Just a minute. (SHE *puts her hand over the receiver)* Gem. It's for you. Danny.

JAMES This kid is going to have a hell of a phone bill.

GEM I . . .

JAMES Oh for heaven's sake, take it in the bedroom.

GEM *goes into the master bedroom without a word.*

JENNY *(On the phone)* She'll be right here.

JOSH *returns with a guitar in its case.* HE *and* MICHAEL *open the case and take out the guitar.* JENNY *stands with the receiver until* SHE *hears* GEM *pick up the phone in the bedroom and then hangs it up.*

LOUISE James, what did you mean by that?

JAMES What?

LOUISE "This kid."

JAMES It looks like Gem is going to make a real fool of herself this time. In love with a kid.

LOUISE For heaven's sake, how old is he?

JAMES His mother is only three years older than Gem.

LOUISE What!?

JAMES That's what she said. I figure he must be the same age as her son.

LOUISE Good heavens!

JOSH You're kidding!

JAMES He must be some kind of sicko.

LOUISE James!

JAMES Well I mean really, what kind of kid would fall for Gem when he could . . . well, you know what I mean.

LOUISE Yes. I do.

MICHAEL I can see it. I mean she's a very attractive woman and well . . . I didn't mean that I . . . (HE *finds himself in another hole)*

LOUISE *(To* JAMES) When Gem gets off the phone, maybe I should call the hospital.

JAMES Didn't they say they'd call when . . . They'll call.

LOUISE Should I go down there?

JAMES That's up to you.

LOUISE I really don't want to.

JAMES   She wouldn't even know you were there.
LOUISE   No.

JONATHAN *and* ANNE *appear walking slowly and talking on the patio.*

LOUISE   *(Continued)* Do you think Anne will get cold?
JAMES   How can she get cold in that thing?

MICHAEL *plays the guitar and sings* "We Three Kings of Orient Are." PEOPLE *listen drinking coffee, sipping brandy and smoking.* MICHAEL *plays and sings very well.* LOUISE *moves restlessly around the room.* SHE *seems to be taking a kind of inventory of her possessions.* SHE *picks up one of the candle holders.* JENNY *goes to the dining table and notices* LOUISE's *absorption in the object.*

JENNY   It's lovely.
LOUISE   Yes. It was my mother's. Is my mother's. No was. It's mine now. When we sold her things and closed her apartment, you know this was the only thing she had that I wanted. Nothing else would have looked right here.

ANNE *and* JONATHAN *have paused in their walk to stand and argue.*

JENNY   Your home is lovely, Louise.
LOUISE   I like it. I wonder if Anne will.
JENNY   Michael plays very well.
LOUISE   Yes.

THEY *move to join the others and sing along with* MICHAEL.

LOUISE   *(Continued)* Lovely Michael.
JAMES   Very nice.
MICHAEL   Thank you. I guess . . . I . . . (HE *pauses, then plunges*) There's something I want to tell you. I don't know whether I should or not, but I really . . . I love Jon a lot and I want to be part of his life and his family too.
JAMES   *(Clears his throat)* Well, Michael . . .
MICHAEL   There's something I should tell you. It's not a big deal, really, but you should know about it. I have been married. I have a child.
LOUISE   Oh.

MICHAEL   It was all a mistake of course. I mean I was so young I didn't
know . . . I didn't know anything. Except my son, he's not a mistake.

LOUISE   How old is he?

MICHAEL   Three.

JAMES   Your ex-wife has custody?

MICHAEL   Yes.

JAMES   You have visitation rights?

MICHAEL   No. She was vindictive.

JAMES   But California courts . . .

MICHAEL   Unfortunately it wasn't a California court.

JAMES   I see.

JENNY *makes a noise of disgust.*

JOSH   Hey, what's the matter with you?

JENNY   It's disgusting and irresponsible. People spreading their legs and
dropping children all over the country. A little thoughtless heavy
breathing and out pops a toy to toss around.

MICHAEL   My son is not a toy.

JENNY   Are you sure? (SHE *stands suddenly, controlling herself)* Sorry
Michael. Excuse me. I suppose the bathroom is still in the same place?

JAMES   Sure. Hasn't budged.

JENNY *goes out to the guest bathroom.* JOSH *whistles at her
volatility.*

MICHAEL   I'm sorry, I . . .

JAMES   Not your fault. She's always been like that.

LOUISE   You don't see your son?

MICHAEL   She let me have him for a weekend last summer. I can talk
to him on the phone whenever I want. She thinks that's safe. My disease
is not communicable by telephone.

LOUISE   It must be difficult for you.

MICHAEL   Yes. Well. We're going to change all that.

JAMES   How do you mean?

MICHAEL   Jon and I have decided. I'm going to sue my ex-wife for joint
custody.

JAMES   Wow. That's going to be a toughy.

JOSH   How come Dad.

JAMES   Custody decisions are traditionally, well traditional.

MICHAEL   Our attorney says we should be set for a long court battle and
just keep appealing.

JAMES   Your attorney?

> JONATHAN *and* ANNE *enter through the sliding glass door.*

JONATHAN   It's started to rain a little. It smells wonderful.

> *Indeed the sound of rain on the roof is heard in the silence.* JONATHAN *turns off the patio light.*

LOUISE   Anne are you cold?
ANNE   No. It's hot in this thing. I'm really tired. I'm going to my room. (ANNE *goes to her room*)
LOUISE   *(To* JONATHAN) Have you upset her?
JONATHAN   No. We just talked. You know she's an amazingly honest person.
LOUISE   About what?
JONATHAN   She faces things.

> *There is a startled scream from the hallway to* ANNE's *room followed by a pause and then* JENNY's *urgent voice.*

JENNY   Anne! I'm sorry, Anne. You startled me.

> *We do not hear* ANNE's *muffled response.*

JENNY   Goodnight.
LOUISE   *(To* JONATHAN) What are you talking about?
JONATHAN   Nothing. Don't worry Mom, she's all right. Just tired. It's been a big day.
JAMES   We were having an interesting conversation here Jonathan. We've heard the news about Michael's son and your court plans.
JONATHAN   *(Looks with surprise at* MICHAEL) Oh?
MICHAEL   I thought they should know.
JONATHAN   Why not?

> JENNY *comes into the room.* SHE *wanders around restlessly and ends up at the kitchen window looking out.* JAMES *is hurt, but as always* HE *keep his hurt private.*

JAMES   Michael tells me that you've hired an attorney.
JONATHAN   Yes.
JAMES   May I ask why?

JONATHAN   We thought we needed a specialist on gay rights.

LOUISE   Jenny, anything I can get you?

JAMES   Are gay rights different from anyone else's rights?

JENNY   No thanks, Louise.

JONATHAN   No. But we don't always get them.

JAMES   You think I'm not competent in that area?

JONATHAN   No Dad, it's not that . . . I just didn't think you would be interested.

JAMES   Not interested in my son's legal affairs?

JONATHAN   I didn't even know if you would approve.

JAMES   I see.

JONATHAN   Dad, it's a long way from real estate contracts. I didn't think you would be sympathetic to the arguments.

JAMES   I understand the law.

JONATHAN   I'm sorry. I didn't mean to . . .

JAMES   When were you planning to tell me? Or was I just going to open the newspaper some morning and read that the Supreme Court was going to hear the case?

JONATHAN   It won't get that far. We can't afford it.

LOUISE   Brandy, Jonathan?

JONATHAN   No thanks, Mom. I think I'll have a beer.

JOSH   Hey, Michael. Play, huh?

MICHAEL   All right. Any requests?

> MICHAEL *plays an instrumental folk song and the* OTHERS *stare at the fire and listen. On his way to the refrigerator* JONATHAN *sees* JENNY *looking out the kitchen window.*

JONATHAN   Jenny?

> SHE *turns to look at him, then moves past him to the dining table.*

JONATHAN   *(Takes a bottle of beer from the refrigerator and goes to her)* Is something wrong?

JENNY   I'm ornery, grouchy, touchy, and horny. I think I know a cure.

JONATHAN   Jenny. Don't.

JENNY   I never have liked that word! Never!

JONATHAN   I know.

JENNY   I'm sorry. Sorry sorry sorry. I'm even embarrassing myself. And that's hard! It's just a little too much for me, this day. Even Gem . . . (SHE *inhales deeply, reaching for control*) I . . . Jonathan, the fact is, I'm lonely.

JONATHAN   I know. I'm sorry. It's temporary. You're beautiful. (HE *tries to jolly her along)* Smart. Gorgeous. Witty. Sexy. Etcetera. Etcetera.

JENNY   I've always felt strange about us. Unfinished. We didn't break up, we just sort of dissolved, slowly. And we never really talked about anything.

JONATHAN   I've never been good at self-revelation.

JENNY   And I always need to say things or they haunt me. I've got a horror of things left unsaid, even when I know they're better left unsaid.

> JONATHAN *has decided to ride out the talk and get the inevitable over with. Nothing will upset him.*

JENNY   *(Continued)* You haven't changed you know. Except you're better looking. The butch look becomes you. You remember when you touched my breast the first time?

JONATHAN   Of course I remember.

JENNY   I thought I'd break my back, sticking my boobs out so far your hand couldn't miss. And now. Now you have other inclinations. Do you never have . . . stirrings? Now that you sleep with boys, do you fantasize about girls? Michael is very . . . attractive. I quite fancy him myself. Maybe the three of us . . . Or maybe I could watch . . .

> JENNY *stands suddenly and moves to the sliding glass door. After a moment* JONATHAN *follows, turns her to face him and* SHE *collapses in his hug.* MICHAEL, *who is still playing, sees the embrace.*

JONATHAN   OK?

JENNY   Yes. I just . . . It's raining. I remember the sound of rain on the car roof. It was never very good, but it was always best when it was raining.

JONATHAN   Jenny, don't dwell there. It's dead.

JENNY   I know. It's self-indulgence. Emotional wallowing. What a state I've gotten myself in. What do I do now?

JONATHAN   Mom would be happy to have you spend the night.

JENNY   Maybe I should move in with Anne.

JONATHAN   All jokes about nunneries are off limits.

JENNY   *(Laughs. SHE squeezes his hand)* Come on, friend, let's join the party before somebody gets worried.

> JENNY *and* JONATHAN *go into the family room area to join the* OTHERS *as the song ends.*

JAMES   That beer looks good.

JONATHAN   You want one?

JAMES   I'd rather have a scotch and soda.

LOUISE   I'll get it. I have to do Anne's drink too. (SHE *goes into the kitchen*)

MICHAEL   (*Hands the guitar to* JOSH) Your turn Josh.

JOSH   Oh no! I'm really bad.

MICHAEL   Oh come on.

JOSH   (*Takes the guitar and plays a comic song to the tune of* "Green, Green Grass of Home")
THE OLD HOME TOWN LOOKS UPSIDE DOWN
AS I LAY HERE ON THE GROUND
AND THERE'S THAT OLD FREIGHT TRAIN
THAT I JUST FELL OFF OF.
DOWN THE LANE I LOOK
AND THERE COMES BESSIE.
DAMN GOOD COW BUT SHE SURE IS MESSY,
GRAZING ON THE GREEN, GREEN GRASS OF HOME.

THE OLD OUTHOUSE IS STILL STANDING,
THOUGH THE CATALOGUES ARE USED AND GONE,
AND THERE'S THAT OLD OAK SEAT
THAT I USED TO SHIT ON.
DOWN THE LANE I'D RUN
AND HOPE TO MAKE IT,
THERE WERE TIMES I HAD TO FAKE IT.
THAT'S WHY WE GOT SUCH GREEN, GREEN GRASS AT HOME.

> *During the song* LOUISE *has brought* JAMES *his drink and returned to the kitchen.* GEM *has slipped in from the master bedroom, trying to be inconspicuous and hoping to avoid comments.* SHE *seems to be very happy and somehow shy as if hugging a private thought of great value.* SHE *sits down and laughs with the* OTHERS *as the song ends.*

JONATHAN   Really classy, Josh, really classy.

JAMES   Yup. No doubt about it, Josh is the intellectual of the family.

> JOSH *offers the guitar back to* MICHAEL.

MICHAEL   No way I can follow that.

LOUISE   *(Calls from the kitchen)* Anybody hungry? How about a piece
of pie?

A chorus of groans attests to still full stomachs.

JOSH   Sure, thanks Mom. (JOSH *puts away the guitar, then cuts himself
a piece of pie and takes it to the dining table where* HE *sits down to eat
it)*
JAMES   So tell me Gem, how's Danny?
GEM   He's fine.
JAMES   Does he always call twice a day?
GEM   James, please. Don't. I'm not a child to be teased.
JAMES   No. Tell me, when are we going to have the pleasure of meeting
the child groom?

GEM *stands in confusion and goes into the kitchen.*

JAMES   *(Continued)* I thought so. The impossible isn't as impossible as
she thought it was.
GEM   Anything I can do, Louise?
LOUISE   No. I don't think so. I'm just going to get Anne settled for the
night. (LOUISE *has just poured a glass of pinkish liquid from a scientific
looking bottle.* SHE *turns and looks at* GEM *and smiles)* Did you have
a nice visit?
GEM   Very . . . interesting.
LOUISE   Good.

LOUISE *is about to go to* ANNE's *room when* JENNY *moves to
her.*

JENNY   Louise, thank you for a lovely dinner.
LOUISE   You're leaving?
JENNY   I think I'd better. Thanks again.

JOSH *goes to the guest room to get* JENNY's *coat.*

LOUISE   You're welcome dear. Say hello to your folks if they phone
again.
JENNY   I will.
LOUISE   Good night. See you soon.
JENNY   Good night.

LOUISE *goes to* ANNE's *room.*

JENNY *(Continued)* Michael, it's really good to meet you.
MICHAEL Same here. Come by and see us when you're in the city.
JENNY Thank you. I'll do that. (SHE *shakes hands with a surprised*
   JONATHAN) Jonathan, good to see you again.
JONATHAN Yes.

GEM *comes into the family room and sits down near* JONATHAN
and MICHAEL.

JENNY Good night, Gem.
GEM Night Jenny.

JAMES *stands and puts a fatherly hand on her shoulder.* JOSH *is
waiting to help* JENNY *on with her coat.*

JAMES I'll walk you across the street.
JENNY That isn't necessary.
JAMES Never know. Suburbia isn't as safe as it used to be.
JENNY OK. Good night, Josh.
JOSH Night. (JOSH *watches them leave*)
JONATHAN *(Looks out the sliding glass door)* It's stopped raining.
GEM Good. I hate to drive in the rain.
JONATHAN We should start back. But I don't want to go without talk-
   ing to Mom.
GEM Her cruise.
JONATHAN Somehow I have to make her understand why I think it's
   so important for her.
GEM I don't think you can do that. Or should do that.
JONATHAN What do you mean?
GEM Your view of why it is important is, well it's your view. It doesn't
   take into account her view of things. I thought it was a good idea too,
   but I think I was wrong. Anyway she won't go.
JONATHAN But why not? We've made all the arrangements, there's no
   reason she can't go.
GEM Jonathan, what would she do?
JONATHAN She'd have a rest at least.
GEM She doesn't need a rest. And she doesn't know how to spend time
   doing anything but running the house. It's her profession. If she
   thought she wasn't needed, well it would remove the point of her whole
   life.

JONATHAN   It's depressing.

GEM   It's just the way it is. Don't project your own ideas onto it. Every-one's life is depressing from *someone* else's point of view.

JONATHAN   Even yours?

GEM   Maybe. I, of course, would find that hard to believe.

JONATHAN   How'd you get so smart?

GEM   Who knows, I may have it all wrong. After all, it's from my point of view.

JONATHAN   You think I should forget about the cruise?

GEM   It was a very sweet thought, and I know she's very pleased.

JONATHAN   Right.

>   JOSH *quietly goes to his room.*

JONATHAN   *(Continued)* Well, Michael. Shall we collect our loot and get going?

MICHAEL   Whenever you say.

>   JONATHAN *and* MICHAEL *start to pile up their Christmas pre-sents.* GEM *picks up empty coffee cups and brandy snifters and takes them into the kitchen.*

GEM   I'm going to be in the city Thursday. Can I take you guys to lunch?

JONATHAN   We don't close for lunch. We take turns eating in the back room.

GEM   OK. Can I bring a picnic basket?

JONATHAN   Sounds good.

GEM   I . . . It's just the I'm about to do something stupid and I want to talk to you about it.

JONATHAN   OK. You're on.

LOUISE   *(Comes in and looks around)* Where's James?

JONATHAN   He's walking Jenny home.

LOUISE   Oh.

JONATHAN   Mom . . .

LOUISE   Jonathan I really can't . . .

JONATHAN   Mom, the ticket is there. If you want to go, go. If you don't want to go, don't worry about it. I just thought you would have a good time.

LOUISE   Thank you. You're very sweet and I do appreciate it. But I can't.

JONATHAN   OK.

LOUISE   How long has he been gone?

JONATHAN   What?

LOUISE   Your father. How long has he been gone?

JONATHAN   Oh he . . . just left.

LOUISE *carries* JOSH's *pie plate into the kitchen and talks there out-of-focus with* GEM *who is putting glasses in the dishwasher.* ANNE's *face appears on the TV monitor.* SHE *sounds tired and subdued.*

ANNE   Hi Michael.

MICHAEL   Hello there. Uh. Just about ready to tuck in are you?

ANNE   I just wanted to say good night. Is Jonathan there?

MICHAEL   Jonathan!

JONATHAN   How you doing Annabelle?

ANNE   I'm going to be OK. It's just strange. It's the first time I can remember going to sleep without saying my prayers. What do people do before they go to sleep if they don't pray?

MICHAEL *chuckles but stops on a look from* JONATHAN.

JONATHAN   Why have you stopped praying?

ANNE   Because I don't know what I believe any more. I thought Michael would be . . . that the sin would somehow show. But he's so nice, and . . . normal. But the church says you're going to burn in hell because you sleep with Michael. And that just can't be true. I don't know. I'm tired. All I know is I love you, and anybody who says you're dirty and bad is wrong.

JONATHAN   Thank you Annabelle. Now go to sleep huh?

ANNE   OK. Good night Michael.

MICHAEL   Good night Anne. Sleep tight.

ANNE   Oh by the way. I've been wanting to ask. It says in the book you gave me that mutual masturbation and fellatio are the two most common homosexual experiences and I was wondering which you and . . .

JONATHAN   Good night Anne!

ANNE   But it seems to me that fellatio . . .

MICHAEL   Good night Anne!

ANNE   *(With a sigh)* Oh all right. Boy, it sure is hard to get information around here.

ANNE *turns herself off.* GEM *has gone into the guest room to get her coat.* JONATHAN *and* MICHAEL *are laughing, then embrace.* JAMES, *coming in the front door, sees them.*

LOUISE   *(From the kitchen)* There you are.
JAMES   Yes. You know it's turned into a fine night. Moon and all.
LOUISE   How romantic.
JAMES   Anyone interested in a nightcap?
JONATHAN   No thanks, Dad. We're going to get started back.
JAMES   Oh. Jonathan. About the custody suit. Perhaps you're right about the expertise. It's not exactly my specialty. But keep me informed, eh?
JONATHAN   Of course, Dad. We'll need to discuss it with you as it develops.
JAMES   Good. And see here. Take it from me, justice is a very expensive business.
JONATHAN   I know.
JAMES   I'd be happy to help out . . . with a contribution.
JONATHAN   Dad we couldn't.
JAMES   Well, a loan then.
GEM   *(Comes into the family room)* I think I'll just grab my gains and steal off into the night.
JAMES   What's your hurry?
GEM   I'm tired.

LOUISE *comes out from the kitchen while* GEM *is picking up her presents.*

LOUISE   Thank you Gem, for the presents, the champagne, and the help. Everything.
GEM   Oh you're welcome. My pleasure. Every year I get better at those damn beans.
JAMES   Next year how about a little more bourbon in the sweet potatoes?
GEM   *(Laughs, waves at* JONATHAN *and* MICHAEL*)* See you guys on Thursday.
MICHAEL   Right.
JONATHAN   Good night Aunt Gem.

JAMES *is walking with* GEM *toward the front door.*

GEM   James, I was uh . . . just wondering . . .
JAMES   What?

GEM   When will my divorce be final?

> JAMES *groans and his answer is lost as* THEY *go out.* LOUISE *turns to* JONATHAN *and* MICHAEL.

LOUISE   Are you sure you don't want something to eat before you go?
JONATHAN   Oh no thanks Mom, I really couldn't.
MICHAEL   Same here. It really was good, Louise.
LOUISE   I'm afraid there's not much turkey left. I should have gotten a bigger one and you could have taken some back with you.
JONATHAN   Don't worry about it, Mom.
LOUISE   Your father doesn't like leftover turkey.
JONATHAN   To be honest, neither do I.
LOUISE   Where's Josh?
JONATHAN   I don't know. He must have gone to his room.

> JAMES *returns from seeing* GEM *out.* THEY *are standing awkwardly.*

JONATHAN   *(Continued)* Well . . .
LOUISE   I hate to think of you driving back to the city tonight. It's not safe when you're tired.
JONATHAN   I'll stay awake. Michael will entertain me.

> MICHAEL *makes a snoring sound and pantomimes sleeping.*

JONATHAN   *(Continued)* Ah ha. It's going to be like that is it?
JAMES   Why don't you stay?
JONATHAN   Dad . . .
JAMES   No need to disturb Josh. You two can take the guest room.
LOUISE   The bed is already made up.

> JONATHAN *looks at* MICHAEL *and* MICHAEL *nods.*

JONATHAN   OK. Are you sure?
JAMES   Yes.
LOUISE   Do you need anything? James has extra pajamas.
JONATHAN   No. We'll just need to borrow your razor in the morning Dad.
JAMES   Sure.
JONATHAN   Well, good night then.
LOUISE   See you in the morning. What time should I wake you?

MICHAEL   We'll need to leave by eight.
LOUISE   Breakfast at seven-thirty then.
JONATHAN   *(Kisses his mother)* Good night Mom.
LOUISE   Good night Jonathan, Michael. Sleep well.
JAMES   See you guys in the morning.
MICHAEL   Good night. Thanks again for everything.

MICHAEL *and* JONATHAN *go out toward the guest room.*

JAMES   Well I guess that does it.
LOUISE   Yes.
JAMES   Quite a day.

JAMES *sits on a stool at the counter and watches* LOUISE *as* SHE *picks up glasses, turns off the fireplace fire, straightens up pillows, etc. as* THEY *talk.*

LOUISE   I thought it went well.
JAMES   You must be tired.
LOUISE   Yes.
JAMES   What's going on with Anne?
LOUISE   I don't know. She didn't want to talk about it.
JAMES   She all right?
LOUISE   Seems to be. Michael plays the guitar very well, don't you think?
JAMES   Yeah. You know, if he's been married . . . maybe, maybe he's not a . . . firmly committed. Maybe it's just a phase.
LOUISE   Oh James.
JAMES   It was just a thought.

JOSH *comes in from his room.* HE *is carrying a suitcase, an electric blanket, and a very long extension cord.*

LOUISE   Josh!
JAMES   What's going on here?
JOSH   I was hoping you'd be asleep.
JAMES   Where do you think you're going?
JOSH   I was going to leave a note.
LOUISE   A note!
JOSH   I've been thinking about this for a long time, and I . . . I've been talking to Jonathan and I've decided that it's the only thing for me to do. I'm going to follow his example.

JAMES   You're going to what!

LOUISE   Oh Josh!

JOSH   I kind of figured you'd be upset. But you've still got Anne.

JAMES   Great!

JOSH   Well it can't be all that surprising. I mean I am twenty, you must have known it would happen soon.

JAMES   No. No, we didn't.

JOSH   I'll see you all the time. It's not as if I was moving away exactly, but I mean it's important to me. I gotta take a step. I need to be on my own.

JAMES   What are you talking about?

LOUISE   Josh we don't understand what you're saying.

JOSH   OK. Well it's just that Jonathan sort of made me see that it's time I got off on my own. I'm too old to be still living at home.

JAMES   You're . . . you're talking about moving out?

JOSH   Yeah.

JAMES   *(Goes to* JOSH *and puts his arm around his shoulders)* Well. So you're moving out eh?

LOUISE   Where on earth are you going at this time of night?

JOSH   My car.

LOUISE   What?

JOSH   My car. I'm going to move into my car.

JAMES   Why on earth . . .

JOSH   I don't expect you to understand. But it's important to me.

LOUISE   But your car . . .

JOSH   You know how I've got it fixed up. There's everything I need.

LOUISE   But you'll be cold.

JOSH   No I won't. (JOSH *plugs the extension cord into an outlet and uncoils it as* HE *walks to the sliding glass door)* I hope it's OK. I took the electric blanket off my bed.

JAMES   Jesus Christ.

LOUISE   But Josh, you've got a perfectly comfortable room, I don't see . . .

JOSH   It's time, Mom. It's time I was on my own.

JAMES *and* LOUISE *are silent.* THEY *look at each other.*

JOSH   *(Continued)* I've made up my mind.

JAMES   Yes. Well.

JOSH   It's just temporary of course. When I get the car going I'll move out of here.

JAMES   I see. Well, no hurry.

JOSH   I left my toothbrush in the bathroom. OK if I still use that?

LOUISE   Don't be silly Josh.

JOSH   Well, good night.

LOUISE   Michael and Jonathan are having breakfast at seven-thirty if you want to join us.

JOSH   Oh sure, thanks Mom. See you in the morning.

LOUISE   Good night, Josh.

JOSH   Good night, Pop.

JAMES   Good night.

JOSH *goes out and disappears to the Left.*

JAMES   *(Continued)* Well well well.

LOUISE   I hope he'll be all right out there.

JAMES   He'll be fine.

LOUISE   I guess it's better than having him off in an apartment somewhere.

JAMES   It's certainly cheaper. Anyway, what can we do? *(Chuckling)* I'll be damned.

LOUISE   Do you want a nightcap?

JAMES   No, I don't think so. Louise, about that trip. You aren't going to go are you?

LOUISE   No. I told Jonathan I couldn't.

JAMES   Good. Well, I think I'll go to bed. Are you coming?

LOUISE   In a minute. You go ahead.

JAMES   You sure?

LOUISE   Yes. I'll be there in a minute.

JAMES   OK.

JAMES *goes into the master bedroom.* LOUISE *goes into the kitchen and turns on the dishwasher, then shuts off the light. All is quiet except for the sound of the dishwasher swishing.* SHE *comes into the family room, turns off the Christmas tree lights, straightens a chair, and is about to turn off the family room lights when the telephone rings.* SHE *turns to answer it. It rings again.*

Blackout.

About Theatre Communications Group/TCG

Theatre Communications Group, the national service organization for the nonprofit theatre, was founded in 1961 to provide a national forum and communications network for the then-emerging nonprofit theatres, and to respond to the needs of both theatres and theatre artists for centralized services. During the 1960s, TCG sponsored programs for about 20 evolving resident companies, enabling them to benefit from sharing common experiences and helping them to solve common problems.

By 1972, the burgeoning of diverse theatres throughout the country created distinctly different challenges, and TCG set about finding both the common denominators and the differences. Today, TCG is considered a unique national arts organization, managing to include creatively both the activities of a service organization and a national professional association, to address both artistic and management concerns, to serve both individual artists and institutions, to act as advocate for a field diverse in its aesthetic aims and located in every part of this country, and always to encourage excellence in the art of theatre.

A structure has been created that allows TCG continually to reassess, improve and expand; to pioneer and respond to changes while providing continuity. Today, TCG's almost 200 Constituent and Associate theatres, as well as thousands of individual artists, participate in more than 25 programs and services. Institutions and individual artists, administrators and technicians are served through casting and job referral services, management and research services, publications, literary services, conferences and seminars, and a variety of other programs.

TCG's main goals are to foster cross-fertilization and interaction among the many organizations and individuals comprising the profession as a whole; to improve the artistic and administrative capabilities of the field; to improve the visibility and demonstrate the achievement of the field by increasing the public's awareness of theatre's role in society; and generally to encourage and support a nationwide network of individuals and non-profit theatre companies that collectively represent the "national theatre" of the United States.

TCG is supported by the Alcoa Foundation, American Telephone and Telegraph Company, Robert Sterling Clark Foundation, Equitable Life Assurance Society of the United States, Exxon Corporation, Ford Foundation, William and Flora Hewlett Foundation, Andrew W. Mellon Foundation, National Endowment for the Arts, New York Community Trust, New York State Council on the Arts and Scherman Foundation.

Publications from TCG

Theatre Communications

The national monthly journal of news, feature articles and opinion about the American professional theatre. Regular columns cover a wide range of artistic and managerial topics, including reports on new plays and playwrights, arts legislation, funding, marketing, innovations in technology, book reviews and current production schedules from theatres nationwide

Theatre Profiles

The fifth edition of TCG's biennial illustrated reference guide to approximately 170 of America's nonprofit professional theatres contains complete artistic profiles, repertoire listings (including new plays) from the 1979-80 and 1980-81 seasons; financial information; contact names, addresses and telephone numbers; types of Equity contracts; touring contact names; performance schedules; seating capacities and types of stages; and more than 200 photographs. Complete index of artists' names and play titles, historical chronology of theatres, listing of theatres that tour and regional index. Introduction by Alan Schneider; Foreword by Sara O'Connor.

Plays in Process

TCG's national script circulation service distributes at least 12 new scripts annually. Chosen by a selection committee of distinguished theatre professionals, each script has received a full production at one of TCG's constituent nonprofit professional theatres during the season in which it is distributed to subscribers. Subscribers also receive *Play Source,* an information bulletin listing other new plays. *Plays in Process* scripts are available only to nonprofit theatres, educational institutions and other noncommercial organizations.

Dramatists Sourcebook

The basic guide for playwrights, translators, adapters, lyricists, librettists and composers working in the theatre includes: script submission guidelines for more than 100 professional theatres throughout the U.S., contests and awards, professional membership and service organizations, selected books and periodicals, script services and publication opportunities, conferences, festivals, workshops, residencies, artist colonies, emergency funds, college and university training programs, video and radio resources. Introduction by Arthur H. Ballet.

Theatre Directory

TCG's annual pocket-sized guide to 200 theatres nationwide lists telephone numbers, addresses, names of artistic and managing directors, public information officers and performance seasons. Also included is a listing of professional theatre service organizations and descriptions of their programs and resources.

Theatre Facts 81

TCG's annual financial and statistical survey presents production activity of more than 120 theatres viewed against five-year trends in earnings, donations from individuals, foundation grants, corporate contributions, and support from local, state and federal government. Introduction by Edwin Wilson.

Graphic Communications for the Performing Arts

An interdisciplinary collection of outstanding examples of graphic design including posters, display advertising, subscription and fund-raising materials, playbills and photography from the worlds of theatre, music and dance. Leading designers, artistic directors and marketing specialists discuss their insights into effective graphic design.

ArtSEARCH

The national employment service bulletin for the performing arts is rushed to subscribers biweekly by first-class mail and lists current administrative, production, artistic and educational job opportunities in theatre, opera, music and dance companies; educational institutions; arts councils, foundations and service organizations.

Subscribe Now!

Danny Newman's book, subtitled "Building Arts Audiences through Dynamic Subscription Promotion," is the basic audience development text on subscription and promotional campaigns for ticket-selling organizations. Chapters analyze subscription goals, renewals, conversion of single-ticket buyers, discounts, brochures, mailing lists, public service time on radio and television, bloc sales, telephone solicitations, subscription parties, door-to-door selling and the relationship of subscriptions to fundraising. Introduction by W. McNeil Lowry.

Toward Expanding Horizons and Exploring Our Art

Aesthetic themes are juxtaposed with current global issues in a permanent record of TCG's landmark 1980 conference at Princeton University. Among the featured speakers are playwrights Edward Albee and Lanford Wilson, actors Jane Alexander and Fritz Weaver; directors John Hirsch and Alan Schneider; designers Ming Cho Lee and Desmond Heeley; political scientists Richard Falk and Sheldon Wolin; sociologist William Simon; molecular biologist Boris Magasanik; anthropologist Kenneth Brecher; marketing experts Danny Newman and Charles Ziff; and many more.

Computers and the Performing Arts

The first national survey of TCG's National Computer Project for the Performing Arts describes computer technology and programming now being used by over 40 companies either in-house or through service bureaus. Conversion from manual to automated record-keeping systems is described in layman's terms, and experts from the computer field and performing arts institutions discuss the development of computer software programs for marketing, development and accounting. Includes sample printouts, case studies and a comprehensive glossary of computer terms.

Performing Arts Ideabooks

The latest, most effective management techniques comprise this report series. In each Ideabook an experienced professional outlines an innovative and successful approach to fund-raising, marketing or management of dance, opera, orchestral and theatre companies. The first two reports cover how to conduct a telephone campaign for subscription sales and how to organize a performing arts tour.

TCG Program Collection

TCG's 20-year collection of 3,000 playbills from nonprofit professional theatres is available on microfilm together with a bound companion index of all plays, authors and directors.

For information on TCG publications, contact:

Publications Department
Theatre Communications Group/TCG
355 Lexington Ave.
New York, N.Y. 10017